CONTEMPORARY FEMINIST THEATRES

UCD WOMEN'S CENTER

GENDER AND PERFORMANCE
Series Editors
Tracy C. Davis and Susan Bassnett

Gender and Performance is a new series that reflects the dynamic and innovative work being done by feminists across the disciplines. Exploring both historical and contemporary theatre, the series seeks to understand performance both as a cultural and as a political phenomenon. Key issues discussed will include conventions of representation, the politics of the theatre industry, the constructions of gender affecting professionals' working and personal lives, changing interpretations of gender and the contributions of women to theatre history.

ACTRESSES AS WORKING WOMEN
Their Social Identity in Victorian Culture
Tracy C. Davis

CONTEMPORARY FEMINIST THEATRES

To Each Her Own

Lizbeth Goodman

London and New York

First published 1993
by Routledge
11 New Fetter Lane, London EC4P 4EE

Simultaneously published in the USA and Canada
by Routledge
29 West 35th Street, New York, NY 10001

© 1993: Lizbeth Goodman.
Typeset in 10/12pt Baskerville by Intype, London
Printed in Great Britain by T.J. Press (Padstow) Ltd, Padstow, Cornwall

British Library Cataloguing in Publication Data
Goodman, Lizbeth
Contemporary Feminist Theatres: To Each
Her Own. – (Gender & Performance Series)
I. Title II. Series
792

Library of Congress Cataloging in Publication Data
Goodman, Lizbeth
Contemporary feminist theatres : to each her own / Lizbeth
Goodman.
p. cm. – (Gender and performance)
Includes bibliographical references and index.
1. Feminist theater – Great Britain. I. Title. II. Series.
PN2595.13.W65G66 1993
792'.082 – dc20 92–23802

ISBN 0–415–07305–7 ISBN 0–415–07306–5 (pbk)

This project was made possible by and must therefore be dedicated to the many women who devoted their time and resources to the interviews, discussions, and workshops which enrich the material of this book.
Thanks alone are not enough; yet, to each her own . . .

. . . And to the memory of Andrea Dunbar, whose first play *The Arbor* was produced at the Royal Court Theatre when she was 16 years old, and who died at the age of 29 in December 1991.

KEYNOTES

There is a saying that women have always made spectacles of them-selves. However, it has been only recently, and intermittently, that women have made spectacles themselves. On this difference turns the ambiguous identity of a feminist theatre.

(Loren Kruger, 'The dis-play's the thing: gender and the public sphere in contemporary British theatre', *Theatre Journal*, vol. 42, no. 1, March 1990, p. 27)

I don't think we're in Kansas anymore, Toto.

(Judy Garland as Dorothy, in *The Wizard of Oz*)

CONTENTS

CONTENTS

SERIES EDITORS' PREFACE

During the past two decades, the advent of feminist criticism has ensured that large numbers of previously unknown or forgotten women writers and artists have been recovered from the past and are now being read and recognized. The history of culture is in the process of being redrafted, as the input of hitherto unrecognized women has started to come under scrutiny and the whole concept of the Canon, already under attack from other quarters (Marxist criticism, New Historicism, Deconstruction) has been brought into question. In this ferment of critical activity, however, one area has been conspicuously absent until very recently: there has been remarkably little work on women's contribution to the history and development of theatre practice.

Gender in Performance is a new series which reflects the wide range of women's theatrical work past and present. It includes books that explore both historical and contemporary theatre, understanding performance as a cultural and political phenomenon. Key issues include conventions of representation, the politics of the theatre industry, performers' working conditions, the relationship between biography and performance changing interpretations of gender, and the intersections between feminism, feminist philosophy, and theatre practice. It offers new insights into the contributions of women to theatre history and cultural studies.

Susan Bassnett
University of Warwick

Tracy C. Davis
Northwestern University

ILLUSTRATIONS

ACKNOWLEDGEMENTS

Because this is my first book, there are many people to thank. Because it's a book about co-operation and collaboration, it's important to list the credits. Thanks to John Thompson, Susan Bassnett, Clive Barker and Peter Holland, whose support and encouragement were invaluable. Thanks also to Michelle Stanworth, for listening; and to Cicely Palser Havely, Gillian Beer, Graham Martin, Trevor Herbert, Tony Giddens, David Held, Jo Whaley and Jim Moore, who offered sound advice when I needed it most.

Several people offered valuable criticism on earlier versions of the material in response to seminar papers, articles and draft chapters; these were Susan Bassnett, Jill Davis, Clive Barker, Simon Trussler, John McGrath and Alan Sinfield. Susan Bennett introduced me to the work of Djanet Sears, and Dennis Walder to the work of Gcina Mhlophe. Lesley Ferris, Janet Goodridge and their MA students in 'Gender, Self and Per-formance' (1990–2: London) heard and commented on some of this material in lecture form. Polly Thomas at the New Playwrights Trust and Eric Sanders at the Theatre Writers Union (London) were invaluable contacts at many different stages of this project. Internationally, Barbara Lanati and Teatro Settimo in Turin, Susan Bennett and Kathleen Foreman in Calgary, Tracy Davis in Chicago, Vaskresia Vicharova and Mariana Tosheva in Sofia, Bulgaria all helped to open out the scope of the book by inviting me to take part in international debates and by responding to my ideas in ways which inspired new ones.

I am also indebted to a number of advisors and friends in the United States, both at the University of Rochester in New York and at Washington University in St Louis. Some of those people may no longer remember me but without them, I might not have continued my work in feminism and the theatre. Thanks to Russell Peck, Bette London and Kenneth Gross; and to Carol Kay and Joseph Roach. Most importantly, one group of children at the Baden Street Settlement in Rochester and another at the Central Institute for the Deaf in St Louis taught me about difference, privilege, silent communication and body language; they inspired my first writing for and about the theatre.

St John's College, Cambridge provided a generous postgraduate research studentship which made the bulk of this work possible. The nucleus of the short-lived Cambridge Feminist Theory Group offered support and feedback at early stages of the project, as did the Cambridge Women and Literature and Graduate Drama Seminars. The Judith E. Wilson Fund of the Cambridge University Faculty of English supported numerous aspects of the overall project, chiefly by sponsoring the production of my own plays and the visits of several important feminist companies to Cambridge. Better Half Women's Theatre Co-operative offered space for trial and error. The Cambridge Footlights Women were always, but always, there to deflate my theories and translate them into living material for comedy sketches.

As the final revisions to the book were being made, the Open University's Faculty of Arts, Department of Literature, and Women's Studies Course Team offered considerable stimulus, support and encouragement. Thanks are due to all those who read or listened to parts of this work, and especially to Cicely Havely, Catherine King, Joan Bellamy, Lorna Hardwick, Frances Bonner, Linda Janes, Richard Allen, Michael Rossington, Anne Bullman and Lydia Chant. The Open University's Research Committee provided funds for overseas travel to Eastern Europe, which opened up a new dimension to my work. Valerie Bishop, Literature Department Secretary, was an enabler of a different and very valuable kind.

In publishing this book, it seemed most appropriate that I work with women committed to feminist ideas and theatre work. Routledge showed commitment to this project in both respects. Thanks to Janice Price, Talia Rodgers, Julia Hall, Helena Reckitt, and to the series editors extraordinaire: Susan Bassnett and Tracy Davis.

Many of the women who are the 'subjects' of this book engaged quite actively in the process of examining our differences and working through our ideas about feminist theatre. In addition, many other friends and roommates, flatmates and housemates lived with this work and shared coffee and advice, including Prema Popat, Liz Klein, Bethann Easterley, Roland Pohlman, Philip Jakubowski and Craig DeLancey in various parts of the United States; and Gabriella Giannachi, Mary Luckhurst, Rob Phaal, Angie Tavernor, Ben Brogan, Sophie Tomlinson, Helen Small, Alison Smith and Sarah Wood in England, Scotland and beyond.

Very special thanks to my sister Jenny.

Finally and crucially, a handful of people saw me through a difficult period of personal and political upheaval. They encouraged the development not only of the book, but also of my life in the UK. For more than

ACKNOWLEDGEMENTS

words can say: to my family in New York. And to my new family of friends in Cambridge.

For all of the above, and much more . . . to J.B.T.

INTRODUCTION

This book is concerned with the evolution and development not of 'women's theatre', but more specifically of 'feminist theatre', defined as political theatre oriented toward change, produced by women with feminist concerns, a definition which is challenged, revised and expanded in these pages. The study focuses on British feminist theatre groups and individual practitioners working since 1968 in relation to contemporary feminist theory and critical practice, and also in relation to the social and economic circumstances of the period. While most examples are taken from British feminist theatres, international comparisons and contrasts are drawn where appropriate.

Personal interviews, performance notes, and studies of unpublished scripts make up a large part of the research base for this book, which was four years in the making. The research process involved extensive interviewing of women in the theatre, while the last year's work was primarily concerned with revising the material after checking draft sections of the manuscript with many of the women I had written about. Aside from Catherine Itzin in *Stages in the Revolution* (1980), I am not aware of any other author who has used this methodology to such an extent, nor of any book which was read and responded to, prior to publication, by so many of its subjects.

While it is always difficult to find a workable balance between the academic and the practical, the dedication and enthusiasm of the women involved in this project made that balance a fairly comfortable one. My own work in the theatre gave the project a certain sense of immediacy, proving that work in feminism and theatre studies is – as Nicole Ward Jouve has argued in relation to academic criticism – closely related to the form of cultural representation known as autobiography.[1] This recognition of the divided and multiple position of the academic voice in relation to theatre work enriched this book considerably, for the study of feminist theatres is, as I shall argue in these pages, the study of many different forms of representation made by many different women in many different public spaces.

1

Thus, while conflicting definitions of key terms like 'feminism' and indeed 'theatre' complicated this project considerably, they also had a positive effect: they confirmed the diversity of feminisms and of approaches to 'staging feminism', the complex idea which this project was designed to explore. What was not in dispute, either in the theatres I studied or in the academic context from which I worked, was the importance of recognizing new work on 'difference' in relation to texts and performances as well as to theory.

THE BOOK'S THEMES

This book has two main themes: the study of different feminist theatres in relation to their cultural contexts and to concurrent feminist and performance theories; and the larger theme of exploring differences within feminist theories and practices as they are 'performed' in the theatre and in everyday life.

These themes are not unrelated to the ideas expressed in the two keynotes to the book: one of the most important aspects of feminist theatre is the ambiguity of the very term 'feminist theatre'. It seems to mean something different to nearly every practitioner, critic, academic and spectator (or audience member). Mary McCusker, a founding member of Monstrous Regiment – one of the British theatre companies discussed at length in this book – has found this ambiguity frustrating, both in terms of its implications for audiences and in terms of the critical reception of feminist theatre. In interview in 1985, she said:

> Women arrive with a set of questions: doesn't it upset you that you might be offending men doing this? And why aren't you more political on the stage? We had hoped that all of those messages and all of our politics would have become apparent in ten years.
>
> Feminism is being presented, as if it were identifiable. It's like there's ten commandments and you believe in all of them and so I'll come and see your next show, and I'll come and see if you've succeeded in telling those ten commandments and I'll write you up. . . .
>
> It's not theory that's strutting around – but recognizing that it's a theatrical form you're investigating as well. And it's sad that after ten years there are so many people looking at it from totally the wrong angle.[2]

Years after that interview, there are still those who 'look at' feminist theatre from 'angles' which weren't intended or foreseen by its makers. Many people approach feminism and feminist theatre, even today, as if these terms had clearly defined meanings which would not change over time and could somehow be applied to the lives and work of all kinds of women.

2

Not so. As Dorothy wisely observed: 'We're not in Kansas anymore.' But were we ever? If there was ever any agreement on what feminism is, that agreement was not adequately recorded in any source book I can locate. I know from experience that the term is used differently in the United States and Britain, and from one generation of women to another. This being the case, it is not practical to expect (much less demand) clarity or uniformity of opinion in a cross-cultural study of feminist theatres. Even if there was once some agreement on the definition of the term 'feminist theatre', there is no such agreement in the 1990s. The goal posts have moved. The landscape has changed: no more flat fields but lots of rocky terrain, littered with discarded definitions and in need of a bridge – or several bridges – over what has come to be known as a 'gap' or 'divide' between theatre practice, performance studies and feminist theory.

But enough metaphors. The point is simple: there is not one feminism, nor one feminist theatre. Each form of feminism and of theatre can be studied in relation to the idea that 'feminist theatre' is itself a form of cultural representation influenced by changes in the geographies of feminism, women's studies, economics, politics, and cultural studies.

To begin at the beginning: when I began the research for this project in 1987, comparatively little academic research had been conducted on the topic of feminist theatre, either in Britain or in the United States. The work of Sue-Ellen Case and Helene Keyssar was widely read, as was Michelene Wandor's. The ideas of feminist theorists such as Jill Dolan were only beginning to make waves in Britain. Yet in the past few years there has been a significant expansion of the field, evidenced in the establishment of several excellent (academic and practical) gender and performance programmes, as well as in the increasing application of gender issues to theatre studies, and of theatre and performance theory to women's studies. The British publishing industry has also recognized the market potential (partly fuelled by growing academic interest) of 'women's theatre'. As a result, the playtexts of several feminist theatre companies were published in 1990 and 1991, while others are forthcoming in 1992. Yet all of this is relatively recent. When this study was begun, the plays of Women's Theatre Group, Monstrous Regiment, Gay Sweatshop and Siren were available only in unpublished form.[3]

Many of the plays discussed in this book were first read by me in the form of working playscripts, often author's or actor's copies, marked with stage directions and highlighted in fluorescent shades of yellow and green. While this project began as the study of an underrecognized field, it became something more: a study of the factors which make certain subjects 'marketable', if not 'legitimate' in terms of more stuffy conservative academic values. Thus, what I call 'valuing', or the study of the social and cultural measures of value assigned to certain kinds of work, is a key theme in this book. It is developed throughout in relation to factors such as popular cultural value, the status of the theatre as an art form and 'plat-form', and the relationship between women's work in the theatre and in academia. The valuing of women's work is, of course, an area of consider-able feminist concern in many different contexts. It is one which I consider quite critically in this book, but always with a humorous undertone, for as Lily Tomlin said in Jane Wagner's *The Search for Signs of Intelligent Life in the Universe*: 'I worry that whoever thought up the term "quality control" thought if we didn't control it, it would get out of hand.'[4]

I think also of the San Francisco Mime Troup's motto: 'We try in our humble way to destroy the United States.' In late 1987, I copied those words onto a scrap of paper and stuck it up on the wall. I pencilled in the words 'and England' in the manner of a covert bathroom graffiti artist. I paired this motto with a cartoon image: a postcard depicting a man with bulging eyes gazing in dismay at a Mr Coffee automatic drip coffee machine, which 'says' to him (in cartoon bubble format): 'Ms Coffee: Make it Yourself.' The cartoon reminded me of the line in Sarah Daniels' play *Ripen Our Darkness*, 'Do it yourself', used ironically within the play in a suggestion from wife to husband regarding the washing up but which has a more common context in Britain – DIY being the shorthand phrase for 'Do It Yourself' home improvements, a phrase which conjures up images of gung-ho young men reading 'how to build a cabinet' brochures ordered from the Sunday supplement.

I read the postcard's message – 'Make it yourself' – as a motto of a different kind, for it seems appropriate to the project of studying feminist theatres. That simple motto can be applied to a number of situations: if your politics are not being represented on stage, make your own theatre, or write and speak about the need for your kind of feminism, your kind of staged representation; don't expect anyone to do it for you; make it yourself. And then know that your reaction may well be bug-eyed astonish-ment, like that of the cartoon man on the postcard, wanting his coffee made for him.

The San Francisco Mime Troup's motto is now filed in an envelope of 'important ideas' next to the word processor, lest I should forget the origins of this project. On the same piece of paper is another phrase borrowed from an account of the 'guerilla' tactics of the San Francisco Women's Street Theatre. In describing their agitprop device/play called 'This is a Cranky', they advise their readers and audience to *write their own*.[5] Such words can be adopted as mottos for feminist theatre work, in many different cultural contexts and generations. They are didactic and perhaps also naive, yet both express a desire to subvert expectation, to enable or initiate positive change for women through political and theatrical representation. The mottos adopted by others are no doubt different. To each her own.

Which leads back to the subtitle of this book: To Each Her Own. Virginia Woolf's early perception of every woman's need for 'a room of

1 A theatre of her own: Gillian Hanna as *Shakespeare's Sister*, Monstrous Regiment, 1982

one's own' has, in the twentieth century and particularly in the second wave feminist movement(s), taken on new meanings and implications. In the theatre, as Peter Brook demonstrated in his now legendary *The Empty Space*, the room needed by theatre makers is open space.[6] For feminist theatre makers, that space must be open to new political intervention and interpretation as well. The space to make theatre, to sit down and write or to get together to devise and improvise or to stand up and perform: this space is necessary for the creation of theatres. The space to do all this within feminism(s), or from within feminist perspective(s), is one which narrows and fills with other problems and agendas very quickly. It's a space which needs constant clearing. Each feminist theatre opens out to create others; each generation leaves a diverse and flexible legacy to the next.

With this idea in mind, I have written this book with an overriding concern for the representation of the voices of the women who make feminist theatres. Throughout, I am concerned to present a realistic picture of feminist theatre, rather than to construct an abstract theoretical approach which could not possibly be representative of the views and experiences of many of the women who are the subjects of the study. Nor do I present a merely statistical or descriptive account of feminist theatre practice. Either of these approaches might be interesting but by themselves would be inconclusive, unoriginal and unchallenging. Differences between Anglo-American and French feminist schools of criticism are highlighted where such distinctions are relevant, but more emphasis is placed on distinctions between the particular branches of feminist thought from which playwrights, directors and companies approach their own texts and performances.

A materialist feminist analysis provides the best framework for this kind of study, though the influence of socialist and cultural feminist approaches is also relevant. Rather than filter the study through any one feminist perspective, I consider a multiplicity of different perspectives and positions. This approach allows the work of individual playwrights to be evaluated on its own terms. While feminist theories of cultural representation do inform the study of feminist theatre in important ways, they may also overshadow the theatre by imposing values not necessarily shared by practitioners. The (hypothetical and sometimes real) 'divide' between the practice and theory of feminist theatre is one of the main subjects of this book, which focuses in part on the difficulty of defining the term 'feminist theatre' in a way which might incorporate the views of practitioners.[7] Yet this 'divide' is often overstated. In Britain at least, the gap is neither as wide nor as treacherous as it is sometimes made out to be.

My approach to the material emphasizes relatively recent feminist critical debates such as the representation of women in theatre and popular culture, the positioning of the female performer within the physical and theoretical dynamic of the 'gendered gaze', and the attempt to construct and define new ways of reading, watching, and performing theatre texts. In regard to this last aspect of the project, I refer to Adrienne Rich's notion of a necessary feminist re-vision process, which she defines in this way: 'Re-Vision: the act of looking back, of seeing with fresh eyes, of entering an old text from a new critical direction'.[8] Throughout this book, however, I use the term 're-vision' in relation to texts and contexts which tend to expand upon the cultural feminist base of this idea.

Theoretical arguments are grounded with empirical information, including the results of an original survey of British feminist theatre groups which studies some of the common working practices, company structures, memberships, sources of funding, and theatrical and political aims of a wide variety of feminist theatre groups. Empirical information is thus compiled and presented as a base for, and possible counter to, the plethora of theories which can inform the study of feminist theatres.

The argument can be summarized as follows: the feminist theatres which initially emerged in or around 1968 have since broken off into many different feminist theatres, including theatres which incorporate elements of several feminist schools at once. A number of factors have contributed to this diversification of feminist theatres, including market forces and shifts in political and cultural climates. Such factors have contributed to realignments of women in cultural politics, which have in turn encouraged realignments of women in the theatre. The changing conception of the role of feminist theory in theatre practice further complicated the definition of 'feminism' and thereby of 'feminist theatre'. I argue that potentially divisive social movements and feminist ideas have influenced the development of feminist theatres with the result that diversity and difference have created a range of very different forms of feminist theatres and cultural representations of women.

A BRIEF ACCOUNT OF OTHER WORK IN THE FIELD

Of the existing body of literature on themes relating, even marginally, to contemporary feminist theatres, most has focused on women's roles in the theatre prior to the twentieth century and on 'writing women into theatre history'. More recently, scholars have applied feminist perspectives to the work of Shakespeare and the established literary canon. Even in the body of writing on contemporary work, most published sources have taken as their subjects 'women's theatre', 'plays by women', 'gender in the theatre', and 'sexual politics in the theatre', rather than 'feminist theatre' as such. That work which does explore contemporary feminist theatre is often limited to magazine and periodical interviews and articles. Published academic studies are rare, and published studies of British feminist theatre even more so. Information on contemporary theatre theory is more readily available, as are texts by and about European and American women in the theatre.[9]

The two most comprehensive contributions to the field are by Keyssar and Case.[10] Helene Keyssar's *Feminist Theatre* serves as an 'introduction to feminist plays': it relies almost exclusively on published sources and, as such, tends to focus on 'mainstream' work at the expense of more radical and less 'canonical' or even 'marketable' feminist theatres. Sue-Ellen Case's *Feminism and Theatre* provides a much more valuable account of developing feminist perspectives on theatres of the past as well as on modern feminist theatre. It takes its contemporary examples primarily from American theatre, and as such might be read as an important sister volume to this book. Yet while both Keyssar and Case have used 'feminism' or 'feminist' in the titles of their books, the terms have been applied to different cultural and political contexts in both. Their approaches are not uncontentious. Loren Kruger has questioned the terminology of critics such as Helene Keyssar, asking whether it is possible to take for granted the identification of 'feminist theatre' and the 'representation of women' by way of the 'creation of significant stage roles for women, a concern with the gender roles in society, exploration of the texture of women's worlds and an urge towards the politicization of sexuality'.[11] In this book, I argue that it is possible to take nothing for granted; or less ambiguously, that it is not possible to take anything for granted. The basic ambiguity of feminist theatre is precisely what renders it so intriguing and timely a topic.

Lynda Hart's anthology *Making a Spectacle* brings together several important essays on feminist theatre – including two by Susan Carlson and Jill Dolan – but again, the anthology includes work primarily by and about American women in theatre.[12] In a different vein, Sue-Ellen Case and Janelle Reinelt have recently edited a collection of essays which examine a range of subjects in relation to contemporary theoretical discourses and performance theories, with relevance to issues of gender, race and power.[13] In addition, a few recent articles (particularly Loren Kruger's and Barbara Freedman's) in *Theatre Journal* have contributed substantially to the international study of feminist theatre, as have a number of articles published in *Women and Performance* and *TDR: The Drama Review*.[14]

The book adds to a body of scholarship which, in Britain, has been recorded primarily in the work of five authors: Susan Bassnett (Susan E. Bassnett-McGuire), Michelene Wandor, Catherine Itzin, Jill Davis and Lesley Ferris (though Ferris is an American who returned to work in the United States in 1990).[15] Of these authors, Bassnett and Ferris have contributed the most to debates about international and cross-cultural women's theatre, Bassnett focusing on European contexts and Ferris on transhistorical studies of representation. Several other women have contributed to the study of women in British theatre, including Susan Todd (with her collection of interviews with women in British theatre), Jan

MacDonald, Linda Fitzsimmons, Geraldine Cousin, Vivien Gardner, Joanna Scanlan, Susanne Greenhalgh, Gabrielle Griffin and Elaine Aston. This list is not indicative of an exhaustively studied field, but rather of a little-studied field in which it is still possible to list the majority of contributors.

In terms of the existing 'canon' of women's and feminist theatre studies, Susan Bassnett's work is most substantial: she offers the first coherent applications of semiotic theory to women's theatre (as opposed to feminist theatre), as well as critical and historical accounts of the Magdalena Project, and original theories of British and international women's theatres. Both Michelene Wandor and Catherine Itzin have also made important contributions to the field, though some of their work is now somewhat dated. Wandor has studied post-war political theatre, and the relationship which sexual politics may bear to the politics of production. Itzin has contributed a history of political theatre informed by a feminist perspective. Jill Davis has compiled the first comprehensive accounts of lesbian theatre and performance and has edited two important volumes of lesbian plays. Lesley Ferris has written – from a combined American and British perspective – a history of 'acting women' which traces women's absence from the stage in various cultures and at various points in history, and theorizes a relationship between men's perceptions of women in life (as dissemblers, perpetual actors) and the conflation of the costume with the actress. Ferris argues that all these developments informed the process of creating a semiotic 'sign' designating man's view of woman, as exemplified in traditional representations of that infamous invention, the 'New Woman'.

This book begins where the existing scholarship leaves off.

THE STRUCTURE OF THE BOOK

The book is divided into eight chapters, collectively providing a survey and study of different (primarily British) feminist theatres from 1968 to the present, with due regard for social, historical, theatrical, economic and political factors. The focus is on *theatre* rather than on *drama* throughout. The term 'drama' is often associated with a certain degree of literary integrity which much feminist theatre does not necessarily aim to achieve. The focus here is rather on theatre as an action-oriented genre, and on feminist theatre in particular as a form of cultural representation. Particular attention is paid to the active elements of theatre: interaction between written text and performance, extrascenic communication between performers and audience, redefinition of the dual role of theatre both as art form and as 'platform' – as medium for social change.

The first chapters focus on the development of feminist theatres and of feminist theatre as modern genre. They are concerned primarily with the development of British feminist theatres for two reasons: because the documentation published to date has not adequately contextualized these theatres in terms of British politics and cultural change in the period; and because a study of feminist theatres influenced by socialist feminism informs the study of feminist theatres in other cultures. Later chapters examine 'texts and contexts' by comparing plays and the views of playwrights from various cultures and by extending the scope of discussion from 'theatre' to theatres as individualized forms of (feminist) representation, 'performed' in the public sphere.

In Chapter 1, different approaches to the term 'feminist theatre' by playwrights, practitioners, and critics are compared by way of introduction to the idea of a multiplicity of feminisms and feminist theatres. In particular, feminist theatre as term and as genre is considered *vis-à-vis* the development of the 'alternative politics' and the corresponding 'alternative theatre' which emerged in Britain in and after 1968. This section discusses the development of feminist theatre, arguing that similarities can be traced between types of individual and collective participation in different alternative theatres of the 1970s and participation in feminist theatre groups of the same period. The term 'sexual politics' – common to much of the relevant literature – is evaluated in relation to different kinds of feminist theatre, and the term 'politics of gender' is proposed as an alternative way of expressing the sexual politics of feminist performances in plays by men. Most importantly this first half of the chapter compares different definitions of the terms 'women's theatre' and 'feminist theatre'. It argues that any purely theoretical definition of 'feminist theatre' will be limited; that a new definition of 'feminist theatre' would most usefully be informed by the views of practitioners and the working practices of operative feminist theatre companies.

Chapter 2 begins with analysis of an original survey of feminist theatre groups operative in Britain since 1968, and compares the results with those of published surveys on the West End and subsidized sectors. The role of the audience and the role and status of women in the British theatre are also examined. It is important to know who makes feminist theatre and who attends it, in order that theories of performance and spectatorship may be grounded satisfactorily. Thus, the empirical information in this chapter provides the base for later, more theoretical discussion.

In chapter 3, the empirical material put forward in chapter 2 is extended and analysed in terms of the effects of logistic factors on the shaping, and continual reshaping and restructuring, of post–1968 feminist theatre. The chapter begins with a study of theatre groups in the context of the political and social agitation of the late 1960s and early 1970s. It focuses on the development of collectives and co-operatives as potentially liberating working contexts for women in the theatre. The chapter then examines the agitprop street theatre protests of the late 1960s and the subsequent formation of the first feminist theatre groups, and ends with a discussion of four of the earliest British feminist theatre groups which are still in operation in 1992: Women's Theatre Group, Monstrous Regiment, Gay Sweatshop, and Siren. Women's Theatre Group has changed its name twice since this study was begun: first to The National Theatre of Women (in early 1991), and then to The Sphinx (in late 1991). These changes are discussed in the chapter. The problematic positioning of Gay Sweatshop, known primarily as a mixed company of lesbians and gay men, within this set of 'key feminist groups' is explained by means of focus on the years (1977–84) when the group was divided into separate women's and men's companies under the umbrella organization of the Sweatshop. Consideration of the various factors leading to both the division and the eventual reunification of Gay Sweatshop is instructive in its implications for the larger study of division and development in other feminist theatres.

Chapter 4 addresses the most common methods of feminist theatre production, beginning with the working contexts of representative groups and playwrights. This includes Caryl Churchill's career development from devising and collaboration to commissioned work; devised work and the problems of defining authorship and ownership of texts for collectives and cooperatives such as Trouble and Strife, Gay Sweatshop and Women's Theatre Group; and collaboration between individual women such as Maro Green and Caroline Griffin.

The next two chapters move from discussion of the development and working methods of feminist theatres to the development of themes and images in feminist plays and performance pieces. Though the primary focus is still on British theatres, these chapters look to other cultures and their theatres as well. Chapter 5 applies some of the theoretical ideas of feminist film and literary criticism to feminist theatre as genre. More specifically, this chapter is concerned with the culturally produced image of 'the feminine', and with possibilities for redirecting the 'male gaze' or 'gendered gaze'. This chapter analyses the issue of marginalization and its expression in lesbian feminist theatres. The relationship of lesbian experience *vis-à-vis* heterosexual experience is 'theatrically' expressed through the socially subversive act of 'coming out'. Coming out and the struggle of some lesbian and heterosexual mothers for 'care and control' of their children are two common themes in lesbian feminist theatre. Both are discussed in the context of women's changing roles in the theatre and society, and with reference to the notable differences of style and theme between contemporary British and American lesbian theatres.

Chapter 6 begins with a brief examination of some prevalent representations of black women, and develops through analysis of images of women created by black women in different feminist theatres. Throughout, it looks at the issue of marginalization and challenges the notion that there might be one feminist theatre or even one kind of black feminist theatre. Interview material is particularly important in this chapter, as one of the aims is the inclusion of black women's voices. The term 'feminist' tends not to describe adequately the theatres made by black women in contemporary societies. The work of Theatre of Black Women, Talawa and Sistren is discussed, and that of Black Mime Theatre Women's Troop is examined in some detail, as it illustrates many facets of feminist theatre work: it draws on new forms and styles, while exploring common experiences such as motherhood, self-consciously directed at a 'new' audience composed of black and white people, women and men. Finally, two plays by black women – both performed by the authors – are discussed in relation to the idea of 'performing self': Gcina Mhlophe's *Have You Seen Zandile?* and Djanet Sears' *Afrika Solo*.

Chapter 7 discusses several 'new directions' in feminist theatre. The chapter begins with a consideration of the development of performance art/theatre techniques employed in the work of artists such as Rose English and Annie Griffin, and by feminist performance art/theatre groups such as Tattycoram. Then, the rehearsed reading is shown to contribute to the development of feminist theatre, as well as to the development of the work of individual playwrights such as Sarah Daniels. Feminist work for 'new audiences' is also considered, including work in Theatre in Education (TIE), Young People's Theatre (YPT), multilingual theatres and theatres by and for the differently abled. This section focuses on the work of theatre companies such as Neti-Neti and Graeae (mixed companies with pro-feminist politics) and Clean Break (an all-women's company founded by ex-prisoners). This chapter ends with discussion of some of the implications of multimedia projects and television drama as 'alternatives' which have become more attractive to feminist (and other) theatre practitioners as cuts to theatre funding have limited the opportunities for creative growth within the theatre itself.

Chapter 8 pulls together some of the main arguments of the book by looking closely at British feminist theatre in an international context. It compares some of the academic approaches to feminism and theatre with associated ideas about the making of plays and performance pieces. It also considers some of the most important contributions 'toward a theory of feminist theatre', and offers a list of plays and performance pieces which might be considered 'feminist' according to different criteria for assessment. The chapter concludes with an outline of the main findings of the book. These findings are evaluated and drawn upon as support for a modest proposal: an outline of ideas toward 'a new theory of feminist theatre'.

The international contexts in which women's theatres are made, viewed and criticized are diverse and sometimes at odds with the notion that there is an identifiable entity known as 'feminist theatre'. The cross-cultural implications of such a totalizing concept, however defined, have to date been glossed over in most writing on the subject, my own included. That larger picture is my main research concern, yet the focus of this book is

British, for this is the area which is currently in most need of detailed study. In offering this account of the development of British feminist theatres, I hope to extend the boundaries of the frame within which feminist theatre is viewed, in the hope that in future, the landscapes of pan-national feminisms and theatres may come into sharper focus as well.

1

CONTEMPORARY FEMINIST
THEATRES

In the study of contemporary feminist theatres, developments in both practice and theory must be taken into account. This book addresses both. But while practice and theory may work together on paper, they rarely do so in the street or on the stage. The discrepancy between vocabularies and priorities which has often been labelled 'the theory/practice divide' does complicate any study of feminist theatre. The disjunction between academic and practical approaches to the making and viewing of feminist theatre becomes evident even in the attempt to define the terms for discussion. For example, though nearly all of the women interviewed for this study were supportive of the project, many were reluctant to have themselves and their work pigeonholed into what they tended to view as sterile academic categories, and many were also sceptical about the relevance and value of such theories in general. Several women interviewed were particularly wary of a university-supported study, the subject of which (let alone the women who create it) rarely receives comparable financial and/or creative support; therefore, it was necessary to establish some personal contacts before academic work could begin. Such tendencies are indicative of a situation – acknowledged in areas of sociological enquiry but not so widely recognized in the Arts – whereby some of the women who might benefit most in the long term from a study of this kind are in a poor position from which to offer support in the short term. The resulting set of possible divisions between practitioners and academics or theorists is the subject of this chapter, in which the focus is on finding a workable definition of the term 'feminist theatre' which incorporates, or at least considers and represents, the views of practitioners.

DEFINING THE TERMS OF THE DISCOURSE

In defining feminist theatre as distinct from other representational forms, Loren Kruger has written:

There is a saying that women have always made spectacles of themselves. However, it has been only recently, and intermittently, that women have made spectacles themselves. On this difference turns the ambiguous identity of a feminist theatre.[1]

This, one of the keynotes to the book, is also one of its central themes. The social valuing of women's public representations is one way of 'placing' the importance of feminist theatre. In all of the work examined, women are making the spectacles, though they may also be making spectacles of themselves. The role of the audience is important: the spectacle must be interpreted as such, as must any play or performance. Feminisms, theatres, politics and productions: these are the 'spectacles' or forms of representation examined in this book. All of them are made by women. Yet this in itself does not render them 'feminist'.

In fact, the most difficult thing about writing on feminist theatres is reaching a definition, or set of definitions, of the term 'feminist' with which both theorists and practitioners might agree. In this book, the term is defined and redefined whenever it is necessary to distinguish one person's or company's approach to feminism. At the outset, however, it is important to point to the wide variety of approaches to the term 'feminist' among the practitioners interviewed and studied. The following set of quotations should give some indication of the diversity of opinions about the relationship between 'feminism' and women's work in contemporary theatres:

> *Sarah Daniels*: Feminism is now, like panty girdle, a very embarrassing word. Once seen as liberating, it is now considered to be restrictive, *passé*, and undesirable. I didn't set out to further the cause of Feminism. However, I am proud if some of my plays have added to its influence.
> *Pam Gems*: I think the phrase 'feminist playwright' is absolutely meaningless because it implies polemic, and polemic is about changing things in a direct political way. Drama is subversive.
> *Megan Terry*: I've noticed, at these conferences where some men have been speaking out, that a lot of American males perceive feminists as separatists. They want to dismiss all women's work if they think they're not going to be allowed to be an equal part of the audience.
> *Yvonne Brewster*: This feminist thing is always a little bit problematic with me, to be quite honest. . . . I come from a very strong West Indian background, and in the West Indies the word 'feminism' has a really hollow ring, simply because it's a matriarchal society. . . . So entering a European or British situation, one finds the concept a bit difficult. . . . But I suppose in a way [my work with] Talawa is exceedingly feminist, if to be feminist means to look at things from a feminist perspective or a female perspective.
> *Ntozake Shange*: I have been a feminist writer ever since I started. When I was nineteen I worked for the Young Lords Party instead

of the Black Panther Party because in the Young Lords, equality for women was part of the platform of the party. I decided I was a feminist at that point [1968–70] and I've never stopped being one.

Caryl Churchill: When I was in the States in '79 I talked to some women who were saying how well things were going for women in America now with far more top executives being women, and I was struck by the difference between that and the feminism I was used to in England, which is far more closely connected with socialism.

Gillian Hanna: When you talk about [Monstrous Regiment] as a feminist group, you have to make a distinction between the organizational structure of the company and the work that appeared on the stage. The Regiment was established on the basis of feminist principles. . . . It didn't all come together at one moment. It wasn't like a neat jigsaw. We were a disparate group of people who came together, and we had to establish our rules through the collective process as we went along . . .

There are certainly places where women's issues are taken seriously these days – mostly in colleges and universities where 'women's studies' are now an accepted part of the curriculum. But we mustn't assume that we've achieved all our goals. If anything, we have to shout louder than ever: otherwise we will be buried beneath the backlash.

Joan Lipkin: I think you have to take a stand if you make political theatre or feminist theatre. You can pose a dialectic to the audience, but in some ways that's kind of a post-modernist cop out. You can't just say that there are so many points of view that I can't take one. Part of what art, in my opinion, does is to illuminate a situation: not simply to reflect it but to somehow put a spin on it so that we see it differently. We have to, not necessarily offer solutions, but raise provocative questions that help us to think about issues differently.

All of these quotations are taken from recent (post-1986) words by women who have been studied as makers of feminist theatre.[2] All of these women appear and reappear in different sections of this book. Their words, in these brief statements pertaining to their own views of the 'feminism' of their work, are enlightening.

Some refer to socialist feminism, some to radical feminism, some to cultural feminism, though these labels are not explicitly used. The differences in perspective between the British and American women is not surprising, though the emphasis which Shange gives to radical feminist politics and which Churchill gives to socialist feminism is important. Both Gems and Brewster question the relevance of the feminist label to their work. Pam Gems has qualified her published statement (above) with the explanation that she considers herself feminist, and has always written from a feminist perspective, but she also wants to 'steer would-be dramatic writers away from the preaching-to-the-converted, straight explicatory, exhortative, law laying down work that has been so prevalent in committed theatre'. She distinguishes between statements about drama *per se*, and about her own work:

> Being labelled feminist creates disadvantages for the artist ... but what is the alternative when you seek a just society? ... I do not question the relevance of the word feminist to my work. The feminist outlook was my springboard.[3]

Thus, what sounds in one context like a possible refutation of the impact of feminism on Gems' theatre writing is actually a much more complicated and 'committed' statement.

Yvonne Brewster argues from the perspective of a West Indian woman that the term 'feminist' has little or no meaning in her own cultural context, though she sees that her work with Talawa Theatre can be interpreted as feminist, if the term 'feminist' is defined in certain ways. Sarah Daniels jokes about the definition of the term 'feminist' as one which has cultural specificity and temporal or generational validity ('like panty girdle'), yet she accepts the label for her work and for her life. Daniels' remarks reveal a certain awareness of a feminist experience which has been inherited rather than created, and which she therefore sees from a certain perspective. Megan Terry comments on the male valuing of feminist work, while Gillian Hanna argues that it is important to keep the feminist agenda within reach of the theatre, and vice versa. Joan Lipkin argues that feminist theatre, like other forms of political theatre, must be directly and uncompromisingly political in order to effect social change.

All of these women make feminist theatre, according to someone's definition. But whose definition, which definition, is most useful? If there is a difference between working as a woman with a 'female perspective' (Brewster's working definition of feminism for her theatre), then can women's theatre be defined as separate from feminist theatre? If so, several other questions are raised: can men make feminist theatre? Can the term 'feminist theatre' ever be applied in a way which means something concrete, or at least recognizable, to different listeners and readers, in different generations and cultural contexts? Can the term mean the same thing, or mean anything, when it is analysed by, as well as in relation to, women whose experiences are influenced by race and class difference? In what ways can differences between women, and between feminisms and theatres, inform rather than impede the making and studying of feminist theatres? This last question, which involves all the others, provides the focus for this chapter.

In addressing the differences between feminisms and theatres, it is helpful to set up a false dichotomy between the 'mainstream' and the 'alternatives'. The dichotomy is false in the sense that it implies that these two terms have fixed meanings, diametrically opposed to each other. But in fact, the terms only make sense in relation to each other: they are not antonyms, but rather hypothetical points on an imaginary continuum which defines the relative 'legitimacy' of various forms of cultural representation. Thus, it is significant that a certain sense of identification has developed among the members of what are called 'alternative theatre groups', who can hardly help perceiving their own status as outside the mainstream. This is important in that it is precisely the 'otherness' and sense of exclusion generated by opposition to the mainstream which creates the unique atmosphere of alternative theatres, and which gives it its generally politicized, often 'radical' edge. Most feminist theatre is 'alternative theatre' and is located on the 'fringe'.

Some readers may not be familiar with the organization of British theatre into sectors. The term 'mainstream theatre' requires qualifiers, as it encompasses two major varieties of theatre. The body of theatre funded by the state, and not relying exclusively upon public demand for the individual production, is generally known as 'mainstream subsidized theatre'. This is the theatre which has traditionally been valued as 'real' or 'legitimate' theatre; it includes most productions in the commercial theatre, the Royal Shakespeare Company main venues in London and in Stratford-upon-Avon, and at The Royal National Theatre at London's South Bank Centre. In New York, this would include productions at subsidized venues such as the performance complex at Lincoln Centre. The term 'mainstream commercial theatre' refers to that body of large-scale theatre funded and 'sold' in a primarily commercial context. This term refers to London productions on the Shaftesbury Avenue circuit, and French boulevard theatre, as well as their American analogues in New York's Broadway and major off-Broadway venues.

Of course, labels such as 'fringe', 'alternative' and 'mainstream' are themselves loaded: implicit in them is the value system of the British theatre establishment (which defines itself, and sees its own values reflected in the writing of academics and theatre critics of the 'old school'). There is not one 'new school' of academic thinking, nor of theatre criticism. There are many new perspectives, and many writers of different generations who have begun to question the values of 'the classics' and 'the mainstream'. But those who have addressed the issue – practitioners, academics and critics alike – have done so in different ways, in different contexts, for different reasons, and crucially, in different languages (even writings in English may use different vocabularies and dialects). Thus, the issue of valuing is critical: it affects how we read as well as what we read, what gets written, what gets published, and what theatres (and feminisms) get written about.

FEMINIST THEATRE IN CONTEXT

In discussion of the mechanisms and politics of theatre production, Bertolt Brecht wrote that the traditional framing of cultural and artistic standards 'leads to a general habit of judging works of art by their suitability for the apparatus without ever judging the apparatus by its suitability for the work'.[4] The term 'apparatus criticus' refers to the set of literary materials required for the study of a text. In the study of the theatre, however, the 'text' to be studied is actually a set of texts, and also includes the interpretations of readers and spectators. Thus, the apparatus is not clearly defined as the materials needed for literary analysis; it must also include materials for the study of the play in performance. In the study of feminist theatre, the 'apparatus' must be wider still: it must be suitable for the study of the aims and effects of feminist theatre as a form of cultural representation. Furthermore, because there are so many different branches of feminist thought, each of which informs a different kind of feminist theatre, the study of feminist theatre must be undertaken in an interdisciplinary context. This approach need not exclude consideration of literary values, but must not be limited or biased by literary critical concerns.

In Brecht's formulation, the 'apparatus' refers to the qualities of work which render dramatic work 'canonical' or worthy of re-presentation for future generations. Yet Brecht's notion of the 'unsuitability' of the apparatus to judge the value of some theatrical work was based on his awareness of the position of his own work outside the set values of the dominant critical apparatus. Similarly, this book begins with the idea that terms such as 'women's theatre' and 'feminist theatre' are defined in relation to dominant assumptions about 'what theatre is'. Feminist theatre (and indeed 'women's theatre') is defined as 'alternative' because it is created by women in the context of patriarchal culture. It is most appropriate, therefore, to study feminist theatre as a form of cultural representation. Feminist theatre is created within a particular context, and is not most usefully considered in isolation from other forms of cultural representation.

The term 'apparatus' is used throughout the book to refer to the structures and value systems by and through which artistic works are 'judged'. The term is used in a Brechtian spirit borrowed for use in another context, in arguing that while it is true that some feminist theatre does not 'suit' the apparatus of cultural value, it is also the case that traditional measures of value do not always 'suit' the study of feminist theatre. A more appropriate and constructive, though critical, approach to the study of feminist theatre can be arrived at through consideration of alternative sets of values informed by feminist and cultural theories of representation. There is no single set of values which can be applied to all feminist theatre, but rather there are certain values which pertain in general terms, and others which vary with different forms of theatre and different varieties of feminism.

These can best be extracted from a study of the theatre itself, rather than by setting out any preconceived hypothesis which could only be 'proved' by manipulating the study.

Janelle Reinelt argues that the Brechtian conception of the function of the dominant apparatus is appropriate to the study of feminist theatre for two reasons: first, because both Brecht and feminist theatre foreground political agendas in what might be called 'platform theatres,' and second, because 'the task of Brecht and also of feminist theatre is to interrupt and deconstruct the habitual performance codes of the majority (male) culture'.[5] Contemporary feminist theory relies heavily upon permutations of this idea, variously formulated in debates about subjectivity and objectivity, otherness and positionality, agency and experience in gender studies.[6] All these debates recognize the position of feminist representation in relation to the 'apparatus' of mainstream cultural values. And of course, different feminist perspectives such as the radical or cultural, the socialist and materialist, all assign different values to that 'apparatus'.

The study of feminist theatre draws upon a range of disciplines, including but not limited to literary critical analysis. A brief reference illustrates the difficulty of applying literary theory to the study of contemporary feminist theatre. One critical idea which has been applied to both literary and performance theory is Roland Barthes' concept of 'the death of the author'. This concept has particular problems in the study of contemporary writing, when the authors are 'alive' in a critical as well as a physical sense. Application of such theories to feminist study of contemporary work may be particularly problematic due to a potential conflict with the tenets of feminist thought, including respect for women's voices and the questioning of academic and critical 'norms'. Feminist studies should, by definition, respect the views and intentions of authors. Therefore, this study has involved extensive interviews with practitioners. Most of these interviews have not been cited in the text, but have rather been used as background material – as a means of balancing critical and academic perspectives with the views of practitioners. When the intentions of authors are considered as they have been in this study, the concept of 'the death of the author' must be questioned. Yet the concept does have important implications for theories of spectatorship, which inform the study of feminist theatre.

For instance, feminist critics such as Laura Mulvey have contributed to the deconstruction of the 'male gaze' in film and television, while Sue-Ellen Case has applied similar ideas to the theatre space in her arguments for a 'new poetics' of the theatre, and Jill Dolan and others have begun to theorize a feminist spectatorship in the theatre and in everyday life.[7] Jill Dolan, writing on feminism and live performance, has argued that 'the traditional triumvirate of playwright-director-actor has been disrupted by the spectator's insertion into the paradigm as an active participant in the production of meaning'. [8] What Dolan has identified is the partial and complicated relationship between critical theory and feminist theory in performance. In this context, the theory of 'the death of the author' can operate with and for the study of feminist theory and cultural representation in some respects, but not in all respects.

Crucially, the concept of 'the death of the author' will have different meanings in and for theatre production than in (and for) audience reception. For instance, reader-reception theory posits the reader of the text as the interpreter and active subject who translates the words on the page into meaningful images and ideas. Yet the reception of the play by the audience in live performance (as opposed to the readers of the play text) will also be informed and influenced by other factors. In live performance, the spectator becomes the active subject interpreting events and evaluating them from her or his positioned perspective. Donna Haraway, writing on cultural studies, has argued that examination of representations of women must recognize the multiple positions which women occupy in relation to feminism and culture. Haraway argues that feminists should write from a 'situated perspective' foregrounding their differences and personal positions in relation to their politics.[9] In some ways, the idea of a 'situated perspective' – like the concepts of 'positionality' and 'difference' as widely interpreted – may be applied to feminist performance as well as to writing and reading.

As the example of 'the death of the author' shows, the application of theoretical ideas to performance practice is not without its problems. It tends, in fact, to be a dangerous process: it may assume the intentions of playwrights and directors, or suggest that certain interpretations of performances are more ideologically correct than others; it may also prescribe certain modes of spectatorship. Yet the application of theory to practice has many potential benefits, and these are increased when the ideas and needs of practitioners are kept firmly on the agenda. For instance, while the concept of 'identity politics' has now gone out of fashion in many feminist theoretical circles, it is very helpful as a framework for understanding certain kinds of theatre work – some feminist work by lesbian feminists, for instance, and some by women of colour – if the term 'identity politics' is defined in relation to 'the tendency to base one's politics on a sense of personal identity – as gay, as Jewish, as Black, as female'.[10]

But of course, everyone has a multiple identity of sorts: someone is a lesbian Jewish feminist and someone else a heterosexual Black man, etc. As individuals with multiple perspectives, everyone can be defined according to multiple 'identity politics' of some kind. Those multiple perspectives need not be seen in any essentialist way, but can rather be viewed as resulting from – or at least influenced by – the experience of living in society, and of interacting with cultural biases of all kinds and with other individuals who can also be identified according to factors such as gender,

21

race, class, sexuality, and age. These multiple identities will tend to influence each individual's ways of seeing plays. Each spectator has a different position in relation to the play in performance, depending upon physical proximity to the playing space and influenced by personal and political perspectives. Feminist perspectives influence viewing and interpretation, creating a multiplicity of different 'feminist spectators as critics'.

More work has been done on applying feminist perspectives to the dramatic canon than to contemporary feminist theatres. This is understandable: it is easier and perhaps more satisfactory to study a 'fixed' subject from a complicated theoretical position, than to study a fractured subject such as feminist theatre from a complicated feminist perspective. But no one said this would be easy.

It has been argued that '. . . an issue to which feminist theory repeatedly draws attention, is that discourse has a way of constructing false universals and making them seem natural'.[11] In theatre studies, the term 'false universals' might equally well be applied to a feminist theatre production on the 'fringe' as compared to a revival – for instance, of Shakespeare, Ibsen or even Brecht – at one of the Theatres National. While Brecht might – in the context of 'the British theatre tradition' – be viewed as 'alternative' in relation to the Shakespearean canon, feminist theatre might be considered 'alternative' in relation to Brecht. The alternative, in relative terms, can become the mainstream, as in the main stage successes of several of Caryl Churchill's later plays. Such relativistic positioning of any given playwright, or indeed of any genre such as feminist theatre, is dependent upon the interaction of two elements: the perspective of the individual critic or spectator at any given point in time, and the set of values in operation. This positioning will also be influenced by the operative dynamic of gender and power which frames and fuels the process of valuing any creative work.

The making of some kinds of feminist theatre involves prioritizing feminist concerns over literary and dramatic concerns. Therefore, many of the plays discussed would not be considered to have sufficient 'literary or dramatic integrity' to warrant their critical analysis in other contexts. This is not to say that feminist plays can not be criticized in terms of literary integrity, but rather to say that literary critical analysis is not necessarily the best measure of value for all feminist theatre. While some feminist theatre is 'good theatre' according to traditional measures of value, much is not, nor is it intended to be. The same can be said of 'dramatic integrity': while some plays are 'well made', others prioritize polemics at the expense of form and style. Such plays – including some of the early feminist demonstrations and pageants discussed in chapter 2 – are best evaluated in their own terms.

The standards of literary and dramatic integrity may function as 'false universals' when they are inappropriately applied to some feminist theatre

22

work. But before such examples can be discussed in relation to practice, it is necessary to contextualize and define the terms for discussion of feminism and feminist theatre. Quite apart from a study of the power of such dynamics as 'false universals' in a mainstream context is the question of their place within a specifically feminist discourse. As Toril Moi has observed: 'Over the past decade, feminists have used the terms "feminist" and "female" and "feminine" in a multitude of different ways'.[12] Feminist criticism has analysed and argued for several different kinds of feminism, some of which have dangerously conflated the terms 'femaleness' and 'femininity'. Yet agreement about the meanings of such terms, and indeed of the term 'feminism', would not solve the practical problem of situating specific 'brands' of feminism within the larger movement. Factors such as age, race, class, and access to education (or privilege) intersect with feminist thought to influence the situated perspectives or positions of individual women.[13] The clash between activist and academic feminisms has long been a problem area, and one which has been exacerbated by initial attempts to fit theory to practice in the study of feminist theatre.

The lack of agreement about the meanings and implications of such terms has a significant impact on the definition of feminist theatre. Just as there is little agreement as to 'what a feminist is' even among self-identified feminists, so there is little agreement as to what constitutes 'feminist theatre'. All the working practices of feminist theatre cannot be combined or reconciled; nor can all the branches of feminist thought. But neither is necessary for the study of feminist theatre. What is necessary is a recognition of the differences between women's and feminist theatres. Recognition of difference is also essential to theatre practice. That is, recognition of the contributions of different schools of feminism, and indeed of different women to the larger feminist (theatre) movement are essential to the definition of terms such as 'feminism' and 'feminist theatre'. Both terms are affected by differences in theoretical schools, changing social and economic movements, and varying criteria for funding.

Any early theatre which is claimed as 'feminist' must be evaluated in terms of its own age and context. The suffrage plays staged by the Actresses' Franchise League early in the century can be called the 'first wave' of feminist theatre.[14] Indeed, the demonstrations of the suffrage movement may be seen as some of the earliest feminist theatre productions; they were infused with and informed by dynamics of gender and power, as Lisa Tickner's study of the imagery of the suffrage campaign has shown.[15] Yet while studies based on 'reclaiming women in history' and tracing the roots of contemporary feminism do unquestionably inform the study of feminist theatre, first-hand studies of contemporary theatres are also needed. Before plunging into complicated theorizing, it is important to determine what the subject is: what 'feminist theatre' is, and who makes it.

There is no single, definitive answer. In a British context, theatre workers including Lillian Baylis, Joan Littlewood and Buzz Goodbody all made important contributions to the theatre. Similarly, Hallie Flanagan played a formative role in the development of American theatre. But consideration of the differences between their jobs and working contexts renders the unequivocal application of the term 'feminist' to all these women very problematic indeed. The contributions of all these women might, in some sense and with considerable qualification, be called contributions to an emerging 'feminist theatre'. The scope of this study is, however, much more narrow, and the intent in the labelling more precise. Discussion is here limited to that feminist theatre written, directed and performed by women in the theatre since 1968.

FEMINIST THEATRES SINCE 1968

There are several reasons for choosing 1968 as a starting point. The first is the obvious correlation between the political and social upheavals of that year and the role they played in the evolution of feminist theatre. In Britain as in Europe and the United States, 1968 and 1969 were turbulent years, when issues of sexual and cultural politics were addressed in a variety of ways, in many different public spaces, from academic conferences and university demonstrations to street theatre protests. In Britain, for instance, theatre censorship was abolished by Act of Parliament in 1968, and the first British National Women's Liberation Conference was held in Oxford in 1969. Catherine Itzin chose 1968 as the starting point for her book, *Stages in the Revolution*, in which she observed a connection between social unrest and the organization of alternative theatre groups.[16] The rise of the women's movement in this period influenced the first specifically gender-oriented political demonstrations since the era of the suffragists. Important demonstrations against the Miss World and Miss America Pageants were staged in 1969–71; these questioned long-accepted stereotypes of women as sex objects by denouncing such forms of representation on both personal and political grounds. Early 'women's libbers' participating in these demonstrations discovered the effectiveness of proliferating their messages through the medium of public performance rather than, for instance, through the methods of isolated encounter group discussions and broadsheet distribution upon which they had previously relied. These protests were staged as theatre performances and were motivated by a specific feminist intent.[17]

Demonstrations such as the beauty pageant protests can be seen, in retrospect, as the first stage in a clear progression from early feminist consciousness to organized feminist theatre. The next stage in this development was the emergence of early feminist agitprop groups such as The Women's Street Theatre Group. Of course, this kind of agitprop theatre is not representative of all feminist theatre; other, often more subtle forms of feminist theatre emerged shortly thereafter. The development of more sophisticated forms of feminist (and much alternative) theatre generated a series of associated and ongoing aesthetic debates about their 'artistic worth'.

Evaluation of the artistic merit of various feminist theatre performances – whether they take the form of street demonstration, performance art, or feminist interpretation of classical texts – is a source of tension among practitioners as well as critics. This tension developed both within and outside feminist circles. It initiated some of the ideological/practical disagreements amongst theatre practitioners which resulted in the development of distinct subgenres of feminist theatre. Just as the development of feminism was contingent upon the growth of the women's movement, so the development of feminist theatre from street demonstration to 'theatrical production' was contingent upon the development of 'fringe' theatre. The emergence in 1968 and after of fringe theatre companies allowed for the subsequent development of splinter groups with particular allegiance to women's issues. For instance, fringe companies such as Portable Theatre, The Pip Simmons Group, The Warehouse Company, The Brighton Combination, Welfare State International, and Incubus Theatre were instrumental to the development of The Women's Street Theatre Group (which sometimes performed in theatre spaces), Monstrous Regiment, and Mrs Worthington's Daughters.

Red Ladder produced *Strike While the Iron is Hot* in 1972, and Women's Theatre Group produced their first show, *My Mother Says I Never Should*, in 1974. In Britain, individual playwrights including Ann Jellicoe, Jane Arden, Margaretta D'Arcy, Shelagh Delaney, and Doris Lessing (all of whom were writing and producing in the late 1950s and early 1960s) were followed in the late 1960s and 1970s by a second generation of feminist playwrights including Caryl Churchill, Olwen Wymark, Maureen Duffy, Pam Gems and Louise Page. In the 1980s, Timberlake Wertenbaker, Sarah Daniels, Heidi Thomas, Clare McIntyre, Sharman MacDonald, Jackie Kay, Winsome Pinnock, Charlotte Keatley and Deborah Levy began to write different kinds of feminist theatre. A tendency for women's plays to be championed by women's companies, producing collectives and directors also developed in the 1970s and through the 1980s.

The most immediate context for contemporary feminist theatre is the post-1968 women's movement. Of course, 1968 is not the only year which could be chosen as a starting point. For American feminist theatres, 1972 was an important year, when the Women's Theatre Council was formed in New York by six playwrights: Maria Irene Fornes, Rosalyn Drexler, Julie Bovasso, Adrienne Kennedy, Rochelle Owens and Megan Terry. Another watershed year for British feminist theatres was 1977, chosen by Michelene Wandor as the end of what she calls the 'second phase' of

British feminist theatre. This same year has been identified by Susan Bassnett as an important one in Italian politics and theatre, and as the year in which significant developments in feminist theatre were happening around the world. For instance, Sistren, the Jamaican women's theatre collective, was founded in 1977. In Belgrade, the first Third Theatre gathering was held in 1976 and Eugenio Barba (founder of Denmark's Odin Teatret) drafted the Third Theatre Manifesto. In Bassnett's words:

> [In 1977] Women's alternative theatre may have been in trouble in the industrialized world, but in the Third World it was just beginning, and increasingly the theatre work that was taking place outside Europe and North America came to be a source of energy and inspiration for theatre practitioners who felt constrained by the cultural backwardness of the new right.[18]

Whether we begin in 1968, in 1977, or indeed view the development of feminist theatres in a more flexible, less linear way, it is generally agreed that the political and social unrest of the late 1960s and early 1970s was instrumental in the development of the women's movement and the growth of alternative theatres.

Many theorists and critics have written about the cultural developments of the late 1960s, and many have made the connection between social protest and its representation in the theatre in the 1970s and early 1980s. Very few, however, have written about the direct results of this cultural revolution in relation to women's active participation in the making and interpreting of images of women in the theatre. Only when women's self-representation is considered does it become possible to discuss contemporary feminist theatre as both an alternative art form and a political platform.

Both feminist activism and feminist theory challenge the measures of value associated with traditional theatrical forms. The chosen methods of that oppositional project vary significantly from culture to culture. Even the most consistently linked cultural women's movements, those of Britain and the United States, differ in several ways. Helene Keyssar has argued that American feminism and feminist theatre tend to be action-based, while British feminism and feminist theatre tend to be more theoretically oriented. She also observes that despite differences in cultural contexts, feminist theatre groups tend to be labelled 'alternative' in both countries.[19] The 'alternative' label of feminist theatre is still, in 1992, applied in both cultural contexts. However, Keyssar's first point must be qualified: the past few years have witnessed a rapid theorizing of American feminist theatre with particular reference to developing theories of 'the gaze' and feminist spectatorship, while British feminist theatre has begun to be influenced by the commercialization of the Arts. In both countries, the potential of terms such as 'alternative' and 'feminist' to designate a marginal position

26

is particularly evident in the history of funding to theatres bearing those names.[20]

In Britain, both feminism and feminist theatre were and – in their present forms – are in essence counter-cultural, that is, they are enacted partially through a strategy of constructing alternative sets of values and definitions. The 'angry young men' of the Royal Court's early years are rarely seen as contemporary role models with any significant influence. The alternative eventually *becomes* the mainstream as other 'alternatives' emerge. For the most part, however, feminist theatre is still largely 'alternative'. Only a major structural change in all theatre could transfer feminist theatre as genre into the mainstream, for the emphasis on collective and non-hierarchical ways of working which are intrinsic to feminist theatre mitigate against 'mainstreaming'. Indeed, most schools of feminism are opposed in theory, and most feminist theatres in practice, to the concept of 'mainstreaming'. In any case, canonization and mainstream production of feminist theatre are both rare.

Very little feminist theatre has entered the canon, except on a few reading lists in 'gender and performance' courses. Very few feminist plays have been produced in London's West End or New York's Broadway circuits, though there are a few notable exceptions. Neither academic nor commercial measures of value have judged feminist theatre to be 'suitable' for inclusion. The few Churchill and Gems plays which are occasionally embraced according to both commercial and academic values may be seen as the exceptions which prove the rule. The popularity of playwrights such as Caryl Churchill and Timberlake Wertenbaker – not only in Britain but also in Canada and the United States, and recently in Eastern Europe – also suggests that there may be something 'mainstreamable' about their work. Perhaps part of this popularity is related to the depiction of capitalist issues and values in some of the work by these women.

Feminist theatre in the post-1968 period was enhanced by the emergence of 'sexual politics' as a term in both the critical and popular vocabularies. Indeed, it is difficult to define feminist theatre without distinguishing between the two major forces working within the cultural revolution of the late 1960s and early 1970s, and within the women's movement itself. These two strands can be isolated and labelled 'sexual politics' and 'cultural politics', terms which must be redefined if they are to be useful in discussion of feminist theatre, for they are too often employed without reference to specific ideologies or events.

SEXUAL AND CULTURAL POLITICS

Since 1968, both sexual politics and cultural politics have contributed to changes in the social structure, and to individuals' ways of viewing their own roles in that structure. Students and workers involved in protests during these years formed splinter groups, which led to the development of 'alternative politics' and 'alternative theatre'. Cultural politics can therefore be seen to have influenced the development of a range of outlets for the expression of dissent, including fringe and specifically feminist theatres.

It was the evolution of a common understanding – primarily amongst women – of the oppression of women in society which prompted the first women's meetings as such, and which led to the rise in 'consciousness raising' both as a form of personal and group therapy, and as a political strategy. Cathie Sarachild, one of the founders of 'consciousness raising' (CR), defined it as a radical method of 'getting to the roots of problems in society' with particular emphasis on the status of women.[21] Some women's CR groups became directly politicized and began to specialize in terms of their aims. Some, for instance, began to focus on 'mainstreaming' of various kinds, from promoting the entrance of women into 'politics proper,' to fighting for increased awareness of the numbers of women artists and academics. Others focused on separation – on defining 'women's art' and 'women's roles' in society and in the theatre.

The term 'sexual politics' cuts across genres: it has been applied to cultural representation in the fine arts, visual arts, conceptual arts and philosophy, as well as in the theatre. Since the term was popularized by Kate Millett in 1969, it has been used in a wide variety of contexts.[22] In choosing a working definition for this study, the work of a broad range of critics has been consulted and compared, from Kate Millett to other social and literary critics such as Toril Moi, Andrea Dworkin and Arlyn Diamond. Feminist art and cultural critics such as Gisela Breitling, Lucy Lippard and Mary Kelly have also defined the term, whether implicitly or explicitly, for use in their own work.[23] Of all these various approaches to the term 'sexual politics', however, Michelene Wandor's are the most useful in defining the term for discussion of feminist theatre, as her work has touched directly on the relation of sexual politics to post-war British theatre. Wandor states of British alternative theatre since 1980 that it has 'raised important questions about the way theatre is organized, produced, and distributed' and that 'sexual politics introduces another kind of radical critique to its vocabulary by raising questions about a division of labour based on gender, and about distorted and debasing representations of sexuality'.[24] In the body of her argument, Wandor draws parallels between the situations of lesbians and gay men and that of the working class, pointing to the ways in which these groups have experienced similar struggles for personal expression and liberation. Wandor thus provides a solid base for approaching the subject of sexual politics in contemporary feminist theatre, as well as an introduction to the notion that the lesbian play shares many characteristics of feminist theatre in general.

The working definition of the term 'sexual politics' I employ develops from Wandor's work and incorporates the idea that theory cannot perfectly fit practice. It takes into account the complications of positionality mentioned earlier, by allowing for differences between individual women, their working contexts and associated perspectives on gender and power in performance. This flexible approach to sexual politics in performance allows for discussion of the related subject of gender politics, a term which is useful in discussion of feminist performances of plays by men, or of mixed gender theatre groups. Some theatre groups include male writers and performers, but call themselves 'pro-feminist' or 'mixed groups with left politics, fairly positive for women.' These groups are discussed in chapter 2. Here, a more subtle distinction comes into play: the situation of the feminist woman who performs in plays by men. What is at issue in this situation is the difference between 'feminist performances' and 'feminist theatre'.

Tilda Swinton, for example, is a self-consciously feminist performer who has often performed in plays written and directed by men. Swinton is known for her 'gender-bending' roles and rejection of mainstream theatre, yet she says of her own work: 'I've never been conscious of taking an alternative stance. My position is not alternative to me'.[25] This statement involves more than a situated perspective. It also involves a conscious rejection of both mainstream commercial and canonical values: neither 'suits' her individual way of working. In the making of feminist theatre, Swinton contends, it is the individual woman's interpretation of her own position in relation to operative power structures which determines her attitude toward her work. Swinton effectively renegotiates the audience's expectations regarding gender and power with each performance. In other words, she actively redefines 'sexual politics'.

It is not easy to determine the relationship of this kind of performance to existing terminology. A question raised by Swinton's approach to sexual politics in performance is whether her position as a 'feminist performer' necessarily aligns her performance with 'feminist theatre'. Because many of the plays in which Swinton performs are written by men, definition of her performance as 'feminist theatre', or even as 'women's theatre' is problematic. Whether Swinton's performance can be called 'feminist' depends in part upon her ability to infuse her stage roles with her own situated perspective, and in part upon the interpretation of the audience. Yet conflicting definitions of feminism give different positions to work such as Swinton's. While Swinton might be called a feminist theatre practitioner in the sense that she is a feminist and she is a theatre practitioner (a performer), she is not – in the strictest sense – a practitioner of 'feminist theatre'. It is the label which poses the problem, rather than the work.

The positioning of feminist performances by women in plays by men raises the question of the relationship of men to (and in) feminism. There is not enough space here to address such a complicated issue in any satisfactory way. Yet it is important to say that most definitions of feminism do not allow for the labelling of men as 'feminists', though most accept the idea that men can be pro-feminist. It is in gender studies rather than in women's studies that debates about 'men in feminism' have found their most satisfactory contexts. Similarly, the term 'the politics of gender' may be useful in labelling work such as Swinton's, in that it helps to express the relationship between theory and practice, between existing theories of sexual politics and their active representation in the performance space. The question of gendered authorship is not the only relevant consideration. The views and interpretations of the audience will also influence the reception of the work, as will the political context in which any play is performed. Staging and interpretation, political content and intent must be considered in the process of determining whether any given theatre is feminist, or whether any given performance by a woman constitutes an engagement with either 'women's theatre' or 'feminist theatre.' The differences between these two terms must be addressed.

'FEMINIST THEATRE' VERSUS 'WOMEN'S THEATRE'

The difference between the terms 'feminist theatre' and 'women's theatre' has been the topic of some debate. Susan Bassnett makes a strong case for interpreting the term 'feminist theatre' in a very specific, pointedly political way, and cites Raymond Williams' contention that 'Marxist writing is always aligned' in constructing an argument for definition of women's writing as politically aligned.[26] Bassnett refers to Rosalind Coward's article 'Are women's novels feminist novels?', in which Coward argued that the term 'feminist' should be reserved for discussion of texts which clearly appeal to 'the alignment of women in a political movement with particular aims and objectives'.[27] Coward's criticisms refer specifically to fiction, but Bassnett applies them as important analogues to the theatrical debate, her entrance into which bears quoting at length:

> There is a problem of the term 'women's theatre' as opposed to 'feminist theatre', and although reviewers tend to use the two randomly, it does seem that there is a distinction to be made. 'Feminist theatre' logically bases itself on the established concerns of the organized Women's Movement, on the seven demands: equal pay; equal education and job opportunities; free 24-hour nurseries; free contraception and abortion on demand; financial and legal independence; an end to discrimination against lesbians and a woman's right to define her own sexuality; freedom from violence and sexual coercion. These seven demands, of which the first four were established in 1970, and the remainder in 1975 and 1978 show a shift towards a more radical concept of feminism that asserts female homosexuality and perceives violence as originating from men. The tendency there-

fore is not so much towards a re-evaluation of the role of women within society as we know it, but towards the creation of a totally new set of social structures in which the traditional male–female roles will be redefined.[28]

Here, Bassnett's emphasis on the reviewing and reconstruction of gender roles is important, as is the way in which she takes issue with the terminology of the debate. Her insistence upon a politicized context for definition of feminist theatre is accepted and incorporated in this book, with one qualification: the seven demands have not been as firmly established in practice as they have been on paper. Even those of the demands which may have been effectively established in common practice in the late 1970s were thrown back into question in the late 1980s, when conservative political policies in both Britain and the United States had a significant influence on the economics of the Arts.

The terminologies of both Coward's and Bassnett's arguments merit discussion and evaluation. Two main ideas are presented as support for the use of 'women's theatre' as a general term and 'feminist theatre' as a political one. The first argument asserts that 'women's common experience' is not necessarily sufficient grounds for assumption of political unification or action. Coward writes that a feminist alignment is 'a grouping unified by its *political interests*, not its common experiences.'[29] Bassnett argues that the term 'feminist theatre' developed from and is most relevant to discussion of the 'seven demands' of the organized women's movement. The two positions share many common features. Most importantly, they share the idea that 'feminist theatre' is written and directed by women, and is informed by the issues of the seven demands and common political interests.

Critics and practitioners of different branches of feminist thought would engage with this definition in different ways. For instance, a cultural or radical feminist critic might support the notion of a common 'women's experience' while a materialist feminist might qualify that notion with reference to the forms of commercial and economic discrimination which affect women as a group and influence the valuing of women's creative work. Such differences can not be ignored, but can be reconciled if a broad definition of the term 'feminist theatre' is accepted. The notion of a common women's perspective and range of experience is inherent to the process of 'consciousness raising' which aims to encourage the improvement of social conditions for women. This aim is shared by feminists who do not accept essentialist notions of 'women's experience'. If the emphasis on change is prioritized, the internal conflicts need not subsume the change-oriented goals of feminist theatre.

Whatever the terminology, it remains the case that not all the women involved in the creation, production and (re)production of feminist theatre would recognize or label themselves as 'feminist', any more than all the visual artists now grouped and labelled as belonging to various 'schools' necessarily agree with the labels assigned to them.[30] Attaching the feminist label to women's work in the theatre is complicated, due not only to the shifting definition of the term, but also to the shifting priorities and concerns of individual practitioners at different stages of their lives and careers. For instance, some of the second-generation feminists who founded theatre groups in the early 1970s have been neglected by mainstream theatres. In some cases, it was the active representation of feminist ideas and aims which limited the success of these women in their chosen careers. At the same time, many younger women in the theatre are currently meeting with success, in the mainstream and on the 'fringe', in ways which many women, and most feminists of earlier generations did not. This situation has led in some instances to the expression of a certain cynicism in older women about the motives of younger women, and to an understandable ambivalence and avoidance of the label 'feminist' in others. Here again, the literary critical concept of the 'death of the author' can be seen to bear a potentially problematic relationship to feminist theatre: the concept of 'the death of the author' is not applicable when individual authors and practitioners actively dispute the labels assigned to them and their work.

Yet dispute about the label need not be interpreted as rejection of it. Most practitioners agree that 'there is such a thing as feminist theatre'. What causes confusion is application of the label to any given play or playwright. Applying the label to a specific play or individual involves specifying – redefining the label (or the definition of feminist theatre) in relation to a particular feminist viewpoint. In the process, the individual becomes representative, a situation which contradicts the basic idea that differences within feminist thought should be recognized and respected. At the same time, however, identification of feminist theatre is enabled by the device of the 'label'. Individual practitioners may (and do) intervene in the labelling process by embracing or rejecting the term 'feminist' for themselves and their work, just as women in the 1970s found that it was up to them to determine the extent to which 'the personal was political' in various facets of their lives. It is most useful to develop a definition of feminist theatre which includes and is informed by practitioners' views, as well as by abstract theoretical ideas.

TOWARD A NEW DEFINITION OF FEMINIST THEATRE(S)

The term 'feminist' has taken on new meanings and connotations in the past few years, particularly with the increasing influence of academic feminism and feminist theory. As a result, some women are wary about applying the term 'feminist' to themselves or their work because they are not sure what it has come to mean.

Playwrights such as Caryl Churchill, Pam Gems and Olwen Wymark can appropriately be labelled 'feminist', for they have accepted the label, at different points in their careers and in different contexts. Louise Page has also accepted the feminist label. In interview in 1986, she said: 'I don't see how a woman can live in contemporary society and not be a feminist', and she continued – with reference to her play *Beauty and the Beast* for the Women's Playhouse Trust – by claiming that the label closest to suiting her work was 'socialist feminism – but like any sort of politics, it's like catching a bus: you take the one that's nearest and it never quite gets you to the door'.[31]

Feminist performer Elizabeth MacLennan has defined feminist theatre in a similar way, though in a different context. Writing about her experiences performing with 7:84 Theatre Company, MacLennan positions herself as a feminist working in the theatre, rather than as a feminist theatre worker.[32] More importantly, she refers throughout her book to her multiple roles as mother and family member, as well as those of performer and company member. The intersection of roles such as these informs the work of many women in the theatre, but is rarely so directly and eloquently expressed as it is by MacLennan. In discussion of MacLennan's work, however, as in discussion of Tilda Swinton's, it is important to note the distinction between the feminism of the performer and the pro-feminist context of her work in plays written and directed primarily by men. MacLennan's work is particularly difficult to disassociate from discussion of feminist theatre, despite its pro-feminist context, due to its strong emphasis on issues of class, gender and power as they have intersected with and informed her work with 7:84.

In a different context, the work of Penny Casdagli (also known as Maro Green) and Caroline Griffin addresses issues of class, race and power. Their company Neti-Neti works in English, Bengali and Sign Language to produce original plays which include positive female characters and multi-racial themes. Their work is primarily about language and power. In a larger sense, so is most feminist theatre. Cultural influences affect the style of their work, and also the changing relationship of the term 'feminist' to that work as it develops in different contexts and languages over time.

Similarly, Timberlake Wertenbaker is a feminist playwright who contends that her multinational background (part French, part British, part American) heightens her awareness of the power dynamics involved in language and discourse – a theme which recurs in her plays – yet which also makes her uneasy about the term 'feminist writer'. When asked in interview whether she accepted the 'radical feminist' label often attached to her work, she replied:

No, because I don't think people know what they mean when they
say 'radical feminist.' I don't know how I got that reputation. People
used to ask me if I was a feminist, or a feminist writer. Well, of
course I'm a feminist, but what does that mean? What's so good
about feminism is that it is so broad.[33]

In this interview, Wertenbaker elaborated on the idea that theatre communicates through language and silence charged with a dynamic of gender
and power. She also described the labelling of theatre as 'feminist' as a
kind of rhetorical activity: one which both clarifies and obscures meaning.

Language, gender, power and rhetoric are common topics in feminist
theory of the theatre. As Patti Gillespie has argued:

All feminist theatres are rhetorical enterprises; their primary aim is
action, not art. Each company is using theatre to promote the identities of women, to increase awareness of the issues of feminism, or to
advocate corrective change.[34]

Feminist theatre, viewed as a rhetorical phenomenon and as an action-
based theatre form, can be seen to challenge the values of both the dramatic
canon and of some alternative theatres. At the same time, analysis of both
feminist theatre and of feminism as 'rhetorical phenomena' can assist in
challenging other rhetorical phenomena. Recognition of the power of the
label can encourage both practitioners and critics to challenge the labels
attached to their work.

Gillian Hanna has directed her challenge at the rhetorical use of the
label 'postfeminist'. In an interview, she argued that:

People who try to attach some idea of 'post-feminism' to the theatre
are trying to block something that never fully happened by pretending
that it did. We can't be taken in by this, in our lives or in our
work.[35]

Hanna not only questions the value of the term 'postfeminism', but she
also argues that the term is a sign of a cultural shift away from feminist
ideas, and one which threatens to undermine the work of feminist theatre
practitioners. Hanna's concern is with theatre practice and the implications
of imposing criticism and theoretical terminology upon it.

The same problem has been identified by feminist critics. In relation to
'the problems of feminist criticism' in literary and cultural studies, Sally
Minogue has argued in a manner which supports Hanna's practical view:

The very speed of development of feminist criticism has scarcely
given it time to reflect upon its own disagreements and difficulties,
especially where it has been caught up in the hectic amalgamation
of disparate and often contradictory approaches to language and

epistemology, and hence to literature and to criticism, which characterizes literary theory.[36]

Some work has been done to deconstruct the elitist approach of feminist criticism to the women whose work it describes and attempts to define, but associated personal and political tensions still reverberate in the atmosphere of many theatre spaces.[37]

Sarah Daniels has expressed the tension between being labelled a 'feminist playwright' and being a playwright who is feminist. In the quotation cited earlier, she made a distinction between the intent and the interpretation or political valuing of her work, explaining that she did not 'set out to be a "Feminist Playwright" ' but is none the less proud if some of her plays 'have added to its influence'.[38] Daniels does not deny that she is a 'feminist playwright', nor that her plays are feminist plays. Rather, she argues that the feminist issues she represents in the plays have emerged from her own set of concerns and perspectives, without a conscious decision to shape her work in order to suit a pre-existing label. The label suits the work, rather than vice versa.

As this reference to Sarah Daniels, and indeed most of the quotations in this section suggest, the interests of critics and practitioners may be similar, though the focus on intent and effect is not always the same and the means of expression tend to be quite different. In attempting to unite the views of practitioners with those of theorists, the context of discussion (post-1968 culture) should be kept in mind. In a British context, for instance, definition(s) of 'feminism' were informed in the 1970s by the convergence of the women's movement and the developing Marxist/socialist movement. Much early British feminist theatre developed out of the grass-roots or 'radical' feminism of the late 1960s and early 1970s, and was also informed, if not directly influenced, by the developing activist feminist movement in the United States.

Defining feminism in the context of the United States is another matter altogether. American feminisms have reacted against the 'patriarchy' in actual and symbolic terms, influenced by the capitalist structure of the economy. One result is the prevalence of materialist feminism in America, as opposed to the prevalence of socialist feminism in Britain. But perhaps more importantly, the terminology of all the different schools tends to be used differently. For instance, the term 'radical' has been replaced in the United States, in some cases, with the term 'cultural feminism', to refer to the branch of feminist activism and theory which is 'dedicated to creating a separate and radical women's culture'.[39] The term 'radical feminist' does not, therefore, convey precisely the same meanings in British and American contexts. It has different implications for feminists within the same culture as well. For instance, Audre Lorde argued in 1984 from a radical or cultural feminist perspective that the concept of a 'women's community' is necessary to the struggle for liberation, though the conceptualization and possible actualization of such a community should allow for differences between and among women.[40]

Lorde's position can be contrasted usefully with the materialist feminist position in which, as Jill Dolan has argued, 'the apparatus-based theory, influenced by Brechtian aesthetics, is prevalent'.[41] Dolan continues:

> Cultural feminist theatre criticism and practice, on the contrary, tends to retain the theatre-as-mirror analogy as the locus of its theory. These critics and artists propose that if women's hands hold the mirror up to nature, as it were, to reflect women spectators in its glass, the gender inequities in theatre practice may be reversed.
>
> Continuing to think within the binary opposition of sexual difference, they assume that subverting male-dominated theatre practice with a woman-identified model will allow women to look to theatre for accurate reflections of their experience. Their effort is to define what cultural feminism poses as a feminine aesthetic, which reflects sexual difference in both form and content.[42]

While Dolan's position is materialist feminist, her comments are relevant to a larger study of diverse feminist theatres. She identifies the ambiguous relationship between representing self and representing 'woman' – between representing sexual difference and discussing a 'feminist aesthetic' which would rely upon a scale of values of its own, replacing one 'apparatus' with another. Both cultural feminist and materialist feminist approaches to performance have advantages and limitations. The former engages with debates about the 'gaze' by re-viewing the universal spectator as female, while the latter criticizes the idea of a universal feminist perspective.[43]

One possible means of uniting opposing views of 'women's experience' has been offered by Linda Alcoff. She argues that polarized oppositions within feminism can be united in the process of matching theory to practice.[44] The argument is appropriate here in that it construes feminism as a *strategy*, a project which seeks change. In feminist theatre, the change sought is that of the designated roles of women in the theatre. Women's roles as makers and spectators are emphasized, as well as women's roles (as characters in plays, and as performers) on stage. Alcoff's proposal, when applied to feminist theatre, emphasizes action and allows for differences between feminist theatres. Without such a flexible framework for evaluation, the study of feminist theatre tends to divide between theory and practice. With such a framework, it becomes possible to define feminist theatre as a form of cultural representation made by women, which is informed by the situated perspectives of its makers, its performers, its spectators and its critics.

For the purposes of this book, then, feminist theatre will be defined in a flexible way as that theatre which aims to achieve positive re-evaluation of women's roles and/or to effect social change, and which is informed in this project by broadly feminist ideas. Feminist theatre thus defined may include all the different schools of feminist thought and practice. It allows for a cultural emphasis on 'women's experience', yet it acknowledges that some feminists reject this idea as potentially reductive or essentialist. Crucially, this definition allows for a diversity of approaches and perspectives among practitioners.

A flexible definition of 'feminist theatre' can be employed in a study of the work of particular theatre groups. In this kind of feminist theatre studies, the primary questions are: who are the members of theatre groups? What do they aim to achieve? How do they operate? What do they think of their own work, as well as of the relevance of feminism to their theatre practice?

2

FEMINIST THEATRES 1968–90

Since the 1960s, there have been many feminist theatres developing and producing innovative work in the United States and around the world, while definitions of 'feminism' and 'feminist theatre' have varied from generation to generation, group to group and culture to culture. Of all the feminist theatres produced in this period, however, those of Britain and the United States contributed most to the development of contemporary feminisms and feminist theatres. Many of the most influential American feminist theatre groups have been written about elsewhere. Early agitprop groups such as the San Francisco Women's Street Theatre were chronicled as part of the American Guerilla Street Theatre movement, for instance.[1] The work of American companies such as The Omaha Magic Theatre, At the Foot of the Mountain Theatre, Lilith Theatre Company, Split Britches, Spiderwoman Theatre, The Women's Project directed by Julia Miles and The Women's Experimental Theatre have been discussed, from different feminist perspectives, by Case, Dolan, Keyssar, Malpede, Chinoy and Jenkins, amongst others. But British feminist companies such as Beryl and the Perils, The Millies, Clapperclaw and Charabanc are virtually unknown outside Britain, aside from the brief references to them in Michelene Wandor's work, and in a few scattered periodical reviews. Thus, it seems most important to fill in the gaps by focusing in this and the next chapter on the development of British feminist theatres.

BRITISH FEMINIST THEATRE SURVEYED

Groups in Operation Since 1968

The statistics and data relating to women's status and roles in British theatre since 1968 are recorded only sporadically, even in theatre periodicals and journals. This is in contrast to the situation in the United States where, although the amount of material available is still negligible and in most cases outdated, it does at least make up a short list: cf Rea (1972), Leavitt (1980), and Chinoy and Jenkins (1987). This non-recording of

38

feminist theatre both reflects and reinforces the low-status, marginal placement of women as subjects in theatre 'history', and minimalizes public
recognition of the extent to which women are, and have long been, actively
involved in making theatre (despite the history of women's exclusion from
decision-making positions in that theatre).

Due to this dearth of published information, it was necessary to compile
an original database. An extensive Feminist Theatre Survey was thus
conducted from November 1987 to September 1990. This survey provides
the statistical and background material referred to throughout the book.

The survey methodology, listings and results are too lengthy to be
included here, but have been published in full.[2] The results can be summarized as follows: of 223 theatre companies surveyed (after many groups
were eliminated in earlier survey phases), 161 feminist or pro-feminist
companies were found to be in operation, and 62 were found to be disbanded. Of these responses, however, only 98 provided enough information
to include in the comprehensive survey calculations. Of those 98, 76 were
still in operation and 22 were disbanded. Of those 98 theatre groups,
category headings were chosen in the following proportions (many groups
chose more than one category):

	Total	In Operation	Disbanded (by category)
Feminist Group (all feminist women)	34*	24	10
Women's Group (all women)	30	22	8
Mixed Group with Feminist Politics	33	29	4
Mixed Group with Left Politics, fairly positive for women	33	27	6

*This figure is complicated by the response sent in by Dillie Keane of the now-disbanded
group Fascinating Aida, stating that the question could not be answered as the group
was 'feminist' but not strictly 'all women', since one of the members was transsexual.

The survey showed that feminist theatre groups – as defined liberally to
include non-political women's groups and mixed groups with feminist or
pro-feminist politics – are relatively numerous and distributed across the
UK. No large-scale groups responded, nor were any feminist groups identified as such in published sources.

The most common source of funding for all responding groups was
provided by the Arts Council's revenue and project grants. In several cases,
reductions from revenue grants to project grants reduced the financial
circumstances of companies, thereby affecting both the scale of the work
produced, and the long-range plans of the groups. Only six of the 98
responding companies reported receiving any amount of business sponsorship: of these, three were mixed groups and three were all-women's groups.

Amounts received in all six cases were relatively small, and made up only second or third sources of income. No companies reported extensive (over 50 per cent) reliance on business sponsorship.

All six sponsored companies surveyed were still in operation in late 1991, though one was temporarily inactive. No disbanded companies reported business sponsorship as a past source of funding. Of the six, the three mixed companies which reported receiving some business sponsorship were Solent People's Theatre, Springboard (the National Student Drama Theatre Group) and Volcano Theatre (based in Swansea). The three all-women's companies were all based in London. They were Monstrous Regiment (which has had all-women's status in terms of core membership since 1978, and which received limited business sponsorship in 1988–9), Tear Theatre (which received some business sponsorship on a per show basis), and Trouble and Strife (which reported receiving occasional small amounts of sponsorship, but which is currently inactive due partially to financial circumstances). The most common reported reason for folding among disbanded groups was a loss or reduction of funding (primarily from the Arts Council). Another commonly reported reason for folding was the decision of key members in established companies to form new companies.

Roughly one-third of the surveyed groups, including some mixed groups, considered themselves to be 'feminist', while some all-women's groups did not indicate having particular feminist concerns. A large percentage of responding groups were mixed. Of these, most indicated recognition of the need to promote women's work and to improve the status of women in the theatre. Because many groups chose more than one category or 'label' for themselves, the 98 companies actually used 130 'labels'. The frequency with which each of the four category labels appeared in the total number of responses was nearly equivalent. There was a strong correlation between sets of categories: a number of groups identified themselves as both 'feminist' and 'mixed' (indicating a mixed gender membership with emphasis on feminist ideas), or as 'all-women's' and 'mixed, favourable to women'. These results indicate that many all-women's groups occasionally employ men for particular productions, and that some such groups do not wish to be identified as in any way 'separatist'. Many combinations of these answers appeared.

When these results are broken down into categories by operational status, a slightly different picture emerges. While only 22 of the 98 companies were disbanded or assumed disbanded, there was a markedly higher percentage of 'feminist' and 'all-women's' groups among the responding disbanded companies. While the samples in both categories are too small to support any large generalizations based upon them, and difficulties in obtaining information about disbanded companies renders those results even less reliable, some observations may be made. A higher proportion of disbanded companies identified themselves as feminist' or 'all-women's' than did responding operative companies. The results of the survey indicate that either 'all-women's' groups are becoming less common (perhaps due to an increasingly difficult funding situation), or mixed but 'pro-feminist' groups are becoming more common. The latter suggestion supports a larger set of considerations, such as the increased public awareness of feminist issues, and the increasing visibility of 'women's issues' in a range of public spheres including the media and academia.

In order to supplement the survey findings with personal statements, a series of interviews with practitioners was conducted.[3] When the survey results are considered in conjunction with interview statements, the similarity between groups is further demonstrated. Many feminist groups have relatively short individual life spans, marked by high rates of personnel change within the companies. This tendency has contributed to an observable production cycle in which certain themes, titles and ideas are sometimes repeated, or 'recycled' from one decade to the next, often without the awareness of the members. Feminist theatre companies are very often formed by small groups of women. In fact, in her study of American feminist theatre collectives, Judith Zivanovic found that 'Occasionally the theatre has a leader and some groups have included men among the founders; however, the majority of collaborative theatres have been founded by groups of three to seven women.'[4]

Often, members have experience of working in mixed groups, in a variety of media. Companies often work on a profit share basis. Few groups remain in operation for longer than a few years. Only a minority of companies survive long enough to undergo development sufficient to allow members to be paid adequately, and thereby to ensure the group's self-sufficiency by ensuring the self-sufficiency of its members. Therefore, many feminist theatre practitioners hold one or more other jobs. Sometimes these are within the theatre industry, in other theatre companies or in general administrative or secretarial posts. Others are not related to the theatre (these are often in the blue collar sector), and are regarded as 'first jobs' by the employers, a circumstance which may further alienate the feminist theatre worker from her work in the theatre.

These same factors influence most theatre groups, regardless of politics or gender composition. They do, however, have special significance for women in the theatre. This significance has increased as the theatre itself has been treated increasingly as an industry, while women's work status in most British industries continues to lag significantly behind men's.[5] While job structures and working hours in the theatre are often very different from those of standard nine-to-five jobs, available figures are representative of general cultural trends. The material conditions and limitations which affect feminist theatre groups, particularly those at early stages of their development, can not be underestimated. In addition to

41

material circumstances, another factor which affects the 'politics of production' of contemporary feminist theatre is the 'role' of the audience, not
only in terms of size, but also in terms of gender and age composition,
race, sexual orientation, mobility and class.

The role of the audience

While all theatre is influenced to some extent by audience reaction, feminist
theatre depends for its survival upon audience support – personal and
political as well as financial. Most feminist theatre in Britain is located on
the 'fringe', and much fringe theatre has particular characteristics which
affect the audience-stage dynamic. For instance, fringe theatre is often
staged in pubs and other non-theatre (public sector) clubs with little or
no budget for advertising and less media coverage. The work space affects
the shape of the play, not only in production, but also during the process
of writing. In other words, the lack of an adequate space into which a
playwright can project her ideas may lead to a narrowing of scope or
vision. Practical factors such as numbers of performers and size of sets
must be considered, since fringe theatres often can not provide adequate
space for large sets, or even for large audiences.

Some have argued in this regard that 'good art comes of adversity',
implying that lack of resources inspires dedication and that inadequate
space demands more imagination of the playwright. Gillian Hanna contends that such a perspective is inappropriate for her own, and much
other, feminist theatre.[6] Deborah Levy considers the construction of the
play as intricately related to the space in which the playwright is positioned
as she writes. Levy argues that the positions of the performers and spectators (imagined or real) must be considered in relation to the actual
physical space in which the play will ultimately be performed. In Levy's
words:

> These are the most useful questions for art and literary critics to ask:
> where does the artist place her attention? How does the shape of a
> room structure our attention? . . . The questions I ask myself when
> writing are: what is present on the stage? What do I want to be
> there? And I ask of my central characters: where is their power
> located? What is the difference between what they say and what they
> do?[7]

Taken out of context, this extract might suggest that the kind of 'structuring of attention' which Levy emphasizes can be accomplished in *any* space.
In the context of her larger argument, however, it is clear that the physical
space of performance has implications for the writer and the writing. In
Levy's words, 'the only thing the writer has going for her is that she is
present in a space and therefore potentially receptive, able to tap into

what's around, and to make something new'. Levy argues that the physical space of the theatre has benefits and limitations which affect the conditions of playwriting, and thereby affect the play.

Plays written and produced without a proper 'space' may be subject to the problems commonly associated with limited production budgets: hastily written scripts; inadequate rehearsal time and space; few or no sets, costumes, lights or effects; multiple parts written for small casts (requiring less expenditure on actors' wages, and at the same time demanding that actors renegotiate their rehearsal schedules to accommodate other jobs). All these logistic and practical limitations affect the feminist theatre production, but none is so important – because so immediate, so closely tied to the success of the production in the public sphere – as audience reception and support. Before any theories of the audience can be applied usefully to the study of feminist theatre, however, it is crucial to determine who, and what, that audience is.

According to the Feminist Theatre Survey results, the majority of feminist theatre groups have a positive woman to man ratio in their average audience, broken down as follows: of 98 responding theatre groups, the number reporting having a positive woman to man ratio in the average audience was 62. Of those, the number in operation was 49, and the number disbanded was 13. Responses of 50 per cent in any given category were considered positive. These results were not obtained by surveying sample audiences, but rather by compiling results reported by the companies themselves. Rough as these figures may be, however, they provide the only available information on a specifically feminist theatre audience.

There are very few published audience surveys which might inform a study of feminist theatre, or even of women in the theatre. Even Susan Bennett's significant study of theatre audiences is not directly focused on feminist theatre.[8] Only a few sources provide comparative statistics on audiences in Britain and the United States, information on audiences for the National Theatre and RSC compared with the opera and ballet, and on the public consumption of British Arts as a cultural 'industry'.[9] None of these is particularly useful in a study of women in British theatre. Some research, however, has been conducted on the relationship of audience composition to the nature of the theatre production in general, and a small percentage of this relates to the status of women in theatre (in the audience and on the stage). This information is offered guardedly: its inclusion here is necessary to provide evidence that there are indeed cultural and economic factors which influence women's (and men's) theatre-going habits, and which can be used as a basis for drawing general conclusions about the role of women in the theatre audience. But the available statistics, even when combined with those of the Feminist Theatre Survey, are only suggestive of a certain situation or set of characteristics common to women's theatre-going habits (which is, of course, only tangentially related to the study of feminist theatre audiences).

Caroline Gardiner conducted a survey of the West End theatre audience in 1985/6, which is both larger and smaller in scope than a survey of a specifically feminist theatre audience would be: larger in that it covers the entire population (women and men of all ages) as potential theatre-goers, yet smaller in that it limits the area of study to the West End. Aside from its date, of course, the most obvious limitation of this study is its target: it deals with West End audiences only. The survey has only limited significance to the study of feminist theatre. Yet it is the best source available, and does offer some information of relevance to the study of women's theatres.[10]

Gardiner summarizes the survey material relevant to sex of theatre-goers in one section of her study. She compares two periods – 1981/2 and 1985/6 – and contrasts three sets of interrelated factors – distribution of West End audience by sex, distribution of each area of residence group by sex and distribution of each sex by area of residence.[11] Her findings, briefly, are these: the West End audience in 1981/2 was predominantly female (58 per cent), with women forming the majority of each residence group. The percentage of male theatre-goers increased in the period 1985/6, with the result that, though women were still marginally more active theatre-goers, men were not so clearly in the minority. The increased figures among men were accounted for primarily by a marked increase in male overseas visitors to the theatre, rather than by British men changing their theatre-going habits. Attendances by women increased by approximately 2 per cent in the 1985/6 period. There was a sharp rise in attendance figures among women after 1986. The percentage of women overall (in both survey periods) was highest among London Borough residents and lowest among overseas visitors.[12]

Perhaps the most significant information which Gardiner's survey provides is that which can only be read between the lines. An extract from Gardiner's survey summary can be seen to have special significance for a study of women in the theatre audience:

> The most noticeable change since 1982 has been an increase in the average frequency of theatre-going among the 35–44s, and in their importance among the very frequent theatre-goers. Some of this may be due to the members of the 25–34 age group in 1982, who were the most frequent theatre-goers, now falling into the 35–44 age group, four years on.[13]

There is one possible explanation for this which Gardiner does not consider. In 1982, the age distribution of the most frequent theatre-goers was the 25–34 age group; in 1986, it was the 35–44 age group. These figures do not refer to two different groups of people, but rather to the same group of people, whose age changes over time. These figures refer to one subgeneration of the population, revealing itself to be a group of consistently active theatre-goers. Thus, Gardiner's observation that the shift in age of the most frequent theatre-goers from the 1982 to the 1986 survey 'may be due to the members of the 25–34 age group' can be interpreted in a much more specific way. It is not the entire age group which is of interest here, but specifically the individuals making up the later end of that age group – the theatre-going crowd which was, on average, 32–4 years of age in 1982 and which would have been 36–8 in 1986. This same group would be 41–43 in 1991. This generation, or subgeneration, would have been active in the cultural and artistic revolutions of the late 1960s and early 1970s (its members would have been 22–4 in 1972). Their continued dedication to the theatre is consistent with earlier trends.

The lack of a generational spread in these figures is not surprising. The lower theatre attendance rates and even lower percentage of frequent theatre-goers is indicative of stagnation rather than development. There is not space here to discuss all the factors which have contributed to this trend, such as the increased accessibility and decreasing costs of television, film and video. What is more relevant to this study is the significant lack of development of a politically motivated feminist theatre-going community. Further evidence for this trend can be found in the results of the Feminist Theatre Survey and related interviews, which reveal a strong correlation between women of the age group which has consistently shown the highest level of frequent theatre-going and those who expressed the highest levels of feeling (whether pro or con) about the theatre in the survey and in interviews.

Despite this decline in frequent theatre-going across the board, women's rates of theatre-going have remained relatively high. Women are more frequent theatre-goers than men, though fewer people were attending the theatre overall in 1986 than in 1982. It can be surmised but not 'proved' that these figures demonstrate some relationship between women in subsidized theatre sector audiences, fringe theatre audiences and regional theatre audiences. Such suppositions, however, are supported by observable trends in generational theatre-going habits. One final observation brings this supposition and estimation to a clear point: 'Although the proportion of ticket sales to women has decreased since 1982, and although some local women appeared to have left the West End audience, women remain, as in 1982, slightly more frequent theatre-goers than men.'[14]

Limitations affecting women's status, finances, and mobility all affect women's potential as active theatre-goers. Such factors can easily be seen to relate to women in the theatre audience *per se*, and to feminist theatre in particular if the role of women in the theatre (backstage, on stage and in the audience) is re-viewed. Theory disjointed from practice is not sufficient, and may be misleading in that it implies that the feminist theatre audience is self-selecting for reasons exclusively associated with the individual production or playwright. Available information suggests that, on the contrary, the contingencies of living in contemporary society – and particularly of city life – weigh against women going to the theatre at all, much less going alone.

As important as the actual figures on women attending theatre productions is consideration of the possible reasons why so little information on this subject is commonly available. Perhaps the primary reason for the lack of available information on audience composition for feminist (and most) theatre is logistic: surveys of this kind require time and money. Ideally, they should involve sampling of audiences for the same show over a long period of time, on different days of the week, and comparison with figures on audience composition (studied similarly) for different types of shows in the same period.

Apart from the question on audience composition included in my Feminist Theatre Survey, only two notable attempts at monitoring the audience of explicitly 'alternative' feminist companies have been made. The first was in 1976/7, when Gay Sweatshop conducted a survey of its audiences, just before it divided into separate women's and men's companies in 1977. The Sweatshop survey was not carefully monitored. It was intended as a source of information for the company, rather than for scholars or funding bodies. The aim of the survey was to monitor audience interest in suggested themes for future shows. The age, class, gender and sexual preference of audiences were not recorded.

The second audience survey of a feminist theatre company was conducted by Black Mime Theatre Women's Troop in 1990/1. Because the company was just forming when the Feminist Theatre Survey was completed in November 1990, it is not included in the survey results. The company has not compiled the results, but my own study of three sample sets of audience responses to its first all-women's show, *Mothers*, revealed that at the Oval House in London and at the Mill in Bradford, the most common response to the survey was from white women, aged 21–30 years, who heard about the show through friends and advertising, and who thought the show was excellent or good. Many of the respondents were students, and the majority of students were female. By contrast, the audience at the Base in South London was composed predominantly of black women, many of whom were students aged between 16 and 30 years. Many were mothers who had heard about the show through 'the children's playgroup' and most thought it was excellent or good.[15] Of course the proportion of positive responses to the show may be slanted by the non-response of dissatisfied spectators.

A hypothetical study which might be more revealing for discussion of feminist theatre in particular would also include questions about audience reaction to characters and situations presented, and would benefit from an additional question on factors influencing choice of venue for female and male theatre-goers. A feminist theatre survey conducted by an independent researcher might also compare a range of different kinds of feminist theatres and their audiences, as well as different kinds of productions. Such a study might include a small production by a well-known author at an out-of-the-way pub theatre (a Page, Gems or Daniels play at the Old Red Lion), a play by a woman on a main stage (Wertenbaker's *The Love of the Nightingale* at the RSC's Pit, or Churchill's *Ice Cream* at the Royal Court), a new play by a women's company in a major company's studio space (a WTG production at the Young Vic), a lunchtime performance of a feminist 'classic' (for instance, Jill Posener's *Any Woman Can* at the King's Head Lunchtime), and a TIE or YPT production by a woman or a woman's company.

Other factors which have not been calculated – again, due primarily to logistic problems – which might produce interesting figures on women in theatre audiences include relative numbers of women and men attending any given production, and relative numbers of women and men responding to any given survey or survey question (as well as differences in their responses). Such questions would require a very long research period and very large sample population if the answers were to be representative, and would also require a large number of researchers to be present at each show. All these statistics would still not 'prove' any theories of the feminist theatre audience, or more generally of the position of women in the theatre-going population.

The most important flaw of any theatre survey has been noted by Caroline Gardiner, who points out that 'audience surveys ignore aesthetic considerations altogether.'[16] In this regard, it is interesting to compare survey results with a related observation made by Jules Wright, Artistic Director of the Women's Playhouse Trust and Associate Director of the Royal Court Theatre. When asked about the kinds of audiences that tend to go to the Royal Court, Wright responded with reference to the plays she herself had directed, both in the Theatre Upstairs and on the main stage. She also responded to the question in terms which indicate an interest in audience gender profile:

> The profile of audiences within women's mainstream theatre is over 60 per cent women, though that is true across the board of theatre. They tend to be highly educated, between 25–40 years old and of a very '*Observer*'ish profile.[17]

Such an unsupported observation is not 'authoritative'. When considered in the light of survey responses and observable trends, however, the observation takes on weight. It may also support a hypothesis: namely, that the composition of British feminist theatre audiences – in the West End of London – are predominantly white, middle-class, and of a particular gener-

47

ation. While factors such as ethnicity and class privilege will vary significantly in other areas of London, and certainly in the regions and less privileged areas of the United Kingdom, the generational trend seems to be more stable.

The politics of production

The phrase 'the politics of production' may refer to a wide range of factors such as the composition of theatre companies, the role of the audience and the economics of theatre production. The last factor is briefly discussed in this section, in relation to the idea that canonical standards for measuring the value of plays are rapidly being replaced by commercially influenced concerns.

One major factor influencing the development of feminist (and much fringe) theatre at present is the issue of 'public image'. Business sponsors tend to offer their sponsorship to commercially viable enterprises. The Theatres National have received more sponsorship by far than any other theatre sector, though it is also true that, without adequate government subsidy, no amount of sponsorship is sufficient to bridge the gap between the annual deficit and operating costs, even for the 'Royals'. Similarly, smaller politically oriented companies such as Siren, Charabanc, Red Shift, Trouble and Strife, Red Ladder, ReSisters, Monstrous Regiment, and Women's Theatre Group are placed in an impossible situation: their very names label them as 'political' or 'for women only'. If sponsorship is to be obtained by such groups, then such companies may be forced to change their images to suit the sponsors' expectations and requirements. In such a process of self-conscious image-making, the subversive aims of feminist theatre would themselves be subverted; the politics of production would overrule the politics of feminist theatre.

The effect of inadequate funding for feminist theatre – as well as for alternative theatre, mainstream theatre and the Arts in general – is seen not only in qualitative but also in quantitative terms. It is measured not only by the richness of the costumes and complexity of production designs, but also by the numbers of theatres and theatre groups in operation in any given geographical area and by the number of paid performers per group. In England, the majority of feminist theatre groups are located in or near London, largely due to disproportionately high levels of localized government support for urban centres, exacerbated in recent years by drastic cuts to what were already relatively low rates of funding elsewhere. The 'unrepresentative' proportion of theatres in London, coupled with the Arts Council's and other funding bodies' sponsorship policies and histories (weighing against small-scale, 'alternative' productions), has been a constant source of tension within the theatre community. This tension has precipitated considerable conflicts of interest between companies, and has influenced theatre production in several important ways.[18]

The issues of space and funding affect the economic security of individual practitioners and also the shape and content of the work produced. It is clear that the move toward business sponsorship is beginning to shape the policies of some theatre companies. For example, Monstrous Regiment, due to the varied political and personal allegiances which its very name suggests, is not well suited to flatter the image of the corporate sponsor. Ex-Regiment administrator Sandy Bailey and the company wrote a report in 1984 as a direct response to the Arts Council's policy paper 'The Glory of the Garden'.[19] In their report, Monstrous Regiment explained that their 'decision' to move from the status of a collective to that of a collective management was a necessary strategy for survival, rather than a creative or artistic decision. This statement provides one of the clearest and most succinct accounts of the double bind of the funding situation for feminist theatres.

Summary

The results of the Feminist Theatre Survey indicate that a combination of factors have affected the growth and development of feminist theatre since 1968: these include low pay, low recognition, the dearth of published material on the subject of feminist theatre practice, the 'invisibility' of work by women of previous eras, and the relative lack of visible 'role models'. The most important finding of this section is the identification of a core group, or key generation of women who have composed the main audience for British feminist theatre in the past few decades. Correspondingly, a small group of practitioners has been identified as instrumental in the shaping of contemporary feminist theatres. The survey also provides evidence that feminist theatre work often develops in cycles. Because women's work is undervalued, underpublished and underrepresented in academic history and criticism, some women begin theatre projects which have in some sense 'been done before'. This idea is discussed in more detail in subsequent chapters.

COLLECTIVES, CO-OPERATIVES AND THE DEVELOPMENT OF CONTEMPORARY FEMINIST THEATRES

This section examines the development of feminist theatre groups in relation to sexual politics, cultural politics and the politics of theatre production. Many feminist theatre companies were formed as collectives and co-operatives. It is therefore necessary to begin this section with discussion of the development of the collective and its influence on the evolving genre of feminist theatre.

Changing memberships, politics, structures, theatres

A study of the politics of gender alone does not account for all of the changes influencing the structures of political and feminist theatre groups. A wider contextual framework can be constructed from feminist theatre groups which formed as a result of the fracturing of some of the key socialist groups operative in the 1960s and 1970s. For instance, the lesbians and gay men working in The General Will divided from the heterosexuals in 1971. The AgitProp Street Players became known as Red Ladder Theatre in 1973, but gender-related political differences led to internal factionalization in 1974. Similar factionalization was partially responsible for the separation of most of the female members of Belt and Braces into The Monstrous Regiment of Women in 1975. The decision of several women in Women's Theatre Group to take 'permanent leaves' was caused primarily by economic pressure related to gender; the women with children found it necessary to leave the company when it became a full-time organization in 1976. Sexual politics were also instrumental in the subdivision of the women from the men of Gay Sweatshop in 1977.

There are several different ways of approaching these examples. It is tempting, and in some circles common, to suggest that sexual politics played only a minor role in the development of these factional divisions. This approach implies that women's formation of their own groups was an extreme reaction to 'normal' levels of gender pressure. It is difficult to give an objective view of these structural changes, partially because they were potentially divisive for the feminist project. The image projected of developing factionalism was, in part, a creation of the media, but the deeply politicized roots of that factionalism must be acknowledged.

While the influence of sexual politics in the 1970s was substantial, the theatre of the period was influenced by other kinds of tensions as well. Such tensions became evident in disjunctions between political groups and theatre groups – disjunctions in terms of philosophies, memberships and structures. Some of this tension was explicitly party political, as Catherine Itzin has argued.[20] In response to the low spirits of the workers in the Labour Party, the first alternative political theatre group was formed in 1964. This group was called CAST: Cartoon Archetypical Slogan Theatre. CAST worked in an agitprop style, in the street and other non-theatre spaces. CAST was deliberately provocative and propagandist.

The AgitProp Street Players emerged from within CAST in 1968, and later became Red Ladder. The evolution of this series of groups is indicative of the turbulent atmosphere of the times. In 1968, CAST called a meeting of people who were 'both political and also into culture' and proposed the organization of a new group which would 'mediate between cultural groups' and act as a 'booking agency' for groups such as CAST.[21] The AgitProp Players was the group which formed in order to do this 'mediating'. That it was a theatre group, rather than a political action group, is significant. John Hoyland, one of the founding members of the AgitProp Players, claimed that the group was formed 'for the application of the imagination to politics and the application of politics to the imagination'.[22]

The company known as the AgitProp Players was broadly socialist, though no official party line was adopted. The company changed its name to Red Ladder in 1973, and produced *A Woman's Work is Never Done, or Strike While the Iron is Hot* in 1974.[23] The play was collaboratively devised and performed by a mixed group of politically motivated women and men. The topics addressed included women's roles in the workforce, equal pay, and women's rights. This play can be seen to have marked a turning point from early 1970s agitprop to the 'social realism' which prevailed in feminist theatres of the mid- and late 1970s. The stylistic shift was accompanied and partially caused by a shift in the political climate:

> Agitprop that may have been sophisticated in 1972 had, by 1974, become a strained hectoring to all but deaf ears. The political climate had changed. The mass confrontations of the past four years were over.[24]

In 1974, Red Ladder subdivided again. One group kept the name Red Ladder, and the other became Broadside Mobile Workers Theatre. A founding member of AgitProp, Kathleen McCreery, moved on to work with Broadside. McCreery described the new technique developed by the group as more subtle than the previous agitprop work:

> We went on to develop a multi-faceted, multi-pronged approach, the result of demands from the movement and also our own analysis of what was needed. We eventually came to use continuous characters who develop throughout the entire play, realistic scenes (in the Brechtian sense), dealing with complex issues not tied up in slogans.[25]

The refashioned Red Ladder moved to Leeds, and continued to work in a vein styled by *Strike While the Iron is Hot* (which also became known simply as 'Red Ladder's women's play'). Red Ladder soon staged two more plays with feminist undercurrents: *Taking Our Time* (1976/7) and *Nerves of Steel* (1977/8). In both of these plays, the members of Red Ladder confronted a common problem: 'how to maintain the critical awareness of an audience without "correct-lining" them to sleep.'[26] In confronting this problem, Red Ladder was influenced by the 'situated perspectives' of its members. The same problem has since been faced by many other feminist and alternative theatre groups and has been complicated with each new development in feminist theory and cultural studies.

For Red Ladder more than for previous alternative theatre groups, concern about the level of critical awareness of audiences was associated specifically with feminism. Red Ladder went through a pressured period of tension between the divergent values and positions of company members. The feminist members of the group argued for feminist content to the plays, while others argued that 'broader' or more 'generic' issues should be the focus of the work. The discrepancy illustrates one of the common sources of tension within alternative groups of the period: the 'generically' defined conception of politics included but did not prioritize feminism. Of course, Red Ladder was not alone in experiencing these internal pressures. During the period which saw both the production of Red Ladder's 'women's play' and its subdivision into separate companies, the large umbrella group known as Inter-Arts was also dividing into factions. The Inter-Action festivals produced in this period included important women's and gay theatre festivals which, as will be shown, contributed to the development of women's and gay theatre companies.

In continuing its examination of work relationships and gender divisions in the economic sector, the new Red Ladder was similar in some respects to feminist companies such as Women's Theatre Group (WTG). WTG was founded in 1974 and produced its second play, *Work to Role*, in 1976–7 on the subject of women at work. Gay Sweatshop was experiencing its own factional divisions in this period, culminating in the creation of a separate Women's Group and production of the first play about the rights of lesbian mothers, *Care and Control*, in 1977.

As these examples show, the idea of 'difference' had real implications, both as a concept in feminist theory and, at another level, as an unavoidable element of group work in the theatre. In each case, tensions were specific to company membership and group dynamics. Yet overall – to quote Kathleen McCreery, quoting Brecht – the same basic tenet held: 'The means must be questioned by the ends they serve.'[27] The ends of feminist theatre are (and were) change-oriented in terms of cultural representation, as well as theatrical. The means, the theatre itself, is therefore best evaluated in terms of both cultural and theatrical criteria. When women's roles within mixed gender theatre groups were marginalized, some women began to form new groups in which their interests might be prioritized. Collectives emerged as a popular alternative, particularly for emerging feminist theatre groups.

Theatre collectives from the 1970s to the present

The earliest theatre collectives operative in Britain included Red Ladder, Joint Stock, Welfare State International, 7:84, Avon Touring, Belt and

Braces, Women's Theatre Group, Monstrous Regiment, and Gay Sweat-shop, all formed in the late 1960s and early to mid-1970s. Members of some of these original collectives often worked with more than one group. Issues of authority and accountability proved problematic in those early years. As a result, internal struggles over issues such as gender and power led to the development of the first post-1968 women's theatre collectives.

In the mid-1960s, many women's increasing awareness of their marginal-ization in the political left corresponded to their marginalization in left-wing alternative theatre collectives. 'Consciousness raising' (CR) was influential in the development of women's theatre groups, just as it was in the development of the structure of the collective.[28] In recent years, as Sue-Ellen Case has noted, women of colour have pointed out that these CR groups were largely white: they did not include, nor reflect the interests and values of, women of colour.[29] In a British context, it should also be noted that these groups tended, on the whole, to include few working-class women who (especially in the 1970s, before the women's movement had influenced the distribution of waged work and 'housework' to any great extent), tended not to have the time for such seemingly passive political gatherings, though of course women were visible and vocal in working-class political activism of other kinds, such as the organization of trade unions. But even there, women's voices were often silenced, as they were in some early socialist theatre groups.

The differences in viewpoint which led many women (and some men) to leave the new left were basically the same as those which led women to leave mixed co-operatives in order to form their own companies: that is, a general recognition of women's 'second class' status in these supposedly liberal groups and structures. The separation of the lesbians from the gay men of the Gay Liberation Movement, for instance, was paralleled in the separation of the women from the men of Gay Sweatshop, when the separate Gay Sweatshop Women's Company was formed in 1977. In short, some women in the early 1970s began to realize that men had occupied most of the positions of power in the liberal left, and on a smaller scale, within alternative theatre collectives. They responded by forming all-women's theatre companies. These often took the form of co-operatives, a term denoting the assumed equality of all members of the collective.

By working in mixed companies in the 1960s and early 1970s, women had gained experience of both the benefits and the limitations of collective theatre work. This experience proved invaluable when they moved on to form companies organized around feminist concerns. Reference to a dis-cussion paper by seven collective members of various (often overlapping) groups during this turbulent period traces the evolution of the feminist theatre co-operative. The discussion, published in *Platform* in 1982, involved Jennifer Armitage (then of Monstrous Regiment and Red Ladder), David Bradford (of Belt and Braces), Claire Grove (of Avon Touring and WTG),

Liz Mansfield (of Red Ladder and Pirate Jenny), Ian Milton (of Pirate Jenny and 7:84 England), Tony Robinson (of Avon Touring) and Steve Trafford (of Red Ladder).[30] Each of these practitioners was involved in several – up to six or seven – different groups in their careers before 1982, and all have since worked with many other groups. Grove in particular is known for her work in contemporary feminist theatre, through her continued work with WTG.

Of the seven, four (Grove, Mansfield, Robinson and Trafford) directly addressed the issue of the hierarchical structure of theatre companies, and its effects on group dynamics. Mansfield and Grove spoke primarily from a feminist perspective, while Robinson and Trafford were more interested in what might have been referred to as the overall problems for theatre in general. In other words, the collective issues were men's issues and women's issues were viewed as marginal considerations, to be noted only when women raised them. In terms of group dynamics, it is significant that Robinson and Trafford were the directors, Grove and Mansfield the performers, though Grove would later work primarily as a director for WTG. The balance of 'collective' directorial power in this discussion group was in the hands of the men.

Liz Mansfield identified the common denominator between the various groups working as collectives or co-operatives (rather than in more traditional theatre structures) as 'to do with control over content. . . . Groups got together because they wanted to say particular things. It was actually out of that that a collective way of working emerged, rather than people saying that they wanted to oppose hierarchical structures.'[31] Mansfield's observation is not original, but rather representative: her emphasis on the importance of collective structures was also stressed by women working in groups such as Monstrous Regiment and WTG in the same period.

Another common observation was that the collective way of working was not (is not) necessarily the best means to making any strong, unified statement. The diversity of perspectives within any given group tended to expand and enrich the emerging 'voice' of any given play, a development which was sometimes viewed as a weakness. In the case of women's collectives, for instance, some reviewers criticized devised or collectively written plays as 'weak' due to what they perceived as overt politics superseding artistic form. A case in point was the RSC Women's Group's 1986 production of *Heresies*. The play was praised in theory (as a noble idea which 'answers a heresy expressed within its own ranks', i.e. the low profile of women within the RSC), but was also criticized in practice, particularly by the press, as a 'sludgy concoction' composed in a 'committee-style collaboration,' the best that can be said of which is that 'it cannot be blamed on a man'.[32]

In the *Platform* discussion, Claire Grove observed that: 'Quite often it [collective work] completely cut against what you wanted to say because, having set up a structure like that there's a feeling that everyone can contribute . . . and you ended up with a sort of gap in the middle of a group of people that was the play. All your intentions were right and the play was dreadful.' In the same discussion, Ian Milton described the dynamic of collective work in terms of a phenomenon of 'ultrademocracy': a good idea leading to mediocre results.[33] Despite the potential problems of the form, most of these practitioners continued to work collectively for some time, choosing to risk the potential flaws of the means in favour of its possibly liberating ends. But it is significant that it was the women in this group of practitioners who first became dissatisfied with the collective as form, and helped to develop a different form: the theatre co-operative.

The original theatre collectives were organized on the principal of equal responsibility among members for all aspects of production, a system which does not take into account the particular skills of individuals and which may therefore lead to construction of 'the gap which is the play'. In order to bridge that gap, it might be necessary for an individual to intervene and 'take control' of a given script or production, thereby invoking a hierarchical system. Yet as Grove noted in 1982, collectives were formed in order to oppose traditionally paternalistic structures within mainstream theatre, wherein the director (commonly known as the 'Old Man') was the authority figure who shaped the performance as a product of his own vision. Ironically, the potential flaw in the collective structure was its lack of provision for adequate safeguards against the imposition of paternalistic authority.

When individuals took more than 'equal' shares of power within groups, some group members began to be dissatisfied, and to attempt to find new ways of working which would allow them to regain control over their forms of representation. Women were among the innovators who formed the first theatre co-operatives. This is not surprising; assertion of control over the representation of self was central to women's struggles in many cultural domains, whether the issue was control over women's bodies in reproduction and representation, or of self-representation in society and in the theatre. Not finding adequate freedom of expression and control over the means of that expression within some alternative companies, many women (and men) turned instead to the co-operative. Co-operatives rejected structures which allowed for authoritarian control, whether by men or by women. The co-operative working system retained the ideal of the non-paternalistic power base, but allowed for exploitation (in a positive sense) of individual skills, without assigning different levels of worth or status to those skills. The transition in some companies from collective to co-operative status was never officially recorded. The transition did, however, mark an important shift in the nature of accountability of the members for various aspects of performance.

Defining the intended audience for the work of the women's co-operative was and is as important as the choice of the director and style of direction. At the base of women's collective work is the idea that women's theatre should be directed by women, at women and, arguably, about 'women's experiences'. The problematic relationship which any theory of feminism bears to a concept of 'women's experience' was raised in chapter 1. Here, the problem can be seen to be related directly to the area of 'women's writing', or the double bind of feminist practitioners aware of the diversity of 'situated perspectives' of individual spectators, and of the desirability of reaching the widest possible audiences for their work. To reach a wide audience, funding is necessary, but as Ian Milton noted in the *Platform* discussion, 'The Arts Council was very much against collective work, they always wanted to push people into having limited companies and Artistic Directors and so on, in order to make them respectable'. Respectable theatre, in the Arts Council's view, was hierarchically structured. Women's co-operatives did not fit this model. When theatre co-operatives were clearly informed by feminist concerns, the gap between the work and the requirements for funding was extended. The funding criteria did not change to 'suit' feminist theatre.[34] Thus, the theatre itself changed.

The subdivisions and factionalization which characterized alternative and feminist theatres of the 1970s and 1980s can be seen, at one level, as reactions to shifting structures and ideas within cultural politics, related to the economic climate of the period. The structures of alternative theatres have continued to shift in response to the changing cultural climate, influenced by developments in mass communication and changes in aesthetic fashion. The strongholds of the Theatres National and the West End commercial sector have not, on the whole, been as radically affected by these shifts as have fringe and feminist theatres. The Theatres National have had some (though not adequate) subsidy and have also attracted commercial sponsorship. The West End operates as a commercial enterprise, bending with the winds of economic change and charging high seat prices in order to keep up with inflation. But small theatre companies, and particularly those – like feminist theatres – informed by non-hierarchical principles of co-operation and relying on attendance by people of different social classes, have not fared so well. In recent years, co-operative status has tended to be replaced by collective management status as companies have found it necessary to compromise in order to remain viable. The majority of feminist companies in Britain at present operate on a profit share basis, 'hiring' (often without pay) directors who are members of their core groups, and, crucially, who are women.

The subgenres and factional divisions

Even in the earliest years of their formation, both the women's movement and feminist theatre groups experienced subdivisions based on differences of perspective between groups of women, as well as between women and men. These divisions resulted in the early formation of several different 'brands' of feminism, and thereby in several different 'brands' of feminist theatre. It is the definition of these subgenres as distinct entities which is both highly problematic and absolutely fundamental to the study of feminist theatre.

In her introduction to *Strike While the Iron is Hot*, Michelene Wandor recorded the events of the 1960s protests, and the development of the Women's Liberation Movement and the Gay Liberation Front. Both organizations were founded in 1969–70, and both were based on a perceived ideological struggle with its immediate roots in the student movement of 1968. In terms of a development from political consciousness to theatrical performance, Wandor observed that 'from the very beginnings theatrical self-expression was part of the feminist and gay movements.' She cites the beauty pageant protests of 1970 and 1971 as examples of feminist self-expression in cultural representation.[35] Feminist theatre was defined in terms of feminism, which was in turn defined in terms of political perspectives and activities.

As argued in chapter 1, feminist theatre has shifted its boundaries in accordance with social and economic movements. An example from 'first wave feminist theatre' illustrates the point: the Actress' Franchise League (AFL), formed in December of 1908, initially as a political suffrage support group and then as a playwriting group dedicated to furthering the suffrage cause.[36] The AFL can clearly be seen as a precursor to contemporary feminist theatre, in terms both of its means and its ends. While the AFL dealt in its work primarily with practical issues such as women's rights, the women involved in fringe and political theatre groups of the late 1960s and 1970s had more rigidly defined feminist issues in mind (as defined in relation to the term 'sexual politics'). Post-1968 feminist theatre took up some of the ideas of the AFL, but was more extreme in its demands, and (in time) more subtle in its tactics.

The development of style(s) in feminist theatre can be seen to have been channelled through a few roughly defined phases: from agitprop and street demonstrations, to social realism and docu-drama, to a range of contemporary approaches. More importantly, the development of feminist theatre has been influenced by a few key individuals. The same generation of women was involved in the street protests and demonstrations of the late 1960s as later helped to found a variety of feminist theatre companies. Among those women were Susan Todd, Kathleen McCreery, Anne Engel, Maggie Wilkinson and Gillian Hanna. Todd was involved in the street demonstrations which led to the formation of the Women's Street Theatre Group in 1970, and she was later involved in writing, producing and directing for groups including WTG, Monstrous Regiment and the short-lived RSC Women's Group (1984/5–7).[37] McCreery, as previously noted, was active in the AgitProp Street Players, Red Ladder and then Broadside Mobile Workers' Theatre; she eventually opted to work as a feminist in socialist theatre, rather than in feminist theatre as a socialist. After the Women's Street Theatre Group, many feminist theatre companies and mixed groups with pro-feminist politics emerged and regrouped, including Monstrous Regiment in 1976, and Mrs Worthington's Daughters in 1978.

To study the chronological development of feminist theatre companies is to recognize not only an issue-based difference of perspective between groups of women and men, but also – more disturbingly – a factionalism between groups of women. Most notably, a series of Women's Festivals – the first held in 1973 at the Almost Free Theatre, another in 1975 at the Action Space/Drill Hall (organized by Nancy Diuguid and Kate Crutchley) and a third in 1977 at the Drill Hall (organized primarily by members of Gay Sweatshop and WTG) – were the first all-women's theatrical events of their kind in post-war Britain. The first festival was sponsored by Ed Berman, director of Inter-Action, who invited women to take part in a season of women's work at the Almost Free, the Ambiance and King's Head Theatres. The success of this festival resulted in the production of several women's plays at lunchtime theatre clubs. The work of Pam Gems, Michelene Wandor, and Olwen Wymark was brought to public attention in this way. The 1973 season at the Almost Free also involved the members of what would soon become Gay Sweatshop, The Women's Company, and Women's Theatre Group. But as Catherine Itzin notes, there was considerable strife among women involved in the organization of that festival. The decision not to work in accordance with what were viewed as 'masculine' hierarchical structures was taken early on, but the alternative collective organization did not function satisfactorily. Internal tensions developed over the level and nature of involvement of various contributors, yet despite these internal tensions, the project was successful in public terms.[38] In Anne Engel's words: 'Despite all the problems, the event was exciting in focusing attention on the work of women.'[39] The factionalism of the season was political, but also structural. It was related to a view which aligned 'professionalism' with the (male) establishment.

As a result of the discrepancies over approach and structure which developed during the organization of this first season of women's work, the participants divided amongst themselves and formed two new companies: The Women's Company (composed of the 'professional' theatre practitioners) and Women's Theatre Group. Both companies were founded in 1974, but the Arts Council took a decision to provide funding for only one of the two companies: Women's Theatre Group. This decision forced the disbanding of The Women's Company. As no records or published explanations as to the reasons for the Arts Council's choice of recipients are available, it can only be surmised that the decision to fund only one of the two groups was intended to quell demands for funding without actively encouraging further proliferation of women's work, or indeed of feminist work.[40] Despite selective funding, several other feminist groups were founded in this period. Significantly, Monstrous Regiment was founded and also gained Arts Council support in 1976.

Of the groups which developed in the mid- to late 1970s, Mrs Worthington's Daughters was perhaps the most influential in the mid-1970s. Founded in 1978 by Anne Engel (also a founding member of WTG), Mrs Worthington's Daughters were not only women: they included Engel, Maggie Wilkinson, Julie Holledge, Stacey Charlesworth and one man: Stephen Ley.[41] The company was original in its choice of material: it produced plays by women of the past, thereby literally enacting the cultural feminist projects of 'rehistoricizing women's experience' and 'writing women into history'. The activities of the group are not well chronicled, but Holledge, Engel and Wilkinson have all contributed to the body of available information about the group.

> The company grew out of the Feminist Theatre Group which we set up in 1975 or 1976. . . . The FTG met once a month and provided a much needed network for women theatre workers. The steering committee turned into Mrs Worthington's; we'd done so much organizational and political work particularly in Equity that we decided we'd like to do a theatre project together.
>
> . . . We originally wanted to do experimental feminist work, a sort of women's hit and run theatre and the 'plays from the past' scheme was intended as a reliable income. At that time reclaiming women's 'herstory' was very popular, but no one was doing it in the theatre so we got funding quite easily.
>
> . . . We never wanted to become a permanent company. All of us had been in long term collectives and preferred the project nature of Mrs Worthington's. . . . All of us, except Steve for obvious reasons, had been in the WTG. . . . In some sense the histories of the two companies were intertwined in the seventies.[42]

This excerpt raises several important points: the group's emphasis on 'plays of the past' was a safety net of sorts, intended not only to 'reclaim women from history' but also to secure funding. This is the only known reference to the Feminist Theatre Group (FTG): none of the published sources so much as mentions the existence of such a group. The lack of available information is not altogether surprising, as it would be relatively easy to confuse or conflate FTG with WTG. The identification of the FTG is significant: it not only adds to the list of companies in Britain, but also adds the key term 'feminist' to the discussion as a term used by practitioners in order to label their own work.

In personal correspondence, Holledge explained that Mrs Worthington's Daughters developed as a separate and distinct company, although the members had previously worked with FTG and WTG. Mrs Worthington's Daughters was a mixed group known primarily for contemporary productions of historical plays by women. Anne Engel provided details about Mrs Worthington's operational status and eventual (market-initiated) demise. From 1978 to 1981, the company received grants from the Arts Council, Regional Arts Association and private sponsors; those grants were doubled each year for the first few years. The company was middle-scale, with average audiences of between 200 and 400 people. It operated six months of every year, thereby allowing company members to continue work on other projects. Engel reports that the company had both feminist aims and content, was a mixed group with feminist politics and was set up to 'rediscover work from the past by or about women'.[43] While there was no written Affirmative Action Policy, there was a positive woman to man ratio of members and participants in all areas of the company's work, including the audience. Then, in 1982, the grant from the Arts Council was cut completely; other grants were not sufficient to allow Mrs Worthington's Daughters to continue. In Engel's words:

> The reasons were never adequately spelled out, but the implication from the Arts Council was that we had been funded long enough. Even though we did try to comply and come up with some 'matching funds' from elsewhere, this was not enough. We tried making ourselves more marketable in a very direct sense: we re-named ourselves 'Mrs Worthington's Daughter's Daughters', and we did live adverts to earn money at the King's Head. They were successful with the audiences, but didn't raise enough money to keep the company going. We disbanded in 1982.[44]

Engel's account does not contradict that given by Holledge. While the company was not permanent, it was envisioned as one which would continue as long as the material and energy were available; the 'surprise' thus resulted from the sudden and unexpected loss of funding. Because Mrs Worthington's Daughters was disbanded, it is not included in the following 'case study' section. Nor has any space been allowed for discussion of the short-lived RSC Women's Group, though that project was unique both in its development within mainstream theatre, and in terms of the controversial nature of the group's eventual demise.

One last feminist company deserves brief mention here, as it was a direct predecessor of Women's Theatre Group. Catherine Itzin has noted that 'while the Women's Theatre Group did not formalize itself until 1974, there had been a loose, *ad hoc* group since 1971 operating as a women's street theatre called Punch and Judies, performing for demonstrations and similar events'.[45] The Punch and Judies performed a street theatre show called *The Amazing Equal Pay Play* in 1972 (later filmed by the Women's Film Group). The work of the Punch and Judies – like the work of the

Women's Street Theatre Group, Red Ladder and the AgitProp Street Players before them – was significant not only in terms of content and intent but also in terms of style and the development of extrascenic effects. The Punch and Judies' *Amazing Equal Pay Play* had a tremendous impact on changing social expectations about what, or who, a theatre audience could be. The show played to working men's clubs, tenants' associations, schools, women's groups, and trade union meetings; it exposed all those various audiences to its controversial themes of women's rights and abortion. In the words of Chris Rawlence: 'We began to broaden our audiences . . . and with this broadening the context of performance shifted'.[46] With this expansion of the audience came the first signs of a widening social tolerance of 'women's issues' as performed on stage. With this tolerance for 'women's issues' came a demand for theatrical representations of women and women's work by women and for (among other groups) women. Only in such an atmosphere could groups such as WTG, Monstrous Regiment and Gay Sweatshop be established. More to the point, only once this kind of staging of 'women's issues' was popularized could such groups secure funding.

3

FOUR COMPANIES

This chapter provides detailed case studies of four long-running feminist companies: Women's Theatre Group, Monstrous Regiment, Gay Sweatshop and Siren, all of which were founded in the 1970s by women who had been active in the theatre and politics of the late 1960s (Anne Engel, Susan Todd, Michelene Wandor, Gillian Hanna, Mary McCusker, Kate Owen, Nancy Diuguid, Tash Fairbanks and others). All four groups are still in operation in 1992, though all have been threatened by funding cuts and Siren is temporarily inactive. As noted in the introduction, Women's Theatre Group has recently changed its name to The Sphinx; the name WTG is used, however, in discussion of the company's work. The first three of these companies have received critical attention, particularly in Itzin, Case, Keyssar, and Wandor.[1] Siren has received less attention, at least in 'academic' sources. This chapter adds to existing sources by investigating issues such as the nature of women's levels of involvement in the defining and negotiating power dynamics within the groups, approaches to the redefinition of styles and themes for feminist theatre, and responses to the current funding crisis.

While these four companies are by no means representative of all the feminist theatre work which has emerged in Britain since the early 1970s, they have all played central roles in the development of feminist theatre as genre, and have been instrumental in the founding of other groups (key individuals from all three have moved on to initiate and encourage the work of women in other companies). These four companies, and their members, have contributed significantly to the process of cross-fertilization which is crucial to the continuing development of feminist theatre as an active, change-oriented genre.

WOMEN'S THEATRE GROUP

Women's Theatre Group (WTG) was one of the first all-women's theatre groups to gain national recognition. Founded in 1974, WTG is one of the few women's companies to have survived the past decade's legacy of cuts to theatre funding, and to have developed as a small- to middle-scale touring company with stringent positive discrimination and equal opportunities policies, and a strong commitment to promoting lesbian and multiracial work. The group best expresses its own origins and goals:

> Our beginnings coincided with and were part of the growing Women's Liberation Movement in Britain. Feminism insisted that links be made between outside and inside the home, between the world of politics 'out there' and what was happening in relationships, friendships, families and so on. In our work we attempt to explore these links in terms of the concept 'the personal is political'.[2]

This statement of aims was printed in the 1980s, but is consistent with the company's founding principles as well.

WTG developed directly out of the earlier women's street theatre and agitprop groups of the late 1960s and early 1970s, in terms of membership as well as of structure and intent. The group demonstrated a continuity of personnel from earlier feminist companies. For example, Anne Engel was a founding member of both WTG and Mrs Worthington's Daughters, while other WTG members had taken part in the Women's Festivals and had been involved with the Punch and Judies.

The content of WTG's material has always been informed by feminism, and often by specifically radical or cultural feminist ideas.[3] For instance, the material has employed themes of 'rehistoricizing' typical to the feminist critical practice of the 1970s and early 1980s, as in Clare MacIntyre and Stephanie Nunn's *Better a Live Pompey than a Dead Cyril* (1980–1, an examination of the life of poet Stevie Smith); as well as in Timberlake Wertenbaker's *New Anatomies* (1980–2, a dramatization of the life and adventures of the explorer Isabelle Eberhardt); and in Joyce Halliday's *Anywhere to Anywhere* (1985: about women workers in the Air Transport Auxiliary). Even in the first decade, the group's work covered topics ranging from contraception (their first production, *My Mother Says I Never Should*, devised by the company and produced in 1975–6), to women in the workplace (the second production, *Work to Role*, group-devised and produced in 1976–7), the peace movement (Kate Phelps' *My Mkinga*, produced in 1980), and pornography and the issue of representing women's bodies (Jacqui Shapiro's *Trade Secrets*, produced in 1984).

WTG was one of the first groups to identify feminist issues as appropriate for representation in the theatre. It was also one of the first companies to include lesbian plays (such as Libby Mason's *Double Vision*, described in *City Limits* in 1982 as 'like a Woody Allen script for lesbians') in its feminist repertoire.[4] The lesbian feminist perspective of some of the work was not, however, made explicit in press materials: the 1985 company brochure described *Double Vision*, along with Elizabeth Bond's *Love and Dissent* (1983), and Libby Mason and Tierl Thompson's *Dear Girl* (1983), ambiguously

63

as 'plays . . . which have looked at the relationship between women's personal and public lives'. Since 1985, though funds to WTG have increased at rates below the rate of inflation, the company's output has remained steady, and themes have expanded to include emphasis on lesbian issues, notably in two plays by Bryony Lavery: *Witchcraze* (1985) and *Her Aching Heart* (1990). That lesbian work was explicitly advertised as such after imposition of Section 28 is in itself significant.[5]

In the area of stylistically experimental work, the company has produced plays such as Deborah Levy's *Pax* (1985). *Pax* was recognized by the group as the first of its plays to mark a departure from naturalism in terms of company style and, appropriately, the first to take feminist issues into the public and even the global sphere. The theme of *Pax* is 'the future of women's culture in the nuclear age'.[6] WTG's experimental style carried over into other types of work, such as the group-devised production of *Lear's Daughters* (1987/8), scripted by Elaine Feinstein with WTG; this play is discussed at length in chapter 4. An experimental style was also evident in the WTG production of *Mortal* by Maro Green and Caroline Griffin (1990). Both *Lear's Daughters* and *Mortal* show that feminist ideology can be artfully and successfully enacted on stage. Both deal, in a sense, with mother-daughter relationships and with the idea of inheriting 'false fathers'. *Lear's Daughters* is the 'prehistory' or 'prequel' to Shakespeare's story of King Lear, told from the perspective of the three daughters. *Mortal* is a surreal play which depicts daughters searching for their mothers and for appropriate partners. The play takes place in a timeless twilight space, and deals with the mother–daughter theme as well as with a range of other themes including lesbianism, homophobia, friendship, desire and death.[7]

Economically and politically, the style of WTG has shifted through the years with changing company memberships. In the early years (1974–7), the group consisted of six members: Lynne Ashley, Clair Chapman, Sue Eatwell, Anne Engel, Julia Meadows and Mica Nava. The themes of the first shows were definitively issue-based, dealing with contraception and women and work. Social realism was the most common form or style of this early work. All the plays were group-devised by the WTG company up until 1978, when Eileen Fairweather and Melissa Murray were commissioned to script *Hot Spot*, which dealt with the complex nature of sexual stereotyping through the representation of ideal female and male archetypes relating to the ideal of 'normal girlhood'. Thereafter, all plays produced by WTG were scripted, though the process of production usually involved a period of devising or collaborative input from the company before the script was written. Partly, this change of approach was contingent upon the skills and interests of the company members, who described themselves in 1985 as 'a collective of six women who jointly implement the artistic and general policy of the group, to produce theatre about the many aspects

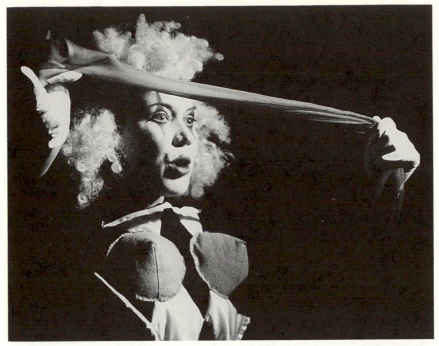

2 Hazel Maycock as the androgynous Fool in *Lear's Daughters*, WTG, 1987/8.

of women's position in society and to create more work and opportunities for women'.[8]

By 1985, the group had effectively changed hands, though a complete change of management did not occur. Libby Mason, Eileen Fairweather and Melissa Murray were instrumental in the development of WTG in this period. The 1985 brochure describes the company's policy on devising and scripting, as well as on performing in non-theatre spaces, encouraging work by new writers and doing rehearsed readings.[9] Just as these innovative techniques were being announced, however, the Greater London Council, co-sponsor of WTG's series of rehearsed readings, was being abolished. The 1985 brochure and some of the production programmes printed at the time urged audience members to support WTG and other groups by writing letters to MPs and to the Minister of Arts, Lord Gowrie. These displays of support had primarily symbolic value. The Greater London Council was abolished and, as predicted, funding cuts soon followed for many art organizations, including fringe theatre companies – such as women's companies – with 'minority' interests.

WTG's response to the Feminist Theatre Survey, received in March 1989, illustrates the long-term effects of these and other funding cuts. The company reported operational status and plans to remain operational in the foreseeable future. Responses also indicated that the group was, in 1989 as in 1985, small- to middle-scale in size, and composed exclusively of feminist women working toward feminist achievements in society through the theatre. A continued emphasis on devising and commissioning was reported, along with affirmation of the group policy of producing rehearsed readings as 'a way of developing work'. Interestingly, the survey does not list Theatre in Education (TIE) as a working method, though the group's first play was the definitive feminist TIE production. In fact, *My Mother Says I Never Should* was so well received that it was taped and distributed to schools as educational material on sex education and contraception.[10]

In response to this seeming discrepancy, Jenny Clarke (company administrator in 1990) explained that the company's general policy on theatre for children is one of indirect support. While particular plays are performed in schools, and while workshops (open to students) are offered in conjunction with each new production, WTG prefers to leave TIE work as such to professional TIE companies and member companies of SCYPT (The Standing Conference of Young People's Theatre).[11] Hence, when WTG commissioned Julie Wilkinson's 1989 production of *Pinchdice and Co.*, the commission was specifically intended to cover rewriting the play for an adult audience. The play – which depicts a group of women fighting in the twelfth-century crusade battlefields – was originally written as a TIE piece for the Theatre Centre's Women's Company. Despite the decision not to do TIE or YPT (Young People's Theatre) work as such, WTG has retained strong links with young people in its workshops and tours of schools and community centres. The last point on the list of WTG policies reiterates the aim of providing 'a resource centre to all women, and young women in particular'.[12]

Changes in group policy since 1985 fall primarily in two areas: group composition, and funding. The company policy on multiracial work had been made explicit by 1985, and the policy on equal opportunities had been defined as an attempt to 'offer positive discrimination to all women in our employment practice and in our work, and . . . to positively discriminate in favour of Black women and Lesbians'.[13] Further changes came into effect in 1989, in a complete reorganization of the company from collective status to that of a small management team. In addition, the company created a Board of Directors which consisted in 1990 of four women: Caroline Falkus, Myrtle Kirton, Maria Warner, and Clarie Middleton, each with her own area of expertise (one a solicitor, one a financial administrator, one a performer and one a specialist in equal opportunities Policies).[14] One of the major responsibilities assigned to the new board was the rewriting of the equal opportunities Policy, which covers multiracial issues as well as anti-discrimination factors regarding sex, sexual preference and age.

The abolition of the Greater London Council had the adverse effects on funding which WTG had predicted in 1985, resulting in the company's increased reliance on the Arts Council for support. WTG received a 2 per cent increase in Arts Council revenue funding in 1987 and another 2 per cent increase in 1988, but was transferred to annual funding for 1989/90, necessitating applications for three-year funding packages. WTG receives some support from the London Borough Grants Scheme, and some project funding for touring productions from various Regional Arts Associations. In 1989, Jenny Clarke indicated that if the application for three-year funding from the Arts Council were to fail, project funding would be the only remaining option. Clarke reported in 1990 that an effective 8 per cent increase was awarded by the Arts Council in 1989, but that as this 'increase' did not exceed the rate of inflation, it amounted to stand-still funding for 1990/1. The company therefore began to consider strategies which might increase its market earning potential. WTG decided on two main strategies in 1990/1. It decided to attempt to 'raise its profile' by moving to new offices and designing a new logo, in order to attract sponsorship. This first plan was recognized, even at the time, as a difficult one to achieve since, in Clarke's words, WTG is 'not what the sponsors want to fund, and [WTG has] already tried numerous times to raise funds through sponsorship, without success'. WTG also decided to attempt to upgrade its market appeal by booking tour shows into 'quality venues' in order to increase earnings at the box office.

Clarke reported in 1990 that the announcement of devolution of Arts Council funding to the regions would not affect WTG too radically at first, since, like other small- and middle-scale touring companies, it would temporarily remain an Arts Council client. While these economic changes continue in 1992, WTG must attempt to maintain the quality of its work, without expanding in terms of size or funding. This will mean 'working more and more with the same resources and the same number of staff, producing plays with two to five performers, and doing no more than three productions a year'. This describes the current working conditions not only of WTG, but also of many other contemporary feminist theatres.

Later in 1990, WTG announced a decision to change its name to The National Women's Theatre Company. The name change was scheduled to take effect in late 1991, and was decided upon for a combination of marketing and artistic reasons:

> Firstly, the name no longer reflects the truth about the company – we are no longer a co-operative, but have a small fixed management structure. . . . We have found in the past that the name 'Women's Theatre Group' has given the wrong impression about the company both within and outside the profession – we are confused with other women's companies ('Which Women's Theatre Group?') and

assumed to be an amateur or umbrella organization. . . . We have therefore considered both this problem and the resolve of the company to broaden its artistic vision and raise its public profile in the choice of the new name.[15]

This statement suggests that the feminist co-operative may not be a tenable structure in the current economic climate. The proposed name 'The National Women's Theatre Company' would have been more likely to attract commercial sponsorship in the sense that it includes the key word 'national', a word which seems to have nearly as much power as the word 'royal' in terms of attracting sponsorship. But the company decided against this rather conservative move. In late 1991, the name of the Women's Theatre Group was changed to The Sphinx. The brochure advertising the first production of the newly titled company explains the decision in this way:

Why The Sphinx?
As the original national touring women's theatre company, the Women's Theatre Group has been developing and commissioning new theatre writing by women since 1973. Following a summer of extensive research into audience perceptions of the field, in which a number of our mailing-list members took part, the company marks a new phase in its life with a new name, The Sphinx, and with the artistic maturity to take its place in the mainstream of British theatre. The Sphinx reflects the work of the company in all her qualities:

She is:
FEMALE – placing women's experience centre-stage;
CLASSICAL – proud of her past, developing the canon of women's writing;
STORY-TELLING – producing original, spectacular, high-quality theatre;
MULTIFORM – reflecting women in all their diversity and subjectivity;
DANGEROUS – challenging and risk-taking theatre;
ORGANIC – nurturing the development of women's writing.

She has:
A WOMAN'S HEAD – to be a leading voice in addressing the cultural disenfranchisement of women;
A LION'S BODY – to fight for the creative freedom of women artists.[16]

This set of 'qualities' reflects an obvious bias toward the cultural feminist perspective in the company's newly revised image. Other changes include the appointment of the first Writer-in-Residence in January of 1992 – Charlotte Keatley – whose play *My Mother Said I Never Should* also reflects cultural feminist concerns with the mother–daughter role and its construction in society. It is a play which, in many ways, is about the 'cultural disenfranchisement of women' and which ends with a hopeful tableau depicting the young woman, Rosie, involved in making a business of her art work. Significantly, the new patrons of the company include Marilyn French – an academic and critic as well as a writer – and a director (Janet Suzman), a television producer (Linda Agran) and a 'renowned classical actress' (Dorothy Tutin). Cultural and economic influences have certainly affected the company's way of presenting, or representing, itself and of appealing to as wide a circle of women as possible.

MONSTROUS REGIMENT

Monstrous Regiment was formed as a feminist theatre collective in 1975 by a small group of actors who 'wanted to make exciting political theatre based on women's experience', because they were 'tired of seeing that experience marginalized or trivialized,' and they 'wanted to take it out of the wings and place it at the centre of the stage.'[17] One of the earliest British feminist theatre groups and one of the few original groups still operating in Britain, the Regiment was set up as a permanent collective committed to both feminist and socialist ideals. Initially, the group had no permanent artistic director and all policy decisions were made 'democratically'. This structure has changed in recent years due to financial restrictions limiting numbers of full-time staff, but the working practices developed in the early years of the collective can still be seen to shape the Regiment's work.

The history of Monstrous Regiment is the history of its members. Directors who have worked on Regiment shows include Pam Brighton, Penny Cherns, Kate Crutchley, Sue Dunderdale, Ann Mitchell, Nancy Meckler, Nona Shepphard, Sue Todd, Clare Venables and Hilary Westlake. Writers who have contributed to Regiment productions include Caryl Churchill, Wendy Kesselman, Bryony Lavery, Claire Luckham, Honor Moore, Melissa Murray, Franca Rame, Rose Tremain, Michelene Wandor and Susan Yankowitz, in addition to Bowler, Hanna and McCusker. Performers who have worked with the Regiment since 1976 are too numerous to list, but include women (and men) known for their involvement in a wide range of British theatres, from Paola Dionisotti (known for her work with the RSC) to Susan Todd (known for directing the RSC Women's Group, as well as for work with the early Women's Street Theatre Group) to Ann Mitchell (known primarily for fringe, feminist theatre work).[18]

Three key members have had a tremendous impact on the development of Monstrous Regiment: Gillian Hanna, Mary McCusker, and Chris Bowler. Hanna, like Anne Engel of Mrs Worthington's and WTG, is one of the women identified in Chapter 2 as having been instrumental in the development of a wide range of British feminist theatres in the past two decades. Hanna worked with 7:84 Theatre Company and with Belt and

Braces from 1971 to 1975, before co-founding Monstrous Regiment in 1975. She worked exclusively within the Regiment from 1975 to 1981/2, and is one of the three original members (with McCusker and Bowler) who still actively participate in Regiment management, production and perform-ance, though Hanna currently works extensively outside the group as well. Her work extends to mainstream feminist plays such as her role in Caryl Churchill's *Ice Cream* at the Royal Court Theatre (Spring 1989). Also in 1989, Hanna translated Dario Fo's *Elizabeth* and began work on a com-mission to translate (and retranslate) the complete *oeuvre* of the one-woman plays of Franca Rame and Dario Fo. Three of the Rame/Fo plays – under the umbrella title *A Common Woman* – were performed by Hanna in 1989.[19] Similarly, both McCusker and Bowler have been involved in a wide variety of feminist theatre projects since the mid-1970s.

Of all the feminist theatre groups operative in Britain since 1968, Mon-strous Regiment has had the most consistently international base under-lying its work. European experimentation has been given considerable space, as in the company's adaptation of plays such as Dacia Maraini's *Dialogue Between a Prostitute and One of her Clients* in 1980, Théâtre de l'Aquarium's *Shakespeare's Sister* in 1982, and Franca Rame and Dario Fo's *Fourth Wall* in 1983.[20] The situation of imprisoned women in Chile was the subject of the 1986 production of Jorge Diaz's *My Song is Free*. American feminist plays have also been produced by Monstrous Regiment, including Honor Moore's *Mourning Pictures* (1981), Susan Yankowitz's *Alarms* (1986) and Wendy Kessleman's *My Sister in this House* (1987). Thus, Monstrous Regiment has avoided the Anglocentric emphasis of so much British thea-tre, and has enriched British feminist theatre by incorporating international perspectives in many different contexts. Unfortunately, however, funding for the company has not allowed it to produce much of its work abroad.

Monstrous Regiment was unique among the early feminist groups in its inclusion of men, both in the early collective structure and in individual performances. The group began with a commitment to foregrounding the work and experiences of women, but did not exclude men on principle. However, by 1980 there were no longer any men working with the group. The shift to all-women's status was a result neither of conflict, nor of political or personal tension. As Hanna explained in interview: 'The shift from a mixed to an all-women's group was more of a process than a decision; it was something that evolved.'[21] It is significant that the Regi-ment experienced a shift in working practices once the men had left the group. When interviewed in 1978, Hanna described the working practices in some mixed theatre groups and observed that women's opinions and perspectives tended to be respected only up to a point: as long as women were willing to raise them continually, and until deadlines loomed and concerns shifted back to the 'major' concerns of production.

In the 1989 interview, Hanna added that though this negative dynamic could still be seen in other groups, it had not affected the Regiment's recent work, although the 'men in feminism' question was, and is, problematic even for an established group such as the Regiment:

> In the early days, . . . it had a tremendous impact on the way we viewed ourselves as a company, and as individuals within a company: a framework which seemed to be replicating the values of the world outside the theatre. And indirectly, that contributed to the evolution of the Regiment as an all-women's feminist group.[22]

Monstrous Regiment responded twice to the Feminist Theatre Survey. The first response (1988) identified the group as a middle-scale company of feminist women, funded by the Arts Council, working with a variety of different methods including commissioning, collaboration, devising and rehearsed readings (but not TIE), with both feminist intent and content and with positive ratios of women to men in terms of membership, playwrights produced and directors employed, but not in terms of audience. No affirmative action policy was reported. In the second survey, returned in 1989, these were the responses: the company defined itself as middle-scale, funded by the Arts Council and by revenue grants. The company was granted £72,400, an increase of 2 per cent. It noted: 'We have only ever had an increase of 2 per cent, which is effectively a cut, due to inflation.' It chose the label 'mixed group with feminist politics' and added that it tends to solicit new material primarily by commissioning work. It indicated that it has both feminist intent and content, an affirmative action policy, and a positive woman to man ratio of members and contributors in all areas, including the audience.

The discrepancies in these survey responses are most directly attributable to individual interpretation of the questions, rather than to changes in the brief period from 1988 to 1989. Discrepancies in most questions can be seen to be caused by differences in approach: the first set of answers reflects more general company policies and exhibits a hesitancy about generalizing (e.g. on audience figures), while the second set of responses seems to refer to a particular individual's view of current company policies (e.g. on commissioning work, and the operative but undocumented affirmative action policy). What is most interesting is the discrepancy in responses to question three. The fact that the same company can be described as 'feminist' and 'all-women's' on the one hand and 'mixed with feminist politics' on the other, though men have not been active in the group for years, is indicative of the flexibility of all those labels and the complexity of the term 'feminist'.

Despite all the various sources of input and changes in company policy over the years, the core membership of Monstrous Regiment has remained fairly stable: unlike WTG, the Regiment has remained within the hands of a few key women who have hired others for input and support on particular projects. In the 1970s and early 1980s, when the group was larger, hiring and commissioning could be done primarily from within the group. In recent years, however, members of the collective have not been paid, with the result that core members are few. The Regiment management collective has therefore built up a network of writers, directors, designers and performers who can be called upon to work with them on particular productions.

Of the women who worked with the Regiment from the beginning, only Susan Todd eventually withdrew. Writers including Bryony Lavery and Caryl Churchill moved on to work with other companies, but have retained links with the Regiment. After the financial changes of the past decade, however, the Regiment has been forced to reshape itself from a collective to a management collective. The company described this restructuring in the report produced in response to the 'The Glory of the Garden', in which it presented an image of itself as a group withstanding government pressure.

> That there should no longer be a permanent Monstrous Regiment collective was a painful economic choice. That we should have restructured ourselves, within economic strictures, as a collective management, was a creative positive decision that is already bearing fruit.[23]

Hanna has since described a marked decline in political energy in the theatre generally, which she sees as a result of two factors: 'the unfashionable status of feminism and ideology on the one hand, and the unfashionable status of theatre on the other'.[24] Monstrous Regiment has survived the cuts to arts funding of the past few years, though it has found it necessary to reduce the numbers of permanent staff and the scale of the projects and some projects have been waiting over five years for production.[25] The move from collective status to that of collective management parallels the move within WTG from collective status to that of a 'small management team'. Both companies have been forced to adapt, both in terms of structure and of scale, in order to survive.

Other Regiment initiatives in recent years are the attachment of a new writer's residency (assigned to Tash Fairbanks, a founding member of Siren Theatre) and the development of a workshop series, the stated aim of which is to 'meet the needs of new writers'.[26] The Regiment, like WTG, sometimes makes Sign Language interpretation of their plays available, and makes a consistent effort to incorporate the work of black women and women of colour whenever possible. Accessibility, however, is not always compatible with market forces.

The Regiment has long served as a role model for feminist theatre. It is ironic, therefore, to reread the optimistic 'conclusions' of its response to the Arts Council's 'Glory of the Garden' report, and to compare them to statements made the following year. In the 1984 report, the company stated its larger aims in these terms: 'Although smaller in size than, say, the RSC, our aims are no less ambitious. We too wish to create a pool of actors, writers, directors and designers who, by working with the company over long periods with shared ideas, achieve a distinctive style'.[27] In 1985, Monstrous Regiment was already experiencing difficulties resulting from the uneven distribution of wealth assigned by the Arts Council's 'gardeners'. They told Clive Barker in interview that funding policies were not allowing them the 'right to fail'.[28] This statement is indicative of the situation of feminist theatre companies in general: when even the most established are affected (as both WTG and Monstrous Regiment so clearly were, and continue to be), then smaller companies are sure to be affected as well.

Cuts to funding have meant a decline in the number of performers, the scale of shows produced and the number of productions mounted by any one company in any given year. Gillian Hanna has explained in detail what all these changes have meant in practical terms, not only for the Regiment, but also for most feminist and fringe theatre. She ended philosophically:

> We may seem in some ways to be at a bit of a standstill, but there is always movement. I've talked an awful lot about financial problems, but of course the changes that have come about since 1975 have been influenced by a whole range of other factors as well: cultural, political, ideological, social; everything is up in the air, and there isn't any way to know where it will all land, or to what effect.[29]

Monstrous Regiment continues to promote the work of women artists. The work has been largely successful, and the collected reviews show that the critical responses the group has elicited through the years, like the shows themselves, have been political as well as 'artistic', and often highly controversial.[30] Perhaps the most valuable contribution of Monstrous Regiment to the feminist theatre movement is its longevity – its tenacious survival, and its support of women's 'right to fail' as well as to succeed in the act of making feminist theatre. Whether it will continue to do so will depend as much upon changes in patterns of theatre funding in the next few years as upon any factors within the control of the company itself.

GAY SWEATSHOP

Though Gay Sweatshop is known primarily as a mixed company of lesbians and gay men, it must be included as one of the four most influential 'feminist' theatre companies, as it has contributed substantially to the development of lesbian theatre as genre. Though some definitions of 'feminism' and 'feminist theatre' would not allow for inclusion of a mixed gender group, it is, in the case of Gay Sweatshop (as it was in the case of the early Monstrous Regiment), both impossible and inaccurate to exclude the group from discussion of feminist theatre. The majority of feminist theatre groups in Britain would not have developed in the same way without the earlier contributions of groups such as Monstrous Regiment and Gay Sweatshop.

Sweatshop did not always promote and provide a positive atmosphere in which women might work, and the history of women in the company, and of the short-lived women's group within the larger company, is complex. A separate women's group formed in 1977 and then rejoined the mixed management company in 1984. A Sweatshop Women's Group as such is no longer in operation. The company currently produces all-women's shows on a regular basis, and is managed by a mixed artistic directorship. The mixed company known as Gay Sweatshop developed out of extensive collaboration by gay and lesbian performers taking part in the Women's Theatre Festival sponsored by Inter-Action in the autumn of 1973. Later festivals – including the one organized by Nancy Diuguid and Kate Crutchley, held over a three-week period at the Action Space/Drill Hall in 1975 – inspired many other events and initiated the development of women's companies of all kinds, from Sisterwrite Booksellers and RPM music, to the Women's Company and WTG. Diuguid and Crutchley, both of whom were to become active members of Gay Sweatshop, defined their motivation for organizing the event as an attempt to begin 'breaking down the barriers between so-called feminists and so-called non-feminists, which is something the media built up. . . . To encourage women to talk again and break down myths that are created on both sides'.[31] Just as the first Women's Festival inspired a women's theatre season at the Almost Free in 1973, so the second festival in 1975 inspired Ed Berman to develop and direct a Gay Theatre Season. Only one play by a lesbian was proposed for possible inclusion in that season: Jill Posener's *Any Woman Can*. The play was rejected by Berman on the grounds that it was not 'theatrical' enough. The gay plays from this season were published but the women's plays from the festival were not.

Gay Sweatshop was founded in 1975, after the success of the first gay theatre season. Many women were active in the company from the beginning – Jill Posener, Kate Owen and Nancy Diuguid among them. Posener's *Any Woman Can* was eventually produced in 1976 by the Sweatshop company, and was, in a sense, the first play to be produced by the women of Gay Sweatshop; that is, it was the first Gay Sweatshop play written and performed entirely by women. But when the play was produced in 1976, the women's group 'proper' had not yet separated from the larger company. Several concurrent events and circumstances led to the division of the women from the men. When the Sweatshop formed during the 1975 season (opening with *Mr X* by Drew Griffiths), many women in the audiences expressed concern because there were no women involved. *Any Woman Can* was then produced in 1976. In its next season, Sweatshop as a mixed company produced two shows: *Jingle Ball* (1976), a pantomime spoof on the story of Cinderella, and *Age of Consent* (1977, for the Royal Court's Young People's Scheme), a play which explored the relationship of the law and homosexual acts between consenting adults. The phrasing of the title *Age of Consent* testifies to the long-term effects and echoes of the wording of the British Sexual Offences Acts.

Even at this early point, public representation of lesbians and gay men was becoming a political issue, and one which bore a problematic relationship to the theatre. Nancy Diuguid, an organizer of the 1975 Women's Festival and a founding member of Gay Sweatshop, prepared a short answer to the hypothetical question 'Why a gay theatre group?' which is illuminating in this context. Diuguid wrote: 'We hope to make an artistic contribution to the theatrical scene; if we can attract people to us, professional theatre people and others, who are *not* ashamed of being gay, or see no horror in being assumed to be gay, then we shall have made a political contribution also'.[32]

This short statement encapsulates several important points: the Sweatshop formed as an action-oriented political theatre company composed of both women and men. The company made an early distinction between various uses of political theatre – for entertainment's sake, as an art form, and as a forum for political action – and also recognized that the same play could perform several functions at once. There was no single party line within the Sweatshop, nor did the group set out to create one. Instead, Sweatshop encouraged the representation of differing points of view. Some writers who were asked to work with the group were not (or were not 'out' as) lesbians or gays. This structure allowed women like Michelene Wandor, for instance, to contribute material and to script one of Sweatshop's most influential plays, *Care and Control*, without declaring any allegiance to or identification with lesbianism as a personal politic: it was enough that the work produced presented alternatives to the heterosexual viewpoint represented in so many other forms of cultural representation.

From the beginning, the work of Gay Sweatshop has been pro-lesbian and gay, but not anti-heterosexual or inherently separatist. In terms of women's representation within the company, the fact that non-lesbian writers and theatre workers have occasionally chosen or been invited to work with the Sweatshop is clearly indicative of an alignment with feminism which may override, at least at some points, the particular concerns of lesbianism. Finally, the wording of the passage suggests that what defines lesbian or gay theatre *per se* is not the level or variety of allegiance with lesbian and gay concerns, but rather public perception thereof. As Diuguid's statement implies, the fact that anyone working with the Sweatshop could be 'assumed to be gay' and that this is further assumed to be a negative incentive is indicative of the pervasive heterosexual bias of British theatre and society.

Even within the Sweatshop's flexible framework, the representation of women and particularly the representation of the lesbian was extremely problematic. The situation became so inflamed that in 1977 the women in the company left the main company in order to form their own group. The division, Michelene Wandor explains, was accomplished for two practical reasons:

> The first was similar to the split that had occurred within the Gay Liberation Front itself, in that lesbians felt that many features of their oppression were shared more with other women than with gay men. One of the consequences of this was to be seen in a conflict between theatrical styles, in that the men drew on an already familiar camp and drag tradition, which they both celebrated and tried to stand on its head, whereas the women leaned more towards the newer agitprop, documentary-based styles, as a means of showing hitherto suppressed lesbian experience. The problem of male dominance in the organization of the group and the clash of styles was acknowledged on both sides, and the plays done in 1977 reflected this divergence of emphasis.[33]

When the group divided, both the women's and the men's subgroups were sheltered by the umbrella organization of Gay Sweatshop, though both retained artistic autonomy. That same year, Gay Sweatshop was instrumental in organizing two festivals: the women assisted in organizing the third Women's Festival, and the men organized the Gay Times Festival (both held at the Drill Hall). A considerable conflict of interests was apparent: the women in the company aligned themselves with other theatre women, while the men aligned themselves with other gay men. The emphasis was thus on feminist and cultural concerns for the women, and on issues of sexual (gay) politics for the men. The 'men's play' of the first 'split' season was Noel Greig's and Drew Griffith's *As Time Goes By*, structured into sections dramatizing in turn the overt repression of homosexuals, the Oscar Wilde trial and its repercussions, Berlin in the 1930s and the beginnings of the Gay Liberation Front in 1969.

The women's play, or the first play produced by the Sweatshop Women's Company as an autonomous group, was *Care and Control*, scripted by Michelene Wandor after extensive periods of research, workshops and devising with the company. This play is discussed at length in Chapter 5. Here, it is important to note that, like some of the earliest plays by both WTG and Monstrous Regiment, this first play by the Sweatshop Women's Company was issue-based and social realist in style. Like *Work to Role* and *Scum*, it also incorporated real-life events (historical and contemporary) in its material. Partly, these similarities in style and intent can be attributed to the period in which all these plays were first produced: alternative theatre was undergoing a period of experimentation with social realism, while the recent political and cultural uprisings were still fresh in public memory. Agitprop had recently been fashionable, and the use of some agitprop techniques was not at all unusual in this period. Partly, however, the similarity in style and intent of these early plays can be attributed to two specific factors: the unique positioning of the groups' members as women in a period characterized by factionalization and division of feminist women from male-dominated companies, and an extended sense of post-war rebellion against perception of the domestic sphere as 'women's domain'.

To put this trend toward social realism into context, after the war, many women who had been encouraged to work in the public sector were suddenly encouraged to stay at home again. It is not surprising that women's plays of the period tended to reflect a certain sense of rebellion against enforced domesticity; these were the 'prefeminist' plays of Shelagh Delaney, Ann Jellicoe and Doris Lessing. With the next generation and its associated cultural shifts, women's plays began to focus not on politics in the global sense, but on personal politics. This trend is often discussed in wider terms, but rarely in terms of particular plays such as these earliest issue-based pieces by WTG and the women of Gay Sweatshop. These early plays have more than style in common. They also share themes including child care, mother–daughter relationships, women's work and power relationships between women and men.

For instance, in taking 'care and control' as the theme of their first all-women's play, the women of Gay Sweatshop employed a social realist style in order to represent 'women's issues' in the public sphere. They created a play which dealt with issues specific to single mothers and lesbian mothers – measures of 'care and control' which were at issue in child custody cases. *Care and Control* was written in response to a request for such a play from Sweatshop's audiences, a request which emerged in the responses to Sweatshop's audience survey (mentioned in chapter 2). After the success of *Any Woman Can*, the Sweatshop conducted a large-scale survey of the women (predominantly lesbians) in their audiences, asking for thematic suggestions for their next play. 'The runaway favourite was court custody: the battle facing (mainly though not exclusively) lesbians who wanted to retain parental custody of their children.'[34] The production of *Care and Control* was thus significant in terms of its cultural context – as the first feminist play requested by a specific audience – as well as in style, content and reception. Of course, many theatre groups in the 1970s encouraged post-performance discussion and suggestions from the audience, but pre-production suggestions for themes were not commonly taken.

In both *Care and Control* and in the earlier *Any Woman Can*, the content of the plays was not exclusively relevant to lesbians. Both plays took lesbian experience as a priority, but depicted lesbian experience *vis-à-vis* heterosexual experience. Because the plays were not separatist in any sense, they – and the important issues they addressed – became accessible to wider, mixed audiences of homosexual and heterosexual women and men. The 'performance' of lesbian feminism was identified in Sweatshop's work as an important and integral part of the Women's Movement and the roughly corresponding development of feminist theatre – neither separated from it nor easily subsumed within it.

The Women's Group was reintegrated into the mixed Sweatshop company in 1984. Sweatshop has since begun to work toward the goal of producing equal amounts of women's and men's work. After it was accorded full union status, the company recombined as a mixed group. Plays produced fall into two categories: mixed, and all-women's. Thus, the company as a whole demonstrates its commitment to redressing the gender balance in its work. Suad El-Amin (Sweatshop Administrator) explained that the 1990 company policy incorporated principles of balancing out the male-oriented work of the 1970s 'by using mixed and all-women's companies, and alternating between "female-focused plays" and male-focused plays'.[35]

The women's plays produced by the mixed Sweatshop company in the mid- to late 1980s included *Pinball* (by Alison Lyssa, 1985) and *More* (by Maro Green and Caroline Griffin, 1986). Jackie Kay's *Twice Over* (1987/8) is similar in some respects to *Care and Control*, though the styles and themes are very different. While *Care and Control* was an issue play, *Twice Over* was a 'coming out' play which relied to some extent on autobiography (Kay's) but did not employ the social realist techniques of using actual court cases, as did *Care and Control*.[36] In terms of the audience addressed, however, the plays have something in common. Both presented the situations of heterosexual and lesbian women, and both appealed to mixed audiences. In 1990, Sweatshop reported an average audience composed of approximately 50 per cent women and 50 per cent men (though this 'depends on the content of the plays . . . *Twice Over* had 60 per cent women in the audience').

Sweatshop's continuing interest in its audience is significant. Some possible explanations for a particular emphasis on the role of the audience in lesbian theatre are discussed in chapter 5. Another major innovation in *Twice Over* was the emphasis on a multiracial perspective. While the multiracial casting of the play was required by Kay's script – based on her own multiracial family upbringing – it 'suited' Sweatshop's multiracial policy as well.

Gay Sweatshop's response to the Feminist Theatre Survey, received in 1988, gives the clearest indication of the status of the women within the group (the company declined to update the survey responses in 1990, as its answers 'had not changed'). In 1988, the company defined itself as 'a mixed group with feminist politics'. That choice of label was qualified with the information that productions were either mixed with positive images of women (particularly lesbians), or were all-women's productions. There was a mixed artistic directorship and a high proportion of women workers running the company on a day-to-day basis: 'Staff are all women, and voluntary management is 50/50'. In terms of plays produced, the company reported in 1988 that some 80 per cent of plays were commissioned, and women's plays were produced less often than men's because fewer plays by women were submitted. The percentage of directors was reported as half women and half men. The company has an affirmative action policy, and considers its material to reflect that policy in terms of direct feminist concerns: with feminist aims and feminist intent.[37]

In interview, Suad El-Amin explained the observable cross-fertilization between women in Gay Sweatshop and other feminist theatre groups in this way:

> There are two reasons why the women in the Sweatshop are also visible outside the Sweatshop company: the first is that if you are an out lesbian and you work in the theatre, there is a small family of companies which will express interest in working with you at some point. That's why the same names crop up again and again. It has taken a long time for Gay Sweatshop to be recognized as a legitimate theatre group, on artistic as well as political grounds, and now that women are known as legitimate members of that legitimate group, we are often invited to work with others as well.[38]

Bryony Lavery and Jackie Kay, for example, are both known for their work with companies other than Gay Sweatshop.

In terms of working practices, it is significant that Gay Sweatshop, like WTG, was one of the first companies to develop the rehearsed reading as form. The x10 Festivals which began in 1985 have been beneficial for several feminist women. They have nurtured young (predominantly lesbian) writers including Tash Fairbanks, Michelene Wandor and Alison Lyssa (1985), Catherine Kilcoyne, Maro Green and Caroline Griffin (1986) and Adele Saleem and Jackie Kay (1987), among others. In the 1988 survey response, Sweatshop explained: 'Rehearsed readings give the company the opportunity to assess the unsolicited work we receive in an atmosphere of performance before deciding whether to develop a particular script and raise the funding to produce it at a later date.' In an era when funding is limited, it is not surprising that the feminist companies which have survived are dedicated to finding means of developing new work at low cost. The rehearsed reading as form has been instrumental in keeping women's work viable, even when budgets for full productions are not available. The rehearsed reading is discussed at length, with reference to the work of Sarah Daniels, in chapter 7.

79

Sweatshop's most important achievement is its continuing viability. It attributes this tenacious success to the strength of the feminist principles upon which it was originally based:

> If there had not been a feminist movement, there would be no Sweatshop. Or to be more precise, there would be no Sweatshop, as we know it, without feminism. Gay Sweatshop is and has to be feminist; if it were not, it would be about boys, about men's experiences, and so would be a different company altogether. All the members of Sweatshop have defined themselves as feminist from the very beginning. The company grew as a result of that temporary split in its early history. Since then, in all good faith, Sweatshop could not produce a play that was not feminist.

This exemplary status has not been sufficient to shelter Sweatshop from the effects of funding cuts. In 1991, Bryony Lavery was called upon to write a new play as a tribute to and fund-raiser for the company. She wrote *Kitchen Matters*, a spoof on Greek tragedy which involved cross-dressing and the representation of both women and men in various roles. The publicity for *Kitchen Matters* read:

> Gay Sweatshop remains Britain's only professional lesbian and gay theatre company. However, *Kitchen Matters* could be their last production as their public subsidy struggles to keep up with inflation. This, perhaps their 'last supper', is . . . an epic comedy production of truly small-scale proportions.[39]

The play was strategically as well as artistically successful. The Arts Council announced that it would reconsider the possibility of revenue funding for future years, and awarded project funding for 1991/2.[40] But even as Sweatshop's success is celebrated, it is also recognized as a threat to other lesbian theatre groups. The Arts Council and other funding bodies have supported various lesbian theatre companies over the years, but none has received as much support as Gay Sweatshop. The implication in 1991, as in earlier years, seems to be that it is not deemed necessary to provide substantial support for more than one lesbian theatre company. The success of one company may therefore lead to the demise of others. This same kind of competition for funding and status within the limited budget available for women's theatre was also reported by WTG and Monstrous Regiment. It has particular effects on lesbian theatre companies.

The Feminist Theatre Survey found several operative lesbian theatre companies, some of which are discussed in Chapter 5. Some companies did not survive long enough or provide sufficient information to enable their inclusion in the survey. One such company was the Coventry Lesbian Theatre Group, founded in 1977 and assumed disbanded in 1979. Groups such as Hard Corps and Dramatrix Productions have had a significant impact as well. But perhaps the most consistently productive lesbian group of the 1970s and 1980s – apart from Gay Sweatshop – was Siren Theatre Company.

SIREN

Founded in 1979, Siren Theatre Company has received much less attention than Gay Sweatshop. Founding members Tash Fairbanks, Jane Boston and Jude Winter have since made up the core of the company, though others have occasionally participated in Siren productions: Deb Trethewey joined in 1981 for the production of *Curfew* and continued working as company technician; Hilary Ramsden joined as performer and musician in 1984; and Rose Sharp became company administrator in 1985/6 (a post previously shared by all the company members). Sharp is also administrator for Monstrous Regiment. The two companies' work and personnel overlap in several ways. Notably, Fairbanks was appointed by Monstrous Regiment as Writer in Residence for 1990, an indication of the relatively poor funding situation of Siren, but also of Fairbanks' recognized status as an independent writer.[41]

Siren incorporates punk music and culture into the fabric of its work. The group began by doing explicitly feminist work with an emphasis on popular (particularly punk) music and on strong political narratives, and produced one show per year from 1980 to 1988. Each show toured nationally. Siren members shared administration until 1985, and continue to share responsibility for writing, direction, technical work and performance. Fairbanks writes or scripts nearly all of the plays, the music is jointly devised, Jane Wood writes the song lyrics, all members help with direction and all company members perform.

Siren defined itself in 1979, as it does in 1992, as an all-women's theatre collective.[42] In the words of the company:

> Established in the climate of the late 1970s Punk explosion in the music scene and the growth of the Women's Movement in the West, Siren developed a theatrical style which owed much to both. Work usually included the interweaving of live electric music, visual humour and serious narrative to make pertinent political and social comments. In this way, the early plays drew their energy from the immediacy of street theatre techniques and the Women's Movement itself. The issues of women's oppression and resistance became the starting point for Siren Theatre.[43]

Siren, like the previous three feminist groups, began with a conscious decision to change the position of women in the community through the theatre. Like Gay Sweatshop, Siren began with a consciousness of homosexuality as a viable position from which to begin that process of change.

Siren was established as a lesbian theatre group and has very publicly and radically promoted lesbianism as an integral part of its company identity:

> Siren's work is *always* informed by a lesbian perspective, but it does not necessarily overtly depict lesbianism as an issue. It is there in the content as symbol, humour, relationship and so on, but increasingly *not* as an object of study. It is part of our lives and therefore of our work generally.
>
> In structuring our plays for particular audiences, we tried to be inclusive rather than exclusive, partly due to funding and booking considerations and partly because it ain't no fun in a ghetto. However, we also wanted to provide a forum for self-recognition to contribute to the creation of a visible lesbian aesthetic.
>
> Our early work consciously addressed lesbian feminist issues and we would have defined ourselves as such. In the last few years it has been necessary to move away from the confines of that labelling in order to insist that the universality of our themes is taken seriously.

The earlier shows were specifically 'lesbian feminist', but the personal politics became more influential in terms of the productions as the company's work developed:

> Siren's work took a turn inwards from 1984 onwards, in order to examine the internalization of the external social values which occurs in women and to see the points of collusion with the *status quo*. In other words, Siren began to explore the contradictions and the ambiguities in women's position; looking at grey areas as the more obvious. The theme of personal relationships amongst women became the focus of the work in the mid-1980s.[44]

This shift in the group's focus is significant in more than one way: it signalled a shift in the content of the plays, but more importantly, it matched the shift in the political climate of Britain.

While the group began only two years after the women split to form the Women's Company within the Sweatshop, these two years made a tremendous difference. In 1979, the shift from feminist politics based on the notion that 'the personal is political' to feminisms informed by more recent emphasis on difference and on 'identity politics' was becoming apparent. When Siren performed its first piece in 1980, the beginnings of this shift and the growing popularity of punk music was already evident. The company's awareness of its roots in this very particular phase of the development of British feminism and popular culture has been articulated by Fairbanks, who wrote in 1989 that Siren 'began as a way of popularizing and gaining access to the discourses of the late 1970s women's movement.'[45] Fairbanks has since updated that comment in this way:

Company members of Siren are, on average, seven or eight years younger than members of the Regiment, for instance. So Siren's origins were very clearly rooted in the 'grass-roots' feminism of women's groups and organizations in Brighton in the late 1970s and early 1980s. Siren members were involved very early on with that world of Punk Sound, Devils' Dykes . . . and then as Siren Band.

In 1979, to a greater extent than in 1977, current debates in feminist theory were developing as more and more sophisticated and internationally focused theories began to be applied to British media and culture. Factionalism among feminists had also begun to develop, and to divide various segments of the feminist community. As a result, Siren's work articulated specifically personal and lesbian experiences just at the time when the relationship between lesbianism and feminism was being reconsidered. It is not insignificant that when Siren began its 'inward-looking' emphasis on lesbian experience in its work, the women of Gay Sweatshop had gone back to working with the men. Here again, feminist theatre can be seen to develop in cycles as, year by year, slightly younger women begin to develop their own feminist theatres, thereby influencing the shape of the overall project. In this case, Jackie Kay (a young independent writer joining a much larger and well-established group) first worked with Gay Sweatshop in 1985/6, just at the point when women of a half-generation before her (including Fairbanks and the women of Siren) were beginning to try a very different approach to the staging of lesbian experience, in a smaller company which they had been involved in from the outset.

What is interesting is the way in which 'the gaps' seem to be filled automatically, without too much overlap in terms of content but with considerable cyclical development of styles and genres from one generation to another, one theatre company to another. One of Canada's contemporary feminist theatre companies is called Company of Sirens. Even within Britain, the name Siren has been adopted by a new women's company (which was not aware of the existing company with the same name): the *Guardian* theatre listings of 10 July 1990 mention 'a debut performance by the new all-woman black theatre company, Siren'.[46] This is, of course, a different company, as the original Siren company affirms. The lack of published information about feminist theatre groups in general, and particularly about small-scale groups such as Siren, results in a lack of communication between women of different age groups working in the theatre. New groups sometimes choose similar titles, or even company names, unwittingly imitating those who have gone before. For instance, to cite a 'mainstream feminist play', Charlotte Keatley was unaware of WTG's play by the name of *My Mother Says I Never Should*, when she gave her play a very similar title.

In terms of content, Siren's plays have dealt with subjects as diverse as

83

deconstructing myths of women and reclaiming history (*Mama's Gone a-Hunting*, 1980), the hunt for the Ripper and the larger issue of male violence, in relation to the 'institution of heterosexuality' (*Curfew*, 1981), militarism, patriarchy, gender and power in the context of the Falklands war (*From the Divine*, 1983) and the effects of Thatcherism (*Now Wash Your Hands Please*, 1984). In 1986, Siren produced *Pulp*, billed as a lesbian thriller. The explicit forwarding of lesbian experience in conjunction with an awareness of popular culture and its market trends, and of the growing body of feminist theory, all make this period in Siren's history important. Siren says of its work on *Pulp*: 'the thriller genre . . . provided the language and style from which to explore a female narrative position, and to express lesbian desire' (a phrase which would not have been part of the cultural vocabulary a few years earlier). In 1987, the group produced *Bubbles*, which was their first highly experimental work in terms of visual and linguistic form, and in 1987–8 Siren produced *Hotel Destiny*.

Here, the work of the group came full circle, back to representations of women *vis-à-vis* definitions of self and society as defined in popular music. This play explored the genre of Country and Western music in relation to its framing of female images and the concept of 'star status'. In this, the group was working along the same lines as was solo performance artist Annie Griffin, who in 1987 experimented with the same themes in her acclaimed performance piece *Almost Persuaded*. But Siren's approach to this theme was unique in its multilayered, self-conscious construction of contrasting and ostensibly coexisting realms of fantasy and reality (and, in Fairbanks' words, 'the confusion between the two').[47]

The status of the group has not changed significantly since its inception in 1979, though the focus of the material has shifted to suit the times. The majority of work is commissioned from within the group. In fact, Fairbanks wrote most of the shows, and was assisted by the group in collaborative work and devising for one show only: *Swamp*, produced in 1989. This marked a new departure for Siren, in that the piece was directed by Théâtre de Complicité, with an emphasis on physical theatre techniques which had not informed previous Siren productions. The story of *Swamp* was based, in the words of Fairbanks and Boston, 'around the myth of the Three Fates, and it explored the moral inertia after a decade of Thatcher'.

In response to the Feminist Theatre Survey, Siren defined itself as both a feminist company and an all-women's company ('and more: we are lesbians and have left wing politics'). Siren's work has both feminist intent and content, but the company qualified the statement of intent by explaining that its aims used to be more explicit. As the political climate has changed and it has become less fashionable to be overtly political, the tone of the shows has changed, and the early 'aim' or feminist goal has been remodelled into a slightly more subtle style of feminist performance, concentrating its politics in its underlying intent:

> Siren has been together for ten years, with all its original members, and has been almost entirely unsubsidized. . . . Over the years it closely reflected and commented upon the changes in the women's movement and the political climate in Britain. . . . Siren toured the UK, Europe and America, returning year after year to the same audiences who, especially in non-metropolitan centres, regarded us often as a link to the wider women's movement, as well as a funny and stimulating night out.[48]

Siren's international touring has been relatively extensive. Fairbanks believes that part of the reason why Siren has received less media attention in Britain than other key groups is related to the radical politics of the work. In her words:

> Our explicit presentations of radical feminist politics and lesbian sexuality were considered shocking, inappropriate, and 'not artistic enough' by Arts Council standards; yet our shows were particularly powerful – for this very reason – and particularly for women in our audiences.

Siren did have some all-women's audiences, particularly in the early years. But one of the consequences of national touring is the inevitability of diverse audiences. On tour, it is difficult, if not impossible, to exclude men from audiences in regional venues with rules of their own.

Of the three key groups previously discussed, Siren may have most in common with Gay Sweatshop. Yet in terms of the age range of the company membership – and indeed of the segment of the population to which the plays have most appeal – Siren has more in common with Women's Theatre Group. The membership of Women's Theatre Group has changed over the years, with the result that a 'third generation' of women currently runs the company. In contrast, the management collective of Monstrous Regiment is made up of Gillian Hanna and other founder members. There is also some similarity between the memberships of Siren and Monstrous Regiment, in the sense that the two companies have employed some of the same members, at different points in time (particularly when Fairbanks was Writer in Residence with the Regiment). But the generational considerations linking the work of Siren to a group such as WTG should not be overlooked.

In 1990, I (provocatively) asked Siren to list the most important aspects of their work, along with some possible explanations as to why these things have not been said (or made available in any written form) before now. In response to the subsidiary question, the reply was:

1 Our funding positions meant that we had a small profile in London (although not regionally).

2 We were poorly funded because we were uncompromisingly radical and lesbian.

3 We formed at a time when WTG and Monstrous Regiment existed, and so women's theatre was 'taken care of'.

4 Perhaps the writers of previous books on women's theatre were very London-identified and perhaps heterosexual?

This brings the discussion full circle and reinforces some of the comments made by other groups – WTG and Monstrous Regiment included – about the ways in which funding patterns have streamlined feminist work, so that only a few groups are funded, while many others form and perform in their shadow(s).

For Siren as for virtually all theatre companies, future plans are influenced, if not dictated, by the availability of funds. As Monstrous Regiment observed in 1985, the lack of funds to groups such as Siren results from the competitive structure of the Arts Council's funding policies, which had in the past effectively allowed for the survival of only two feminist companies: WTG and the Regiment.[49] In effect, this has meant that the number of plays produced by Siren has remained relatively small – an average of one play every two years.

In interview in 1991, Tash Fairbanks summarized Siren's aims for the future in this way: 'to support each other in our individual creative endeavours, to find new ways of funding our projects, to publish the plays we have already produced'. Such a statement of intent might read as the banner for all the key groups discussed, and for many others as well.

Siren did not shift to co-operative status, mainly because it never expanded sufficiently to risk developing power struggles within the group. Like the previous three companies discussed, Siren's work is based on the feminist idea that women's roles in life are worthy of representation on stage, and indeed, that such representation may effect positive social change. Like Gay Sweatshop, Siren began with a consciousness of homosexuality as a viable position from which to begin that process of change. Siren was established as a lesbian theatre group and has very publicly and radically promoted lesbianism as an integral part of its company identity.

The problem of public recognition of Siren as a contemporary feminist theatre group may be related to generational factors. The women who were responsible for the development of so much early feminist theatre were, on the whole, half a generation older than Siren's members. Fairbanks and company may be seen to belong to a 'third-generation' feminist audience, not so much because of the women's ages, but because their work is based on more recent cultural developments (punk music, etc.), and is intended to appeal to a younger audience. Siren can, in this sense, be more easily compared to groups such as Trouble and Strife than to Monstrous Regiment or Gay Sweatshop. As the Feminist Theatre Survey showed, however, a matter of a few years is quite important in terms of the theatre-going public. Siren has been hindered not only by limited funding, but also by the changing trends of a slightly younger audience, seeking forms of cultural representation outside the theatre.

Siren's temporary inactivity is a sign of the times. While it is encouraging that a collection of Siren's plays is soon to be published, it is also important to remember that while the company remains 'temporarily inactive' due to lack of funds, the possibility that the 'temporary' will expand into a 'permanence' is all too real.

The Feminist Theatre Survey identified some 246 feminist or feminist-sympathizing companies in Britain, 185 of which were in operation when this survey was completed. This number will inevitably have decreased in the interval due to a range of factors, many of which are beyond the control of small companies such as Siren. Yet feminist theatre companies, in Britain and in the United States, Canada and Australia, do have control over the working methods they employ and the types of theatre they choose to make.

'Control over the means of production' is a phrase with complex meanings in social and historical contexts which can be applied to the study of contemporary feminist theatres in a useful way. By looking at the areas which feminist theatre companies can and do control, it is possible to talk more precisely about the similarities and differences between feminist theatres, women's theatres and alternative theatres of other kinds.

4

COMMON WORKING METHODS
OF FEMINIST THEATRES

There are many different means of working toward the desired 'end' of the theatre text, whether written script or text for performance. Such aspects as financial backing, availability of space, and consideration of intended audience all play their parts in determining the ways in which any particular theatre group, playwright or director might choose to work. In the case of feminist theatre, factors such as time constraints (imposed by personal/domestic factors specific to women's lives), limited availability of space and low budgets may also enter into the equation.[1] The political nature of feminist theatre as genre often sets it apart from the mainstream, and thereby creates a certain set of working conditions, and a certain range of possible working methods. The position of feminist theatre, while similar in some ways to that of political or alternative theatre in general, is also distinct in its approaches to these working methods. Though there are no 'feminist working practices' which are completely unique to feminist theatre, there is an identifiable set of working methods which tends to be used in the making of feminist theatre. Some of these methods are explored in this chapter.

Current working methods common to feminist theatre groups include small-scale commissioning of new work by women; the devising and collaborative writing processes used by many collectives and co-operatives; the rehearsed reading (whether it functions as a trial run before production, or as an alternative to production); and the 'performance art' approach (largely based on 'visual texts' compiled through improvisational exercises). According to the Feminist Theatre Survey, the ways in which these types of working practices intersect with feminist politics in any theatre group varies significantly, depending upon factors such as group composition and size, and sources and amounts of funding. Of the theatre groups responding to the survey, nearly all reported using a combination of working methods, and these included groups identifying themselves according to all the different categories (feminist, women's, mixed) and with vastly differing statements of policy and political intent. Of the total groups responding (of 98): 54 used commissioned work; 57 used collaborative work; 69 used devising as a method; 13 had done some TIE work; and 23 had done at least one rehearsed reading. The percentage of operational and disbanded groups using any combination of these methods was roughly proportional.[2]

Survey findings further indicate that these working methods overlap in practice: some collectives, when adequately funded, commission independent work. Of the 69 groups which use devising and the 57 which work collaboratively, there is a great deal of overlap (most groups using one method also use the other). TIE companies and community groups tend to devise their own work. Individual women and collaborative teams with low budgets seem to be increasingly turning to performance art as an alternative to (more expensive) approaches to the theatre. While a large percentage of groups use commissioning, devising and collaboration as working methods, relatively few are in positions to commission writers from outside. Of the 54 groups which commission work, most also indicate that some or all artists commissioned are group members: in other words, few groups can afford to, or choose to, commission 'outsiders'.

Of companies using rehearsed readings, most reported their reasons as mixed: partly financial due to the cost-effectiveness of the reading as form and partly artistic due to the opportunities which readings open up for developing new work. The smallest number of responses by far was in the area of TIE (while this is not a 'working method' as such, it was included here as an indication of the kinds and varieties of work in which the same company may be involved): only 13 companies reported having done TIE productions, and of those 11 are operative companies. Even taking into account the specific targeting of several TIE companies in the survey, it seems clear that TIE is becoming more common as a means of reaching new audiences, and is increasingly being used, among other methods, by theatres which are not TIE companies as such. The use of rehearsed readings also seems to be increasing: only 3 disbanded companies reported using readings, as opposed to 23 positive responses from operative companies. Most companies (operative and disbanded) reported using a combination of two, three or more of these methods and approaches, with the most common combination being (predictably) collaboration and devising.

The implications of both rehearsed readings and TIE for women in the theatre are discussed in chapter 7. Here, the various combinations of the first three working methods (commissioning, collaboration and devising), and the development of performance art/theatre are outlined. The chapter provides a range of 'case studies' detailing some of the strengths and weaknesses, or potential problems, associated with these working methods. These examples have been carefully chosen, as they reflect working dynamics which are symptomatic of wider trends in the area of feminist theatre.

COMMISSIONED WORK

Commissioned work is the most financially rewarding of the working methods available, and it offers the added advantage of allowing the playwright the time to write the script on her own, with the knowledge that she will be (or has already been) paid for her efforts. With funding for playwriting becoming increasingly limited, receipt of a commission is a sign of recognition and status, as well as a financial reward. With the promise of a commission, the playwright enters the public market and presents her playscript as a purchased commodity. At present, it seems that only the 'top girls' (those who have already established a reputation of commercial success) can be confident of receiving commissions (at least, reasonably paid commissions) for their work. The present economic climate militates against widespread commissioning, which in turn affects all theatre. The specific effects on women's and feminist theatre can be observed in the increasing tendency of groups to produce work by core members, in the reduced output of many companies and venues, and in the worst instances, in 'closing stages'.[3]

Some playwrights prefer not to work to commission, as they find that in writing only for themselves, they produce their best work. For instance, Charlotte Keatley reports that she prefers not to work to commission because she 'wants to be free to change [her] own mind in the process of writing, which is a process of exploration', but also admits that without commissions, the material needs of the playwright may not be met.[4] For most, however, the commission functions in a very basic sense as prepayment for work produced. Caryl Churchill is regularly commissioned, as are Louise Page, Timberlake Wertenbaker, Olwen Wymark and Pam Gems among others (most of these are among the older and better-established of Britain's women playwrights). Wymark has in recent years been commissioned primarily to write adaptations rather than original scripts – a sign, she contends, of the effects of the funding crisis on the shaping of the theatre, *vis-à-vis* a certain creative 'self-censorship' imposed on writers and practitioners by the need to produce commercially viable plays.[5] Caryl Churchill's career is the most illustrative in this regard, for she is generally accepted – in commercial and artistic terms, in the mainstream and on the fringe, by practitioners, other writers and critics – as a 'success story'.

Caryl Churchill

Early in 1976 I met some of the Monstrous Regiment, who were thinking they would like to do a play about witches; so was I. . . . Soon I met the whole company to talk about working with them. . . . I left the meeting exhilarated. My previous work had been completely

90

solitary – I never discussed my ideas while I was writing or showed anyone anything earlier than a final polished draft.[6]

A survey of Churchill's career shows her to have experimented liberally with a wide variety of forms and techniques, and to have worked her way through the list of practices, media and approaches available to women in the theatre today. This is not a hierarchical list: it does not imply that independent writing of a commissioned script is in any way superior (artistically or ideologically) to devising, for example.

Churchill's career to date can be viewed as a three-tiered one: 1) a period of solitary writing, mostly for radio, beginning with her student productions in Oxford in 1958 and ending with her first major stage production, *Owners*; 2) the period from 1972 to 1979 which extended through a series of independently scripted plays to a period of collaboration with Joint Stock and Monstrous Regiment, beginning in 1976 and culminating in 1979 with the production of *Cloud Nine*; and 3) the period from 1979 to the present, which has produced Churchill's greatest successes in all genres and writing contexts, from *Top Girls* and *Fen* to *Serious Money* and *Ice Cream* and *Mad Forest*.

Churchill began as many women (and indeed, most writers) begin: writing part-time, for little or no money and to mixed reviews. The plays of the middle phase marked a testing period in Churchill's career which led to the finding of a distinctive voice and the development of confidence in that voice, which in turn allowed for the innovations in language notation (overlapping dialogue, etc.) for which Churchill is known. This 'voice' developed during that middle period, in the context of her collaborative work with Monstrous Regiment and Joint Stock: 'Working closely with actors and directors on an approach to performance which encourages innovation and flexibility has facilitated the daring experimentation with structure that is a notable feature of her plays.'[7] Once the collaborative work had encouraged this 'flexibility', Churchill began to be offered commissions – the first came from Max Stafford-Clark for Joint Stock. Indeed, most of the commissioned plays were produced, predictably, in the middle and late periods of Churchill's career.

To put the commissioned plays into context, it is necessary to examine Churchill's working history as a whole. Churchill's first student production opened in Oxford in 1958. With the exception of her early student productions, Churchill's first plays (over a dozen) were written between 1961 and 1972, for the radio and television. They were short scripts written in short periods of time, in between the performance of other social roles such as motherhood, and that of 'acting self' in the very public role of barrister's wife. In a discussion of Churchill's early work, Colin Chambers and Mike Prior attribute Churchill's choice of writing primarily for radio and television in this period to her social position: they argue that the shorter amounts of time (presumably) required to write short radio and television plays, combined with a decreased emphasis on author involvement during production, account to some extent for the disproportionately high number of women writing for these media.[8] Such an argument is not particularly convincing.

Churchill herself accounts for her slow break into writing professionally for the stage in several ways. She describes her early work as 'depressed plays about depression' and explains in this way:

> I was fed up with the situation I found myself in in the 1960s . . . it seemed claustrophobic. By the mid-1960s, I had this gloomy feeling that when the Revolution came I would be swept away.[9]

In the early 1970s, Churchill began breaking out of her claustrophobia by doing local research on the poor housing facilities in Islington; she refers to this research as the first widening of perspective leading to her later collaborative research and writing projects, though several references cite her husband's simultaneous move into low-status community law practice as her primary influence.[10] In 1972, Churchill's 'widened perspective' encouraged her to write her first full-length play for the London stage, *Owners*, which (appropriately enough) was about a strong-minded real estate agent who refuses to be defined and confined by her husband. *Owners*, once begun, was written in three days. Churchill recalls:

> *Owners* wasn't my first play, more like the twentieth now I count them up, and certainly the fifth full-length stage play. But the earlier stage plays were student productions or unperformed, and most of my work had been on radio for the previous ten years. Since *Owners* I've worked almost entirely in the theatre. So my working life feels divided quite sharply into before and after 1972, and *Owners* was the first play of the second part.[11]

Most of Churchill's collaborative work was done with two companies: Joint Stock and Monstrous Regiment. The history and main working methods of Monstrous Regiment were outlined in chapter 3. The crucial difference between the two companies, apart from gender composition of the groups, was Joint Stock's emphasis on company input and workshops. Thus, as Elizabeth Taylor notes, the influence of the particular actors involved in any given Regiment production may have been less than that in a Joint Stock production, where individual experiences were company material.[12] Yet Churchill contends that her early work with the Regiment had a measurable influence on her perception of her own role, as a writer and as a woman, in the collaborative work process:

> . . . this was a new way of working . . . which was one of its attractions. Also a touring company, with a wider audience; also a feminist

company – I felt briefly shy and daunted, wondering if I would be acceptable, than happy and stimulated by discovery of shared ideas and the enormous energy and feeling of possibilities in the still new company.[13]

In other words, Churchill was centrally and beneficially involved with the performers in Monstrous Regiment, and the benefits of that collaboration affected her approach to future work. In addition, the process seems to have been of value to Churchill personally. The progression of her work after this important collaboration was markedly affected by it: the plays became progressively more feminist, and more overtly political. Churchill's view of the writer's context during this middle period (of working in collectives and in collaborative ways) can thus be seen to have been influential in the development of her later work.

Of all Churchill's commissioned plays, one is particularly illustrative in this regard; Cloud Nine, Churchill's first commission, was offered by Max Stafford-Clark and Joint Stock. In 1978–9, after serving as the Royal Court's first female resident dramatist, Churchill began work as a tutor for the Royal Court's Youth Theatre Project. While there, she was asked by Stafford-Clark to write another play for Joint Stock. The idea for the play developed from a rather vague starting point: Stafford-Clark wanted to base a project on the idea of emigration and the uprooting of people, setting the first half in Europe and the second in America, and holding workshops on both continents. When arrangements for this idea fell through, Churchill suggested writing a play on the theme of sexual politics (since in 1979 the women's movement was frequently represented in the media). Stafford-Clark and Churchill decided to explore sexual stereotyping, with research focusing on the actors involved and their attitudes and differing approaches to sexual role-playing. In part, this choice of subject may be attributed to the topicality of sexual politics, but it also seems to have been influenced by Churchill's development as a playwright in a feminist collaborative framework.

Churchill's belief in the possibility of breaking down limiting sex role stereotypes through re-evaluation of the masculine precepts of language, increased attention to body language and forwarding of the unstated, were all developed in Cloud Nine. Her interest in the theme of sexual politics, and the development of new notations for language patterns in her later texts, are indicative of a concern with the gendered politics of expression – a concern which became more evident, because better expressed, with each new play from Cloud Nine to Top Girls. Churchill's post-1987 plays, however, have tended to reflect cultural politics as well as sexual politics, in dealing with themes such as commercialism (Serious Money), and the effects of shifting international boundaries and the concept of democracy (Mad Forest).[14]

By the time Churchill had introduced the silent image of the embrace in the closing scene of *Cloud Nine*, she was well on her way to the realization which led her into the third (independent, often-commissioned) phase of her theatre-writing career: 'So often, dialogue works better if you just take lots of it away.'[15] This minimalist approach to dialogue is the key to the writing of Churchill's recent plays, including *Mad Forest*, a political allegory inspired by the Romanian revolution, written after extensive workshopping, devising and touring with the students of the Central School of Speech and Drama.[16] *Mad Forest*, or rather, the collaborative context in which it was produced, and the young people by and for whom it was performed, mark yet another turning point in Churchill's career, from large expensive commissions for the West End and Broadway, to small-scale productions for the educational sector. This is the antithesis of the career path followed by many writers, but it should be remembered that Churchill wrote this play with and for young people because she thought it appropriate to do so, not because she lacked a more 'profitable' option.

In conclusion, it can be said that Churchill's experimentation with and within the structures of the early theatre collectives, combined with her use of the devising and workshopping processes, marked a turning point in her career, both in terms of a shift in medium (from radio and television to work for the stage), and in terms of her relationship with the process of producing plays. Churchill's early experience of collaboration and co-operation with the director and actors clearly influenced her own working methods, and led her to a phase of collaborative work in the mid- to late 1970s. The shift to collaborative work (paralleled by a shift from writing exclusively in the context of the home) was one which may have had greater effects on both the language and imagery of the later plays than has yet been taken into account. This is the development which the middle, collaborative phase of Churchill's career opened up to her. The increased confidence of creative voice which grew out of that collaborative phase was reflected in the plays, resulting in a growing public perception of Churchill as a 'successful' playwright. With the reputation for success came a series of commissions; with the commissions came the increasing freedom of the writer to choose her own topics, and her own ways of working.

COMMISSIONED-DEVISED WORK

There are cases in which the script commissioned by a group or a director simply is not found satisfactory. If time and funding will allow, that script may be returned for revisions. But often, time and funding do *not* allow, and in these cases a decision must be made either to pay for the script but not to produce it (i.e., to cut losses before further funds are wasted on Equity fees, rehearsal space, etc.), or to work with the script and shape it into something more suitable for performance. The first decision can only be made by a company in a financial position to take the initial loss, a criterion which eliminates most feminist (and women's) theatre groups and which also entails a dead season, potentially damaging to any company's reputation. The second decision requires more time, effort and commitment, but often leads to the creation and production of very original (often successful) theatre pieces. In this case, a group will take the script provided and revise it, or sometimes entirely rewrite it. In this way, commissioned work becomes devised/collaborative work, with the company writing the text for performance alongside, or in spite of, the written script.

The final and crucial step in the developmental process from straightforward commissioned work to devised performance is the polishing of the text in production, a process which is meant to shape all the various narrative strands into a cohesive, unified text. When such attempts to 'save' scripts through collaboration and devising fail, little is known about them (for advertising of such failure creates bad press for the playwright and the group, and is therefore especially dangerous in the current economic climate). There is a distinction to be made, however, between material which is devised and then scripted by an individual, and material which is devised and scripted through devising by a group.

An example of a play which was scripted after group collaboration and devising is *Care and Control*. The play was scripted by Michelene Wandor from material devised by the company, and directed by Kate Crutchley.[17] Wandor's published introduction to the playscript describes the process of research and production. Both Nancy Diuguid and Tash Fairbanks have added further information, stressing the input of the research and devising done by Diuguid and Kate Crutchley, with help from the company.[18] To quote from interviews with Nancy Diuguid:

> *Care and Control* . . . was very much a collaborative effort, a collaborative piece. . . . In a very real sense, Gay Sweatshop collectively wrote *Care and Control*; in another sense, the women whose lives the stories were based on, whose cases make up the court room scenes of Act II, are also 'authors'.[19]

This account must of course be balanced with consideration of Wandor's position: commissioned as scriptwriter, she was in some sense the 'writer' of the play as script. Michelene Wandor, Nancy Diuguid and Tash Fairbanks have all questioned the term 'author' in relation to group-researched work. The discrepancy of terminology does not undermine the work of any individual woman, or of any given play. Rather, it points out that in devised work or collaborative work of any kind, especially within feminist theatre groups (non-authoritarian and notionally democratic in structure and style), the contributions of all members should be taken into account in consideration of the complex question of authorship. Michelene Wandor has articulated the distinction quite clearly:

I would not in any way claim to be the 'author' of the work. The company researched and devised the play and I 'scripted' it (which is not the same as 'writing'). We also split the copyright, so that further income from the play should be split, which I also felt was right. . . . I think credit should be correctly given where due.[20]

Tash Fairbanks of Siren Theatre was able to contribute information about a play commissioned by WTG which has generated a similar discrepancy over the question of authorship, but which has not been resolved. The play, produced in 1986, was *Fixed Deal*. WTG lists the play as 'devised by the company and scripted by Paulette Randall', while Fairbanks contends that *she* wrote it, after being asked 'to devise the play with the company at short notice [they had three and a half weeks] after Randall's commission fell through'.[21] It seems that WTG failed to make the correction on their promotional material, with the result that accessible printed sources attribute the play to Randall.

The discrepancies over the question of authorship in *Care and Control* and *Fixed Deal* are illustrative. Other devised plays have been subject to a different, but associated problem: when they did not succeed in performance, their reviews included phrases (such as 'sloppily pieced together') which are indicative of the reviewers' discomfort with the devising process, as well as with the plays themselves. A case in point was That's Not It Theatre Company's production in 1982 of Natasha Morgan's *By George!*, a performance piece which could not be neatly categorized as a 'play', and which employed experimental techniques in the depiction of characters and time frames. The reviews were mixed, and several seem to suggest that the piece was not 'polished' enough.[22] Whether this means that it was genuinely in need of further work, or rather that it did not match the expectations of reviewers, is an open question. Similarly, the RSC Women's Group's 1986 production of Deborah Levy's *Heresies* received mixed reviews, polarized around a similar issue: critics applauded the 'idea' and the intent, but criticized the collaborative input which preceded scripting of the play.[23] While *Heresies* was not 'devised' as such, it is a relevant example, as the Women's Project had been meeting for nearly two years before the play was produced. The play was, in that sense, the product of an on-going project. The input of many women was clearly and purposefully included in the complex interplay of voices which Levy wove into the play.

The complicated question of authorship in devised work causes considerable problems for the researcher and critic. For instance, the commissioned playwright's name will (for contractual reasons) often remain in the credits on advertisements, programmes and press releases, thus obscuring the actual authorship of the finished piece. This can lead to long-term misunderstanding about a text's authorship, as was the case with WTG's *Fixed*

Deal. It can also lead to inequitable distribution of funds, whether in terms of royalties (an issue Michelene Wandor addressed above), or in terms of the process of bidding for grants from the relevant funding bodies. For instance, The Arts Council of Great Britain and the American National Endowment for the Arts tend to fund theatre work which can clearly be identified as 'by' an identifiable writer. In other words, funding bodies like to know who they are funding – to have a name to match to the funds. This is problematic for group-devised work, a situation which is discussed by way of the example of Trouble and Strife, in the next section.

Another potential problem resulting from the attempt to assign an author to devised work is related to the collaborative nature of the devising process itself: devised playtexts are rarely 'written' in finished form. As a result, the accessibility of definitive versions of written texts is greatly limited. Notable examples of devised/scripted plays bearing problematic relationships to the question of authorship are *Lear's Daughters* (1987) by Elaine Feinstein and Women's Theatre Group, and *Now and In the Hour of Our Death* by Sonja Lyndon and Trouble and Strife. The complicated histories, or herstories, of both of these plays deserve individual attention.

Women's Theatre Group and *Lear's Daughters*

Lear's Daughters was first commissioned in 1987 by WTG.[24] Elaine Feinstein was offered the commission as writer to work with members of the company, which at that time consisted of Gwenda Hughes, Janys Chambers, Hilary Ellis, Maureen Hibbert and Hazel Maycock. The script was to be a new feminist version of Shakespeare's *King Lear*. Feinstein worked with the company in devising some ideas, and then went away to write the script independently. The script which she submitted, however, was found to be unsatisfactory by the company. A rushed series of workshops followed, out of which emerged a revised version of the script, which was used in the first touring production of 1987. All company members contributed to the workshops, and thus to the revising process and the rewriting of the working script.

As is the case with much group-devised work, it is difficult to determine the 'authorship' of *Lear's Daughters*. Furthermore, there was and is among the members of WTG a certain sense of solidarity, centred around the concept of the integrity of 'collective authorship'. In the case of *Lear's Daughters*, company members were agreed that the script had been the result of a collective effort, and were hesitant to take individual credit (even when credit was due). Yet it seemed clear from the polished finish of the piece – both the written script and the production – that at some point someone must have shaped the individual contributions and devised images into the polished play. In this case, after lengthy discussion with the group, it emerged that it was one of the actors (Janys Chambers, who played Nanny on both tours), who did most of this final 'editing'.[25]

The processes of writing and rewriting *Lear's Daughters* were not visible to the public. Yet the public presentation of the play required some written attribution of authorship. Here again, the role of authorship, or ownership (in the artistic, if not the legal sense) of the commissioned–devised play is highly problematic. This example was further complicated, in that the play was given two separate tours (a standard procedure for WTG). The posters and press releases from the first run of *Lear's Daughters* listed Feinstein as author.[26] In its second run at the Young Vic, however, a few changes were made: a black actress was cast as Cordelia for the Young Vic run, while in the first run Cordelia was played by a white actress. In addition, the second run had what seemed to be a more tightly directed style, a development which may well be related to, if not a function of, a fixed venue. Perhaps most interestingly, Feinstein's name had been dropped from the credits in the programme for the Young Vic run of the play. Unexplained, this sudden omission of authorship shed no light on the origins of the piece, and irritated at least one critic.[27]

The company acknowledged the difficulty of crediting authorship for the play. Kathleen Hamilton, administrator for the second tour, noted that 'with regard to Elaine's original work, this is not available as it was very much a work in progress and fed into the collaborative script. There is only one version of *Lear's Daughters*'.[28] This 'one' script credits authorship in the following way:

Lear's Daughters
by The Women's Theatre Group and Elaine Feinstein
copyright 1988 The Women's Theatre Group and Elaine Feinstein.

Some official agreement had clearly been reached, and Feinstein's name was included on the script. Unofficially, however, the play as public property was unattributable, or was difficult to discuss in the context of any standard notion of 'authorship'. It is this ambiguous placement of the text in the public domain which seems to influence some critics' difficulty in discussing devised work.

The original formulation of authorship (printed on the first run advertisements) is still to be considered:

Lear's Daughters
by Elaine Feinstein
Women's Theatre Group

Here, the lack of an 'and' or 'for' between the group and the commissioned playwright's name leaves the relationship between the group and the writer unspecified and renders ambiguous the group's role in the authorship.

The third formulation (as it appeared on the second run handbills and programmes) reads:

Lear's Daughters
by Women's Theatre Group

with no mention at all of Feinstein's contribution. Critical responses to these different versions of the credits reveal an underlying discomfort with the notion of devised work. This discomfort may be related to the lack of an individual author, a situation which eliminates the identifiable 'subject' (or individual) to be criticized in relation to the 'object' which is the play. Alternatively, this critical discomfort may be justified, in some cases at least, by a genuine need for further editing and shaping of the play. In the case of *Lear's Daughters*, the former explanation is more creditable. The reviews of *Lear's Daughters* may not be typical, but they are worth considering here, as they raise issues also faced by Trouble and Strife and other feminist companies in their experiences of devised work.

The *London Theatre Record* reprinted five reviews by female reviewers of *Lear's Daughters*: two reviews from the first tour, both very positive and both by women (Lyn Gardiner and Peggy Butcher), and three reviews during the second tour production, one favourable (by Barney Bardsley) and two unfavourable (by Jane Edwardes and Paula Webb). Edwardes was clear about her discomfort at the omission of Feinstein's name, and Webb mentioned her efforts to disassociate her experiences as a woman who thinks herself a feminist from her viewing of this admittedly feminist, group-structured play. Edwardes, in effect, was perturbed by a perceived slight to an individual author (not, presumably, out of any particular allegiance to Feinstein), and Webb reacted to the non-hierarchical structure of the collective by expressing discomfort at some unstated notion that she should, as a 'feminist', be able to place herself at least vicariously within that collective dynamic. Both women were reacting, in some sense, to the difficulties of reviewing a production based on a text for which no single author could be identified.

The field of feminist criticism has so infused and influenced the media in the past few years (whether implicitly or explicitly) that issues of personal politics in performance are criticized, not only in and of themselves, but also in relation to the politics of the critic. The operative popular assumption that female critics are inherently sympathetic to women's work is thus complicated by the politics inherent to feminist work: that is, the female critic of the feminist piece may find herself uncomfortable with her own position *vis-à-vis* a given production, and may therefore be more critical, because more directly implicated, than would be a male critic of the same piece.

The politics of the individual critic may influence the reception of any given play, just as the politics of the author and of the audience can be seen to do. This dynamic might be extended to consider the situation of the lesbian critic of a feminist but heterosexist play, or the gay male critic of an all-women's play, etc. The notion of a gendered criticism, coupled with the operative concept of critical distance, can thus become a double-edged sword. In subsequent chapters I cite reviews of feminist plays, written by male critics. In these reviews, the language and tone used by the critics suggest that they are reacting against the authors as women and the feminist content of the plays, rather than reviewing the plays themselves. The critical/political implications of this dynamic warrant much more extended analysis in conjunction with current debates about feminist spectatorship and 'the audience as critic'.

COMMISSIONED-DEVISED-COLLABORATIVE WORK

Trouble and Strife

A similarly difficult placement of text in public context emerges with any attempt to discuss Trouble and Strife's *Now and in the Hour of Our Death*.[29] The play's theme and central metaphor are constructed around the symbolic 'no-wash' protests among women prisoners of Northern Ireland's Armagh prison. The original idea and the title were the company's. After a period of discussion, the group brought in a friend, Sonja Lyndon, to take part in workshops and to script the piece. After extensive devising and workshopping with the group, Lyndon went away and wrote one scene, which the group approved. She then went away to write the rest of the play. When the complete playscript was submitted, however, the company (as was the case with WTG and *Lear's Daughters*) was not satisfied: they had expected something different.[30]

By this time (1987), the play was scheduled to open in four weeks. A hectic series of workshops and rewriting sessions followed, in which Lyndon was not encouraged to participate 'because there was no time for sensitivity to author's wishes and feelings: we had to be brutal and get the play done'.[31] Lyndon revised her own version and renamed it *Poetry in Motion*, but it was the collectively 'written' version which was produced. Lyndon and the group agreed that, due to this complicated situation, Lyndon's name should be removed from the publicity materials for the show. However, the posters and prepublicity materials were already printed. Her name was removed from the programme. Publicity for the play thus credited authorship in two different ways. The five-woman show toured extensively from January to October 1988, and Lyndon's name remained on the posters and most of the press notices throughout.

Confusion over the issue of authorship had, in this case, more than incidental effects. When Abigail Morris revised the play and submitted it for the BBC Radio Young Playwright's award, the play was short-listed, and the company was informed of its success. Before the award was received, however, a member of the awards panel discovered the discrepancy in the credits of the promotional materials, and questioned the authorship of the piece. Because Lyndon was not under the age limit specified by the contest, the play was disqualified and the offer of the award was revoked.[32]

Trouble and Strife's dilemma differs from that described for WTG in two important ways: in this case, Lyndon had been commissioned to write the play from ideas developed in company workshops (hence the base material and ideas were unquestionably group property), and Trouble and Strife discarded Lyndon's script altogether (*Poetry in Motion* is a very different play). As was the case with WTG, however, the real conflict developed not in devising or even in performance, but in relation to the play's reception in the public sphere. In both cases, the discrepancy was related to the question of the public crediting of authorship for devised work. Finola Geraghty (Trouble and Strife member) explained the group's perspective on the situation in this way:

> We originally enlisted a writer to script a play from our improvisational workshops, etc. (hence publicity materials bearing her name). She received our £800.00 writers' grant from the Arts Council (at this stage we were operating on loans, promises, etc.). As it turned out, we did not use her script (*Poetry in Motion*) and WROTE [sic] our own play. It thus seems that our way of working may be a problem – in that it is not widely recognized. Companies either have a writer to transcribe (and create), do plays already written, or devise pieces (as opposed to WRITING) [sic].[33]

Geraghty's letter supports the supposition that one of the primary difficulties of devising is a definitional one: that of distinguishing between 'writing' and 'devising'. The ambiguous status of both 'copyright' and 'authorship' are further complicated in this case by a set of funding policies that are not geared toward acceptance as legitimate of working methods such as devising and collaboration. The problem of authorship was actually initiated by the Arts Council, in that it was the need for funding, which could only be acquired in the form of a writer's bursary (and which could not be allocated, according to Arts Council policies, to the group members as collective 'writers') which led the group to commission Lyndon in the first place.

Trouble and Strife work as a collective, using the basic techniques of devised work and employing a collective approach to the writing process as well. Aside from their commissioning of Lyndon for *Now and In the Hour of Our Death*, Trouble and Strife works in this way: 'We write our own plays collaboratively. In effect this means a long period of research and discussion, workshopping and improvising, culminating in a period of writing, all sitting around a table with papers and pens.' As the set guidelines of their Arts Council grant allowed funds specifically for a writer, a writer was commissioned. It is significant that both the group and Lyndon refrain from blaming each other for the difficulties they encountered, and rather account for their predicament in terms of the company's 'mistake' in attempting to fit its preferred working methods (in this case, group devising without an outside writer) to funding guidelines. The result was negative both for Lyndon, the 'outside writer', and for the group. As this kind of dilemma is becoming increasingly common, it is worth examining the issue of funding criteria in relation to the concept of 'artistic control over the means of production'.

Trouble and Strife first came into conflict with the Arts Council before *Now and In the Hour of Our Death* was fully conceived, when they estimated and applied for funds to cover their wages during the lengthy period needed for workshopping, writing and rehearsal. Their request was refused:

> The Arts Council stipulate very strictly how the money is to be distributed, and the wages, under their stipulations, covered a six week rehearsal period, three weeks of performance and six weeks touring. . . . This is a problem we have come up against with publishers as well. They are reluctant to accept that a play is written by a company.

Here again, a certain conflict of interests between a theatre group and a second party (whether it be an individual critic or a funding body) can be seen to have arisen in relation to a dispute about the concept of authorship. The Arts Council stipulated, in essence, that it would prefer to fund plays which could be attributed to identifiable authors. The same critical discomfort which arises with the ambiguous placement of the devised text in the public domain, as illustrated through the WTG example, is thus shown fundamentally to be related to a question of origins – of ownership, and of credits.

That such conflicts of interests have direct economic implications is apparent. What is not apparent is a tenable solution. Increased awareness and publicizing of the benefits of working methods such as devising and collaborative writing might, in time, lead to increased awareness among critics and funding bodies, and might thereby influence the economic viability of these working methods. At the moment, many theatre companies find themselves caught (like Trouble and Strife was in 1987) in a vicious cycle: funds are needed to produce a play, but cannot be obtained without paying an 'author', while other groups carefully avoid commissioning authors in order to cut down on financial output.

Current funding patterns tend to subordinate artistic decisions to economic ones, not only in feminist theatre, but also in British theatre *per se*.

The Feminist Theatre Survey, however, suggests that there may be a particular dynamic at work in all-women's and feminist companies: because devising and collaboration are so common among these groups (and indeed, because these working methods are aligned with the non-hierarchical structures and ideologies of feminism itself), it seems that funding policies which discourage these kinds of work may thereby discourage feminist work in particular.

DEVISED WORK BY COLLECTIVES AND CO-OPERATIVES

Some theatre groups work almost exclusively by devising their own material. Of groups surveyed in 1987–90, 69 (of 98) identified devising as a common working practice. Some of the reasons for choosing to devise are obvious: devising tends to reduce the amount of capital investment spent outside the group itself (and may eliminate the need to commission an outsider, etc.), while allowing for the benefits of improvisation (including spontaneity) without the hazards of unpracticed performance (i.e., unpredictability or under-rehearsal). Further, devising ideally produces scripts based on collective rather than individual experience. Some of the dangers of devising have already been mentioned: primarily, devised plays may run the risk of structurelessness, that is, too many writers may 'spoil' the play. Even in the best of working relationships, there is a danger that a group-devised play will not ultimately find a single voice through which to express the multiple contributions of the group. While all these factors may also affect traditionally scripted and rehearsed plays, the intense, personal and non-hierarchical nature of the collective or co-operative tends to intensify both the positive and the negative aspects of these working conditions. Lack of a unifying voice, or of tight editing and direction of the devised script, is a fundamental problem for collectives, based as they are on the notion that no single member should exercise powers greater than those of her equals. But – as was seen to be the case with *Lear's Daughters* – at some point, in order to produce a coherent play, an individual within the collective almost inevitably takes charge.

Monstrous Regiment has also had its problems with group-devised material. A notable example is the 1977 cabaret, *Floorshow*. Co-written by Caryl Churchill, Bryony Lavery and Michelene Wandor, the show was a tremendous public success. Privately, however, there were problems within the group, relating to the collaborative-devising process, in conjunction with issues such as control of the written text and equal representation in performance of the finished script.[34] The Regiment now tends to use a combination of working methods much like that used by Trouble and Strife: it commissions work from individual writers, based on and/or supporting its own ideas. It sometimes uses improvisation and workshopping as part of the process, later employing a director to bring the process to

103

its fruition in the form of a unified and focused play.[35] As was the case with Caryl Churchill's positive and fruitful relationship with Monstrous Regiment during the process of writing *Vinegar Tom*, this has been and still is a viable combination of working methods and one with the potential to benefit both the company and the individual writer.

The working methods of both Monstrous Regiment and WTG have been discussed here and in chapter 3. In shifting focus to a lesser-known company, it is illuminating to discuss the influence of feminist working methods in relation to a feminist theatre group which has developed and changed through the years: Common Ground.

Common Ground to Meeting Ground

As devised work for the theatre is written or at least conceived in a shared space, so the final devised or collaborative theatre piece incorporates, at least to some degree, a shared perspective. Such was the case with *The Fence*, devised by six women from Greenham Common (only two of whom had previous theatrical experience) who, in 1984, formed their own theatre company: Common Ground. Common Ground's roots in public political protest illustrate both an ideological and a stylistic connection to early feminist street theatre protests. In fact, the group's one and only show (the term 'play' is not strictly appropriate for this piece, though the script has been published), *The Fence*, was intended to intervene in the arenas of sexual and cultural politics. *The Fence* was based on improvisational exercises from the members' own experiences, loosely structured in a series of fifteen short, highly visual vignettes. The topic was 'peace'; the theme was the need for solidarity among women against the 'patriarchal structures of men' (embodied in the presence of the military on one side of the Greenham Fence) and the need to tear down this and other fences (cultural, social, political and economic divides). The theme of this performance piece matched its intent: an intervention in society through public demonstration of a theatrical nature. Performance spaces for this piece were similarly non-traditional: *The Fence* was first performed at St Paul's Church, Hammersmith, London in 1984, and then at the Greenham Fence itself.

Images generated by the show are closely related to the image of the Greenham Fence. Indeed, the fence as the show's central metaphor pervades every element of language and setting: 'The Fence was built collectively and performed in London and at the Greenham Fence itself in 1984', according to the production details in the published text.[36] In this same text, perhaps to replace the lively post-show discussion which was an important element of *The Fence* in performance, the script (which is nine pages long) is followed by five printed pages of commentary by the members. This functions not so much as explication of the script, but rather as a testimony by the company of its reasons for writing and performing it, and indeed of its reasons for forming Common Ground.

The *idea* of the collective – of women working together for peace – was inspirational to the women of Common Ground as feminists, while their roles as mothers and potential mothers imbued their work with an orientation toward the future. In this sense, Common Ground was a feminist theatre group dedicated to social action. Common Ground's emphasis on motherhood and the potential for change inherent to the generational cycle was stressed by company members in their published postscript to the play, and was also contained in and enacted through the metaphor of pregnancy (the pregnant performer as the ultimate initiator of change).

The collective format was not only an ideological preference for the group, but also its intrinsic structure. The group's working relationship was dependent upon a view of the collective as a non-hierarchical group, impervious to external pressure so long as internal relations were harmonious. Thus, when personal conflict disturbed the group dynamic, the balance of the group was shifted in a fundamental way, and the work was adversely affected. This is true of most collectives, but especially so for a group like Common Ground which relied on an image of itself as unified in direct political opposition to forces outside the company – in this case, to nuclear weapons and the political sphere in which such weapons are created.

The Fence was co-devised by all the members of the group: Tracy Boden, Carmell Caddell, Max Holloway, Tanya Myers, Fiona Wood and Sally Wood. The group originally included a woman known as 'Zouffi', who participated in some of the workshops for the piece and then dropped out due to a certain tension between members – a tension often develops in small (political) working groups. The example is instructive, not only of an uncompromising view of the function of the feminist collective as structure, but also, in larger terms, of an element of the feminist movement itself. In losing a core member in order to reduce conflict, the group demonstrated in microcosm what the feminist movement demonstrated in larger terms: political aims were advanced, and those with 'clamorous voices' found it best to leave rather than disturb the balance of the group dynamic. This example can hardly be seen as representative of feminist theatre *per se*, but it is indicative of one of the potential problems of an idealistic emphasis on a personal/political ideology – one which can be seen to have affected various segments of the women's movement(s) from the outset. The potential for developing factionalism which has been exhibited in the development of many different feminist theatres is not necessarily destructive, but is clearly rooted in potentially divisive political/personal conflict.

Common Ground's allegiance to feminist principles took precedence over the style or 'aesthetic' of its work. In Myers' words, 'we knew we wanted to work collectively and that would mean finding alternatives to structures we knew'. In addition to the close working relationship of the group, Myers stressed the importance of the spaces in which it worked: churches, fields, friends' flats, the Riverside Studios (once it could afford heated rehearsal space), but most importantly, Greenham Common, a space which was an intrinsic part of the work in ideological as well as physical terms. Myers also emphasized the role of the audience, both in the preview run in the church, and in the performance on the Common: 'The audience at St Paul's Church in Hammersmith was both men and women. The audience at Greenham was also mixed, except this time the men stood behind the fence with guns.'

Such a critical configuration of audience-as-participant, or as active spectator, is one of the clearest examples in evidence of a revisionist view of the role of the spectator in contemporary feminist theatre. In the case of Common Ground at least, the audience was charged with participation – active or passive, violent or nonviolent – in a play of huge proportions, on 'the world as stage'. The audience was divided into opposing camps: those with guns and those without; people disrupting the environment and the peace (with little regard for future generations), and people striving for peace. The gender divide was made explicit: women as creators and men as destroyers; in both cases, gender was constructed as actively performative. Feminist activists in the audience were aligned with the performers. Thus, it was the performers who judged the 'value' of the actions and alliances of the audiences, in a context (the theatre) which is traditionally structured in precisely the opposite way. Yet this analysis must, in Tanya Myers' view, take account of the difference between the text and the way that text developed in performance. In Myers' words:

> We started off with the premise that it was them and us. That's how the script looks. But in performance, there were overlapping voices, a certain hesitation in some voices and a powerful determination in others. In performance, there was no way to tell from moment to moment who might fall on which side of the divide created by the fence. And as we, the performers, became the fence, we also became our fathers, who were part of us and who might have had a different position to our own.
>
> In this way, our positions changed and developed during the performance, and we identified and met the fences within ourselves, and tried to transcend them. In that sense, you could say that *The Fence* was about challenging the divide, about using improvisational exercises as rites of passage, using performance as a means of transport for our internal and external journeys, and in the connection of images and ideas.[37]

The Fence was agitprop performance in several senses: it was theatrical, image-based and episodic. The fence, as metaphor for the structure of feminist theatre itself, functions as a self-conscious analogue to the 'fences' (hierarchical structures) of traditional theatres and texts.

Significantly, Common Ground disbanded a year after it formed. Tanya Myers and Tracy Boden had been the only members of Common Ground with theatre training. Myers moved on to join Stephen Lowe and others in the established (mixed gender) company called Meeting Ground in 1985. Thus, Common Ground disbanded but Meeting Ground benefited from the addition of a member who had been instrumental in the political performance of *The Fence*. Meeting Ground is still operative, and has recently developed into an international company involved in the exploration of images of women. Meeting Ground's membership is not fixed; it involves different numbers of women and men for different projects.

The international scope of Meeting Ground was first extended when in 1990 the company produced Zofia Kalinska's *The Sale of the Demonic Woman*. This performance piece was inspired by Kalinska's workshops at the first Magdalena (Women's Theatre International) Project and, like *The Fence*, was concerned with iconography and symbolism, with women's bodies and myths of the idealized and simultaneously 'monstrous' image of the feminine.[38] To some extent, Meeting Ground's turn to international work was a symbolic 'act' in itself, corresponding to developments in feminisms and theatres in other cultures.

COLLABORATIVE WRITING

A working method which combines positive elements of both the commissioned and the collectively devised processes is the collaborative script writing method, in which two or more writers pool their efforts toward creation of a single script (as opposed to the devised method in which performance takes precedence over the written script). It should be noted that the products of some mixed gender collaborations (such as those of Franca Rame and Dario Fo, and Caryl Churchill and David Lan) have been 'feminist' in many important respects, and have received critical attention in this regard.[39] In addition, several feminist (collaborative) comedy duos have emerged in recent years, including Parker and Klein, Donna and Kebab, French and Saunders and Lip Service (Maggie Fox and Sue Ryding). Focus here, however, is on British women's collaboration in the theatre. Two particularly productive feminist collaborative teams deserve attention: Cordelia Ditton and Maggie Ford, and Maro Green and Caroline Griffin.

Cordelia Ditton and Maggie Ford

Cordelia Ditton is a performer, director and writer with experience in touring and repertory companies, as a director for the self-styled feminist group Beryl and the Perils (now disbanded), and as a performer in film, television and radio. Maggie Ford has been involved in various aspects of fringe theatre from its emergence in the early 1970s, has worked with Joan Littlewood, and as a performer in repertory, at The National Theatre, and on television. Both are key figures in the development of feminist theatre in Britain, in so far as both are among the small circle of friends and acquaintances composing the 'subgeneration' of active women identified and described in chapters 2 and 3. In 1980, Ford devised and performed her own one-woman show, *The Rising of The Moon*, and took it on a large-scale international tour. She later wrote and produced several other one-woman shows, before she met Cordelia Ditton and began working collaboratively. Since 1985, Ford has also contributed to theatre projects with Graeae, Clean Break and Gay Sweatshop.

Ditton and Ford's first collaborative piece was *About Face*, a performance piece which addressed working-class women's experiences of the coal strike in Nottingham/Derbyshire in 1984–5.[40] The play involves thirty-five characters (including The Thatcher, a Mad Scientist, an Oil Sheik, a Rubbish Tip, and an Indian Cow), all played by Cordelia Ditton. The central character is not a woman, but a horse. Ditton and Ford refer to this choice of casting, tongue-in-cheek, as an 'alienation device':

> *Ford*: In a lot of ways, the style's really quite anarchic. We don't take any particular theatrical convention and stick to it. There are very strong Brechtian alienation devices – I suppose you would call them.
> *Ditton*: It has to be said, we are very keen on Brecht.
> *Ford*: And Dario Fo devices are there too. And you can find that they used to develop argumentative theatre in Ancient China.

The references to theatrical predecessors are strategically placed. They both defy the critics to deny the 'serious intent' of the work, and simultaneously mock the structures and conventions of 'serious' theatrical criticism. Ditton explains that this preference for what might be seen as a mild form of 'canon-bashing' is one of the keys to writing successful collaborative women's work. In the absence of enough female role models and in the present economic and political circumstances, the duo believe that the best approach is to 'set up your own conventions and break them all over the place'. In a sense, this is an instance of judging the apparatus by its suitability for the work.

What is significant about this particular type of collaboration is the crucial role of comedy in Ditton and Ford's collaborative work. Several of the most successful feminist collaborative writing teams in operation in 1990 work or began working in the stand-up comedy and cabaret circuits, including French and Saunders, and Maggie Fox and Sue Ryding (of Lip Service).[41] While collaborative comedy teams are not uncommon, collaborative comedy which is written and staged as theatre, rather than as cabaret or stand-up, is relatively rare. It is significant that Ditton and Ford insisted on directing their own play, albeit through the mouth of a horse, and to the ears and eyes of an audience of specifically working-class women. They evidently knew not only how they wanted to convey their message, but also who they wanted to convey it to.

Ditton and Ford worked together again in 1986 in researching and writing *The Day The Sheep Turned Pink*, a play which serves as a direct response to the crisis of the nuclear age, similar in terms of intent, but not in terms of content or style, to Common Ground's *The Fence*. Both plays serve as vehicles for the expression of direct political statements. Rather than choosing agitprop, however, Ditton and Ford chose satiric comedy as their vehicle. Since 1986, however, the collaboration has effectively ceased, as each of the women has moved on to work with larger feminist groups, and to give occasional workshops for the Women's Playhouse Trust on, among other topics, collaborative writing skills. Such a situation is not only ironic, but also indicative of the destructive effects of funding shortages, particularly on small-scale alternative work, which is not easily labelled, and therefore does not correspond to the categories and criteria of the funding bodies.

Maro Green and Caroline Griffin

I will devote more space to the collaborative work of an operative team: Maro Green and Caroline Griffin. Green and Griffin are well known for their collaborative feminist theatre work on such projects as *More* in 1985 and *Mortal* for Women's Theatre Group in 1990. They founded The Nitty Gritty Theatre Company in 1987, which produced *The Memorial Gardens* in 1988 in response to the controversy over Section 28. In conjunction with the founding of Nitty Gritty, they also founded a company producing multilingual theatre work for young people: Neti-Neti. In Neti-Neti's work, Green goes by her given name of Casdagli. In looking in some detail at one of the plays which Green and Griffin wrote collaboratively, some of the strengths of the collaborative working method become apparent.

More tells the story of Coquino, 'a failed escapologist', and Mavro, who 'hopes to be invisible'. It explores the themes of disability, anorexia, bulimia and agoraphobia, ritual, religion and love.[42] These are more than 'themes' for the authors. Griffin is a 'practising' agoraphobic, as is the character Coquino, while Green is a lapsed bulimic, as is the character Mavro. The exploration of agoraphobia as a 'theme' within the play is strengthened by the insights which Griffin's experience gives the character. The play, like other work by Green and Griffin, was inspired by the writers' lives as women and feminists, and was influenced by Griffin's poetry. In particular, the poem which deals with agoraphobia, 'Call This A Life Lived Backwards', was inspirational in both *More* and in *The Memorial Gardens*.[43]

When the play was performed in 1986, Maro Green played the character of Mavro, but Caroline Griffin (who, like the character Coquino, is agoraphobic) did not perform. Yet in a sense, Griffin is represented in the character of Coquino. The rope which is tied to Coquino in the opening of the play can – at one level – be seen as a symbol representing the identification between the character and the writer. However, Griffin explains the significance of the rope in this way:

> The rope only relates to Coquino's experience. At the opening, Coquino is tied to the rope: she hasn't been born properly at all. The moment when she loses the rope is very important. This not being born feeling is partly the agoraphobic experience: i.e. not being able to believe the possibility of the self surviving as separate. That's very important.[44]

The realistic side to the character of Coquino charges the comedy of some scenes with an element of tragedy as well. The play is a tragicomedy of sorts, in which comedy allows serious statements to be made.

For instance, when Coquino mimes her false birth, she holds onto the rope which functions both as a prop and as a figurative umbilical cord, tying her to the safety of existence off-stage. But while the rope functions for Coquino as a tie to safety, it also represents or demonstrates her fear. The rope connects the character of Coquino (on-stage) to the performer (also on-stage), created by the writer, Griffin (off-stage, or in the 'real world'). At the same time, the rope provides a connection between the two characters as Mavro and Coquino discuss its importance as a symbol of power:

> *Coquino*: One way or another, whoever holds the rope is in charge.
> *Mavro*: You can never say you haven't heard this. From now on, you're responsible too, or culpably naive.

In reinterpreting the rope as a symbol of power (of being in charge) rather than as a sign of weakness, Green and Griffin ask the audience to accept a different scale of values. The audience seems to be implicated in the power dynamic contained in these lines as well. Thus *More* both implicates the audience and also keeps the rope physically as well as symbolically limited to the playing space of the stage. The audience is implicated, but indirectly.

More takes place, like much of Green and Griffin's collaborative work, in a timeless, placeless space. Griffin explains that this setting and tone may 'suggest the performance of a ritual, which could take place anywhere. We don't posit any location in the play: they are just there'. Both writers observed in their published notes to the play: 'Maybe the most subversive element of the play is that in its direct address, the audience are given an opportunity and a choice – to identify themselves as part of Mavro and Coquino's world unequivocally and without apology or to stay outside.' The authors explain that their aims in writing and producing the play were neither to entertain nor to please, but to represent some of the real conditions which are specific to Mavro and Coquino's lives. In so doing, they set out to make feminist theatre according to their own definition of the term, as 'that theatre which puts girls' and women's experience first'.

Women's experience is at the centre of most of Green and Griffin's collaborative work. Their work is also unusually aware of the position of the audience in relation to the play. *More* actively subverts the theatrical transformation scene. The moments in many traditional narratives and dramas, such as those found in fairy tales and pantomimes – when frog turns prince and hag turns raving beauty, are themselves transformed in this play. For instance, Green and Griffin offer this dialogue:

Mavro: Why do we want to jump so much?
Coquino: Because we're happy.
Both: The transformation scene! [They wait. Nothing happens.]
Coquino: Has it worked?

It does 'work' in the sense that there is a transformation of sorts, but one which relies upon the imagination of the audience. Green and Griffin allow for the possibility of a transformation, but do not insist upon or impose one.

The scene, like the entire Godot play, is imbued with a sense of waiting for something which never happens. Also like the Godot play, the scene is ritualistic, set in a timeless nowhere land. There is no explanation of how or why the characters have arrived in this space on the stage. They wait, but it is not clear what they are waiting for. In *More*, however, it is not so much the characters' or even the performers' waiting which is emphasized and challenged, but rather the expectation of the reader and audience. Green and Griffin are careful to ask the final question which the Godot pair do not ask: has it worked? The answer depends upon audience interpretation and reception. As the authors explain: 'The play was an experiment to see if anyone was out there'. The people 'out there' are necessary to the play's performance. And, Green and Griffin argue, the transformation does or can 'work' in *More* if the audience and performers allow themselves to take part in the ritual, to accept a new set of rules, to use their imaginations.[45]

Feminist theatre of this sort emphasizes extrascenic communication in order to instigate personal responses. In terms of response to early versions of the show, Green notes that: '*More* came out of a woman's writing workshop, whose members, despite the contract to be supportive, gave this unpromising first draft a rough ride'. The contract to which Green refers is the unwritten, unstated notion that women will unite and support each other in their efforts to find their own ways of writing. That early criticism may have 'worked' for the play by helping to shape it into a more cohesive and effective piece of theatre. In early 1985 *More* was performed in the South London Women's Hospital, 'while it was still occupied and before it was closed'. Intervention in political arenas, emphasis on the personal elements thereof, the choice of alternative performance spaces: all these were elements of this performance.

Performance in non-theatre spaces always complicates the performer–audience relationship in some way. When *More* was performed in the Women's Hospital, the audience dynamic was influenced by the setting, just as Common Ground's performance of *The Fence* was influenced by its setting on Greenham Common. The hospital setting was appropriate to *More*, which seeks to implicate the audience with the characters' emotional and physical problems in such a direct way. As was the case with Common Ground, the early stages of the rehearsing and writing were done in truly 'alternative' spaces. In *The Fence*, Common Ground's audience were viewed as 'outsiders', or as 'the opposition'. In *More*, by contrast, the audience (as a whole) is viewed as a potential collaborator – potential agoraphobics and escapologists, perhaps temporarily 'escaping' to the theatre.

Green and Griffin collaborated again in 1989, when they co-wrote *Mortal* for Women's Theatre Group. *Mortal*, like *More*, experimented with the boundaries of theatre convention in presenting a surrealistic setting and a skewed time frame. It also offered characters who 'created themselves' within that performance space. Green and Griffin's play of 1988 was also concerned with representation of the self on stage. *The Memorial Gardens* was produced in response to the then-current controversy surrounding Section 28. Like their earlier work, *The Memorial Gardens* was a ritual play of sorts. It had a realistic set, but one which could be transported any-where. The play could take place in any garden. It operated in several time frames and frames of mind – present and past, reality, memory and imagination – each created and expressed by characters very closely aligned with the authors.

They employ this same assumption of extrascenic collaboration in work for Neti-Neti, their theatre company producing work for young people. Neti-Neti's work is briefly discussed in Chapter 7. In Neti-Neti's work, as in *More* and *The Memorial Gardens*, the working method shapes the final product. Green and Griffin explain the importance of their collaborative working method as related to their position as feminists:

We are not a traditional theatre company. And we are not a collective. But we support each other in overlapping, complicated ways. This is how we work best. . . . There shouldn't be a contradiction between the process and the content of theatre work. That is . . . a feminist idea.[46]

In the authors' notes to the published version of *More*, Green and Griffin identified themselves as 'radical lesbian feminists'. Their identification with a particular feminist stance is clear. But *More*, like *The Memorial Gardens*, is 'feminist' in many different ways. Both plays experiment with several ideas which are central to the development of feminist theatre, including an emphasis on collaboration between women, and a respect for audiences of critical spectators.

As argued elsewhere, changing definitions of feminism have complicated the definition of feminist theatre. Green and Griffin have worked in the theatre, individually and collaboratively, for many years. To them, the term 'feminist theatre' is both resonant and empty, fixed and flexible. It has meant different things to them, as to other women, at different points in their lives and careers. This is how Maro Green articulated her definition of feminism in relation to her collaborative work with Caroline Griffin in early 1991:

I am feminist, and so is Caroline. All our work is explicitly feminist. And we're tackling issues of racism as well as sexism, communication problems as well as gender issues, ability and disability as well as sexuality. . . .

Our feminism is developing, and has been qualified by our experience. I can't answer for new definitions of feminism these days. I am not sure how other women working in the theatre are defining their feminism. But I haven't stopped being a feminist.[47]

The words are those of one woman whose work might be described with the help (or hindrance) of many different labels, including 'lesbian' and 'feminist'. Yet Green's statement can also be applied to the larger, perhaps depersonalized subject of feminist theatre. In fact, the statement supports the main idea of this book: that feminist theatre should be defined flexibly in order to take account of differences between women, and also to allow for differences in the same woman's (women's) perspectives over time, and in different social contexts. Yet feminist theatre always, by definition, promotes change in society. In Green and Griffin's words: 'The way in which we are each viewed and valued in society has profound effects on the ways we see ourselves, and on what we can achieve. Changing those social views is the aim of our work, and part of our equal opportunities policy.'

5

LESBIAN THEATRES AND THEORETICAL PERSPECTIVES

The contradiction to compulsory heterosexuality is lesbian existence.
Sue-Ellen Case (*Feminism and Theatre*, 1988).

LESBIAN THEATRE AND FEMINIST THEATRE

Of the body of published scholarly work on the subject of lesbian theatre(s), most has focused on American rather than British or other theatres, and on theoretical approaches to the representation of lesbians in feminist performance. Plays have not been the primary focus of most such work; rather, lesbian performance – the activity rather than the 'product' – has been studied.

This chapter focuses on the gaps in the existing scholarship – on plays and performance pieces and on the ways in which individual women view their own work in lesbian theatres. A number of plays are considered, most of which were written by British women and most of which are 'issue plays' of sorts. One of the most striking differences between British and American lesbian theatres is the British focus on the play as the form for expression of lesbian themes. It seems that, in moving so far from the white male heterosexual 'norm', lesbian theatre practitioners have found something else to hold on to. This 'something' is the play, a structure which has been subverted in several provocative ways by women of different generations, in the making of different lesbian theatres.

Of course, there are many different kinds of lesbian theatre and performance, and most lesbian plays deal with much larger issues than sexual preference. Lesbian theatre of many different kinds tends to experiment in original ways with 'the role of the audience' as complicit in the performance, and with construction of a self-conscious female (to female) gaze. In fact, lesbian theatre is a particularly rich source for the analysis of one of the key concepts of feminist theory in media and performance studies, that of the 'gaze'.

The concept of the gaze is relevant not only in theory but also in practice, as it may be analysed in relation to the audience-stage dynamic of any given play, and also in terms of the dynamics of desire which may influence scenic interaction. More importantly, the theory of the gaze is relevant to a study of lesbian theatre as a subgenre of feminist theatre, which is itself a form of cultural representation. As Elizabeth Wilson has proposed:

> The persistent cultural representation of the lesbian seems to suggest that lesbian and gay experience is the lens through which hetero-sexual-biased society is desperately peering at its own problematic practices.[1]

The element of voyeurism which Wilson detects is reflected in many aspects of the representation of the lesbian. The study of lesbian theatre, however, is not the study of the lesbian in theatre, but rather of theatre made by lesbians. The positioning of lesbian experience as the active creative subject is crucial.

The term 'contemporary British lesbian theatre' refers primarily to the work of a very small network of women, and primarily to the few individuals who have founded various lesbian performance groups or management collectives.[2] In chapter 2, a group of women was identified as those who had consistently – for some fifteen years – been the most frequent theatre-goers. Some of these same women have also been the most productive creators of lesbian theatre. Women including Gillian Hanna (of Monstrous Regiment), Bryony Lavery, Kate Crutchley (of the Oval House), Kate Corkery, Julie Parker and Mavis Seaman (of the Drill Hall), and Karen Parker and Debby Klein have contributed substantially to the development of British lesbian theatre. This same group of women has been influential in the creation of a significant proportion of British lesbian theatre produced since 1968. It is only since the 1980s that a slightly younger group of women including Tash Fairbanks, Maro Green and Caroline Griffin have begun to make 'new' lesbian theatres.

Thirteen British lesbian theatre groups were identified in the Feminist Theatre Survey, including The Character Ladies, Gay Sweatshop, Hard Corps, No Boundaries, Outcast, Shameful Practice and Siren. Of the thirteen, ten were operative in November 1990. Thus, the study of lesbian theatre is a very specific one; it has a great deal in common with the study of feminist theatre (where, again, one generation of women is extremely influential), but it also demonstrates crucial differences in terms of the potential for separatism which is inherent to the lesbian performance (regardless of the particular positions of playwrights, directors and performers).

Jill Davis has conducted the most important and extensive research on the subject of British lesbian theatre. Her two edited volumes of lesbian plays are the only ones published in Britain.[3] The first includes an introductory essay by Davis, in which she discusses various factors affecting the production and publication of lesbian plays.[4] Since so little has been written on the subject of lesbian theatre, it is necessary to refer to current criticism of lesbian literature and film. This seems the best way forward, when entrance into some theoretical discourse is necessary to the project of setting lesbian theatre in context (rather than considering it on its own, as if it developed without influence from social or economic factors, for instance). This frame of reference also allows the discussion to escape the trap of continually reaching backwards toward comparison to the 'norm' of traditional theatre – a method which would defeat the purpose of discussing lesbian theatre as a subgenre of feminist theatre, which itself attempts to offer an alternative to such male-defined norms. At the same time, this approach takes into account the tendency of lesbian theatre to define itself in relation to the forms of alternative theatre, including agit-prop, performance art and political cabaret. It thus provides a base for comparative study of lesbian theatre and other alternative art forms, with due consideration for the peculiarly British focus in lesbian theatre on 'the play'.

Here, two ideas may assist in the contextualizing of lesbian theatre. The first is from Judith Butler, and the second from Teresa de Lauretis, referring to the work of Marilyn Frye:

> *Butler*: Gender reality is performative which means, quite simply, that it is real only to the extent that it is performed.[5]
>
> *De Lauretis*: There are some people in the audience who do see what the conceptual system of heterosexuality, the Play's performance, attempts to keep invisible. These are lesbian people, who can see it because their own reality is not represented or even surmised in the Play, and who therefore reorient their attention toward the backgrounds, the spaces, activities and figures of women elided by the performance.[6]

The situation described by Teresa de Lauretis is based on Marilyn Frye's notion that lesbian representation is performed in relation to both 'background space' and 'foreground space'. Butler's contention that 'gender is performative' can be seen to support this notion, in the sense that it identifies lesbian identity as that which is not performed in society biased by a heterosexual 'norm'.

De Lauretis evaluates the role of the lesbian in the theatre audience, depicted by Frye as complicit with the stagehands (gendered people moving backstage, unseen). Butler's view can be seen to extend and reframe the argument. By focusing on the stagehands and the lesbians in the audience, the critic 'is doing for feminist theory what Pirandello, Brecht and others did for the bourgeois theatre conventions': that is, the critic is questioning and testing the limits of the stage–world divide, refocusing the gaze of the critic on the active and essentially political audience–stage interaction of

116

both theatre performance and gender as performance.[7] This critique omits one crucial factor: the lesbian's agency as a maker and performer of the 'Play'. What remains to be seen is the way in which the lesbian frames and directs her own 'spectacle' – the way in which the maker or performer of lesbian theatre positions herself in terms of gender, agency, and positionality in relation to her (gendered, and therefore complicit/performing) audience. The positionality of the lesbian theatre maker, and of her audience, is tested in performance in the 'act' of coming out.

The performance of coming out

The action involved in the act of coming out for lesbians in society can, under some circumstances, be a political act of rebellion against a recognized norm of heterosexuality as well as a personal act of denouncing the patriarchal assumption of the male right of access to women – of reclaiming and naming self. In Foucault's terms, a 'speaking of sex' effectively makes possible a strong advance of social controls in the area of 'perversity'.[8] Since sex and sexuality are often defined in relation to political domains, the 'speaking' or publicizing of homosexuality, when defined as 'transgressive sexuality', may be particularly prone to such increased emphasis on social controls. Hence the recent implementation of Section 28.

Of course, lesbianism is a socially constructed category which emerged at a particular historical point (in the late nineteenth century), but it was not recognized in a positive sense as anything other than a measure of 'deviance' until very recently. A study of lesbians as 'romantic outsiders' suggests that lesbianism as such may not have been fully recognized until the early twentieth century.[9] The American Psychiatric Association removed homosexuality from its official list of diseases in 1973.[10] According to the laws and ordinances of the British Commonwealth as of 1992, lesbianism simply does not exist; it is not legally recognized in any form, 'deviant' or otherwise. Gayle Rubin locates some of the more recent periods in which women's sexuality in its various forms has taken centre stage in cultural discourse as 'the campaigns against prostitution in the 1880s, discourse in the 1950s and 1960s over homosexuality, and more recently, hysteria over AIDS, sex education and Clause 28.'[11] While Rubin's list is potentially misleading in that it compares, and runs the risk of conflating, some very different social movements which themselves emerged in very different eras and under vastly different circumstances, still the basic comparison is enlightening: there have been particular historical points when women's sexuality was clearly on the agenda. Significantly, these have been moments when performance techniques were utilized in order to make political points.

The connection between sexual politics, cultural politics and performance is most evident in relation to socially constructed views of lesbianism. Celia

Kitzinger argues that the view which interprets lesbianism as a 'sickness' or 'perversity' has been largely replaced in modern society by the equally debilitating liberal perspective which labels lesbianism an 'alternative lifestyle'.[12] Such a label, she argues, depoliticizes the act of coming out by conflating it with other choices of lifestyle (such as vegetarianism and communal living). The reception and interpretation of the 'act' of being self is emphasized, just as it is in heterosexual feminist theatre work. Just as feminist theatre focuses on roles played by women in everyday life as represented (and representable) on stage, so lesbian theatre focuses on the role or 'act' of being lesbian. So long as being lesbian is considered 'deviant', the representation of self in lesbian theatre is bound to reflect images of self in relation to a set of artificial values or 'norms'.

Lesbian imagery has been obscured in the history of representation, but has emerged in contemporary feminist theatre in many and varied ways. One important form of (theatrical and political) representation is the act of coming out: as a lesbian, as an active subject in the world, and on the stage. The representation of coming out can be read in terms of political struggle and theatrical performance simultaneously. Nancy Diuguid, one of Britain's most influential feminist theatre directors, was raised in the Southern United States in a social and familial structure which expected her to 'come out' as a debutante. She has subverted those expectations in the most creative way through her successful work in the theatre, directing women and men who choose to represent themselves in a variety of ways. Diuguid has compared her coming out as a lesbian to her entrance into British feminist theatre, referring to her 'coming out as a lesbian performer and director'.[13]

While most women's experience of 'coming out' as lesbians is not quite so metaphorically charged, the dynamic is often similar. To extend the metaphor, the coming out of the lesbian can be seen as the antithesis of the socially acceptable (and even desirable) coming out of the debutante, which represents in a radically different context the coming of age, social saleability and sexual availability of the young woman groomed within the feminine stereotype of high society. The metaphor is complicated. Many lesbians do not 'come out' but lead private lives very different from their public ones. Though the consequences of coming out have, in many contexts, become less extreme as advances in civil rights and women's liberation have become influential, the act of coming out has not been disassociated from all negative cultural implications. The act of coming out is highly personal, even when ritualized into the most public of performances. If 'gender is performative', then cultural representations of lesbian and gay orientation – which often involve an experimentation with sex and gender roles – may be even more so.

Despite cultural pressure, or perhaps because of it, many British lesbian playwrights of the 1970s and early 1980s wrote coming out messages into their plays. But interestingly, many of these messages appeared in clearest form not in the texts of the plays themselves, but rather in authors' introductions to and comments about their plays. The tendency toward pushing polemic to the borderline in lesbian theatre scripts, as well as the comic tone prevalent in much lesbian theatre, both suggest that it may be precisely that which is the most private and personally significant which cannot be presented 'straight', which must be distanced from its importance to the author.

Perception of distance and marginalization, comedy as a vehicle, and an appeal to a specifically constructed audience: these three elements are often included in lesbian plays, and particularly in British lesbian plays. Perhaps the use of humour is, in fact, a reaction to the British theatre tradition, in the sense that lesbian plays oppose traditional 'norms' in so many different ways that, paradoxically, they may be in a good position to look back with a sense of humour at the culture from which the authors and subjects have been figuratively (and sometimes literally) outcast. The view of coming out as a 'subversion' (and mockery) of social expectation can easily be extended, and exemplified in terms of performance. The debutante analogy illustrates the point: just as it is the author's perceived distance from the acceptable position of the debutante which must be taken into account, it is also the author's perception of a common bond with the debutante, with the carefully framed and moulded image of self which she represents, which is defined and confined by awareness of the power of the gaze. But while the debutante seeks out the approving male gaze (or the male-defined way of seeing self which is associated with upper-class paternalistic society), the lesbian may only see or represent herself as her self when that male gaze is escaped or subverted.

The marginalization of lesbian experience in society is directly reflected in theatre hierarchies. The same distinctions and values operate in both. Similarly, differences of perspective among lesbian theatre practitioners have not yet been adequately addressed. As Kate McDermott notes in her introduction to the first published anthology of American lesbian plays, significant attention has not been paid to the triple distancing which lesbian women of colour might bring to their plays.[14] Similarly, studies have been done (or begun) on the ways in which society tends to represent the perceived deviance of lesbianism as its primary point of interest, relying on sensationalism and sometimes going so far as to 'sell' such triply deviant images as that of the lesbian nun and the lesbian vampire, both of which have begun to appear with alarming frequency in popular fiction, film and theatre. Such extreme images may reinforce the notion that lesbianism is 'deviant' and may also effectively make examples of lesbian women in the negative sense of scapegoating lesbians for larger cultural taboos.

Elizabeth Wilson has suggested that the popular fascination with such extreme images of lesbianism may reveal an indirect and voyeuristic gaze at heterosexual experience. In this view, representation of lesbian experience as 'deviance' serves the purpose of reaffirming, by contrast, the heterosexual 'norm'. Similarly, Tucker Pamela Farley has described the function of lesbianism as social taboo.[15] The same idea has been contextualized by Jeffrey Weeks, who argues that discussion of lesbianism even in legal contexts has been effectively censored.[16] Weeks identifies a common problem for lesbian social critics and theatre (or film) critics: the lack of legislation about the lesbian reflects a lack of social awareness of the lesbian position, and thereby forms the base for a very powerful, because covert, attack on the lesbian and all forms of lesbian representation. In other words, refusing to recognize lesbian experience is an effective means of silencing or suppressing it. This strategy effectively limits the forms of public protest available to lesbian representation as well: more forms of protest could be conceived in relation to a more overt form of discrimination. The exception which proves the rule is the tendency to represent lesbians in terms of extreme stereotypes such as that of the lesbian nun and the lesbian vampire, which further displace cultural focus on 'real' lesbian experience. Depicting lesbians in these ways makes it possible to ignore (and to seem to be justified in ignoring) lesbian experience and its implications for heterosexual culture.

Live performance of lesbian experience created by feminist women does not allow for the kind of voyeuristic and negative stereotyping common to many other forms of cultural representation of the lesbian. The double or triple marginalization of the lesbian act of coming out, of acting the role of self in a society with a vested interest in not seeing that self, places lesbian theatre in a separate category from gay theatre. Lesbian playwrights have not only to assert the value of their work, but also first to assert their value (and very existence) *as people*. Thus, lesbian existence is 'performative', and as such, is well suited to demonstration (in both senses of the word) and representation in the theatre. The theatre is a public forum appropriate to the staging of lesbian and gay 'coming out'. Feminist theatre may be the most appropriate forum.

Like all feminist theatres, lesbian theatre is change-oriented. The images and values it seeks to change are clearly defined. More importantly, its strategy for self-representation is clear-cut. The primary aim of lesbian theatre is the representation of lesbian experience, created by lesbians. The stage is the platform upon which self as subject may be declared and represented in a number of different ways. It is therefore interesting that, in Britain more than in America, many lesbian feminist theatre workers have written and produced plays informed by but distinct from the genre of performance/art theatre.

Directing the gaze in lesbian theatre

Two factors common to many lesbian plays are a certain polemical edge and a reliance on gender-specific but non-camp humour. These two factors are most often (and most successfully) combined. Lesbian theatre tends to attack the 'fourth wall' convention, often arrived at by framing of the plays' issues in polemical language. Political messages may therefore be communicated through a brand of comedy which involves the audience in recognition and reaction. The ability to laugh at self which results from the continual distancing of self from experience is part of some lesbian theatre performances, whether the laugh takes the form of personal farce or irony, political agitprop or the 'cheap laugh' of comedies and cabaret.

There are several distinct kinds and forms of lesbian theatre, each of which is directed at a specific audience. The first is that which is made by lesbians and which borrows the techniques of experimental collectives, directing itself at women spectators, but with no specific lesbian content. British examples of this kind of theatre are Sarah Daniels' earlier plays and some of Bryony Lavery's less overtly political material, including her recent TIE play for Theatre Centre, *The Two Marias*.[17] This kind of lesbian theatre assumes that lesbian experience can be subsumed into that of all women. As Kate Davy notes, this kind of lesbian theatre is indicative of an underlying functional assumption that social change is its first priority and best achieved by reaching the largest audience regardless of sexual orientation.[18] An American play which adheres to this same philosophy is Joan Lipkin's *Some of My Best Friends Are . . .* , discussed at the end of this chapter.

A second predominant form of lesbian theatre is separatist theatre: that which assumes not only an all-female audience, but also an all-lesbian audience. Nowhere but in the atmosphere of the playing space are such assumptions recorded. The transgressing spectator may sense that she or he does not belong, but will sense this in an indirect way. The non-lesbian spectator at a separatist performance is automatically and actively cast in the role of the voyeur. The issue is complicated, and best discussed with reference to theoretical work on the subject of 'the gaze'.[19]

According to Laura Mulvey, the male gaze in film has been rooted in three separate perspectives: the eye of the camera(man), the eye(s) of the men in the shot or frame who gaze at female characters in an objectifying manner, and the eyes of the spectators – the audience who, in traditional male-directed film and theatre, are assumed to be either specifically or 'generically' male.[20] The lesbian role tends to refuse the gender-defined status of object to the subjective male gaze; the separatist role always, by definition, does so. The separatist lesbian theatre piece will not include the male gaze; it will erase or ignore its perspective as the gaze itself has traditionally erased or ignored lesbian (and much women's) experience. It will not deny or present a male perspective in order to subvert it (as do many of the classic 'feminist films'), but will simply not represent it, as if it were not relevant, or not worth taking into account. Such a deconstruction of the male gaze might, in theory, lead to the construction of a directed gaze in separatist theatre which is neither generically female, nor a-gendered. A specifically lesbian gaze might be constructed.

Like lesbian film, lesbian theatre is written and directed by women, acted by women, and directed at a predominantly or exclusively female audience. As such, it has the potential to escape some of the problematic dynamics of the male gaze. Yet theory can not be translated into practice so easily. The very notion of a specifically lesbian gaze is inherently complicated by the gender construction of sexuality, by the idea that the 'dominant' partner in a lesbian relationship (imagined or real) may take on some elements of the desiring 'male' gaze, and that in the very construction of desire, a 'desirer' may be seen to be controlling a gaze in some 'masculine' way which renders the 'desired' the object of that gaze.[21] The implications of this gender/power dynamic were comically depicted in the artificial insemination debate ('who's on top') in Green and Griffin's *The Memorial Gardens*, for instance. In an ideal situation, the construction of sexuality between lesbians would eliminate the gender differentiation of the male to female gaze, but in reality (and in theatrical action) the same problematic elements might interfere.

While, ideally, the lesbian gaze would direct attention in primarily (if not exclusively) liberating ways, it does not operate in an ideal world. Both scenic and extra-scenic factors may interact with the gaze in lesbian performance. For instance, desire may be manifested in a woman-to-woman gaze. This desire may only escape the objectifying, commodity/exchange model of the male-to-female gaze if women's sexuality and desire are viewed as biologically determined (i.e., if women's desire is assumed to be less aggressive and 'selfish' than men's). If, more practically, an emphasis is placed on the socialization process which plays some role in gender construction, and hence in determination of sexuality as gender-defined, the problems inherent to the male gaze might be introduced into the lesbian gaze as well. The photograph from Siren Theatre Company's production of *Pulp* (Fig. 3) illustrates this point: the woman in the photograph looks out, as if at the audience, in a mock imitation of a stereotypical 'male gaze' (with obligatory raincoat and stand-up collar included). In contrast, the photograph from Bryony Lavery's *Her Aching Heart* (Fig. 4) depicts two women as courtly lovers: aristocratic Lady Harriet (looking out) and working-class Molly (looking at Harriet). In the context of performance, they alternate taking subject and object positions in relation to the gaze.

A second possible complication could develop in performances in which the lesbian gaze is directed exclusively for an all-lesbian audience, as in

3 Jude Winter in Siren Theatre Company's production of *Pulp*, by Tash Fairbanks, 1985/6.

4 Nicola Kathrens and Sarah Kevney as lovers in *Her Aching Heart*, by Bryony Lavery for Women's Theatre Group, 1990.

separatist theatre. In this case, the notion of woman-to-woman attention to experience could be narrowed to lesbian-to-lesbian desire, while the role of the audience's 'desire' is magnified, due to a combination of two factors: the directed gaze of the audience (at the performers) and the active role of the audience in the feminist theatre production (since the 'performance' of sexual orientation requires a subject and an object, each oriented toward the other). Lesbian theatre may represent active and equal subjects demonstrating active desire.

All this makes interesting theory, but in practice, more often than not, lesbian theatre deals with social issues rather than, or in addition to, issues of desire and personal politics. For this reason, it is crucial that in discussion of the non-gendered gaze, a clear distinction be made between 'femininity', 'femaleness' and their cultural 'performance values'.[22] E. Ann Kaplan argues that when a woman takes on the subject or 'I' (eye) position in a male-directed film, she tends to lose her 'feminine' characteristics; she retains her beauty, but can not be kind, humane and motherly as well.[23] A radical feminist critique of 'Lesbianism and the Social Function of Taboo' rephrases these arguments in order to focus on the lesbian role as defined by and in opposition to the dominant (heterosexual) culture. This critique argues that the role of the lesbian in society, and particularly the lesbian artist or critic, is one which insists upon public representation of self.[24] According to this argument, the lesbian is 'performing transgressive acts' simply by existing in society as herself (i.e., by acting self). In acting self on stage in lesbian feminist theatre, lesbian performers thereby engage in a doubly transgressive act. Transgressive acts of self-representation are performed in many different lesbian theatre texts and performances. In the next section, I shall look at a selection of lesbian plays which all involve indirect reference to the notion of acting self in lesbian theatre.

THEMES AND VARIATIONS

Lesbian theatre deals with many of the same themes as does feminist theatre *per se*, including sisterhood and friendship as well as love, lust and desire. But one of the most interesting contexts for 'acting self' in lesbian theatre is the representation of the mother role *vis-à-vis* traditional notions of the nuclear family. The situation of lesbian mothers (who are generally excluded from any such model) has been commonly expressed in relation to the phrase 'care and control'. The phrase is derived from the vocabulary of the legal system; it is used in divorce and child custody settlements, wherein the court system makes decisions about individual people's lives based on a set of values associated with the venerated model of the nuclear family. The phrase became associated with lesbian representation in the 1970s, when the first publicized lesbian child custody cases were heard in the British courts.

The theme of 'care and control' is common to several contemporary lesbian plays, from agitprop to satiric comedy. *Care and Control*, devised by Gay Sweatshop and scripted by Michelene Wandor, is the primary example. Sarah Daniels' *Neaptide*, and Alison Lyssa's *Pinball* are two more obvious examples. Michelene Wandor's *Aid Thy Neighbor* was the first feminist play about Artificial Insemination by Donor (AID), while Maro Green and Caroline Griffin's *The Memorial Gardens* examined the problem of choosing 'roles' in relation to lesbian parenting, when one partner can be a biological mother yet the other can not be a biological 'father'. Of course, all lesbians (and indeed, all women) do not wish to be mothers; nor do all mothers seek to gain 'control' of their children in custody settlements. But the care and control issue is clearly infused with a dynamic of gender and power, associated with paternalistic ideas about women's roles and biased by economic circumstances weighing in favour of men. In this sense, the extensive legal and cultural implications of care and control make it an issue of general feminist concern, as well as an example of the role of traditional (heterosexual) motherhood as the 'norm' against which the lesbian is seen to transgress.

The care and control theme takes the notions of the mother role and the myth of the 'fit father' (as opposed to that of the 'unfit mother') and transposes them into real situations. Thus, the care and control play is a crucial, though minor, subgenre of lesbian theatre. Discussion of the 'care and control' play is problematic in that it emphasizes the mother role *vis-à-vis* that of the lesbian, setting up a model which posits the mother as a member of a patriarchal unit, in contrast to the rejection of patriarchal structures which is inherent to the lesbian feminist position. But in discussing this unrepresentative example, it becomes possible to discuss a wider range of lesbian roles, without allowing them to be subsumed into the larger topic of feminist theatre.

Three of the plays chosen for discussion deal in various ways with the 'care and control' theme, and two deal more generally with the performance of lesbian coming out. All of the plays discussed in this chapter offer examples of lesbian theatre wherein a female spectatorship is assumed, and a lesbian gaze is constructed, while allowing for the interaction of a heterosexual gaze as well. Each of the plays illustrates some of the ways in which coming out as a self-declaratory and defining act can be represented in feminist performance.

Care and control: performing the personal

Care and Control, scripted by Michelene Wandor for Gay Sweatshop in 1977, focuses on the problems facing lesbian and heterosexual mothers in child custody cases. It also highlights the similarities between coming out in private (at home, among family members) and in public (on the theatri-

126

cal platform or stage of the courtroom). *Care and Control* was first produced ten years after the Sexual Offences Act was amended and the Abortion Law Reform was put into effect, and ten years before the Alton Bill and Section 28 became national news.[25] While there is no direct causal connection between the play and these social factors, they do help to 'position' the play in terms of cultural circumstances of the time.

The style of the play reflects the company's perception of lesbian issues as symptomatic of wider issues for all women. Structurally, the play is divided in two: Act 1 presents three parallel stories of women in different living situations, at different levels of economic security, all facing the same problems and prejudices. All three women locate the source of their problems in the structure and terminology of the court system to which they must appeal for support. This system grants parental custody to the person in the best position to provide 'care and control' and considers financial status as the determining factor; furthermore, it fails to provide adequate childcare facilities and full-time paid jobs for women, and then punishes them for their financial dependency on men. For example, one of the mothers, when confronted by a hostile ex-partner (the father of her daughter) and challenged with the words 'there are alternatives', replies that 'you have to be rich to be an alternative'.

Similarly, Chris (another lesbian mother) points to the phallocentrism of many linguistic terms of abuse applied to lesbians. She observes a social punishment for the transgression of coming out which is directed at lesbians: 'It's not just the names. It's all this shit about not being a real woman, and couldn't get a man. Mostly I can ignore it – but there's one thing that always gets to me. . . . Someone using "lesbian" as a term of abuse.' This pejorative labelling is indicative of a heterosexual bias in society, operative in the courts. But heterosexual women also experience battles over care and control when men control the economic means within the family. The appeal to both lesbian and heterosexual experience provides a broad social backdrop for the play.

The second half of the play is a stylized montage of actual custody cases, set in the court where these women's cases are eventually heard. The Act is more loosely structured than Act 1; its quick scene and character changes are indicative of the anonymous and sterile bureaucracy of the court, alienating the women involved in the custody cases from their lives by discussing their situations openly in the specialized jargon of the legal system. The third of the play's mother figures, Carol, is not only penalized for being lesbian, but is also required to defend herself against the judge's personal accusations in regard to her sexuality. The judge contends that Carol's lesbianism is 'a deliberate rebellion against the marriage contract'.

Carol defends herself by pointing to the absurdity of defining a woman's life solely in terms of her contractual sleeping arrangements with men:

> It wasn't that I decided to adopt a homosexual way of life. I was trying to find a relationship. You see, in the marriage ceremony, my husband said he would love and cherish me, and he didn't.

The voice of patriarchal authority, vested in the court, replies that 'women like Carol' bring trouble unnecessarily upon themselves and that 'it should be brought home that there is a grave danger that they will lose their children, if they choose to behave in this way'. Only one of the three mothers is awarded custody, not for ideological reasons but on the grounds of 'bricks and mortar' – because she is in a better financial position to support her children.

This example is depicted within the play as an exception to the rule. The judgement is favourable for Carol, but not for Sue (her lover), nor for lesbian mothers in general. The male authority figure qualifies his decision by attaching strict social controls, that is, the stipulation that the women should keep their relationship 'as private as possible'. Carol's lesbianism is not recognized as a valid position, but is rather overlooked, in light of financial considerations. Lesbianism is depicted as tolerable only when invisible, or when strictly prohibited from public 'performance' (a view which ominously preshadows the judgment that homosexuality must not be 'promoted' – the official ruling of Section 28).

Care and Control was both theatrically successful (critically well received) and politically effective. The style was a cross between agitprop and social realism. The long-term success of the play may be related to theme rather than to style. Because the play focused on motherhood and women's rights, as well as on the particular relation of the lesbian 'role' to those issues, it appealed to a very wide range of contexts and feminist positions.

Discussion of a lesbian playwright from a different generation introduces another element to the 'care and control' theme *vis-à-vis* contemporary representations of lesbians in theatre and society. Sarah Daniels, like Tash Fairbanks, is half a generation younger than many of the original feminist theatre practitioners. Daniels does not write theory; instead, she writes political plays. Of all the playwrights interviewed for this book, she was by far the most willing to discuss the ideological roots of her work as intrinsically related to her radical feminist perspective. Daniels locates her position within the published and produced body of feminist theatre by referring to her own belief that the writing of 'safe' plays and traditional plays is not what feminist theatre should be about; she says: 'I don't like plays where the audience goes out feeling purged. . . . I like challenges. . . . I write issue plays.'[26] Daniels' work is often controversial, centring on themes such as pornography and violence (*Masterpieces*), rewriting of myth and re-viewing of archetypal images of women (*Ripen Our Darkness*), male appropriation of women's bodies in the birthing process (*Byrthrite*), and the rights of lesbian mothers (*Neaptide*).

In *Neaptide*, Daniels recreates the earthmother-goddess in the form of a contemporary character named Claire. Claire is a teacher in a small secondary school, torn between defending the rights of a few lesbian pupils and remaining silent, thereby keeping the secret of her own sexuality from her peers.[27] While she is involved in a potential child custody case, the pressure to 'appear normal' is great. Meanwhile, she reads the myth of Persephone. The myth functions both as a bedtime story for her daughter, and as an allegorical subtext to the play. Daniels' version of the story begins with the Greek tale of Demeter (mother/earth) and Persephone (daughter/spring). It then re-views the story in the present tense. On the one hand, the story focuses on the lives of a contemporary lesbian mother and her struggle to keep her young daughter. On the other hand, it focuses on Claire's comic conflict with her well-intentioned but misinformed mother, Joyce, and her friend and flatmate, Jean.

Hades is present in the figure of the remarried father, anxious to take his daughter and start a new life elsewhere. The familiar and recurrent theme of child custody (a form of possession) and inequity under the law is presented not only as a feminist or even a radical feminist issue, but also as a lesbian issue. The ending of the play is optimistic, but not overly so. The male order remains in place; conservative social reactions to lesbianism are revealed but not significantly challenged; the father retains the power of his threatening presence. In this play (as in *Care and Control*) only individual women transcend such limitations: the lesbian pupils are saved when the principal of the school is embarrassed into a confession of her own homosexuality, and the mother comes out of the proverbial closet and decides to fight for her child. The myth functions as a convenient analogue to contemporary problems, but not as an oversimplified model of a social corrective, nor as an all-encompassing statement about the function of roles.

Lesbian feminists have long criticized heterosexual feminists for constructing an alternative literary history 'which appears to be almost as selective and ideologically bound as the same male tradition which excludes non-white, working-class and lesbian women.'[28] Similarly plays like Lillian Hellman's *The Children's Hour* have been widely criticized (by lesbian and non-lesbian theorists alike) because they present lesbianism as a painful, defeating experience and because the lesbian relationships occur not within lesbian communities, but within heterosexual ones. In some respects, *Neaptide* can be criticized on similar grounds. Daniels admits that *Neaptide* is very much an issue play. She criticizes her characterization of Claire as the archetype of the lesbian mother in hindsight as 'too good to be true'. She explains:

> Looking back, I see that I felt censored. Claire always had to say the right thing, explain everything to her daughter perfectly. . . .

129

Society is so stacked against women that I felt I had to make her so good that there wasn't a chink. . . . I was speaking for a lot of women and I didn't want to blow it.[29]

It is significant that even in this explanation, Daniels identifies with women's issues rather than lesbian issues. She further explains that she deliberately pushed the situation in *Neaptide* to the limits of thematic credibility. For instance, Claire has no sexual partner in the play; there is no character on whom the court can fasten any blame. Similarly, the daughter is seven years old; were she eight, or even seven and a half, her stated desire to stay with her mother would probably have been considered by the court in the British legal system. Thus, Claire is deliberately depicted as a woman in extreme circumstances.

The characterizations of both Joyce and Jean are also significant in this respect. The comic presentation of the older mother figure (Joyce) adds the perspective of someone sympathetic to but not in the same situation as Claire. The tension between mother and daughter is of a well-meaning but misunderstanding sort: it both adds to and detracts from Claire's serious situation, and the comedy of the scene undercuts and thus allows for representation of the more serious implications of Claire's situation. Jean, the 'straight' flatmate, is the play's straight-(wo)man, through whose eyes it is possible to re-view the character of Claire. Jean is the sarcastic figure – the educational psychologist who, when bothered by her son's squirming while she is cutting his hair at the breakfast table, threatens to cut off his head.

A final quote from Daniels' discussion of *Neaptide* removes Claire from exclusive association with the playtext, and allows her character to be viewed in larger terms, in relation to the social context in which, in some sense, she is a prototypical lesbian mother. As such, Claire becomes more than a character: she becomes a means through which Sarah Daniels can articulate her political position on feminism and the representation of women:

I'm not interested in feeding into prejudices or writing something that could have been done in mainstream entertainment. If there was no prejudice, no violence against women by men, I probably wouldn't be a writer. I didn't allow myself the luxury of making that woman [Claire] more real – and that was my mistake. I didn't let *her* make mistakes. I forgot in the pressure of trying to put her beyond reproach that we most identify with others' mistakes.[30]

Here again, Claire is presented as a representative of 'womanhood' and 'motherhood'. Her lesbianism is incidental to her other roles, but is the lens through which her situation is focused. Lesbianism is the example, but prejudice against women is the real issue of this issue play.

The final problem of the play is related to the playing context in terms of audience expectations. No surveys were conducted on audience composition during the run of *Neaptide*. At the National Theatre, as elsewhere, audiences are largely self-selecting. Yet two factors are unique to the National (and other highly subsidized venues): the extent of the publicity, and the reputation for producing plays which uphold 'standards of excellence' (the latter contributing to a general profile of upper-middle-class and relatively highly educated audiences). In this case, the audience for *Neaptide* would have had extensive advance press regarding the play and its author. The publicity materials for *Neaptide* did not label it a 'lesbian play' or even use a convenient euphemism such as 'a play about women's relationships' or 'a play about friendship, mothers and daughters'. In fact, the programme provides a few lines about each of Daniels' other plays, but includes only one line about *Neaptide* itself – a definition of the term ('Neaptide is the lowest tide, occurring when the sun and the moon are in opposition').[31] It seems that references to lesbianism are not acceptable in National Theatre publicity material: the symbolic is described instead.

Neaptide is the only British lesbian play of this order to be produced in a mainstream venue. No other lesbian play has since been produced there, though a major 'gay play', *Bent*, was staged and restaged, both times to critical acclaim. *Neaptide* reached a very wide audience, and addressed stereotypes of the lesbian (and the mother role) in a mixed, rather than a separatist, context. That the audience for this play might not have known what to expect from the play, in thematic terms at least, due to the ambiguity of the press materials, is indicative of the marginalization of the lesbian role in public representation, as in performance. It is not likely that the National Theatre was unaware of the lesbian theme in *Neaptide*, nor that the theatre was aware but thought the theme too insignificant to warrant attention in the publicity. It is more likely that the press office judged it to be a potentially risky commodity, and chose not to mention it in the advance press materials.

The introduction of comedy into the text and context of *Neaptide* distinguishes it stylistically from the polemical approach of plays such as *Care and Control*. Consideration of another play on the theme of 'care and control' illustrates the potential effectiveness of an even more radical shift to the medium of comedy. Alison Lyssa's *Pinball* is an example of an 'outsider's play', not only in the sense that it is written by a declared lesbian consciously writing against mainstream norms, but also because Lyssa is Australian. Her play was ultimately published in England.[32] *Pinball* is a retelling of the biblical story of Solomon – a story of two mothers fighting for one child. In the biblical version, the 'real mother' is assumed to be the one who will not agree to settle the dispute by cutting the child in half and 'sharing' him. In Lyssa's version, the lesbian mother and lover are given custody in the court battle.

Thematically, *Pinball* can usefully be compared to Brecht's *Caucasian Chalk Circle* which, in a sense, is also a care and control play, in that it depicts two women fighting for custody of one child. Class issues are of primary importance in both Brecht' and Lyssa's plays. In Lyssa's play, however, it is lesbians who are treated as a lower class. Lyssa constructs the happy ending in which the lesbian finally 'wins' the child, but she does not deconstruct the hegemonic system of patriarchal power within the play. Instead, she allows an outsider to win, but does not allow the outsider to enter the mainstream. Thus, the recognition scene of traditional drama is rewritten and that which is ultimately recognized is a value system in operation outside the play – a system which interprets the granting of care and control of a child to its natural mother, when that mother is known to be a lesbian, as somehow 'unnatural'.[33] When the nuclear family is the 'apparatus' according to which 'normality' is measured, then the subordination of lesbian and gay culture is endemic to the system.

Lyssa, like Wandor and Daniels, writes parts for male as well as female actors. The possible reasons for this are numerous. One reason may be that a male presence can best be represented on stage by men; another that the complex dynamics of sexual politics are best presented – particularly in social realist theatre – in relation to cultural 'norms'. In any case, the physical presence of men on stage distinguishes these three plays from a great deal of other lesbian theatre. Other feminist playwrights present only female characters, arguing that the lack of a male presence on stage allows the female and the lesbian gazes to be constructed. Such an argument obviously supports the idea that all-female spaces are necessary to the production of some kinds of theatre.

Of course, it is not only lesbian theatre which has attempted to eliminate men from the playing space. Charlotte Keatley did so, purposefully and comically, in her recent Royal Court production of *My Mother Said I Never Should*. Her reasons for the non-representation of men were as much to do with a balancing of power relations as with a balancing of the sexes on stage, and with the pleasure derived from experimenting with audience expectations.[34] Such experimentation with expectation is contextual as well as textual, extra-scenic and scenic at once. It challenges the relationship between gender and power, suggesting that it may be the case in practice – as Dolan and Butler suggest it is in theory – that power bears a problematic relationship to gender, and not solely to the issue of sexual orientation.

There is an obvious danger in confusing the lack of a physical male presence on which to focus blame with the lack of a blaming or questioning perspective. Lyssa articulates the difference herself, in an essay in which she expresses alarm at a male theatre critic's published perception of his views on feminist theatre. Lyssa quotes Mel Gussow from a review on the subject of 'the new women's theatre,' which includes his controversial statement: 'They [women playwrights] have moved past the need to blame men, even though it may be justified. For the most part, this theatre is free of polemics.'[35] Lyssa deconstructs Gussow's argument, interpreting it as a statement to the effect that women's work has progressed from issue-based agitprop to deeper exploration of characters, enhanced by women's growing knowledge of theatre craft. This would imply first that the use of agitprop is categorically bad form, which necessarily pushes character development and 'artistic integrity' into positions of secondary importance (a statement which many theatre practitioners would insist on qualifying, if not denying), and second, that it is women's coming to terms with male-defined theatre craft which renders them 'professional'.

Lyssa took issue with Gussow's views, and re-viewed them by asking a rhetorical question:

Does what Mel Gussow is saying also mean that once the work of women becomes accepted on the main stage it becomes absorbed by the system and loses its power to challenge? The male can take it in and praise it, but somehow it is contained, he no longer feels threatened. It is no longer a polemic, no longer is there urgent demand for change.[36]

Lyssa's question addresses the 'positioned reviewing' of feminist theatre work. The criticism of this particular critic seemed to be aimed at the politics of the playwright, rather than at the play itself. Lyssa's statement above is an expression of her awareness of this bias in the reviewing which damns with faint praise and loaded phraseology. She was justified in her wariness: in his review of the first performance of *Pinball*, Brian Hoad dismissed the play as 'yet another piece of tedious female chauvinist pig-gery'.[37] Irrespective of the formal qualities of the play, Hoad's phrasing suggests that his approach to the reviewing of feminist work was clearly positioned in a gendered (male) perspective. Lyssa's play, and her response to Gussow's differently positioned review, may have challenged that perspective to some degree. But the problems of situated perspectives in theatre reviewing – and indeed in academic criticism – are too large to be dealt with by any one playwright.

Another subgenre of lesbian theatre is the 'coming out play'. Two such plays are discussed in the next section.

Comedy, satire and lesbian self-representation

Jackie Kay's *Twice Over* is a coming out play by a black woman, in which three of the six female characters are black and three white.[38] In

133

5 Pamela Lane as Cora and Adjoa Andoh as Evaki in *Twice Over*, by Jackie Kay for Gay Sweatshop, 1990.

performance, the words at times overtake the action, and the story seems too episodically structured. Yet, at its opening night at the Drill Hall, the play received three standing ovations.[39] The audience, as is usual for lesbian plays at the Drill Hall, was composed primarily of women, and largely of lesbians. The audience reacted to the intent, as well as to the content and presentation of the play.

The play conveys a story of family relationships in a stylistically experimental form – one which presents the performance of gender identity *vis-à-vis* sexual orientation. The pivotal character, Cora, is dead. The play opens with her funeral. Cora's granddaughter, Evaki, finds an old letter and some diaries while going through some personal effects after the funeral, and discovers that Cora was lesbian. Cora's 'ghost' haunts the stage (in the person of Pamela Lane), talking to all the characters, urging them to discover her lesbianism so that she may be free of the secret. Cora's story is one of a lesbian 'coming out' after death. Cora's lover, Maeve, is left to deal with her grief alone, since no one (as far as she knows) is aware of the nature of her relationship with Cora.

The entire story is recalled through the interplay between these two generations of women, and the middle figure of Evaki's mother (Cora's daughter) never appears. She is referred to and played through, but not

134

represented on stage. Instead, the story is progressed by the characters of Jean (Maeve and Cora's friend and co-worker) and two of Evaki's girlfriends at school. The grandmother and granddaughter are separated from each other by two generations, by race (Evaki is black, Cora white) and by sexual preference. Evaki is separated from Maeve by all of these factors, and by a resentment about her close relationship with Cora. Yet Evaki learns to accept and, slowly, to embrace Maeve in friendship. In so doing, however, she forces Maeve to 'come out' in terms of her lesbianism. Thus, Cora's *post mortem* act of coming out (accomplished for her by Evaki) is less theatrical and personally painful than is the coming out of the living lover.

The dissolution of the fourth wall is more than a critical description of the play's style, but is actually a part of the play. For example, in some sequences, all the characters speak at once, with Cora engaging first with one character and then another, acting even in death as the invisible, omniscient narrator and editor of her own life story. The staging allows no spatial divisions: the coffin out of which Cora emerges in Scene 1 is a trapdoor in the floor, centre stage. It is also the 'chest' out of which Evaki pulls her grandmother's belongings (the truth of the past, the heart of the secret, etc.). All characters remain on stage at all times. Their seemingly arbitrary movement in and out of the playing space at the interval enhances the sense that the actors are part of the audience, but the ones who happen to be aware of the details of this particular story. On opening night, the level of audience participation was obviously central to the play's reception (as was, no doubt, Jackie Kay's presence in the audience). Equally important was the escape from over-seriousness (and over-identification between staged issues and the personal lives of the audience) which the play's comic moments allowed. Consideration of the play as a whole benefits from analysis of three of these moments.

Cora urges Evaki to tell her schoolfriends what she has discovered but Evaki (who can not hear Cora, though the audience can) stubbornly refuses. Evaki is embarrassed, disgusted and angry. Rather than redirect that anger at Evaki, Cora turns to the audience and comments: 'I wish I were the kind of ghost that makes an impression, you know, like Cathy in *Wuthering Heights*.' The 'you know' may invite participation, in which case the joke simply relaxes the dramatic division of the characters from the audience via the colloquial address. But it may also serve to diffuse the intra- and extra-scenic stress of the situation, though this depends upon the way in which the line is delivered. The invitation to audience identification thus functions in the performance context of *Twice Over* in much the same way that an emphasis on audience recognition and sympathy functions in Sarah Daniels' work.

Later, Evaki and her friends privately discuss the subject of 'boys'. Sharon (the sexy and rebellious type) has recently lost her virginity to a boy she 'trusted to respect her' and is left wondering whether she is either pregnant or infected with AIDS. She delivers a sweeping statement to Tash (the shy, sensitive type) about the worthlessness and treachery of boys and men in general. Tash replies: 'All men aren't like that, some are OK', to which Sharon responds, 'Yeah? Name one.' Tash's answer is a blank look at the audience. Her silence says enough. The moment is played down and the conversation on stage quickly takes another turn, but Tash's silence evokes an enthusiastic burst of laughter from the audience. The complicit laughter and the fact that no one will 'name one' (even silently) is indicative of the personal nature of the comedy. The humour operates on two levels simultaneously: on the first, the joke between friends is recognized and shared; on the other the audience response evoked by Tash's silent stare crosses through the 'fourth wall', by inverting a standard joke on the predictability of sex-role divisions, and by addressing it in a way which indicated that a silent reply from the audience would be appropriate. The wall must be in place before it can be knocked down. For a play like this to work, the audience must be willing to work as well, in that each audience member must be aware of her or his own gendered and 'situated' role and part in the larger script.

Like the other two discussed, the third significant laugh in *Twice Over* is not directed exclusively at lesbians, but at women in general (and much more pointedly at heterosexual women). In this case, however, a certain tension is revealed in a direct reference to the mother role (or its potentiality) for women as a source of conflict. This tension has a range of unique meanings in the lesbian (arguably separatist) playing space. The situation is a common one: Sharon gives herself a home pregnancy test. She waits for it to develop as the play develops, then takes centre stage while she checks the results. She reads the instructions on the disposable test package aloud: 'If the indicator turns a definite blue colour, the results are positive.' Then she repeats: 'a definite blue colour'. She looks at her indicator. She reads the instructions for a last time. She looks back to the indicator, then to the audience and demands: 'What colour is *this*?' There are different shades of blue, just as there are different shades of meaning encoded in the scene, and in the play as a whole.

The audience responds with appreciative laughter; many have evidently also experienced this moment of tension and indecision, this feeling that all the future relies on the outcome of a litmus paper test. Such tension needs release; in this play, the release comes from the female audience members, through recognition and identification with the character's situation. The expression of release, of catharsis, is the laugh. This is a distinctly female identification, a distinctly female joke, though men may well understand the joke and find it amusing in a less personal way. Sharon is not pregnant, and the action develops along other lines.

In all three examples from *Twice Over*, the laughs elicited in the audience are laughs of recognition. The polemic is not written into the text but is rather present in the context, in the notion that the performance of coming out is a social act inextricably linked to the assumed demands and expectations of an audience. If that audience is not present, or not assumed, then the act need not be performed in the same way.

Twice Over is a lesbian comedy. By contrast, Jill Fleming's *The Rug of Identity* is a cross between feminist political drama and satire – a comedy of contemporary manners, infused with a grotesque black humour (seemingly derivative of Joe Orton's work in both tone and style). As Jill Davis notes in her introduction to the play, '[it] takes for granted an audience of lesbians secure enough in their identity to watch "The Rug" being pulled from under it and from under the shibboleths of feminist politics, and to find it very funny'.[40] The complex and utterly unrealistic scenario of the play is complicated by the shifting gendered perspectives of the characters. Laurie and Joanna are lovers, pretending to be 'just friends' in front of the looming mother figure, Mrs Proctor. Mrs Proctor is actually Laurie's father – a transsexual transvestite, capable of and eager to offer advice to both sexes (like the prophet Tiresias of Eliot's *Wasteland*), since s/he has had the experience of having both sexes and genders. This situation allows Mrs Proctor to mock traditional gender relations in such lines as: 'A man has to have experience . . . and a woman has to get pregnant. . . . I'll tell you what men are like – quite happy to wear women's clothes, but none of them would ever want to be one, and I should know.'

The scenario also mocks the inverted mother–daughter relationship. Both the desired and desiring subjects are women. Laurie explains: 'My mother is absolutely in love with men. It was much easier for her when she had a penis.' Joanna jokes back: 'Her [Mrs Proctor's] name must never come between us. My problems must consume you utterly. Oh Laurie, I could not even bear it if you were breastfed.' When this complicated subject–object relationship is introduced, the feminist theoretical attempt to reclaim language breaks into the very structure of the play. The characters define themselves as the subjects of their own histories. They re-view their relationships with other women accordingly and 'perform' their new awareness via the means of comedy. Thus the play invokes feminist sympathy by calling values, rather than individuals, into question. The comedy releases the characters from the confines and standards of realistic presentation. It allows them to play many different roles at once, to put on multiple masks representing different versions of the archetypally oversimplified (and therefore semiotically complicated) 'feminine' image.

In *The Rug of Identity*, Mona (who is both friend and mother to Joanna) is a key 'straight' character, just as the mother figure of Joyce (combined with the straight friend figure of Jean) was central to the characterizations in *Neaptide*. In both plays, the mother figure operates not through preaching, but through humour. Whereas Joyce's and Jean's presence and perspectives provide a quietly humorous yardstick of 'normality' in *Neaptide*, Mona's jokes are macabre, and her situation completely unrealistic. Mona is in prison for murder, awaiting her own hanging on death row when this play opens. She laughs about it. She takes 'the myth of everybody else's mother' over the brink of absurdity, with lines such as, 'Oh, I see. Everybody else's mother can be a professional assassin, but not yours.'[41] The stereotypical eyeball-rolling and deep sigh are written into her language. At the same time, Mona defies simplistic pigeonholing into character types: she combines aspects of several different stereotypes (the concerned mother, the overbearing mother-in-law, the oversexed middle-aged woman, etc.) and thus reduces the power of the stereotype, at least within the framework of this play.

Mona reacts humorously to difficult and unrealistic situations. She is one of the most likable characters of the play. In addition she is instrumental in the structuring of its hidden agenda; she makes directly political statements which connect the abject farce to the social/mythological structures it mocks.

Fleming, like Daniels, indulges freely in the cheap joke; her characters discuss the social effects of the act of coming out in this way:

> *Mona*: You take things so seriously. Life is supposed to be fun. Let me see this Gay side of you that's reportedly always been suppressed.
> *Joanna*: I am NOT gay. I consider any sort of enjoyment of life as it is to be in the worst political taste.
> *Mona*: Sometimes, I think you chose to be a lesbian so you could be justifiably miserable for the rest of your life.

Similarly, when Joanna describes to Mona her feeling of being an outsider, she does so in linguistic, even grammatical terms: 'It's even worse when I'm with heteros. I feel like a consonant when I want to be a vowel.' Joanna thus expresses her sense of not fitting in, of being an outsider.

The play is not only peopled with a variety of 'false fathers' and mothers, but is also cluttered with a thoroughly confused list of dramatis personae, played by an all-woman cast supplemented by a dummy named Harvey. Because the play makes no claim to realism, it invites, in Jill Davis' terms, a pulling of the rug from under the cultural expectation of compulsory heterosexuality. The important recognition within the play is that of a need for solidarity in the face of adversity and perversity. Mona expresses her recognition of this need indirectly, when she releases Jo from the necessity of further charades of heterosexuality: 'I believe in a different kind of justice, Jo. We were partners in crime, rather like you lesbians and feminists.'

Here, Mona emphasizes a crucial link between the marginalization (or, in some cases, selective separatism) of lesbians in relation to feminism. Just as she implicitly recognizes lesbians and feminists as groups united both by common problems and a need for common struggle, she also explicitly defines lesbians in opposition to feminists by the negative element of their 'guilt by association'. This is the tension of lesbian experience within the larger feminist movement. Mona's outburst might be reread in the context of the conflation of the terms 'lesbian' and 'feminist' in Churchill's *Cloud Nine*. In Act 2 of that play, the gay man whose lover has left him declares: 'I think I'm a lesbian', and Victoria, the young mother who has recently discovered her own attraction to women, but who finds herself caught up in a charade of heterosexuality due to the need to support her daughter, explains that 'you can't separate fucking and economics'. Here, as in Wandor's *Care and Control*, the word 'lesbian' is defined in opposition to its definition, in common mainstream usage, as a term of abuse.[42] Economics and sexuality, gender and power, language and 'control over the means of production' are all represented as core issues in these different feminist theatres.

When these ideas are filtered through the voices of the authors, as well as of the actors, they may have an increased impact. Self-representation by the playwright in the play may be textual or contextual, scenic or extra-scenic. For example, Maro Green and Caroline Griffin published an endnote along with the text of their co-written play *More*, informing the audience that 'both are radical lesbian feminists' – a contextual placement of the playwrights' views. Sarah Daniels avoids such personal commentary and mentions issues of personal importance only in workshops and interviews. Fleming's situated perspective is not presented in an endnote, but in the text itself. She makes the ironic observation (via her character of Mona) that 'feminists and lesbians are partners in crime'. The statement indicates a recognition of crucial differences between groups of women, but does not imply that these differences need be destructive.

There is nothing mythic or heroic about the female characters in *The Rug of Identity*. There is nothing particularly believable about them either, except that Mona's second-hand wisdom turns out to be legitimate and relevant. The comedy does not undermine the serious issues of the play (lesbian identity and self-recognition, etc.) but rather supports them. Even the borrowed device of the Desdemona's handkerchief/Lady Windermere's fan motif is put to demystifying, comic effect in this play, wherein the missing and all-important object is a person – Mrs Proctor turns out to be both Laurie's mother and Joanna's father. The traditions of classical drama and farce are subverted in this mock recognition scene, wherein gender becomes a text in itself and sexual preference is represented as wholly performative.

Contemporary lesbian theatres

The various 'care and control' and 'coming out' plays discussed above all include some reference to the 'acting of self' in the performance of everyday life in heterosexist society. Of course, it would also be possible to discuss lesbian plays of other kinds: such plays are numerous, but by no means innumerable. Jill Davis lists forty-five lesbian plays as the constituents of the growing lesbian theatre canon (this includes both British and American plays, as well as Lyssa's *Pinball*, an Australian play performed and reviewed in Britain).[43] She divides the 'canon' according to subject matter, labelling seven plays as 'issue-based' (of these, three are by Daniels – *Neaptide*, *Byrthrite*, and *The Devil's Gateway* – and two are by Wandor – *Care and Control* and *Aid Thy Neighbour*), and four as 'coming out plays' (including Posener's *Any Woman Can* and two by Jackie Kay – *Chiaroscuro* and *Twice Over*).

When an American context is allowed to inform this study of (primarily) British lesbian theatres, however, it becomes immediately apparent that a great deal of lesbian theatre is not defined or confined by the recognizable structure of 'the play'. For instance, the work of Holly Hughes, Sande Zeig and Monique Wittig is widely recognized as making an important contribution to contemporary feminist theatres. Similarly, Split Britches is widely recognized as an exemplary lesbian feminist theatre company which performs 'plays' so heavily influenced by performance art/theatre techniques that they are difficult to discuss as plays, and are more appropriately discussed as examples of lesbian (postmodern, post-structuralist) performance. As Kate Davy has observed, like other feminist theatres and most theatre *per se*, their work is influenced by the context in which it is performed. Yet in the performance of a company such as Split Britches, which experiments with gender roles and which incorporates many direct addresses to the audience, the expectation of the audience has considerable impact on the performance itself.[44]

Of course, American feminist theatres have had a tremendous influence on British lesbian theatres, and companies such as Split Britches have a large and loyal following in England. Several important performance pieces deserve brief mention here as particularly well-constructed work dealing with lesbian themes and experimenting with a female gaze. For instance, *The Constant Journey* (1984) by Sande Zeig and Monique Wittig depicts a female Don Quixote.[45] *Donna Giovanni* by the Companias Divas of Mexico represents a female Don Juan in a modern opera 'sung in Italish in a free adaption of the opera by Mozart and Du Ponte, for six actresses and a piano'. The show is performed half in the nude, with a focus on female sexuality, and all the characters are played by women.[46] New York's infamous Split Britches did remarkable things with cross-dressing and gender roles in their production of *Dress Suits to Hire* by Holly Hughes.[47]

In 1992, Split Britches joined the gay male company Bloolips to re-produce ('back by popular demand') *Belle Reprieve*, a show which self-consciously plays with gender roles and comically re-examines Tennessee Williams' *A Streetcar Named Desire* by questioning not only the nature of desire, but also the nature of a society which allows us to assume that we know the sex and gender of those around us, or are absolutely confident about our own sexualities.[48]

In these performance pieces, the position of the actor in relation to the audience was of paramount importance. They included no men in their casts, and few in their audiences. They experimented with explicitly sexual scenes and indulged in partial or complete nudity, but unlike camp theatre (where women's traditional sex/gender role is admired, studied, imitated and often mocked by men), or vaudeville/sensationalist theatre (where exposure of the female body is played up for its voyeuristic appeal to men), or male gay theatre (where audiences are predominantly male), these lesbian performances were directed at a female, predominantly lesbian audience. The exposure of the body, or the change of 'female' for 'male' clothes and vice versa, were used as empowering rather than objectifying acts.

Zeig and Wittig's work has influenced both the theory of lesbian performance and the development of acting styles in British lesbian theatre, in terms of theory as well as practice. As Sue-Ellen Case has written in her work on American lesbian theatres:

> A new generation of lesbian critics have started to create what they hope will be a new lesbian theatre aesthetic. Using plays that embody the lesbian perspective, Wittig and Zeig's new lesbian acting-style, as well as elements of traditional acting-theory, they seek to articulate a lesbian dramaturgy.[49]

Jill Dolan has begun to develop an analysis of the emerging forms of lesbian theatre (the 'lesbian dramaturgy' to which Case refers), working with the notion that the fundamental elements of traditional drama are difference and conflict. According to Dolan, traditional drama is based on the concept of oppositional genders.[50] Her theories expand upon the work of Zeig and Wittig, playing with the cliché that 'opposites attract' (as enacted in society filtered through a heterosexist norm), and such conventions as the traditional ending of plays with the institution of heterosexual marriage. Such structures are obviously not workable for the presentation of single-gender or homosexual experience.

As noted above, the male gaze perceives the lesbian as 'not a woman', as one who does not adjust her image to attract that gaze. Thus, theatrical representation of the lesbian challenges the social constructions of gender as represented in her physical appearance. Dolan, Zeig and Wittig place great emphasis on the role of impersonation in their working out of lesbian

141

theatre gestures; the notion is that the lesbian in society is acting a strange parody or impersonation of herself. The concept of impersonation becomes a central theme for gender-specific comedy as a medium for the representation of acculturated gender-class roles. Thus, when Zeig and Wittig encourage their students to discover their own 'impersonators', they make the claim that the impersonator is more than just a character constructed from fictional information, or that the 'impersonator is oneself, but as the opposite sex'.[51] In a sense, this idea is the underlying theme of *Belle Reprieve*.

In a British context, Jill Davis argued in the introduction to her first volume of lesbian plays that part of the difficulty in creating a space for lesbian theatre (whether on the stage or in the academic canon) is based on conflicts of interest within the feminist and lesbian communities, and consequently between branches of feminist theory as it is translated into practice in the playing space. She describes the consequences of inadequate funding and related logistic limitations on the process of the writing, and thereby on the playtexts themselves. But most importantly, Davis records a conflict between the liberal and separatist means and ends of lesbian theatre production, a discrepancy which is evidenced in the 'mainstreaming' of a few liberal lesbian plays:

> Liberal feminist playwrights, whose work unsurprisingly constitutes the majority of plays by women performed on main stages, seem most often to be preoccupied by the issue of balancing women's demand for space in the public world of work, with their personal destiny as mothers and (heterosexual) lovers. Many such playwrights are heard to be irritated when asked questions about their politics, demanding the same right as male playwrights to write as individuals, rather than as spokeswomen for feminism. That position is totally understandable, but the consequence is that much of the most visible women's theatre writing in the 1980s leaves feminists and lesbians disheartened by its lack of political energy.[52]

Davis' observation not only holds true in 1992, but is further supported by imposition of Section 28. The Section has implemented a host of restrictions on Theatre in Education in regard to the theatrical 'promotion' of homosexuality in schools. These legal restrictions have been further complicated by financial cuts to the educational sector and restructuring of the National Curriculum, as well as by the more generalized effects of continued cuts to Arts funding. Demand for space, public recognition and visibility are important issues in and for feminist theatre, and especially for lesbian theatres. The questions posed by recent critical evaluation of lesbian theatre – the position of the gendered gaze, and the construction of desire within that gaze, particularly when manifested in the (scenic and extra-scenic) communication of lesbian performance – are as problematic as ever.

The study of lesbian strategies for (self-)representation in society and in the theatre can provide certain insights into feminist theatre as genre. The conditions of lesbian theatre production and performance may be seen as extreme examples of the problems of many feminists, and indeed of many women and so-called 'minorities' in their efforts publicly to present images of self. These differences and difficulties have not necessarily weakened lesbian theatre, but have rather contributed a certain strength to the plays and performance pieces, whether they be intended for mixed or separatist audiences, whether they be comic or 'straight' in form. Of course, many such plays and performance pieces do not 'suit' the academic canonical apparatus. They are 'suited' to a different apparatus – one which prioritizes social issues and measures 'value' in accordance with cultural representation and change.

This chapter will be brought to a close with reference to several British and American lesbian plays which were very clearly designed to suit another apparatus, and to appeal to specific audiences. In discussion of the evolution of Gay Sweatshop in chapter 3, I mentioned Bryony Lavery's *Kitchen Matters*, a play about lesbians and gay men which was both entertaining and intended to attract the attention of supportive audiences, critics and funding bodies, when the company faced impending closure. That play was a tremendous success, on many different levels.

Here, I want to end with brief reference to three other lesbian plays which I have found exemplary both as entertainment, and as feminist political theatre. I have discussed two of these at length elsewhere: they are Bryony Lavery's 'lesbian historical romance' *Her Aching Heart*, produced by Women's Theatre Group in 1989; and Cheryl Moch's *Cinderella The Real True Story*, first produced at the Wow Cafe in New York, and premiered in England as the Dramatrix lesbian Christmas panto at the Drill Hall in 1987.[53] Both of these plays work extremely well as comedies: they have a wide popular appeal for heterosexual as well as lesbian and gay audiences. Both plays experiment with traditional theatrical and literary forms (the 'bodice ripper', the romantic novel, courtly love, the fairy tale, the pantomime). Both use gender and sex role-reversal, and some cross-dressing. Both are strongly feminist and have serious political messages, conveyed lightly, through comedy. Both are joys to watch and to read (and, I would wager, also to perform and produce).

The third is an American play which is as yet unpublished: That Uppity Theatre Company's *Some of My Best Friends Are . . .* (billed as 'a gay and lesbian revue for people of all preferences'). Written and directed by Joan Lipkin with music and lyrics by Tom Clear, the play was first produced in St Louis, Missouri in 1989. St Louis is not noted for its progressive politics. In fact, it is located in the heart of the 'Bible Belt', where politics are often influenced by conservative social and religious beliefs. (Author's note: I was born in St Louis and lived there from 1986 to 1987.) The play was written in reaction to the 1986 US Supreme Court case known as *Bowers* v. *Hardwick*, which held that individual states have the right to regulate private sexual behaviour between consenting adults. The Sexual Misconduct Law in Missouri considers homosexuality a 'Class A' misdemeanour punishable by up to a year in jail and/or a fine of $1,000. In other words, the United States rules against freedom of expression for lesbians and gay men. That Uppity Theatre Company chose to challenge this discrimination, not with legal jargon in the setting of the courts, but rather with words and music in the form of a play.

In *Some of my Best Friends Are . . .* , Lipkin's use of the revue format was a deliberate political choice which allowed for a broader cross-section of lesbian representation. As lesbians are typically under-represented in the theatre, any play with lesbian characters often unfairly bears the weight of making the ultimate lesbian statement. Thus, Lipkin chose to depict a multiplicity of lesbian experiences, in order to avoid that reductive kind of representation.[54] The play opens with a song called 'No Billing', which depicts the playwright trying to find actors willing to be 'billed' as participating in a 'gay play', and trying to generate media attention and financial support for the production. This scene is interestingly similar to the opening scene of Bryony Lavery's *Kitchen Matters*, in which the playwright (Lavery) sits and writes the play which may help to save Gay Sweatshop.

Some of My Best Friends Are . . . is composed of a series of vignettes or comic sketches, with key characters and ensemble actors all joining in the songs which punctuate the piece. The play uses the conceit, or running gag, of 'a straight couple trying to make their way in a gay world'. The couple, Sheila and Frank, appear four times. In this excerpt from the end of Act 1, they discuss the difficulties of going out to the cinema as 'hets' in a lesbian and gay world:

Sheila: I just want to go to the movies.
Frank: Well, I don't want to pay $5.50 plus popcorn to see a bunch of gays up on the screen. Why can't they show movies that reflect my reality? Look, why don't we order in a pizza and I'll go to Blockbuster. They've got a special section of straight movies.
Sheila: You're kidding. Where?
Frank: At the Brentwood store. Right next to the Jewish and Black movies at the back of the store. In the ghetto section.
Sheila: Come on. It's Saturday night. Date night. Let's splurge. I want to take my honey to the movies and hold hands like everyone else.
Frank: Are you kidding? On a Saturday night at the Galleria with all those gays making out? No way am I holding hands with you at the movies. It's too risky. You remember what happened the last time.

Sheila: So he called you a dirty het and asked you to step outside. Does that mean that you're never going to the movies again?
Frank: It's bad enough living in a subculture without having our noses rubbed in it. I'm not going and that's final.[55]

This sketch was marginal to the main plot, and was repeated in a series of four interludes as 'one way of subverting the norm and asking people to look at the world a little differently'.[56] Most of the play, or more accurately, most of the sketches which make up the play, are concerned with the lives and experiences of lesbians and gay men. Like Sheila and Frank, most of the characters are drawn in caricature style: they are exaggerated, even ridiculous. In this respect as well, the play is similar to Lavery's *Kitchen Matters*. The comedy is absurd in both, yet the political messages are serious and effective because comedy works as a subversive strategy within the extra-scenic dynamic of the performance.

Because it was co-written by a woman and a man, *Some of My Best Friends Are . . .* does not 'fit' the terms of this discussion in the sense that strictly speaking it does not offer representations of lesbians by lesbians. But the play is not a 'lesbian' play as such. Rather, it is a play which deals with the representation of lesbian and gay characters, and which gained wide media attention and opened up to a wide audience some of the problems facing lesbians. In this sense, the play does what Sandra J. Richards has suggested should happen with regard to women of colour in the theatre and academia: it has got some heterosexuals involved in the project of bringing the work of lesbians and gay men out of the margins. In fact, the play was written as a direct response to the political and social marginalization of lesbians and gay men in the United States.

Joan Lipkin has spoken and written about the issues of personal choice and political freedom, which inform most of her work with That Uppity Theatre. In her own words:

> When I realized that it was the twentieth anniversary of the Stonewall Riots – the popular beginnings of the American lesbian and gay liberation movement – I thought it was an ideal time to make a piece of theatre, and to get involved in what was sure to be a major public protest at the anniversary of that uprising.
>
> . . . We initiated a lot of political action at the theatre: we circulated a petition to repeal Missouri's Sexual Misconduct law, and we threw condoms, as a form of education, at the curtain call. Most of My Best Friends *practise* safer sex. We made it fun and we made it camp. We did a lot of benefit performances for different community groups. We figured that way, we'd keep the money raised through ticket sales circulating through the system back into the community.
>
> Another thing that was interesting was the choice I made, as the primary writer on this project, to direct it at lesbians and gay men

together, and at a wider mainstream audience as well. I wanted all these people to have to come into a space together, to learn about each other's lives, butt up against each other's differences, and to learn to laugh together. This is all part of my own personal philosophy, of what I call the 'politics of inclusion'. I am not any kind of a separatist: I certainly recognize the need for some separate spaces, and the need of some people in certain situations to have separatist gatherings. But I think that ultimately, people have to learn how to listen to each other and to appreciate, or at least tolerate, each other's differences. That's part of what this play is about. So in some ways, and as an ultimate strategy towards wider social change, this approach was more radical than doing something separatist.[57]

It is most significant that Lipkin's theatre is political and directly interventionist – that she discusses her audience and community, their needs and biases – and her awareness that the marginalization of lesbians and gay men is an important and mainstream issue, related to other issues of central concern to feminism(s).

Similarly, all of the plays and performance pieces discussed in this chapter work at two levels: the personal and the political. All involve the representation of gender-coded material. All these plays encourage a revisioning of popular culture and popular performance – one which takes lesbian experience into account and which valorizes women's experience, regardless of the sexual orientation of particular women. The phrasing of this statement is problematic: it implies a commonality of experience among lesbians, which is no more valid than the notion of a commonality of experience among all women. Lesbian theatres, like all feminist theatres, represent the situated perspectives of many different women.

Feminist theatres of many different kinds can benefit from the example of lesbian theatre, which has succeeded in making a spectacle of itself, not despite itself, but in order to verify, confirm and 'perform' its own existence. Some lesbian plays use agitprop, some comedy, and some various combinations of the two. Many lesbian plays use and subvert the very categories through which they are valued as forms of cultural representation. Some lesbian plays also offer positive models for dealing with marginalization of various kinds, for instance in reclaiming the act of coming out.

The lesbian play can challenge the terms of its own discourse and the structures of its own means of production. In different ways, so can most forms of feminist theatre, whether or not any 'play' or 'script' is involved. And as Jill Davis has recently argued, the terms of reference for lesbian theatre are increasingly defined in relation to other forms of cultural representation, including film and fiction but also including the 'reality' of life in contemporary culture(s).[58] Davis argues that the recent popular references to 'queer culture' reveal a significant shift in allegiances: lesbians and gay men have begun to find a sense of purpose in a shared, though separable identity, whereas in the 1970s lesbians and feminists tended to share that kind of mutual identification and support. An increased emphasis on the dress and 'costumes' of lesbianism, and on the forms of representation which are daily (or nightly) enacted in social interaction and most specifically in club culture: these are some of the reference points for the study of lesbian representations today, and are sure to influence future work on the subject of lesbian theatres as well.

6

BLACK FEMINIST THEATRES IN CULTURAL CONTEXT

> You know, nothing exists until a white man finds it!
>> Djanet Sears, from her play *Afrika Solo*, 1990

This chapter explores two related themes in relation to the work of black women in the theatre today: the concept of double marginalization from the white male norm, and the ways in which black women's theatres review myths and stereotypical images of black women, thereby creating positive alternative images and cultural representations of black women, created by black women. While it might seem that this project would be most appropriate coming from a black writer or academic, it is important that white academics also recognize the importance and originality of the work of black women in the theatre. As Sandra J. Richards suggested in her recent paper to the 'Breaking the Surface' conference/festival in Calgary: 'It is time that white women and men began to participate in the project of bringing more black women's writing and theatre work to critical attention.'[1]

Just as women working in the theatres of different cultures influenced by feminism have reclaimed images of themselves in and through their theatres, so women of colour and black women have made theatres which reflect their own images. But it is important to recognize the difficulty of defining the terms 'black women' and 'women of colour'. Discussion of black women's theatre must be cross-cultural or pan-national in focus. Yet in Britain the term 'black' refers to Asian as well as African and West Indian peoples. The tendency to conflate the cultural heritages of people from widely differing backgrounds is itself indicative of a distinctly British form of racism. This does not imply that America is less racist. The American vocabulary includes a considerable number of slang insults for people of non-white/WASP origins, but the term 'black' in the United States generally refers to people of African-American and Caribbean heritages. Chicana and Native American peoples are not often included in the category 'black', and people of Asian descent tend to be discriminated against according to a different set of slang words and racist assumptions. This discrepancy in terminology makes it difficult to discuss the work of black women and women of colour in Britain, as compared to the United States and other countries. Yet is important to do so, keeping differences of terminology in mind.

A few sources do consider the influence of black women in the theatre. For instance, Kathy A. Perkins has published a collection of plays by black women in America, and another collection, *Afro-American Women Writers*, edited by Ann Ellen Shockley, includes a few playwrights. Both these books focus on work from earlier periods, and are therefore not very useful in an exploration of the relationship between contemporary feminism(s) and black women's theatres.[2] The few academic books which discuss black women are focused primarily on American women in the theatre. For instance, several sources discuss the work of Alice Childress, Lorraine Hansberry, Ntozake Shange, Adrienne Kennedy, Maria Irene Fornes and Corinne Jacker.[3] A few source books also discuss the contributions of Caribbean women to the Arts, though little of this material focuses on the theatre *per se*.[4]

Only Sue-Ellen Case explores the issue of cultural representation by examining black women's work in the theatre. Case writes from a perspective informed by contemporary feminist theory and cultural studies. But, as she admits, Case is also limited in her examples to the work of women in America. Of course, my choice of examples is also necessarily limited by my access to the work of other cultures. I will focus in this chapter on the 'gaps' in the published history – on black women's theatre made by British women, and by women of West Indian and South African descent whose work has been published in English and/or performed in England and North America.

Michelene Wandor included one paragraph on the work of black women in *Carry on Understudies*, where she referred to the American production in Britain of Ntozake Shange's *For Colored Girls who have Considered Suicide when the Rainbow is Enuf* in 1979, and to a range of other examples (a range which is inevitably limited by her own access to theatres outside of Britain). Her last reference is to Grace Dayley's play, *Rose's Story*, produced in 1983.[5] Catherine Itzin has contributed to the field with one important fact, which is difficult to trace further: the Black Theatre of Brixton emerged out of the same process of division and subdivision within the alternative theatre community of London in 1978 which led to the formation of Women's Theatre Group and Gay Sweatshop.[6]

But what do these miscellaneous facts about and interviews with a few black women who work in different theatres say about 'black women's theatre'? Is there one useful way of defining 'black women's theatre'? Can some contemporary theatres made by black women be called feminist? If so, which ones, and by whose standards? To what extent is Djanet Sears' comment that 'nothing exists until a white man finds it' true of white women as well? That is, does the privileged position of white middle-

CONTEMPORARY FEMINIST THEATRES

class women academics (self included) also obscure or marginalize the accomplishments and views of black women and women of colour? Is any attempt to define black women's theatre as 'feminist' – a term which has been developed, defined and redefined primarily by white women – problematized by this privileging of perspectives? And if so, what is the best way to ensure that black women's work is represented, and that black women have the opportunity to represent it and themselves?

In this chapter, to a greater extent than in the rest of the book, I have incorporated long quotations from interviews with the women whose work I examine. This seemed the best strategy to ensure that black women might 'speak for themselves' in these pages. But this strategy is only partially successful at overcoming the white middle-class monopoly of representation. This monopoly has been noted repeatedly, and not only by black academics. Many white academics are wary of appropriating other people's experience in their academic work. I am also wary, but am aware that in avoiding the problem, I might ignore a whole range of important theatre work as well. It would be easier not to discuss black women's theatre, since many of the women who make it do not label their theatres 'feminist' in accordance with any definition I can offer. But again, ignoring their work in order to make my task easier would not be good academic (or political) practice: it would amount to choosing a sample in order to illustrate my point. And most importantly, it would amount to judging the work (implicitly, by ignoring it) by its suitability to the apparatus, rather than judging the apparatus by its suitability to the work. I want to look again at the apparatus – at the standards and values of traditional theatre work, and its suitability as a framework for evaluating black women's theatre.

I also want to look at my phrase 'feminist theatre' in regard to a different set of values. If the alternative can become the mainstream – as I have argued throughout – then even my flexible definition of feminist theatre becomes an artificial measure of 'the mainstream' in relation to some of the theatres I explore. It has certainly been the case in the past that, with the best of intentions, white women scholars and feminist activists have marginalized the work and experiences of black women and women of colour.[7] These are huge issues, and ones which I hope to see addressed at greater length, by black women and by white women, in all manner of future work. Here, I will take the issues into account in the study of black women's theatre texts and contexts.

THE REPRESENTATION OF BLACK WOMEN IN CONTEMPORARY THEATRES

Most of the black women and women of colour who have found public success in the theatre have been playwrights, such as Lorraine Hansberry,

Alice Childress, Adrienne Kennedy and Ntozake Shange.[8] Black women directors are not so common, and this situation seems to reflect the inequalities in directing (a very powerful position) discussed in relation to the work of feminist collectives and co-operatives in chapter 4. But when the director is not only a woman but also a black woman, the issue of directorial power is further complicated. After all, the basic issue is that of control over the cultural representation of certain images. Thus, while playwrights may write from their own experiences and depict black women in their plays, the director often has the power to determine whether those plays will be 'played' as situation dramas, or as larger political statements. In deciding who will have the control of the image and the political message, the role of the (black woman) director is very controversial indeed.

The difficulties which all women face when engaging in the activity of directing – defined by traditional theatre structures as an authoritative, powerful position often identified with a 'white male gaze' – are multiplied for women of colour, who are doubly distanced from that white male norm. There have been notable exceptions: for instance, Ellen Stewart founded the Café la Mama in New York in 1961. She was one of the first black women to found her own feminist theatre and to make a name in direction internationally when she opened a second Café la Mama in Paris in 1965. But, as Sue-Ellen Case has observed, 'Stewart is one of the few black women directors and founders of a theatre in the United States to have achieved a national reputation and followed a "colour blind" career.'[9] This suggests that Stewart's reputation flourished in spite of her race – that her individual success was not necessarily linked to any broadening of a cultural acceptance of the contributions of black people and people of colour. By contrast, in the 1990s, there are a number of black women working in theatres around the world, making plays and performance pieces which refer to issues of race and class as well as gender, and which are not 'colour blind' but rather definitively informed and enriched by the experiences of their makers.

One 'black' British feminist play has already been discussed – Jackie Kay's *Twice Over*, also known as a 'lesbian play'. Kay's *Chiaroscuro* was one of the first plays by a British black woman to receive widespread acclaim, all the more remarkable for someone as young as Jackie Kay.[10] Plays by Jaqueline Rudet (*Basin* and *Money to Live*) have been published in Britain, and plays by Maria Oshodi and Winsome Pinnock have been performed to considerable critical acclaim.[11] These playwrights deserve further attention, but are not discussed at length here, as I want to focus instead on the theatres of black women whose work (writing, directing and performing) has received even less attention to date.

Examples of unpublished work by black women in the British theatre can be taken from a wide variety of sources, from the work of Theatre of

Black Women to that of Black Mime Theatre Women's Troop and the Black Theatre Cooperative. The last of these is not discussed here because the company is mixed in terms of gender and replied to the Feminist Theatre Survey in this way: 'We have had no "feminist" theatre involvement and are specifically a black company, not a women's company.'[12] Similarly, Munirah (an 'Afrikan' theatre company based in London), Tara Arts and Temba are not discussed at length here, since they are mixed gender groups, the last two run by men. Tara Arts, led by Jatinder Verma, and Temba Theatre Company, directed by Alby James, are respectively the leading mixed Asian and black theatre companies operating in Britain. Both have contributed indirectly to the development of feminist theatre, in that they have centralized the work of Asian and black artists, and thereby opened doors for black women in the theatre.[13]

Verma's and James' work is often compared to that of Yvonne Brewster, Artistic Director of Talawa Theatre. The three companies (Tara Arts, Temba and Talawa) are currently the most prominent 'black' theatre groups operative in Britain. All three have recently gained main-stage space in major subsidized theatres. Yet Verma, James and Brewster are often singled out for interviews in the press as 'representatives' of black theatre arts. Jatinder Verma has expressed his dissatisfaction with being seen as a 'representative' Asian or 'black' working in the National Theatre, while the real effects of racism and bigotry continue in the streets. In 1988, he wrote an article titled 'Marginalized like me' in which he argued that it is too frustrating to continue to define and redefine the term 'black' (and the question of whether it includes Asians or not). Instead, Verma advocated a shift in focus among theatre practitioners to the common aim of building 'alliances' between marginalized groups of all kinds.[14]

Similarly, I want to argue that it is frustrating and unproductive to continue to define and redefine the term 'black feminist theatre', at least until some basic information has been collected, that is, information regarding the nature of the theatres made by and for black women, and the views of practitioners on the relevance of terms such as 'black theatre' and 'feminist theatre'. To this end, the New Playwrights Trust and the Black Audio Film Collective of London collaborated to commission a report on the status of black playwrights in Britain. The report, known as *Blackwright*, contains listings of plays by black authors (female and male) and of companies, projects and workshops involving or aimed at black writers.[15] Like the New Playwrights Trust's *A Guide to the Writer of Bengali Language and Bilingual Plays*, this is a very useful source of further information on non-white theatres and writers' projects.[16] But in themselves these guides do not provide enough analytical information to begin an informed analysis of black and Asian theatres.

In Britain, the Theatre of Black Women (disbanded in 1988) was one of the most explicitly 'feminist' of black women's theatre companies. Talawa

Theatre Company, directed by Yvonne Brewster, draws upon West Indian and African traditions in re-viewing the classics, while Sistren, a women's theatre collective also originating in Jamaica, focuses on contemporary issues of closer relevance to the daily lives of contemporary women. The Black Mime Theatre Women's Troop is composed of British women from a wide variety of backgrounds, all of whom are considered 'black' in the British usage of the term. These four companies have not been studied at length in any other published academic text. They are the focus of the next part of this chapter, which ends with reference to two plays by women of South African and West Indian descent: Gcina Mhlophe's *Have You Seen Zandile?* and Djanet Sears' *Afrika Solo*.

THEATRE OF BLACK WOMEN, TALAWA, SISTREN, BLACK MIME THEATRE WOMEN'S TROOP

Theatre of Black Women

Theatre of Black Women disbanded in 1988, primarily due to financial pressures. The three founding members of the group are still active writers and creative artists: Bernardine Evaristo writes poetry as well as plays, and is currently concentrating on her poetry. Patricia Hilaire writes both poetry and plays. Paulette Randall is a freelance theatre director.

In a paper she recently published, Bernardine Evaristo – former director of Theatre of Black Women – recorded the history of the company, thereby making accessible some first-hand documentation of some of the problems facing black women working in the theatre.[17] In interview, I asked more specifically about the company's work as a feminist theatre group. Evaristo explained that 'Theatre of Black Women always was a feminist company, because we (the founding members) defined ourselves as black feminists. We still do.'[18]

The company was supported by a variety of different funding bodies. Since funding from the Arts Council was always project funding rather than revenue funding, it was not so much 'cut' in 1988, as 'no longer funded'. The company's project proposal for that year was turned down, which meant that its funding from GLA (Greater London Arts) and LBGS (the London Borough Grants Scheme) was not sufficient to support the project. As a result the company was forced to disband, and Evaristo is not considering reforming it. She says: 'We have moved on now. We might well start another company, but Theatre of Black Women played an important role and is now gone. That momentum is gone, and we have each taken up other projects.'

When the company was active, it functioned in part as a centre for black women's creativity. Theatre of Black Women offered workshops in acting, writing, directing, designing, stage managing and poetry in performance. Its first project was a three-year workshop for unemployed women. It also offered summer schools culminating in performances. In that sense, it was more than a theatre company: it was a larger cultural project as well. Theatre of Black Women worked out of small offices and the private homes of company members. It never had a building base, so it could not provide a physical centre – a space from which the project could operate.

One of Theatre of Black Women's productions was Jackie Kay's *Chiaroscuro*, which was first given a rehearsed reading in a Gay Sweatshop x10 Festival. Evaristo explained that the connection between Kay's reading for Gay Sweatshop and the production for Theatre of Black Women was coincidental: Evaristo was working part-time with Sweatshop organizing the festival, and noticed Kay's script. She suggested that it be given a reading by Gay Sweatshop, and later took the play to Theatre of Black Women for a full production. But Theatre of Black Women considers its most successful and 'representative' production to be *The Cripple*, by Ruth Harris, a play about a black woman which appealed to a large and diverse audience. What the company found particularly satisfying about the play and its success was its perception that 'the audiences really believed that the actress was disabled though she wasn't. Partly that's direction, and partly that's because the author's disabled, and her experience went into the role'. In other words, the self-representation of a talented black woman was what gave the play its authenticity and its value, both for the company which produced it, and for its diverse audiences.

The audiences for Theatre of Black Women's plays were composed mainly of women, but were not mainly black. In Evaristo's words:

> The reasons are complicated. When we started, our audiences were mainly female, but as the topics of the plays broadened, so did our audiences and we started to get a lot of men as well. We rarely had lots of black people in our audiences, I think because there isn't really a tradition in this country of black people going to the theatre. . . . So of those black women who go to the theatre, we had a high proportion in our audiences. But we never had a primarily black women's audience.

It is therefore not surprising that the company did not operate according to any political line or specific policy. It produced mostly non-naturalistic plays ('no kitchen sink drama') and 'used poetry a lot'. Theatre of Black Women experimented with choreopoems as a form, producing Jackie Kay's *Chiaroscuro*, which is similar in some respects to Ntozake Shange's classic choreopoem, *For Colored Girls who have Considered Suicide when the Rainbow is Enuf*. Yet the company moved away from that kind of work in the last two plays, primarily because it wanted to avoid being categorized as a maker of 'overly stylized, agitprop or directly politicizing' theatre.

It is crucial that Theatre of Black Women had only one general policy guideline: to focus on work by black women. It involved very few men in its plays; although at one point it did have a male stage manager, it did not employ male producers, directors or actors. Similarly, white women were only very occasionally involved in its plays. The company employed one white actress in its last play, and one Asian woman actress as well. But primarily Theatre of Black Women was made by black women – women representing themselves and their own perspectives and values.

It is most interesting, in this regard, that Theatre of Black Women considered its work to be 'feminist'. Bernardine Evaristo explained the significance of feminism to the company's work:

> We are black feminists. The two aren't mutually exclusive. Race issues have always informed our work. White groups are starting to tackle race issues now as well, like Women's Theatre Group and their multi-racial casting. But this is a recent development, and those groups rarely have black women writers or directors. As black women and black feminists, we were the driving force of Theatre of Black Women. We were at the steering wheel, in control of what we were doing, the images we created, and how they were presented.[19]

This last sentence is crucial. It answers the question 'What is black feminist theatre?', at least for one theatre company, at one point in time. That Theatre of Black Women embraced the feminist label, according to its own definition, is important. But of course it does not mean that the label can therefore be applied to the work of other black women and women of colour. Talawa Theatre Company and Sistren – two groups with roots in Jamaica – have quite different approaches to 'feminism' in their theatres.

Talawa

The origins and policies of Talawa throw a different light on this discussion of black feminist theatres.[20] Talawa Theatre Company is an example of a successful black (African/Caribbean) theatre company operating primarily in Britain, founded in 1985 and directed by a black woman – Yvonne Brewster. Brewster has problems with the term 'feminist', as the quotation cited in chapter 1 revealed. She said:

> This feminist thing is always a little bit problematic with me, to be quite honest. . . . I come from a very strong West Indian background, and in the West Indies the word 'feminism' has a really hollow ring, simply because it's a matriarchal society. . . . So entering a European or British situation, one finds the concept a bit difficult. . . . But I suppose in a way [my work with] Talawa is exceedingly feminist, if

to be feminist means to look at things from a feminist perspective or a female perspective.[21]

While Brewster does not consider the company to be 'feminist' in some respects, she is willing to accept the term if it is defined in a certain way – as work which looks at things 'from a feminist perspective or a female perspective'. Of course, this definition is problematic: it does not define what it means by 'feminist perspective' and it borders on an essentialist reading of 'female perspective'. But Brewster did not want to pursue this question further, as the defining of the term 'feminist' is not the primary concern of her work.[22]

Brewster's work with Talawa is most widely known in Britain, but she has been active in the theatres of Jamaica, Africa and North America as well. She worked as a drama teacher, television production assistant and presenter, and film director in Jamaica, before taking up her international theatre directing career.

The following extract from a published interview with Brewster brings together three of the central themes of the chapter: the issue of the representation of black women in the theatre and society; the differences in perspective of black women (and white women) in different countries and from different generations; and the representation of black women in stereotypical roles (as 'nannies', etc.). This extract is from a part of the interview discussion which focused on the question of whether feminism in the theatre might be generation-specific, and might be viewed and treated differently in different cultures. In reply, Brewster referred to her experience of devising a play called *Champung Nanny*, or simply *Nanny* at the New York Women's Festival in 1988:

The festival directors invited twelve women from around the world: they had someone from China, someone from Finland, someone from Mexico, from France (Simone Benmussa no less), from South Africa, etc. Well, when it came time to find the representative woman director from Britain, the directors wrote to the British Directors' Guild. And they suggested me. I don't think the Guild told the American festival directors too much about my background. I got invited so I went. And when I arrived, the Americans were, well . . . very surprised when they saw me. I won't say what they *were* expecting in a British delegate, but it wasn't a black West Indian woman. I don't think they expected *me*!

The Women's Component of this festival was that we would all create workshops and performances around the theme of St Joan, and all our work was to be produced by the Women's Project (which is the most wonderful American women's theatre company). They gave us a lovely working space, and told us that our work should be related in some way to the concept of the Woman Hero or Woman

156

Warrior (keeping St Joan in mind). So we ended up with a St Joan from Holland, and a St Joan from France, etc. But I had trouble with this.

I told them that I didn't fancy St Joan but I wouldn't mind doing the Woman Warrior. What could they do? What did they think about the fact that the delegate from England didn't fancy St Joan? I don't know because I didn't ask. But I did what I wanted. I did a piece about Nani (or as the British would say Nanny): the Ashanti woman warrior. Of course, Nani is just like St Joan in many ways. She was called a witch in the eighteenth century, and almost 'got burned'.

. . . My piece got very hot too. But once I clarified the connections between my approach and 'what I was supposed to do', it all worked out just fine. The Women's Project did an audition call and would you believe it, *everyone* wanted to be in this thing [laugh]! We got two women from *Fame* for goodness sake! And we got Rosanna Carter, who played in the original *Raisin in the Sun*: she was cast as my wonderful magical Nani-figure.

We (the performers and I) devised this piece about the spirit of Nani, the true warrior. Ellen Lewis – a young writer at the Women's Project – went away at the end of each day and typed out whatever we had come up with so far, so that we had a working piece to start with each morning. This was an exciting way to work, because it meant that ideas from improvisation didn't get lost, and that the performers' experiences became part of the show. It was quite interesting to see these black American actresses allying their experiences with this Ashanti figure. It turned out that a lot of these actresses' families had come from the West Indies, but perceived their social roles as products of American society. These black women were upfront, socially aware, and recognized as talented; in that sense they were ahead of other black women in many ways. These were not 'nannies' or hired help. These were successful black women, and they identified with my story of the woman warrior.

. . . those women were privileged, and yet *so hungry* for reflections of their own achievement in recognizable forms. They didn't find reflections like that in society, or in most of the parts or 'roles' on offer to them in American theatre.[23]

Brewster's anecdote is interesting at several levels and for several reasons. It is significant that the St Joan figure was not compelling for a black director – that Brewster found a more positive and exciting character in an Ashanti warrior. But the choice of a 'nani' figure is also significant. It was a choice not only of an image of a powerful black woman, but of one who has been interpreted (by white cultures) in stereotypical form – the 'nanny' as a substitute mother figure and lower-class citizen, etc. Brewster returned to the origins of the myth and tapped into West Indian and African cultures in order to find and re-present a more powerful and empowering figure. Significantly, she brought performers and audiences (and indeed, the Women's Project's directors and other participants in the festival) into contact with this powerful figure, and thereby with West Indian and African cultural myths. Thus, it could be said that Talawa's work is quite strongly feminist in one sense, in that it actively seeks to dispel negative stereotypes and images by replacing them with powerful black female images.

In fact, the stated aims of the company are to use the ancient African ritual and black political experience in order to 'inform, enrich and enlighten' British theatre. Talawa is conscious that the work of black women writers does not tend to receive the detailed attention it should, and hopes to redress that balance in its work. The company is primarily female: the artistic director and the majority of employees are women. All designers to date have been women, and technical and stage management staff are predominantly women. The Board is composed predominantly of women, though during production the company employs both male and female actors, and the current administrator is male.[24]

The extract from Brewster's interview is particularly informative in regard to the representation of black women on stage. The performance piece *Champung Nanny*, as described by Brewster, provides an intriguing account of the context of production. The script is unpublished, and is therefore difficult to discuss as a play. Yet perhaps over-emphasis on the script of this piece would be misleading. Brewster argues that it is the piece 'in her living memory' which matters most in that it encapsulates the process and the decisions which went into the making of that performance, as well as the final product. She does find it significant, however, that Ellen Stewart was inspired to record the piece in written format, and to keep it alive in that way. But most of all, Brewster was moved at the commitment which Stewart and all the women involved showed in the piece, seeming – in Brewster's view – to embrace it as a reflection of their own positions in society. It is this aspect of *Champung Nanny* which is most interesting in terms of the idea that black women's theatre is based on black women's self-representations. Even for the Afro-American actresses who took part in the piece, the play seemed to have a special significance – a self-validating relevance.

The economic factors which led to the development of Talawa are also important. It is ironic that whereas the disbanding of Theatre of Black Women was caused primarily by discontinued funding from the Arts Council, the founding of Talawa was made possible by a sudden windfall grant. In 1984/5, one of the people involved in the GLC (Greater London Council) asked Brewster if there was a project she wanted to do. She wrote a large-scale proposal on the idea which later became Talawa's first play:

The Black Jacobins. This was the story of the first Haitian revolution. It required twenty-five people in the cast, several weeks of rehearsal and a great deal of money. Brewster 'proposed the ultimate, assuming that it would all remain a proposal'. That proposal was accepted. As a result, rather than starting on a shoestring, Talawa – meaning 'small but stalwart' or 'strong, female and powerful' – was founded on the relatively firm base of a substantial government grant.

Brewster took the grant and formed a company with three friends: Carmen Munroe, Mona Hammond and Inigo Espejel. They named the company Talawa:

> after the most significant female word coming out of Jamaica. . . .
> Talawa is an old Ashanti or Twi word. It was very appropriate to
> us because we are all of us tiny women in terms of height, but have
> – how should I put it? [laugh] – quite powerful personalities. We
> were none of us ever to be said no to. Let's put it that way.

But despite the emphasis on strong women, Talawa has only (in late 1992) produced one play written by a woman: Ntozake Shange's *The Love Space Demands*. This makes Talawa one of the few companies studied in this book which has produced work written by men. But does this mean that Talawa is not a 'feminist company'? Whether the answer – if there is one – is affirmative or negative, it is necessary to consider the source of the definition of the term, that is, according to whose standards, applied for what reasons? Yvonne Brewster has defined Talawa as 'feminist' in the sense that it works from a 'female perspective' – an ambiguous term which adds to the ambiguous identity of the company, in relation to the larger terms of this discussion. Talawa's ambiguous identity is worth pursuing further, for it is crucial to the questions posed about the relevance of applying definitions from one perspective to another.

Brewster argues that the lack of female playwrights in the company's repertoire is due to the emphasis on an 'epic' style, combined with the company policies of reproducing 'the classics' with black performers, and introducing the work of black playwrights to British audiences.[25] The 'female point of view' has been incorporated into all Talawa's work, including the 1991 production of Shakespeare's *Antony and Cleopatra*, in which Cleopatra's role and 'view' are emphasized. What Brewster did not say, but what is implicit in her responses, is that the marginalization of women's work in previous centuries has limited the number of women's plays which she might choose to direct for Talawa. Furthermore, there are not many plays by women from previous centuries which are not written from a 'white perspective'. In Brewster's words: 'I know that some women in the past wrote large-scale plays, but I never have found one that would be right for Talawa. The Aphra Behns of this world are beyond my ken. I don't understand what the bloody hell she's on about.'[26]

This comic statement has serious implications. Why should the work of a seventeenth-century British white woman have any special significance for black women (of Jamaican origins) working in the theatre today? More importantly, why should the work of any author – female or male, black or white – be *assumed* to have relevance to the women of Talawa? In fact, there are a few young black women whose work Brewster admires: Jackie Kay, Winsome Pinnock, Maria Oshodi and Yazmin Judd. Judd is not well known as a playwright, but Talawa has workshopped her first play – a play which was chosen by Talawa for two reasons: first, because it has an 'epic' scope (it is set in a deserted church and deals with issues of life, death, heaven and the possibility of immortality), and second, because according to Brewster, it is 'very definitely written from a female point of view'.

Talawa's company policies are quite general: to do female-oriented work, to do work of importance to black people and 'to be *general*. Our policy is to do work which is historically and ritualistically important'. Predictably, levels of funding have also influenced the company's choice of plays to some extent. Before 1991, Talawa did not have adequate resources to 'take too many risks'. The expansion of the company into the Jeannette Cochrane theatre space in late 1991 has expanded the range of Talawa's work to three plays per year, which will in turn allow the company to take more chances, particularly with plays by young black women writers, such as Yazmin Judd. In describing her dedication to 'nurturing' young women's work, Brewster compared her way of working in the theatre with mothering:

> We can bring up plays like babies. And that's the kind of theatre work I understand. That's my kind of feminism. In a sense, I don't understand the term in any other way: certainly not in its most strident forms.

But this was not a bald generic statement, nor is it necessarily as 'essentialist' as it may at first appear to be.

Brewster continued, and explained that her view of feminism has been influenced by her generation and origins:

> I suppose I feel that I'm a bit too old to take on the more radical aspects of feminism. But then that's not only because of my age, but also because of my origins, my background. And of course, I'm from a different generation than you young feminists today. We share a sense of the richness of women's contributions, but as far as I'm concerned, men don't have to be excluded from that. In fact, I think men can and often do (in my experience) help and encourage women's accomplishments, just as women encourage men and other women.

This extract from the published interview is telling, in that it emphasizes Brewster's view of herself and her work in relation to larger questions about black women's roles and generational differences in defining feminist theatres. Brewster recognizes a connection between black women's social status and their roles in the theatre. She sees herself as an outsider when working in American theatre, though she is comfortable working in Jamaica, and has grown accustomed to working 'as an outsider' in England. Yet, when speaking from her experience of working in African theatre, Brewster was less optimistic about the status of women in their social and theatrical 'roles', arguing that the male dominance of society is strongly reflected in the theatre, and that the best women's work is 'locked away in the universities' and therefore does not have any significant social impact.

Here, I want to expand the scope of discussion by comparing Brewster's cross-cultural work with Talawa to some examples of women's theatre from South Africa. The theatres of Africa and South Africa have produced very little work by women, or more accurately, very little work by women from South Africa has become known in England or America. One powerful play by South African story-teller and performer Gcina Mhlophe is discussed later in the chapter. But the work of the Vusisizwe Players is probably more familiar to British and North American audiences. The Vusisizwe Players toured their all-women's production of *You Strike the Woman, You Strike the Rock* in 1987. The play depicted the lives of several South African women living in the townships. It employed music and comedy to underline its more serious political points, and it gained considerable critical success on its international tour.

The problem of discussing this play by the Vusisizwe Players is, again, one of defining the term 'black feminist theatre'. There is no question that the play was feminist in some sense – as it was created and performed by women, focused on women's lives and urged political and social change – though the company might well argue with the term 'feminist' itself. Yet because the production was directed by a white woman, it is difficult to call this play 'black feminist theatre'. In Brewster's words:

> This is where we run into trouble with the phrase 'black theatre'. What is black theatre? If we mean theatre played by black women, but directed by a white woman, or by a white man, then is that 'black theatre'? [Is Athol Fugard's work black theatre? Of course he is white. But many of his performers are black and he often co-devises with Ntshona and Kani.] *Conceptually* speaking, whether we like it or not, the director and the designer and the writer – though the writer is probably most important – are the people who shape the play in the most direct hands-on way. So I think that the position – the colour – of the director is very important.

Similarly, of course, the gender of the director is important. Can or should a play which employs several actresses but which is written and directed by men, for instance, be called 'women's theatre'? I think not, and in all the debate about feminist theatre and women's theatre, I have found no arguments to contradict this view. Particular plays can be discussed in terms of gender politics. But what of racial politics? Brewster is wary of the 'feminist label', but not of the term 'black theatre'. She defines black women's theatre as theatre written and directed (and played) by black women.

I want to end this discussion of Talawa's work with one last quotation from the interview with Yvonne Brewster, who defines her work in relation to two cultures: West Indian and British. She says:

> I am a West Indian black woman directing in Britain. That makes me an outsider here, and elsewhere. But being an outsider can be a good thing: it can be a position of power. Because I am an outsider, I'm in a good position to listen to what goes on around me.

This is one way of looking at marginalization, or double marginalization. Other companies have experienced the same kind of double marginalization. For instance, when the Vusisizwe Players took their play *You Strike the Woman, You Strike the Rock* to the Magdalena Project Conference in Cardiff in 1987, they reached an audience of women from many different cultures. Most of the women in the audience were strongly supportive of the play and the company, but also – due to their own backgrounds and perspectives – tended to view it as an 'imported' piece of theatre, interesting for its depiction of another culture. This perception of the 'imported' play is particularly interesting, as it came from within an alternative feminist gathering focused on concepts such as the marginalization of women through dynamics of gender and power inscribed in language. Yet even within this kind of gathering, the women from South Africa were somehow – unintentionally and almost imperceptibly – set apart as 'other'. Similarly, when South African solo theatre artist and story-teller Ghina Mhlophe performed in the London International Theatre Festival in 1991, many people experienced the story-telling narrative style of her theatre. Either of these theatres could be analysed as 'marginalized' theatres trans-planted to British stages. But both could be seen more positively as well – as central theatrical forms of other cultures, temporarily visible in Britain.

Yvonne Brewster has argued that the 'bottom line' in defining 'black theatre' is direction by a black person (female or male). But even if this is the case, there must be more to defining 'black feminist theatres'. Talawa has been very successful in redirecting the classics with black actors. In this, the company has staked a claim in British culture. But is this 'black feminist theatre', or black theatre directed by a black woman? When

Talawa produces Shakespeare's *Antony and Cleopatra*, is this 'black theatre' at all? Sue-Ellen Case posed similar questions about the work of Adrienne Kennedy. She argued that while Kennedy's plays are not explicitly feminist, they can be interpreted as feminist in so far as they demonstrate the effects of racism on central female characters, or between 'black women in the theatre and the white canon'. In this part of her argument, Case refers to several black women performers who have played Shakespearean roles.[27] In a similar context, Talawa's work can be interpreted as feminist, in that it experiments with the real implications of racism in contemporary British society, by putting black people centre stage, in the classics and even in Shakespeare (all the more daring when staged in England, the homeland and heart of the Shakespeare industry).

Yvonne Brewster's work with Talawa has created new stages for black performers in the classics, and in less traditional roles as well. But in order to find black women telling their own stories and representing themselves in the theatre, it is necessary to look to a different women's theatre group with roots in Jamaica. That group is Sistren.

Sistren

Sistren Jamaican Women's Theatre Collective was founded in 1977 in Kingston, Jamaica by a group of women who were interested in the theatre and concerned with social issues of importance to women. These two areas of concern – women's lives and theatrical representation – have always been fused in Sistren's work. The company uses experience from daily life in Jamaica and re-presents that experience on stage. The theatre work produced is not in any sense 'high art' or 'drama', but is rather a theatre of the people. In fact, the title 'Sistren' means:

> more than 'blood sisters' – it means right on, it means from the people, of the people, in the people and for the people. It is a term of high respect and love and this is how Jamaicans and Caribbean people of all walks of life regard the Sistren Theatre Collective.[28]

The company was founded when a group of women involved in an employment programme known as the Impact Programme decided to enact their objectives on stage. The Impact Programme was designed to address the issue of women's work status, in a society where a high percentage of unemployed people are women, yet women are often the sole supporters of families. Here, support is provided for Yvonne Brewster's comment about 'feminism' being an inappropriate term in a society where women 'rule the roost without wearing the pants'. But more importantly, the origins of Sistren are located in practical social action, comparable in a very different context to the aims of Britain's Clean Break Theatre (discussed in Chapter 7).

The Impact Programme was implemented by the Jamaican government in order to provide manual jobs for the unemployed. But when women were not equally admitted to the programme, the People's National Party Women's Movement, led by Beverly Manley, and the Committee of Women of Progress, led by Linnette Vassell, 'successfully petitioned the government that positive discrimination should be applied in respect of the ratio of women to men employed in the Impact Programme, owing to the harsh conditions facing the women and their very great responsibilities'.[29] A small group of women met through their involvement with the Impact Programme – Pauline Crawford, Beverly Elliott, Lillian Foster, Beverly Hanson, Lana Finikin, Lorna Burrell-Haslam and Cerene Stephenson, the founding members of Sistren Theatre Collective. These women shared their ideas about women's roles as workers, wives and mothers in their daily lives, and translated those ideas into performances.

Elean Thomas has written about the development of Sistren's work:

> They started out with mini-dramas mirroring the lives of the working-class women – like their *Belly-Woman Bangarang* ('Belly-woman' means pregnant woman) – and climaxed in this period with their astounding and multiple award-winning *QPH*. In this, they took a legend, that of a famous prostitute Pearl Arbor, who died in the poorhouse. They took a contemporary traumatic happening, the Eventide 'Home for the Elderly' fire in Kingston in 1980 in which nearly 150 old women perished, the same 'home' in which Pearl Arbor died.

Thomas goes on to say that the work was handled sympathetically and with humour, with the effect that the serious issue of the maltreatment and ghettoization of working-class women in Jamaica was presented in palatable form: the oppression was represented indirectly, and humour was used to touch people's sympathies and to stir a feeling of empathy, as well as sympathy. In *QPH*, the theatrical representation of a contemporary social issue was filtered through the figure of one woman with whom the public was already familiar – the prostitute Pearl Arbor, also known as 'Queenie'. Beverly 'Didi' Elliott played Queenie, and said of her relationship to the part: 'The part just fit me. On the night of the Eventide Fire I was living nearby and I ran out and saw everything. So, especially when we do that play at night, it reminds me of the fire and me just put everything into it.'[30]

Elliott's view of her role is strongly influenced by her own memory of the event which the play depicts. In addition to identifying with the character of Queenie, Elliott identified with Queenie's terror, with her part in the larger event. The individual character's position was represented in the play as an emblem of the position of many women (and men) in Jamaican society. The play itself was staged in order to effect recognition of class-based social inequality among audiences. And because the audi-

ences of this play were already aware of this injustice at a larger insti-
tutional level, the play had the effect of motivating a certain level of group
awareness (or 'raised consciousness') of a problem, and of instigating
community thought about possible social action.

Other Sistren work has similarly used real social events as the basis for
devising original theatrical material. In *Sweet Sugar Rage*, the company went
to work as farm labourers and used the experience in developing a play
about the lives of women working in Jamaica's agricultural (sugar) industry. In this play as in *QPH*, the story is focused through the experience
of one central character, Iris, who worked in the fields for twenty-five
years and encountered all manner of problems with male management and
union leaders. This play was filmed and shown in urban centres, to increase
public awareness of the real circumstances of the lives of women working
on sugar plantations. Sistren has explained that the decision to work with
improvisational techniques to create believable characters who are also
slightly humorous, and to film this production and show it in urban areas
of Jamaica, were both political strategies: 'The play sparks off animated
discusson . . . [and] probes sources of women's oppression, and shows how
women, through drama, can explore solutions to that oppression.[31]

Similarly, one strong female character was the focus of Sistren's play
Nana Yah (produced in 1980). The play focused on the life of a 'nani'
figure, much like the one created by Yvonne Brewster in her work with
the New York Women's Project several years later. In this as in all of its
work, Sistren can certainly be called a 'political women's theatre group'.
Whether it can be called 'feminist' depends upon the definition of the
term. Just as in discussion of Talawa, it is necessary to consider the
definition of 'black feminist theatre' in relation to both race and gender.
In terms of gender, Sistren's membership does not pose a problem: it is
and always has been a women's theatre collective, composed entirely of
women. But in terms of race, the issue is more complicated. Though the
membership of Sistren is primarily black, Sistren involves a number of
white women as well. Honor Ford Smith, Joan Ffrench and several other
women have long been involved in Sistren's work. Partly, Sistren's connection with white women is a legacy of the company's roots in government
projects and large-scale community work initiatives. There were white
women involved in some of the same projects, and some of those women
were invited to work with Sistren.

The company is not opposed, in theory, to the term 'feminist theatre',
but does not tend to apply the term to its own work. Rather, Sistren works
on issues of social importance to women in Jamaica. Most of the women
who make Sistren's theatre are black, and most of the women depicted in
the plays are black. But the term 'black theatre' is not strictly accurate.
In discussion of Sistren's contribution to the growing cross-cultural awareness of the differences between life circumstances of women from many

165

different backgrounds, however, Sistren's work is indisputably influential. Its own magazine publication, *Sistren*, is widely read in many areas of the English-speaking world, as well as in Jamaica. Its book, *Lionheart Gal* (a biography of Sistren members, written in 'Caribbean English') has become reasonably well known in England.[32] Some of Sistren's video plays are available for sale, and have therefore been shown in England, Canada and the United States.[33] But most importantly, Sistren's live theatre work has become known in an international context. Representatives of the company often tour and attend festivals and conferences.

Pauline Crawford and Rebecca Knowles, two Sistren members, attended the 'Breaking the Surface' Festival/Conference in Calgary in 1991.[34] They took part as panel participants in several of the discussions about women's political theatre work and social change. They gave a practical workshop session which involved showing two of their videos and discussing the origins and political implications of their work. On the last night of the festival, they also performed an extract from a political sketch about two young girls experimenting with gender roles in child's play, in a cultural context which 'values' the gun as more than a symbol of 'budding masculinity'. The sketch broke into the rhythm of the final night's 'cabaret' and hung heavy in the air – a piece of comedy with serious implications. The same mixture of humour and serious intent is found in a comment made by Annie May Blake, the company stage manager and Theatre Team Leader: 'Sistren is actually doing the work that any interested, people-oriented government should be doing.'[35]

In so consciously bringing together politics and theatre, Sistren's work has been influential in changing views of women's roles in Jamaican society, and in making Jamaican women 'visible' in other cultures as well. This makes Sistren's work, in some sense at least, 'feminist theatre', and possibly also 'black feminist theatre'.

Black Mime Theatre Women's Troop

> We are trying something new: looking for a way to change British culture by enriching it with real Black experience, Black talent. We don't have a British equivalent to Shange's choreopoem/dance/theatre work. We want to develop a theatre which is British and Black and related to our culture here and now (not American, not African, but Black British).[36]

This quotation from an interview with Denise Wong, director of both the Black Mime Theatre and its Women's Troop, highlights the cultural positioning of this 'Black British' mime theatre company, in relation to the more internationally (Jamaican and African) influenced work of Talawa and Sistren. Yet for all the emphasis on the creation of a distinctly

'Black British' theatre, the work of Black Mime Theatre Women's Troop is obviously influenced by other cultures and traditions, just as the 'theatre' element of the work is influenced by developments in mime, physical theatre and dance from the United States and Europe. This is not to say that the Women's Troop has not been successful in expressing a 'British-ness' in its work, but is rather to question the notion of 'Britishness' when there is so much cultural diversity amongst British people.

Just as the American melting pot phenomenon has made it difficult to say what an 'American' is, so it is difficult to use the term 'British' without first acknowledging its outdated associations with a white aristocracy of sorts, and then acknowledging how very different the composition of the population is from that lingering 'British' image. The incongruity of that image is not a result of mass immigration in this generation, but primarily of the migration of earlier generations. That is, many people of African, Indian, Asian, Caribbean, European and Eastern European descent have been born in England and are therefore 'British'. Their cultures inform British culture, though those cultures are not often reflected in the images of the glossy pages of 'quality newspaper' colour supplements.

Thus, I would argue that Black Mime Theatre Women's Troop is uniquely and definitively 'Black British Theatre', because it reflects the cultural diversity which should be more commonly associated with the term, and because the themes addressed in its work are relevant to the lives of people living in Britain today. In the case of the Women's Troop, these themes are relevant to women's lives, and black women's lives in particular. It is therefore significant that Black Mime Theatre is one of the few companies which has surveyed its own audiences and taken account of the ethnicity and nationality, as well as the gender, age and occupations of its audience members (see chapter 2).

Denise Wong joined Black Mime Theatre as an actress in 1984, when the company was co-founded by David Boxer and Sarah Cahn. Wong began directing in 1986, though she had not trained as a director in her three years of drama school at Rose Bruford College. She had done courses in community theatre, and a four-month training programme in Circle in the Square in New York. When asked why she decided to form the Women's Troop, Wong replied:

> I have always been interested in women's roles in the theatre – mainly because I am an actress myself – and I wanted try out the idea of a female group, to explore issues relevant to women. We needed to diversify and to recruit women in order to achieve a mixed ensemble. It needed to be a separate company at first, so the women could develop their own style and not be overshadowed by the men.

The Women's Troop and the larger Black Mime Theatre (composed pri-marily of men) are autonomous, but were envisioned as joint projects, and are intended to merge in future, when the women 'have had enough time to develop their strengths and establish their own house style'. At present, the Black Mime Women's Troop consists of three women performers and a training troop consisting of twelve more women. Wong anticipates that when the two troops merge, the mixed group will continue to produce shows which focus on women. In this, the process of Black Mime Theatre's subdivision into groups according to gender is similar in many respects to that which took place in Gay Sweatshop in 1977 (discussed in chapter 3).

The Women's Troop's first play was *Mothers*, produced in 1990.[37] The show was a critical and popular success, and is interesting in terms of its political function as well. *Mothers* takes place in several time frames and locations at once, all of which are versions of – or projections from – an internal space where women think about and react to their experiences with other people (mainly men and young boys). The action of the play does not develop in a linear way or follow a single narrative line, but uses mime, song and devised sketches to construct a collage of impressions about black women's (and many women's) lives. The show was devised by company members around their experiences of being girls, young women, married women and of course, mothers. Three women play (or act) the parts of both women and men, adults and children.

An excerpt from the middle of the play gives an indication of its overall style. The scene opens with one woman washing dishes and talking to her irate husband, who has come in late for dinner. They argue a bit, then embrace. In the next sequence, all three women participate in a multiple role-playing sketch: they each play various characters in succession, from salesmen at the door, to women answering, to men making emotional and physical (sexual) demands, to children making physical and emotional demands, to women reacting, to men hitting out at the women, to the final embrace framed by the child 'defending Mum' from battery by the husband/father. The emotional intensity of the last image is undercut by a swift scene change, and a song. The 'child' cries out 'Leave my mommy alone!' After a momentary freeze-frame, the same performer slowly rises, snapping her fingers to start the rhythm. She begins to sing. The others join in on the third line of the music, acting as her 'back-up' singers in what resembles a 1950s-style pop song:

> Bum, ba Bum
> Ba ba ba Bum, Ba Bum
> Ba ba ba Bum, Ba Bum,
> Ba ba ba Bum, Ba Bum,
> Ba ba ba
> Ba ba ba ba ba ba
> Ba ba ba ba ba ba
> Ba ba ba ba ba ba

6 Black Mime Theatre Women's Troop in *Mothers*, 1991.

Bum (two missed beats):
Oh . . . Girl,
You know I love you.
Oh . . . Girl,
You know I need you.
I love you,
I want you,
Oh Girl . . .

The song trails off as the 'lead singer' leaps up and falls into 'split' position on the floor and his (her) trousers audibly tear. The 'act' of the pop star is undermined when his (her) trousers split, just as the somber scene of wife abuse in the preceding sequence was swiftly undercut with a change of character and perspective and a break into song. The song itself is both nostalgic and suddenly humorous. Most importantly, the humour of the song relies on gender reversal. All three women sing the song as if they were men, crooning to their female audience. The audience is invited to participate in that event, just as the audience was implicitly invited to sympathize with the child and with the woman being beaten in the preceding sequence. No single emotion or mood is allowed to dominate in the rapid succession from scene to scene, though comedy is a throughline of the play as a whole.

Mothers is worth considering in terms of the process of its development as well as its style. In interview, Wong has described the process of devising the play in detail:

> We have established a process of research, reading, talking to mother's groups and looking at our own personal histories. Personal commitment and investment makes for a better show. We decide what we want to achieve, then start working, researching, devising, trying things out. Sometimes we achieve something very different from what we conceptualized. Once we have a pool of ideas, images, information, ways of approaching our subject, I give it an overview, structure it, shape it. I try to work out the throughline, the scenario. But this sounds easy. Actually, the ground keeps shifting. The scenario changed in *Mothers*: it opened up and evolved, due to the nature of the subject (which encouraged personal input of all kinds). *Mothers* could have fractured off into many different shows – youth and motherhood, the role of the family, growing into motherhood – a different play could be based on each scene, which was a danger.
>
> . . . Our style, scene by scene like the drawings in a sketchbook, is sometimes very crude. Maybe even naïve, if you compare our work to that of a company like Théâtre de Complicité. Complicité are seen as the 'masters' and they do very important visual mime theatre work,

much of which we can learn from. We can not all be Complicité. We are something else.

What kind of 'something else' the Women's Troop *is* is a complicated question, as the genre of mime has been reinterpreted in recent years and now often involves a variety of physical theatre techniques, as well as musical interludes, dance and even words or text. In Black Mime Theatre's work, these disparate forms and techniques are brought together through devising, and interwoven by the director (Wong) in collaboration with the performers.

All the performers contributed to the musical element of *Mothers*, though Challe Charles wrote the music for 'Unconditional Love' – the song which frames the piece. In devising the music, the company found that the themes and subjects of 'male' love songs did not match those it wanted to sing about. Wong said:

> This proves that even in devised work, it is not always the director who leads the actresses. Especially in devised work like ours, it sometimes works the other way as well. . . . The musical element of our work is where I learn the most from the performers. Of the three women in *Mothers*, one was a session singer, and all had some experience of singing. So even when I had a certain kind of music imagined for the piece, I would find that my notion of what the music should be would change when I saw – or heard – what the performers could do, what they envisioned. Sometimes, they didn't believe that what they were offering was good enough. If I would say 'yes, that's good, let's use that', they would look at me like I was crazy, or kidding. It took some time for them to acknowledge the strength of their own contributions. That's partially conditioning of course. As Black women performers in Britain, they haven't exactly been nurtured and trained to the point where they are full of self-confidence.

Wong's observation about the self-confidence necessary for this kind of devising and performance is important. Part of the legacy of marginalization is an effective silencing of certain voices – an underlying feeling that what we (women, or black women, or lesbian women or working-class women . . .) have to say is not important, that our images are not significant. This observation has often been made in relation to women's literature and art, but not so often in relation to women's self-images as represented on stage.

When working in mime – a marginalized form of performance, without the safety net of a text – the identity between performers and characters, events on stage and in 'real life', is enhanced. When the performers are also black women, doubly marginalized by definition from the 'white male norm', that level of marginalization and vulnerability is further enhanced.

Thus, for the women in Black Mime Theatre Women's Troop, performance certainly would require self-confidence. But the marginalization of form and performers is easily overstated. Such potential marginalization can be subverted and employed as an empowering device, as in Wong's positively phrased statement of her conception of the company as a 'Black British' theatre group. Thus, Black Mime Theatre has gained a reputation for using alternative forms and styles in order to represent the issues and images of importance in their lives, and of relevance to Black British audiences. But their work has a much wider appeal, as the results of their audience surveys indicate.

The audience survey which Black Mime Theatre Women's Troop distributed – or rather, the fact that it took the trouble to distribute it, and to take account of the results – is itself an indication that the company is conscious of the 'role of its audience'. The reasons for distributing the questionnaire, according to Wong, included a desire to make people more aware of the issue of this show – motherhood – as 'a permanent role with lots of problems attached', and to change people's ideas about women's roles as mothers – to initiate social change through challenging people's ideas. The play had a pedagogic or 'consciousness raising' element to it as well. In Wong's words, '*Mothers* was for women, young mothers, teenagers who might be becoming sexually active.' In this sense, the play functions in a manner similar to that of earlier ('white') feminist TIE plays such as WTG's *My Mother Says I Never Should*, produced in 1975/6.

I consider Black Mime Theatre Women's Troop's work to be 'black feminist theatre' in that it is made by black women, about black women, and is intended to raise questions of social concern, to represent the issues relevant to the everyday lives of many black women, and to initiate change. In my view, Black Mime Theatre Women's Troop produces 'political feminist theatre' of a sort. Yet in interview, Denise Wong was concerned that application of the term 'feminist' to her theatre work, and to black theatre work in general, may be misleading. She explained:

> The feminist label is not something I necessarily attach to me or my work, though I don't deny it either. It's almost as if being black makes the word a little bit irrelevant. Staunch feminists might think our work too naïve, or not political enough. We talk about motherhood rather than about 'political issues'. But when I called the company 'Black Mime Women's Company' I was told by friends that the name implied politics. And I agreed. The word 'black' implies politics, as does the fact that we're working with women in the Mime Troop. And when we add to that mime is still such a 'white' art form (there is still an appalling lack of black people, or women, working in mime), then what we're doing is very political, very challenging, even provocative.

172

Someone said to me 'black people aren't interested in mime'. I
said it wasn't a question of lack of interest, but that black people
have not had access to mime as an art form relevant to themselves.
In terms of being political and filling a need, inspiring others and
trying to effect change, then our work is definitely political. It's
amazing that in 1991 in a multi-cultural society, an art form [mime]
still remains almost exclusively white, and largely male. So Black
Mime Theatre Women's Troop has to be political and also feminist,
in some sense.

Wong went on to discuss the idea that the Women's Troop is 'doubly
marginalized' when critics and audiences compare its work to that of the
Mime Troop 'proper', which was founded in 1984, and when it is compared
to the work of 'white' companies with access to training and higher education of various kinds. This marginalization was partially overcome by
the use of comedy as a strategy:

The choice of using comedy was partially due to the prevalence of
comedy in mime, but was also a deliberate choice to make the subject
matter accessible. We don't want to depress people, but to give hope,
and present new view points and maybe options. We often use
comedy in our work, because we often tackle emotionally charged
subjects (the men's last show was about schizophrenia). In time we
may choose to use less comedy, but humour as a vehicle to make
points for young people is very important. We don't want to progress
past our audiences.

But as in the comparison to Théâtre de Complicité, our use of
crude comedy (women as exaggerated male pop stars, rather than
highbrow farce) brings up the dilemma between populist theatre and
elitist art. At the moment, we're frowned upon as 'populist' as if
we're poor cousins to the establishment. But I don't see why being
popular, or populist, should be negative.

Two main points raised in this excerpt are relevant to discussion of other
forms of feminist theatre as well. For instance, in the chapter on lesbian
theatres (chapter 5), the idea that comedy is an effective strategy in
representing politics and the theatre was discussed and supported with a
range of examples from very different kinds of feminisms and theatres.
And of course, Wong is quite right to note the nature of much critical
valuing of comic mime work. In arguing that the popular appeal of Black
Mime Theatre's work should not be interpreted negatively, she highlights
the operative cultural apparatus which values 'serious drama' over comic
mime, and particularly over comic mime created and performed by black
women.

The women and the men of the Black Mime Troop, like many theatre workers today, face uncertainty in terms of the funding for their work. Their current level of funding does not allow members to be paid well, nor to train and rehearse for long periods of time. Of course, this is a familiar situation. Just as Monstrous Regiment and other feminist companies have found, so it is the case with the Black Mime Theatre Women's Troop that 'any company forced to do two shows a year in order to keep its funding will not have a break, will not have time to think of the future except in purely practical survival terms. For a small company like us, this has tolls on individuals. And if we're talking about mothers, well . . .'[38]

I asked Wong what she thought was the most important thing to say about the Black Mime Theatre Women's Troop, and the position of black women in the performing arts. She replied:

> So many of these women haven't worked much, and it's not for lack of talent or energy. Black women are assessed in certain ways, by white people with a white vision of what black people are, or what 'black roles' should be. Some groups now try for integrated casting, but then black performers will tend to be rewarded for not disturbing the balance, not standing out too much. Multi-racial productions need black performers who can conform, blend in and just be noticeable, but not agitate. This kind of approach will make British theatre stagnate. Black culture can add a whole new dimension: maybe it's too great a threat.

Perhaps the influence of black culture does pose a certain threat to contemporary British theatre, and to theatres around the world. Many feminist theatres have attempted to keep the issue on the agenda, but have also perhaps put the 'gender question' before the 'race question'. Companies such as Women's Theatre Group and Gay Sweatshop have been unusually attentive to the representation of black and Asian people in their memberships, and in the themes of their work and the perspectives of their audiences. Companies such as Theatre of Black Women, Talawa, Sistren and Black Mime Theatre Women's Troop are made by black women. Yet each is very different from the others, and indeed, while the term 'feminist theatre' is applicable to all these groups according to the definitions of a 'white' feminist perspective, each company sees itself in a different relationship with the term, and with feminism as a social project.

TEXTS AND CONTEXTS: GCINA MHLOPHE AND DJANET SEARS

Finally, I want to give space to the work of two little-known but undeniably strong black women playwrights: Gcina Mhlophe and Djanet Sears. To call either of these women 'playwrights' is immediately misleading, as both work in a non-linear narrative style which defies classification. Comic story-telling is a more accurate label for what these women do, though the theatricality of their stories is evident. These women come from very different backgrounds. Gcina Mhlophe is a South African writer who has performed in England, while Djanet Sears – whose parents were from Jamaica and Guyana – was born in England, and raised in England and Canada. As some of the work of both of these women has been published, it is possible to discuss their texts in the context of the larger issues raised in this chapter.

Gcina Mhlophe and *Have You Seen Zandile?*

Gcina Mhlophe is a South African playwright, poet, actress and teacher. In 1988, her devised play *Have You Seen Zandile?* was published in English. The play is largely and admittedly autobiographical. The first few scenes are set in Durban and the later scenes in the Eastern Cape region of South Africa known as the Transkei. The play depicts the development of black South African women's growing self-awareness, by focusing on an eight-year-old girl who gradually becomes aware of herself as a black woman, and of the political circumstances of her homeland and the social pressures which divide families (including her own).[39] The play is divided into fourteen short scenes, each of which involves Zandile, played by Mhlophe, re-enacting different parts of her life: the separation from her mother when she is quite young, the years spent with her loving and wise grandmother (whom she calls Gogo), the growing awareness of the meaning of her blackness in a culture divided by racial prejudice, and her developing sense of self.

The play is formally associated with the oral story-telling traditions of South Africa. This gives it a certain sound and rhythm. In the first six scenes, some of Zandile's speech is in Zulu, some in English, and some in a combination of the two languages. Later in the play, when Zandile is transplanted to the Transkei, another South African dialect is used as well. The narrative is punctuated by a gentle humour and by the rhythms of South African music. The story it tells is very moving. In order to convey any sense of the play's power, it is necessary to resort to a brief plot summary.[40]

Young Zandile is eight years old in the first few scenes. She lives with her paternal grandmother, though we (the readers/audience) learn that her mother is living with her new husband and four children in the Transkei. The old grandmother is quite happy to have Zandile. The old woman and the young girl have both been lonely, and find comfort in each other's company. They grow to love one another very much, and to see the world through each other's eyes. This mutuality is expressed indirectly, through shared phrases, glances, gestures and bits of song – the story-teller's ways of expressing character. Gogo (the grandmother) takes pains to ensure that Zandile goes to school and learns as much as possible. But the threat of the 'white car' (which seems at first to be a generic symbol of political threat and white power) is mentioned repeatedly, even by Zandile as she pretends to teach a 'classroom' of flowers in her grandmother's garden.

In Scene 5, the threat becomes real. Zandile is walking home from school when a white car pulls up beside her. Mhlophe as Zandile does not present any white men on stage. She does not need to. She lunges forward 'screaming as she reaches the end of the stage'. It is clear that she has been taken. In the next scene, Gogo returns home to find Zandile gone. She sadly packs some gifts for Zandile into a suitcase, an action she will continue for many years, saving gifts for Zandile's return. But it turns out that Zandile has been taken to live with her mother. Young Zandile tries in vain to locate Gogo. She begins by writing letters in the sand with a stick, asking Gogo to rescue her and take her 'home'. Ten years pass before Zandile gets her first clue as to how to find Gogo. She hears through her friend of a family with her father's surname. She fits the pieces together (in a traditionally climactic penultimate scene) and realizes that this is her family, and that they 'have an old woman' who may be Gogo.

In the last scene, Zandile finds her way back to Gogo, but Gogo is dead. An old female neighbour gives Zandile a photograph and the suitcase which Gogo left for her. The last words of the play are stage directions:

> Zandile is on her own in a pool of light, very quiet, separated from her surroundings. She opens the suitcase and takes out all the little parcels her grandmother has been putting away through the years. Zandile holds each of them for a moment, before laying them gently to one side. At the bottom of a suitcase she finds a dress, takes it out and holds it up against herself. It is a little girl's dress, which barely reaches beyond her waist. She puts it down, reaches for a second dress and repeats the action. She picks up a third dress and also holds it against her body. She then holds all three dresses closely to her, hugging them and sobbing. The lights slowly fade to black.

This scene is reminiscent of scenes from feminist plays of other cultures, suggesting that there may be some gestures and images which are cross-cultural or transcultural in their significance for many women.

For instance, the mixture of language and music, and the emphasis on the dress as a distinctively female garment associated with a physical and emotional inheritance from and connection with other women, is also emphasized in the archetypal American black feminist choreopoem/play, Ntozake Shange's *For Colored Girls who have Considered Suicide when the Rainbow is Enuf* (a play which can be compared on many levels with Jackie Kay's *Chiaroscuro*, a black feminist lesbian play written by a British-born Scottish woman). It is significant that Zandile inherits not only the memory of her grandmother when she is given the dress, but also the memory of her younger selves and the many people she has been as she has grown from Gogo's little granddaughter to the young woman of the closing scene.

Echoes from the closing scene of *Have You Seen Zandile?* can easily be found in 'white' feminist plays as well. For instance, Charlotte Keatley used the technique of signalling growth, loss and family ties through the discovery of several generation's women's clothes in *My Mother Said I Never Should*. In *Lear's Daughters*, the final scene captures three daughters in different-coloured dresses, all caught in a pool of light and all trying to catch the airborne crown – the symbol of their inheritance. Zandile's inheritance is not so symbolically charged with power and authority. Hers is the inheritance of a photograph and a few small gifts, a few collected belongings left from the grandmother to the child. It is a valuable inheritance, and a powerful ending for the play. It also recalls a (female) image depicted in a feminist play from Italy – the image of Laura Curino in the final scene of her *Passione*, framed in light, at once representing and looking for a mythic symbol of inheritance, the Virgin Mary. These plays and images come from very different cultures. All offer images of individual women spotlighted in isolated moments – moments of connection with and significant isolation from other women, moments of seeking and gaining inheritances from real and mythic women through legacies and personal reflections.

Have You Seen Zandile? is a moving play, and Gcina Mhlophe's multiple roles as its subject, creator and performer enrich the story it tells, just as Laura Curino's involvement as the subject of her story enriched her performance in *Passione*. But what is most interesting about Mhlophe's play is the cultural heritage which it emphasizes in both its form and content. Story-telling is the frame for the play, just as it is and has long been the primary means of communication between generations of women and men in 'real life'. It is so accessible as a form, and Mhlophe is such an able manipulator of that form, that the story of Zandile is immediately accessible and recognizable to and resonant for audiences in England.

The form reaches beyond the barriers of language and culture. It also re-presents those barriers by bringing them into the play. For instance, when the young Zandile is given a new doll by Gogo, it is a 'pink' doll – a white girls' toy. And when Zandile and her school friend talk of 'what they will be when they grow up', her friend says that she will be a white woman. The imagined white woman is the dominant image for them, signifying the little girls' idea of what it would be to be important, significant. The power of the image is encapsulated in Zandile's immediate association of white women with long hair and high-heeled shoes – glamorous images disassociated from the realities of hard work and life in the townships. The association between 'whiteness' and privilege is presented humorously within the play; it is depicted as the (mis)understanding of the young girl. But of course, the child is correct: she sees the situation quite clearly when she perceives a cultural double standard based on race.

Throughout the play, Zandile's mirror reflects two cultures: that in which Zandile lives, and that which she perceives as 'white' and powerful. In this play, audiences of many races may find reflections of cultural identities other than their own. And because the characters of Zandile and Gogo are drawn so carefully and sympathetically, we (the audience/readers) are invited to see things from their perspective(s) as well. Thus, while Mhlophe's work is not explicitly feminist in that it is neither a product of the 'Women's Movement' as such, nor immediately influenced by contemporary feminist theory, it is a political play based on the personal, and one which focuses on women and urges social change on a large scale. In that, it can be seen as a form of feminist theatre. In a similar sense, Djanet Sear's play *Afrika Solo* can be interpreted as 'black feminist theatre'. It tells the story of a young black girl (also based closely on the author, and played by the author) growing into a complicated but eventually unified image of self. Yet the mirror into which Djanet Sears looks is even more complicated by multi-cultural perspectives and the multiple identities of the author.

Djanet Sears and *Afrika Solo*

This chapter began with a quote from Djanet Sears, and it will end with one as well. In her play *Afrika Solo*, Sears describes her experience of multiple marginalization from a white male norm, as an English-born woman living in Canada, whose mother is Jamaican and whose father is Guyanese.[41] She poses the question of origins, asking whether she can be identified with any one of these cultures. In the play, she tells her own story through flashback and fictionalization:

> *Afrika Solo* falls into a category of writing that Audre Lorde calls autobio-mythography. The play is both fictional and autobiographical, loosely based upon a year-long journey that I took across the breadth and some of the length of Africa. A journey that changed my perceptions of the world; a journey that changed my perception of me in the world.[42]

The play opens with the sound of a drummer playing a traditional West African rhythm. The sound gets louder and builds to a 'full sensual pulse'. Janet Sears (playing herself) and two men – one black and one white – sing together. The lights come up to reveal Janet in the room of her lover, Ben, in Benin, West Africa. Janet is leaving Ben a goodbye note and preparing to return to Canada after her long stay. She is obviously upset. She does not want to leave Ben, but more importantly, she seems hesitant to leave behind the sense of identity she found in Africa. She embraces the culture by signing her name (in the goodbye note) as 'Djanet' – the African spelling. She sings a rap song as she leaves, with lyrics about finding roots and about sharing her new-found sense of identity with others back in Canada and England.

Next, Janet is in the airport waiting to catch a stand-by flight to Paris, London, New York and then Buffalo (where she can catch a connecting flight to Canada). The repetition of this list of cities is a continual reminder of the flow of cultures, one into another. African music blends with rap and old television theme songs to create a cross-cultural blend authentic to Janet's background. As she waits, she recalls bits of a narrative about her childhood and her journey through Africa, mingling stories and pieces of her life in a humorous monologue accented with song. Throughout, the airport courtesy phone rings and a voice-over announcement asks her to pick up the phone: it is Ben, wanting to ask her not to go. She does not answer until the end, when she tells him that she must go – that she must share her experience with others who have not had the opportunity to take this journey.

In this play, which is mildly cynical and punctuated with comic moments, Janet's experience as a black woman looking for the meaning of her blackness is the main theme. The play is not explicitly about being a woman, though it is told by a woman. The theme is not that of finding a female voice, but that of finding roots in a (multi)cultural identity and a voice with which to express it. In this sense, the play is more directly influenced by cultural politics than by sexual politics. Is it a feminist play? Or a black feminist play? Sears does not use the word 'feminist', and it would be deceptive to suggest that she wrote or performed this piece 'from a feminist perspective'. It is also worryingly presumptuous to assign feminist content to a piece which clearly has other aims and another agenda. Still, the play can be seen to be part of the larger feminist project in some respects: it gives voice to a woman's experiences and concerns, it deals with issues of class and race, and it focuses on the hope for social change through individual experience. This may or may not make it 'black feminist theatre'. It certainly contributes and adds an important new perspective to the study of cross-cultural images created by women in the theatre.

Afrika Solo, like Gcina Mhlophe's *Have You Seen Zandile?*, relies on story-telling as a form of theatrical expression. Both plays emphasize a central theme – the young black woman's efforts to find positive images of herself in cultural representations. Both plays make reference to the lack of positive images of black women on television and in film. Both suggest that there are more significant forms of representation to look to: Mhlophe looks to the matriarchal heritage of her grandmother and mother, while Sears ends her play with reference to the original 'negroid' nose of the Egyptian Sphinx, and the unwritten contributions of black women and men to the

179

Western cultures which marginalize them. The term autobio-mythography is an accurate one for both Mhlophe's and Sears' plays.

The term autobio-mythography suits the work of another black Canadian theatre artist as well: ahdri zhina mandiela. Mandiela's work is little known outside of Canada, but may soon be familiar to readers in England and the United States, as her plays have recently been published.[43] One of her plays, *Dark Diaspora... In Dub*, was performed at the third Fringe of Toronto Festival, held 28 June to 7 July 1991. It received a very positive review in an otherwise rather critical account of the Festival:

> ahdri zhina mandiela's *Dark Diaspora. . . In Dub*, shown as a work-in-progress, combines the appealing rhythms and dramatic choral repetitions of dub poetry with choreographed movement performed by six dancers plus the poet herself. The piece chronicles a black woman's experience growing up in the Caribbean and then Canada, dealing both with the racism of her adopted country and her knowledge that she and other black immigrants are 'African by instinct' even though they may never have seen the mother land. Part-exploration and part-celebration, the show wonderfully evokes black women's power and insights. It will only get stronger in its integration of sound and vision as it gets further production.[44]

This review highlights many of the themes and images which were central to the work of the companies and playwrights examined earlier in this chapter: Theatre of Black Women and Black Mime Theatre Women's Troop both used choreography, movement and music; Talawa and Sistren both emphasized the African origins of Caribbean forms, and the inter-relationships between performance on stage and in life; Gcina Mhlophe and Djanet Sears both used costume and visual imagery to trigger memories related to the larger concept of a (black) matriarchal legacy to contemporary women.

The term autobio-mythography might also be applied to the work of Jackie Kay. Kay is one of Britain's most powerful black women writers. A poet and playwright whose natural mother was a black British woman and whose biological father was Nigerian, Jackie Kay was adopted and raised by white parents in the (largely white) context of Glasgow. She writes from the perspective of a young black lesbian woman who is both a daughter and a mother. She embraces several identities and uses them as empowering devices. So, in another sense, do Mhlophe and Sears. Theatre of Black Women, Talawa, Sistren and Black Mime Theatre Women's Troop also approach the issues of multiculturalism, identity and self-expression in different ways. There is no single way of framing, or 'performing' black feminist theatre. The term itself may be meaningless, or so diverse and flexible as to have no meaning at all. But the difficulty of discussing this broad range of work can not be used as an excuse to ignore it.

Similarly, the work of lesbian feminists in contemporary theatres is often difficult to define. Thus, I want to expand on the idea, eloquently expressed by Cecilia Green and others, that 'middle-class white women's feminism' tends to marginalize black women and working-class women (and, I would add, lesbian women) from the 'mainstream of feminism'.[45] Firstly, there is no single feminism in relation to which other feminisms are marginalized, though some forms of feminism – particularly French-influenced feminist theories – have had more influence in certain academic circles. Thus, while I would argue that there is no single mainstream feminism, each culture does have its own systems of power and privilege associated with certain forms of expression. In that sense, Green's argument is supported by the fact that white middle-class women in most societies have had more opportunities to gain access to education and positions of power. But, of course, women as a group have been marginalized from these positions, by virtue of gender. Rather than enter into a debate about who is more marginalized than whom, it is more useful to acknowledge the relative privilege of many white middle-class women, but also to recognize that among those women who think and act as feminists, there is already an understanding of the consequences of such privilege for women of colour, lesbian and working-class women.

In order to work toward a workable theory and practice of feminist theatre, it is most useful to recognize (though not necessarily to 'celebrate') the differences between women and their feminisms, in order to find the most effective ways of eliminating multiple marginalizations and making sure that all kinds of feminist voices are heard. Valerie Smith has begun this project, in her theoretical writing on the subject of 'Black feminist theory and the representation of the "other"', wherein she argues that black feminist (literary) theorists use flexible methodological strategies in analysing black women's literatures – methods which 'are necessarily flexible, holding in balance the three variables of race, gender and class and destabilizing the centrality of any one'.[46]

By looking at some of the ways in which feminist theories (which some consider 'elitist' in terms of their specialized vocabularies and assumptions) can be seen to clarify and advance some of the aims of feminist theatre practice, the development of feminist theatres can be expanded from the study of one particular culture – Britain, for instance – to a larger pan-national study of new developments in feminist theatres and cultural representation.

7

NEW DIRECTIONS IN FEMINIST
THEATRE(S)

Most of this book has focused on the means which women have employed
in working toward the creation of texts, or scripts. But of course, all
feminist theatres are not text-based. Some rely on movement and gesture,
while some use scripts in alternative ways, and others combine scripts with
body language, multilingual performance and dance to create multi-media
and multi-cultural performance work. This chapter looks at some of these
new forms, and the ways in which they have begun to influence the further
development of feminist theatres.

PERFORMANCE ART/THEATRE

The term 'performance art' has been variously defined and is often used
in an imprecise way, designating that which is not quite theatre, not quite
dance, not quite photography, but something else. Sue-Ellen Case has
discussed a range of performance artists influenced by feminism, while
Jeanie Forte has argued that 'women have virtually taken over the post-
modernist genre of performance art'.[1] Here, I want to discuss the origins
and contemporary manifestations of a specifically British approach to feminist performance art in the theatre. In this regard, I use the term to refer
to physical and conceptual theatre which emphasizes the role of the performer as the representer of herself – her body as text, her self as character
or costume, her own movements as symbolic of the gestures and rituals of
everyday life. In this kind of feminist performance art/theatre, the artist's
body becomes a metaphor – a medium through which she invents and
interprets her own sense of self, and with which she negotiates and conveys
meaning to her audience. This emphasis on the personal and on the body
make the form particularly challenging for feminist theatre workers. In
addition, some feminist photographers, painters and dancers have chosen
performance art as a way of expressing certain ideas by incorporating their
own art forms into live performance.

Performance art as a form or genre became accepted in the 1970s, with
roots in the emerging art forms of post-1968 America, France, Italy, Russia

and England. Yet in the past decade, the distinctions between performance art, mime, physical theatre and dance have become increasingly blurred.[2] Some contemporary feminist theatres use performance art as an approach to their work – as a way of moving away from text-based theatre into more physical exploration of body language, gesture and movement. Mixed-media work has become increasingly popular as video equipment has become affordable and accessible, and as audiences have become acculturated to the idea that 'theatre' may include film and video as well as live performance. Of course, the increasing popularity of mixed-media work would not have come about for such pragmatic reasons alone: there must also be something which mixed-media work contributes to the theatre. Similarly, the incorporation of performance art into the work of contemporary feminist theatre artists has come about for a combination of practical and artistic reasons.

The progression to the present mixed-media theatre piece has been a convoluted one, from the agitprop street theatre performances and staged demonstrations of 1968–71, to the first Women's Festivals and staged performances, and to the development of visual theatre and early performance art techniques, for instance, in the work of the Living Theatre (New York) and Belt and Braces (London). Claire MacDonald and Pete Brook's work with Impact Theatre was central to the development of visual theatre in England. Such work was influential, and can be seen to have inspired some popular contemporary techniques such as the use of film and video as increasingly common components of the total theatre performance.

While all feminist theatre is not performance art, all feminist theatre does share some of the performance artist's concerns and approaches. These may include the use of alternative forms of expression (silence, body language, mime, etc.), an emphasis on the body, and a tendency to use non-theatre performance spaces. Ironically, this last tendency is becoming a necessity for feminist theatre in the age of funding cuts. The form is becoming more popular as funding to the Arts continues to decrease. While initial training in movement and physical theatre techniques may be costly, it is possible to make and tour performance theatre work with minimal sets and props, and with minimal casts as well. In fact, as some performance art work is performed to minimal audiences, or no audiences at all, the performances themselves tend to require considerably less space and resources than other theatrical forms, though this is not to say that less training or rehearsal is necessarily involved in the production of performance art, nor that the form is any less engaging than other forms of theatrical performance in terms of an analysis of space, texts or contexts.

In fact, performance art – one of the earliest forms of women's performance – is still one of its most viable forms, both in economic or practical terms, and in theoretical terms. The self-conscious nature of the form seems appropriate to the self-conscious project of making feminist theatre. The performance art which I will discuss in this section is of a certain variety – what I call performance art/theatre – and it requires audiences of some kind (however small, and even if the audience is composed of 'known' people such as friends and other artists).

Performance art/theatre allows for a direct politicization which is difficult to infuse into other kinds of performance media and spaces – into the traditional staged play, for example, or even into an otherwise liberating form such as the rehearsed reading. The emphasis on free performance space, in the various forms appropriated by performance artists for presentation of their work (primarily streets, lofts, and shops rather than galleries or traditional theatre venues), and the view of these spaces as necessary to the representation of living art, allow the artist the freedom to escape many of the financial and economic pressures which have kept some forms of theatre in 'alternative' spaces, in the pejorative sense of that term.

Because performance art has not been accepted fully by the cultural apparatus which values high art and 'drama', the form is particularly accessible to women. It cannot be coincidental that, of the many recognized women performance artists, many are (and call themselves) feminists, including Rose English and Annie Griffin in England, Karen Finley, Holly Hughes, Laurie Anderson, and Lenora Champagne in the United States, and Shawna Dempsey in Canada.[3] Similarly, in the area of contemporary dance/theatre, women have gained relatively high levels of recognition: notable (international) examples are Molissa Finley, Trisha Brown and Pina Bausch, while Peta Lily has a strong reputation as a (feminist) mime theatre artist. Similarly, several British feminist theatre companies have sought to combine a performance art approach with more 'theatrical' methods in their work. Théâtre de Complicité and Trestle Theatre are perhaps best known for this kind of work, but feminist theatre groups such as Tattycoram and Etheldreda have employed the same techniques. The work of Tattycoram is illustrative in this regard, as it borrows from performance art and has been informed by continental sources.

Tattycoram

Tattycoram, the Oxford-based women's theatre group, is currently (though temporarily) inoperative. The group still considers itself a viable entity, however, and so can best be described in the present tense. Tattycoram consists of four women (Susannah Rickards, Kate Fenwick, Victoria Worsley and Caroline Ward), who work co-operatively to devise their own performance theatre. The style of the work is not performance art as such. It calls upon the theatrical tradition in many ways, and relies on a collective scripting process which, while it does not necessarily lead to a finished (written) piece, does lead in some sense to a 'play'. The plays of Tattycoram are better described as 'works in progress' than as finished pieces, though not in the pejorative sense in which the term 'work in progress' is sometimes used.

All four members are experienced actresses, each with some background in either writing or directing. All share the common experience of having been undergraduates at Oxford. (It is ironic that while performance art as a form has the potential to make the theatre accessible in terms of the economics of staging, it also tends to be made by a relatively well-educated and privileged elite.) All four trained with the theatre specialists Philippe Gaulier and Monika Pagneux in Paris. This element of continental mime theatre and movement training informs all of their work, as does their extended contact with Théâtre de Complicité.

The company describes its working process as a product of the devising method, involving the director (Annie Griffin for their first show, Caroline Ward for the last two) from the start. 'The visual comes first, the physicality of the movement; the text comes second', explains Rickards.[4] She further stresses that the lighting design is introduced from the beginning, as a primary element of the final performance. Each show in its entirety, Rickards explains, is planned with the audience in mind; the group begins with an idea (a feminist re-reading of Chekhov, in the case of its last show), and constructs the show by developing improvisations from that idea.

In Tattycoram's last show, *Three Sisters in I Want to Go to Moscow*, the developments of the first five weeks of rehearsals were completely rejected. Even the performance at the Edinburgh Festival (1988) was 'very much work in progress', needing audience feedback for the progress to continue. As Rickards explains, Tattycoram sees itself as a specifically feminist group in its concern for the experience of the audience, and its conception of the ideal audience as female. It considers audience interaction to be a function of the devising process:

> When you devise your work, you say what you want, what hasn't been said before, mainly because there are so few strong roles for women in traditional theatre. You talk right to the audience and your whole purpose is channelled to saying 'listen to this women'.

Of its three shows to date, Tattycoram has had a relatively high rate of success, in terms of critical response from audiences and reviewers, if not in terms of commercial viability. Its first show, *The Very Tragical History of Mary Shelley, Her Husband, and Famous Friends*, was a performance piece constructed around ideas of 'how women are looked at and treated on stage' (directed by Annie Griffin, on tour in 1986). Its second show, entitled *Vesta Tilley, or How a Lady Had Her Cake and Ate It*, took cross-dressing as its theme, and experimented with gender roles by 'trying to be strong without trying to be male' (this show was directed by Caroline Ward, on tour in 1987). *Three Sisters in I Want to Go to Moscow* (directed by Ward in 1988) was Tattycoram's last group production.

The pressures of working on a very limited budget have since forced the group to disband temporarily. Its only production in 1989 was a short piece for the London Institute of Contemporary Art's Ripple Effect Series, described by the group as 'a version of *Three Sisters* – which has come a long way since the Edinburgh show'.[5] Tattycoram is optimistic about the possibility of producing another show together in the future, but also admits that its working method, which combines devising with performance art, is both its greatest asset and worst liability – it both frees the group from reliance on the perform/publish cycle against which many women playwrights must continually fight, and shuts doors in terms of keeping past shows viable in written (semi-permanent) form. The group agrees that one of its next projects will be compiling some collective scripts from its past shows, if only for the benefit of the group.

Tattycoram was fortunate to find a female role model and director for its early work – Annie Griffin, an American-born and British-influenced performance theatre artist, whose work relies jointly on the influences of Lecoq and the European dance/movement schools, and on American-based ideas of women's performance art/theatre (influenced by the work of Café la Mama, the Wow Café and the Living Theatre). Rose English has similarly taught younger women to 'perform gender' in the British theatre. Groups such as Tattycoram and Etheldreda have benefited directly from performance workshops with women like Griffin and English, and from the support of organizations such as the Magdalena Project and the Women's Playhouse Trust.

The function of such role models in the theatre can be illustrated by reference to the recent success of Victoria Worsley's solo performance piece, *Make Me a Statue*. This piece experiments with the relationship between artist and subject, subjectivity and objectivity. The subject is Camille Claudel, a sculptor known primarily as the lover of Auguste Rodin, whom Worsley and Ward recreate as the subject of her own life. The show is part theatre, part performance art, and part modern dance. Tattycoram's training with Gaulier, Pagneux and Griffin is evident in Worsley and Ward's collaborative work.

Make Me a Statue is an example of feminist performance theatre: it focuses on images of women, and uses these images in order to challenge the notion of a patriarchal standard for creation, as if such a standard were engraved, or carved, in stone. In performance, voice and movement belong to the female protagonist alone. She in turn 'moves' both the statues and the audience. A performance such as *Make Me a Statue* relies upon the audience as part of the show, and is clearly aware of and concerned with the gendering of its audience. On tour in the spring of 1990, the reviews were intriguingly mixed, as Ward explained at the time: '*Statue* is getting just the kind of reviews I most appreciate: very mixed, with men, in general, not understanding it, or lamenting the "lack of a storyline", while

7 Victoria Worsley as Camille Claudel in *Make Me a Statue*, directed by Caroline Ward, 1989/90.

women, on the whole, seem to find it engaging, and often comment that it touches them in ways which much mainstream (male-produced and directed) theatre and film tends not to.'[6] A female spectatorship is not requisite to enjoyment of the show, but (as Ward observes) a feminist or pro-feminist awareness may be requisite to enjoyment and understanding of the piece as both 'art form' and 'platform'.

Feminist theatre did not emerge dissociated from other forms of theatre; rather, it relies on the traditions which it subverts. Performance art comes from somewhere as well. Current debate centres on the question of where the form might be going, or how it may be influencing the development of new feminist theatres. In offering an outline of some of the present options (working practices and styles) available to the feminist theatre worker, this chapter has dealt with one aspect of the 'present' of British feminist theatre. This leads inevitably to questions about the future of feminist theatre. Some of the major new directions which theatre practitioners and feminist theorists have recently begun to develop are the subjects of the following sections of this chapter.

THE UNPERFORMED: REHEARSED READINGS

It has been argued that the appeal of performance art/theatre as a 'new direction' for feminist theatre workers may be related to both its formal flexibility and its potential for low-budget production. The rehearsed reading has become increasingly popular in recent years, for similar reasons. Since economic trends have severely reduced the amount of funding available to the Arts, the rehearsed reading has been developing rapidly as an alternative to the staged play. The Feminist Theatre Survey showed 23 of 98 responding theatre groups using the rehearsed reading as a working method.

As shown in chapter 2, Gay Sweatshop and WTG both experimented with the rehearsed reading early in their company histories, primarily as a means of developing the work of young playwrights, and preparing individual plays for staged production. Recently, however, diminishing funding has rendered the rehearsed reading useful, not only as a form of preparation for staged production, but as an alternative to it. In the rehearsed reading, new scripts (often, but not always, by relatively unknown playwrights) are given readings by a group of professional actors. The readings are generally 'performed' on bare stages without sets or costumes. Stage lights are replaced by reading lights. Scripts in hand, the actors sit facing the audience. They often sit in a semicircle – the position which allows for the greatest amount of eye contact, and which thus encourages the actors to engage with the audience as well as with each other. It is significant that the writer is often part of that audience, that the extrascenic interaction of the rehearsed reading tends to include the writer as a spectator, or more accurately as a listener (for the visual element of the rehearsed reading is minimal). Because there is no need to change costumes, to enter or exit, one actor can play multiple parts, designating changes in character by shifts in the tone of voice, posture, or simply by means of verbal exposition between characters (i.e., by naming, greeting and signalling).

Like performance art, the rehearsed reading has firm roots in theatre conventions of the past. Rehearsed readings can be seen as similar in form, if not in intent, to the late eighteenth-century convention of the author's first reading to the company, when prompt scripts were not available, and only cue scripts were provided for the actors. Under these circumstances, the reading may well have been the only opportunity the actors had to hear the play as a whole, and to establish their own parts in that whole. The implications of this kind of reading are discussed in Peter Holland's paper 'Reading to the Company':

> Either as part of the process of getting a play accepted for production or as the opening stage at the process of rehearsal it was – and sometimes still is – the practice of the playwright, who is not an actor, to read the play to a group of actors. . . . This event, which seems to represent a rite of passage, a transfer of control from the playwright to the company, has repeatedly acquired its own strange aura of emblematic significance.[7]

In contemporary rehearsed readings, the author does not read, but is read to. Her words are handed over temporarily to the actors, who read them back to her and to an audience. She is nearly always present, both throughout the rehearsal process and during the reading-as-performance. She has the benefit of hearing her words, learning from actors' insights and doing her own rewrites. If the text is cut, it is usually cut by the author rather than the director (even if at the suggestion of the director, or after discussion with the actors). The rehearsal thus becomes a process whereby actors engage with the playwright, as well as with her words. Questions of the relative status of the author are thus eliminated by the physical presence of the author. The status of the director (the 'Old Man' of old) is diminished, but not negated.

Terry Eagleton expressed these ideas in his analysis of 'the author as producer':

> Drama is not just a collection of literary texts; it is a capitalist business which employs certain men (authors, directors, actors, stage-hands) to produce a commodity to be consumed by an audience at a profit.[8]

It is significant that Eagleton referred to theatre as a business involving men, in an argument which – from a contemporary perspective – can be seen to undermine the role of the 'Old Man' as the authoritarian director.

189

While the authorship of the play in the rehearsed reading may be resolved by virtue of the author's presence in the audience, the critical implications of the theory of 'the death of the author' (referred to in chapter 1) are not. The rehearsed reading of the contemporary feminist play emphasizes the living author. Indeed, it is often intended to act as an aid to her revision of the play. Yet the dilemma identified by Jill Dolan, in terms of a materialist feminist perspective, is also relevant: the 'traditional triumvirate of playwright–director–actor' is disrupted by 'the spectator's insertion into the paradigm as an active participant in the production of meaning'.[9] In the rehearsed reading, the disruption is intensified by the playwright's role as a spectator and critic of her own work; that is, she is actively engaged, not merely in watching her play in performance, but in hearing it read, imagining the possibilities for staged production, and in considering possible revisions to the text.

While it might be argued that playwrights are consulted before script changes are made in staged productions as well, this argument does not always hold up in practice. Many staged plays are changed, slightly and even radically, without the permission or even the knowledge of the playwright. For example, Sheila Yeger contends that her play *Watching Foxes* was so drastically cut without her permission by the (male) director of the Bristol Old Vic production (Spring season, 1983), that she could 'no longer recognize the work as her own'.[10] Once staged, the play became public property, part of the public domain. By contrast, the words of the text in the rehearsed reading remain the author's; they are physically present before her at all times, and also before the actors, who, without the responsibility for learning lines and coping with blocking, are free to concentrate on interpretation of the words before them. The emphasis on the words of the text allows for an emphasis on, and recognition of, the source of those words – the playwright herself.

Thus, the traditional reading by the author to the company can be reviewed as a 'sale' of sorts, a selling of the worth of the play to the director and company (the middle consumers), whose responsibility it would then be to transform the words on the page into images and gestures to be 'sold' in performance to the audience and critics (the ultimate consumers). In the rehearsed reading, the shift in control over the means of production (of the text for performance) becomes a shift in the status of the end product (the text): the author remains the 'owner' of her own words.

In contemporary feminist theatre, the reading remains an important part of the process of preparing the play for production. Yet control of the script is doubly usurped; it is handed from the author to the actors, not after the author's first reading, but before the reading. This shift is emblematic of a repositioning of the author in relation to her work. The author is not present to read to the actors, but to have the actors read her words back to her (a reversal of the process described by Holland). Furthermore, a difference in the relationship between the script, the actor and the audience has been introduced, as the reading is the performance, and the actors are 'on the book' throughout. The physical presence of the text as script adds a certain symbolic significance to the words of the text, and by extension to the role of the author – a significance which undermines the idea behind much modern and postmodern theatre production that the text serves as a blueprint for performance.

The invention of the photocopying machine and innovations in publishing and bookmaking (which created the possibility of mass-production and distribution of playscripts) have contributed to a significant shift in the relationship between the playwright and her script. Like the publication of books and playscripts, rehearsed readings also serve a purpose based on economic rationale: they allow for public hearing of plays which could not be produced in fully staged versions.

Several British theatres and companies have used the reading in this way as a low-budget trial run. The Women's Playhouse Trust, in association with Methuen and the Royal Court Theatre, has been very active in this regard. Yet even this seemingly new alliance has firm roots in theatre history – in the tradition of 'new writing' at the Royal Court, usually linked to the developments of the English Stage Company (ESC) and the influence of the generation of 'the angry young men' in the late 1950s. The first 'reading' in this century was produced at the Royal Court when Charles Robinson's *The Correspondence Game* was directed in 1957 by Peter Coe, as the first 'Sunday Night Production Without Decor'.

In the period between 1957 and 1969, these low-budget productions allowed for the staging of new work on a trial basis, as Terry Browne notes in his history of the ESC:

> The 'Sunday Night' plays were rehearsed up to dress-rehearsal point, but performed with only indications of locale and costumes. . . . [Under these conditions] the play cannot be 'dolled up' by productions, and hence both its strong points and its weak points are plainly visible. It is an invaluable aid to the budding playwright to be able to see his [sic] play in production, even though it may not be considered good enough for a full production.[11]

Women benefited greatly, both directly and indirectly, from George Devine's 'right to fail' and its legacy. Ann Jellicoe was the only woman in the Writer's Group, and enjoyed years of success as one of a celebrated group of young political playwrights (though she has since withdrawn from the main stage to write community and children's theatre, she contends that her role in the Writer's Group was important both for her, and for other women playwrights).[12] Ann Jellicoe was one of the first playwrights to benefit from the 'Sunday Night' productions, when her play *The Sport of My Mad Mother* was directed by Jane Howell in 1959.[13]

191

Anne Devlin, Caryl Churchill and Andrea Dunbar are just a few of the many women who were 'nurtured' at the Royal Court. (Dunbar's death in 1991 was therefore significant in the sense that, although her work was not explicitly informed by feminist politics, she was one of the first young working-class women to make her voice heard on one of Britain's most celebrated stages.) The Theatre Upstairs annually hosts the Young Playwright's Festival, encouraging young people from all over the country to submit scripts, some of which are staged and some of which are given readings. Some small-scale groups use the reading as a forum for new material to be tried out before small audiences, and others use it as their primary form of performance.[14] Particularly since reductions in funding forced Max Stafford-Clark to announce the temporary closure of the Theatre Upstairs in 1989, the rehearsed reading has become one of the staples of the Royal Court repertoire, allowing the Court to maintain its reputation as 'the powerhouse of new writing', even within the limits of a substantially reduced budget.

Other theatres and companies have also contributed to the development of the rehearsed reading as alternative form. Approximately ten new plays are given readings each year in the Drill Hall's x10 Festival, sponsored by Gay Sweatshop. Some of the plays which are most successful in readings are then staged. Jackie Kay was 'discovered' as a playwright (she was already known as a poet) after a rehearsed reading of her first play at the x10 Festival. The Soho Poly and several other venues and companies have also begun to explore the rehearsed reading as form.

The Royal Court is now one of many theatres to use rehearsed readings as a cost-saving device, yet it is still one of the few theatres to encourage women playwrights in particular. The Royal Court initiated the introduction of Methuen playscript-programmes produced in collaboration with the Women's Playhouse Trust, thereby increasing the accessibility of women's plays in print.

Sarah Daniels and the Women's Playhouse Trust

Sarah Daniels' *Beside Herself* was the second play to be co-commissioned by Methuen and WPT; the first was Louise Page's *Beauty and the Beast* (1985). Both plays were directed by Jules Wright. *Beside Herself* (originally titled *The Power and the Story*) combines aspects of several of the working processes described in chapter 4.[15] The play was commissioned by the WPT in the hope that it would be produced jointly by the WPT and the Royal Court Theatre on the main stage of the Royal Court. The first draft was given a rehearsed reading in the Theatre Upstairs. It was understood that what the audience was seeing (or hearing) was work in progress and that the reading was primarily for the author's benefit. On the basis of the rehearsed reading, Daniels rewrote *Beside Herself* following discussions with Jules Wright and the actors. Access to the rehearsal process of *Beside Herself* (as reading) provided me with an inside perspective from which to discuss this particular play.[16]

Sarah Daniels has never devised plays in the same way that Caryl Churchill has done. Yet she often conducts research for her plays: for *Masterpieces*, she read feminist literature on the subject of pornography; for *Byrthrite*, she investigated the role of midwives in the seventeenth century; for *The Gut Girls* she did local research into the history of women's work in the Deptford slaughter houses. Before writing *Beside Herself*, Daniels contacted survivors of child sexual abuse, which is the play's underlying theme.

The rehearsed reading of *Beside Herself* allowed Daniels to incorporate the best aspects of devised work, including feedback and input from actors, without entailing the worst aspects of some devised work. There was no confusion over authorship, nor any loss of the playwright's 'control' of her play. Devised work often begins with a company – in feminist and women's theatre, composed of a group of women (usually the actors) who come together over a certain theme and work through improvisation, word association, workshopping, etc. The finished products are the written text and the performed play. In the rehearsed reading, unlike devised work, the actors are not generally included before scripting but are rather cast to fit the play. In a rehearsed reading, the abbreviated rehearsal period and the author's presence in rehearsals may influence the structure and working relationship of the group. This co-operation between author and actors can be an effective compromise between devised work and staged performance, in that it allows maximum connection between the text and the performance for the author. In staged work, the author's influence is less central to the rehearsal process; even in cases when the author is allowed access during rehearsals, there inevitably comes a point when the director requires the space to direct (i.e., interpret) the text's images into the physicalities of performance with props, blocking, and movement.

A few scenes were amended slightly before the reading. The version which was read before an audience on the evening of 20 August was revised during rehearsals to incorporate actors' comments as well as director's and author's changes.[17] No 'final' version of the script had been collated at the time of the reading, or even months afterward, because Daniels was commissioned to write *The Gut Girls* (about women working in turn-of-the-century slaughter houses in Deptford) by the Albany Empire Theatre, and the commission came while rehearsals for the reading of *Beside Herself* were still under way. Revising of the script of *Beside Herself* was therefore delayed for several months.

In the rehearsed reading, the text as physical material replaced costumes, blocking and movement on stage, and the words of that text took on an added emphasis. The words had a stage presence of their own. The actors' reading of those words became the audience's only means of entrance into the world of the play. Jules Wright's directorial line in rehearsal reinforced a sense of the power of the text. She told the actors: 'Explain, but don't interpret; tell the story, but don't take a stand. The text takes a stand, and *that* is your stand.'[18] In the rehearsed reading of *Beside Herself*, the actors surrendered their right to interpret through action and movement; they became readers, and much more. With no costumes, no elaborate sets, entrances or exits to help them delineate their characters, they had to become expert readers, as well as actors. The text was performed, rather than the play. Thus, the production of 'the gap which is the play' – to borrow the phrase from chapter 2, describing the results of some collaborative work in the 1970s – did not develop. Instead, the reading provided an opportunity to refine the text and prepare for staged production.

The rehearsed reading of *Beside Herself* was exceptional in the sense that it was intended to provide feedback for the author on her work in progress, rather than being the result of financial constraints. Yet *Beside Herself*, like most rehearsed readings and staged productions, was influenced by financial concerns to some extent. Roles were doubled and tripled in order to maximize the skills of the actors and minimize fees (set by Equity contracts). The demands of playing several roles at once are considerable in any setting. Thus, contrary to the assumption that a rehearsed reading can 'make do' with less professional actors, readings may require a particularly high degree of professionalism from their performers. There must be a careful balance between the amount of character doubling initiated by financial constraints and that initiated by a need to serve the spirit of the play. In the case of the script for the reading of *Beside Herself*, there were twenty-four characters (seventeen female, seven male) played by ten actors (seven women, three men). All actors played at least two parts. One actor played four of the minor female roles. This formulation was worked out by Wright and Daniels in a balance of economic and artistic considerations – the smallest number of actors to create the greatest effect. It was necessary to the plot that the seven women performers should each play at least two parts – a biblical character (one of 'the wives': Mrs Noah, Mrs Lot, etc.) and also a modern woman. But the male parts need not have been doubled and most likely would not have been in a staged production. In fact, several of the doublings would not have been either tenable or credible in a staged performance, as the time needed for entrances, exits and costume changes would have been excessive.

Even with all the multiple parts assigned in the reading of a play such as *Beside Herself*, the audience must be able to follow the story-line and the shifts in character. Thus, while the presence of the text frees the actors from the tasks of movement and blocking, this freedom is rapidly encumbered by responsibility for multiple parts, and for intense concentration. The rehearsed reading, in effect, calls for a narrowing and specialization of actors' skills. Rehearsed readings also demand the attention of the audience, not to a play but to a text, and to the subtle gestures and shifts in tone which signal character and scene changes. In this sense, rehearsed readings are best directed at audiences of attentive and critical spectator/ listeners. And of course, audiences at readings tend to be composed of critics and other practitioners (directors, producers, other writers and per-formers) and students of the theatre – those who have attended because there is something they want to learn about a play or a playwright, or about the process of developing a text for performance.

With this background on the rehearsed reading as form, it is possible to make an informed comparison between the reading and the play in production. First, a word about the story-line: the bulk of *Beside Herself* takes place in a community group home in London, in the present day. The first scene offers an analogue to women of the past – seven biblical wives (Eve, Delilah, Mrs Lot, Lilith, Jezebel, Mrs Noah and Mary), who meet in a grocery store, in among the canned goods, to complain about the various ways in which they (or images of them, stories about them) have been preserved and reconstituted through the ages. The women tell stories of blaming (men of women) and of a lack of understanding and unity between women, which has allowed the blaming to continue. In Scene 2, these same women are London residents – social workers, clients, mothers and daughters. Jezebel is a volunteer worker, played by Dinah Stabb; Delilah a hairdresser, played by Lizzy McInnery. Their interactions model those of the biblical wives only in the most superficial ways, yet the doubling of characters emphasizes the parallels. The story-line of the play is detailed, often humorous; it ends with a few of the strongest women back in the supermarket, this time as their contemporary selves but mim-icking some of their foremothers' actions. All of the visual information – even the poses which characters adopt (Delilah leaning against the canned beans with her scissors) – are only described to the audience through the stage directions. Yet the action is clarified in the reading; the play, even in its complexities of doubling and flashback, is 'performed', is made real to the audience, without any physical action on stage.

One set of female characters is particularly important to the play: Evelyn (played by Dinah Stabb in both the reading and the staged version) and Eve (played by Kathryn Pogson in the reading, and by Marion Bailey in the staged version). The relationship between these two characters is sym-biotic; in fact, they are two facets of the same person. Evelyn was sexually abused as a child, but has repressed the experience almost entirely. Within the time frame of the play, Evelyn is in her forties, a volunteer helping in the group home with the others. Eve is the personification of Evelyn's younger voice, the timid and secretly angry voice of her childhood.[19] When Stabb and Pogson/Bailey speak their lines, their words overlap slightly, they contradict each other. They begin speaking as two versions of the

8 Dinah Stabb and Marion Bailey as Evelyn and Eve in *Beside Herself*, by Sarah Daniels for the Women's Playhouse Trust, directed by Jules Wright, 1990.

same person, yet their voices begin to connect and balance each other as the play develops. In the climactic scene when Evelyn confronts her repressed memories, Evelyn and Eve address each other directly. In the articulation of the experience of abuse, the two characters are united. The problem of the reading is the difficulty of conveying this emotional and complicated scene to the audience, when all that can be seen is two actors, sitting in chairs, holding scripts.

This scene required the most rehearsal time. It also created a minor problem in one early rehearsal which, though not significant in itself, is indicative of the primacy of the words of the text in the rehearsed reading. Daniels took the three pages of dialogue in the scene and rewrote them on separate pages, arranging the words on the page so that the last few words of one speech overlapped with the first few words of the next (using the Churchill technique developed for *Top Girls*). Visually, these three pages had a different form from the rest of the script. They were appended to Stabb's and Pogson's scripts only; in these two scripts, the original three pages of the scene were moved temporarily to the end of the script.[20] In the first read-through with this new arrangement, Pogson accidentally read the first line of the speech (now repeated at the end of her script) a second time, into what should have been the final silence of the play. Such are the audio effects of moving pages of the script for a reading, when the reading is the performance.

The visual effects are more significant. During the reading of these three pages (when the rest of the company did not have a matching copy of the words being spoken), the rest of the actors were not obliged to read along. As a result, they seemed to lose partial concentration on the script; they were freed by the lack of text to look up from their copies, to look at the speaking actors. The visual impression elicited was intense: eight people who had previously been looking primarily *down* suddenly and collectively (but spontaneously, in an unrehearsed way) looked *up*. The shift in attention and focus was reflected in increased tension amongst those of us observing the reading: the moving of pages in the script became an action with direct visual repercussions for the audience. The missing pages became an important part of the play.

A similar example can be found in a slight change of wording in one of the stage directions. In the last scene, tension builds around the idea that a few of the stronger women are alone again, thus building toward the moment when they return (as their other selves) to the grocery store, bringing the unstaged action of the play to its close. The problem is the clarification of the solitude of these women, when (lined up in their chairs as they have been all along) all the other actors are still physically present. Expository remarks in the earlier scene accounted for the exits of all but four characters: Rory (William Hoyland), Evelyn (Stabb), Shirley/Mrs Lot (Julia Hills) and Lilith/Lil (Sheila Reid). Rory exits during the scene, and it is the stage direction indicating this exit (leaving the three women alone) which must set the tone for the play's end. In the first version, the stage direction reads 'Rory leaves, awkward silence'. This is replaced with 'Rory leaves, difficult silence'; and then with 'Rory leaves, Shirley and Lil stay, awkward silence'. On Saturday afternoon, during the last rehearsal before the reading, it was established that the extra adjective was no longer needed once the physical locations of the women had been clarified. The stage direction was changed to 'Rory leaves, Shirley and Lil stay, silence'. But between that last rehearsal and the reading, another change was made. The physical placement of Evelyn had not been accounted for. In the reading, the direction read 'Rory leaves, Shirley, Lil and Evelyn stay, silence'.

The wording of stage directions is important when words are all (as in a rehearsed reading). In this play in particular, where the victim is a woman and the abuser/blamer is a man, it was crucial that the audience be told whether that man was present in any given scene, and also where the victim could be located, both in the words of the text and in silence.[21] By contrast, in the staged version, it was the visual placement of the actors on stage which was the most important consideration at crucial moments of emotional intensity for the characters. An obvious example is found in the last lines of the staged version (a completely new scene, not included in the reading). The staged version ends with a scene headed 'World Without'; it draws away from the personal story of Evelyn/Eve, and into the larger realm of women who have been abused, and women who are learning to recognize the needs of their daughters above loyalty to their men. Nicola (Lizzy McInnery) – Lil's abused daughter, estranged for years – goes to the house where Lil's partner Tony (the abuser) sits inside watching television. This is the scene, the last of the play:

World Without
Outside *Lil's* front door. *Nicola* hesitates before ringing the bell. She steps back as near to the balcony as she can, in case she decides to run. *Lil* opens the door, a book in her hand, her finger marking the page.

Tony (off): Who the hell is it?

Lil looks behind her, then drops the book on the floor. Steps over the threshold shutting the door behind her. The two women stand facing each other.

This is the version printed in the playscript-programme (accurate to the performance given on Press Night). But as Daniels has explained, the scene did not work visually, and was therefore altered for the remainder of the play's run. At first, the scene was directed to take place at the back of the stage, with the result that the two women's faces and their expressions were not visible, and the confrontation between them lost some of the emotional power which Daniels had intended it to have. The solution: the house was moved to downstage right, the women's faces thereby made visible. Then, a new last line was added:

Lil: It's for me.

With this line, the world of the play opens out: the reunion of one character with another seems to take on greater significance as a positive image for women within and beyond the world of the play. This placement of the two female characters on stage has implications for the male character as well. Tony is no longer allowed the last word, and is separated from the women's circle of silent communication, highlighted momentarily before the last blackout.

Reviews of the staged version (directed on the main stage by Jules Wright in March 1990) tended to damn the play with faint praise. For example, in the same review in which he called it 'much the best thing Ms Daniels has written', one (male) reviewer added that 'Ms Daniels' feminist anger is the source of the play's weaknesses as well as its strengths'.[22] Such a review says less about the play than about the criticism of feminist theatre work; it focuses on the playwright's feminist perspective rather than on the play. Most significant is the comment that 'one gaping flaw is that she deals with sexual abuse entirely in terms of father/daughter relationships, entirely ignoring the proven fact that there are male victims as well'. In accusing Daniels of setting up straw men, the critic does just that. Daniels does not deny – either in the play or in 'real life' – that there are male survivors of sexual abuse (victimized by women as well as by men). But the point is not relevant to the play, which is quite clearly and deliberately focused on a father–daughter relationship. In reading the choice of this relationship as a denial of other possible relationships which might have been depicted, the critic assumes an anti-male 'anger' not present in the play itself. The criticism thus operates according to a double standard by making demands of feminist playwrights which are not generally demanded of male playwrights or non-feminist female play-wrights. It is difficult to imagine any critic arguing that every playwright should present all sides of every controversial issue in every play. Such a demand would surely result in very boring theatre indeed.

The significance of 'gendered reviewing' of feminist plays is discussed in chapter 8. Here, it is more important to point out that, both as a reading and as a staged production, *Beside Herself* was clearly informed by the processes of interpretation and reception not only of audiences and critics, but also of the author, director and performers who took part in the rehearsed reading. The rehearsed reading itself involved reception and interpretation of various kinds, both scenic and extra-scenic. The most important aspect of this play as a rehearsed reading was the interaction between Daniels as the author and her audience (of performers and spec-tator/listeners). 'The death of the author' is not a relevant concept when the author is part of her own audience, and one of her own critics as well. The author's connection with the process informed her revisions for the staged production. They also inform this larger study of 'the role of the audience' and of the 'spectator as critic'.

REACHING NEW AUDIENCES

Women's work in Theatre in Education, Young People's Theatre and Community Theatre

Feminist theatre work is not only directed at adult audiences and at the audiences surveyed in Caroline Gardiner's West End study. Feminist theatre is also produced for 'alternative audiences' – for young people, for the differently abled and for those with limited access and mobility, as well as for multilingual audiences. Some of this work is made by able-bodied adult women, while some is made by and for young people and for the disabled and multilingual communities.

Julie Wilkinson compiled a report for the Theatre Writers Union on the devised working process as it relates to TIE (Theatre in Education) and YPT (Young People's Theatre) schemes.[23] The report shows that, on average, TIE is a particularly low-funded area of work, and one which relies almost exclusively on devised scripts, either workshopped by the company or scripted for the company by outside writers. In cases where writers are commissioned from outside the company, rates of pay tend to be low (even lower than is usual for devised work). For this reason, writers of community plays may not be professional playwrights, but rather teachers, students, and community workers; or they may be well-established playwrights who may be in a better position to take the occasional financial risk.

The Feminist Theatre Survey showed that 13 of 98 groups reported having done some TIE work. While this may appear to be a relatively small percentage, it is actually quite high given the relatively low status of TIE. Thus, the survey results support that which Wilkinson surmises: much of the devised work used by TIE and YPT companies is devised by women. As group devising for small-scale theatre is one of the lowest-paid and lowest prestige 'opportunities' for playwrights in contemporary British theatre, the economic implications are clear, and can be compared to figures on women's employment and pay scales in other sectors.

The aesthetic and practical issues which such a situation raises are also important. The TIE companies are not to blame; they work with the resources they have and pay what they can afford to the available playwrights. But, as per usual, most of the playwrights 'available' or who can be pressed to make themselves available at such low rates of pay (and with no benefits, no job security, no hope of a residency or higher commission in future) are women. The Theatre Writers Union recognizes the problem which devised work poses in terms of contracts, but notes that 'TWU still has no distinct policy on the devised play, and wishes to consider it a priority'. It was further decided that 'the Union as a whole should take more responsibility'.[24] In the interim, however, the numbers speak for themselves. As shown in chapter 2, women's work in the theatre tends to be undervalued, just as it is in society at large.

A study of the role of women's work in community theatre reveals similar statistics to those of women in TIE and YPT. Ann Jellicoe is a notable exception: she gave up her successful career in London to set up her own grass-roots community theatre project in Dorset, and to write her Jelliplays (plays for children).[25] Overall, however, some young and less experienced women work in community theatre, and in the other lower-paid sectors of theatre work, by default rather than by choice. The indirect effect of the tendency to employ women primarily in low-paid areas of theatre work leads to a subtle restructuring of social value systems. The problem is complex: its effects show themselves in a social stratification which assigns a higher value (in terms of pay and prestige) to theatre reflecting mainstream values, while assigning marginal status to theatre reflecting the values and needs of so-called 'minorities', that is, women, children, lesbians and gay men, people of colour, people of abilities and ages which deviate from the 'norm'.

Just as the techniques of performance art have begun to be integrated in new ways into the theatre, similarly, relatively 'new directions' in contemporary theatre (theatre by and for the disabled, multilingual theatre, theatre for the socially and educationally disadvantaged, etc.) are actually newly emphasized movements which have existed, in various forms, since the late 1960s.[26] These forms have been adapted by many feminist women in the theatre since 1970. For instance, since the success of Berta Freistadt's *The Celebration of Kokura* (1970) as a 'peace play' for young people, TIE has been a major force in British theatre. Women's Theatre Group adapted the idea of using TIE as a vehicle for its first play, *My Mother Says I Never Should*, a play for young women dealing with the issue of birth control. Much later, in its 1982 production of *Time Pieces* by Lou Wakefield and the company, WTG incorporated the stories of different women in generational conflict, all exploring their own 'situated perspectives' in relation to each other.[27]

The development of a thematic cycle, from WTG's 1974 *My Mother Says I Never Should* to Charlotte Keatley's altogether different play of nearly the same name (but with the phrasing in the past tense), attests to the common roots of women in their story-telling: the nursery rhyme/sing-song verse from which the title derives ('My mother says I never should play with the gypsies in the wood') is as resonant for Keatley in the 1990s as it was for WTG in the 1970s. Known primarily as a children's skipping song, the verse is associated with play, and particularly with female play. Skipping rope is primarily a 'female sport', and the song itself incorporates an implied threat related to the notions of playing with 'others', and especially gypsies and 'foreign others', which may be of primary significance to the little girl. The verse itself may not have any special significance for women of other cultures, but the implications of the rhyme are common to people of varying cultures (i.e., threat to body and reputation from contact with 'others'). The stories remain the same, with new additions and twists; it is the means of telling the stories and the opportunities and rewards for the tellers which are changing.

TIE, YPT and community theatre are written for and directed at very specific segments of the population – at children, and at people identifying themselves (at least while they participate in and/or watch any given play) as members of a given community. These theatrical forms may have the potential to avoid becoming entangled, at least to some extent, in the hierarchies of power and privilege inherent to traditional theatre forms.

More importantly, these varieties of theatre can and often are intended to function as lessons, as educational materials for children and adults, presented in accessible form. That these varieties of theatre are created in large proportion by women is interesting. That they are particularly undervalued in economic terms is indicative of women's relative status within the theatre and the larger work-force, as well as of commercialism's impact on contemporary theatre production.

Multilingual feminist theatres and theatres of difference

Theories of difference can be seen to be very influential in contemporary discourse about feminist practice, or praxis. In moving from the purely theoretical to its application in the theatre, however, 'difference' and its performance take on new meanings, and new possibilities. This section examines several diverse 'theatres of difference' from multilingual theatres to theatres by and for people who are differently abled, or differently privileged. This kind of grouping-together runs the risk of conflation, implying that these kinds of theatre, because they are not generally created by English-speaking, able-bodied, white middle-class people, are therefore 'different' in the pejorative sense of the word. This is not my intention. Nor is it my intention to glamorize and valorize these types of theatres as genres: this would be as misleading, and as biased, as the inverse approach. It is the intention of this section to discuss a series of very different kinds of feminist theatres which have not received much media attention, yet which have all contributed substantially to the growing body of feminist theatre. By discussing these theatres together, even at the risk of temporary ghettoization, it may be possible to bring these kinds of theatres – and their creators – out of the margins and closer to the centre of attention and critical debate.

Theatre by and for the differently abled is an important and little-studied form of cultural representation. The Feminist Theatre Survey found only three British feminist companies which work in this way: the Integrated Disabled Women's Drama Group in Liverpool, Neti-Neti Theatre Company and Graeae Theatre Company. Common Stock Theatre also reported using sign language in its plays, but did not report any feminist perspective. The Integrated Group is a small-scale drama project, working mainly in Liverpool without 'professional status'. The two professional companies, Neti-Neti and Graeae, are worth examining briefly, since both have produced explicitly feminist theatre work which combined TIE with issues of disability and race.

Maro Green and Caroline Griffin's work with Neti-Neti was discussed in chapter 4. In their plays for Neti-Neti, such as *More* and *The Memorial Gardens*, the working method can be seen to inform the final product of the play. Green and Griffin describe the company in a way which expands the definition of feminist theatre to include work which offers images of women in a changing society:

> Neti-Neti is an integrated company, rather than a feminist company, but the foundation is in feminism. . . . And we're tackling issues of racism as well as sexism, communication problems as well as gender issues, ability and disability as well as sexuality.
>
> . . . One possible definition of feminist theatre would include that theatre which puts girls' and women's experience first. We have to make a distinction between our way of working and the plays themselves. We certainly prioritize the experience of girls and women in all our work practice, but the female characters' experience is not always put first in our plays.[28]

Neti-Neti's work has included several plays which used multiracial casting of disabled and able-bodied performers (women and men), and the company produces theatre for young people which incorporates three languages: English, Bengali and Sign Language. The most recent play, *Grief*, incorporated some African (Tsetswana and Zulu) and Sylheti (a dialect of Bengali) songs as well. Neti-Neti's work has been featured on television and radio as well as in the press, and is widely recognized for its challenging approach to multilingual, multicultural theatre work. Neti-Neti plays include *Aesop's Fabulous Fables*, performed in London Zoo in 1988/9; *The Beggar in the Palace*, a feminist rewriting of the *Odyssey*, in 1988; *Only Playing, Miss!* in 1989/90; and *Grief* in 1991. The last two plays dealt with themes of gender and power as expressed through language and body language. Both were critical successes.[29] As a result, Neti-Neti has begun to bring multilingual theatres to the attention of a diverse audience of practitioners, critics and reviewers. In publishing its plays and making some of the associated study materials available (including written study packs and videos) Neti-Neti has acted on its feminist principles by initiating learning and change in society.

Graeae Theatre is the longest-running and best known of the three companies. Founded in 1980, Graeae produces theatre by and for the differently abled and sponsors regional workshops and festivals of disabled artists and students. The group was founded by men, and has produced only two 'feminist' plays to date. The first was *A Private View*, a play which explored the relationship between four women artists, their talents and their disabilities. The play was written by Tash Fairbanks of Siren, an able-bodied woman. As Steve Mannix, company administrator, has explained, the choice of Fairbanks as writer was made despite her physical ability, rather than because of it:

> We always try to do plays by disabled people. But scripts are not always easy to find. Access is a problem for disabled people, who

are not often able to get to (or afford) writers' schools, training, workshops. Graeae has only produced two plays by able-bodied writers: *Working Hearts* by Noel Greig, and Tash Fairbanks' *A Private View*. But we received a lot of criticism, particularly from within the disabled community, when we produced plays not written by disabled people. *A Private View* came in for criticism of this kind. Though it was very successful theatrically, politically the ability of the writer was a problem.

. . . Disabled women have so many obstacles in their lives, and so rarely have the opportunity to train as writers. We hope to get over that block by providing writers' workshops by and for disabled people. When access and training are overcome, more plays by and about and for disabled women should also appear.[30]

Graeae does not have an official policy on numbers of women in the company, primarily because company policies are focused on the disability issue. But Graeae does have an unofficial policy which works strongly in favour of women: 65 per cent or more of the company are women, and in early 1991 the Board of Directors was composed entirely of disabled women. The Theatre in Education team is composed of three women and one man (who is the stage manager).

Chances Are (1990/1) was a TIE play, and the second Graeae production about 'women's issues'. Written by Jo Verrent (who is profoundly deaf) and directed by Annie Smol, the play focuses on an 18-year-old disabled (deaf) woman who discovers that she is pregnant. The woman is pressured by her family, friends and the medical community to make a choice: to have the child or to abort. In the words of Graeae's promotional material:

[The play] raises questions about the way society regards mother-hood, about hereditary disabilities, family pressure and the choices surrounding all of us, disabled and non-disabled, concerning pregnancy.

The young woman in *Chances Are*, and those in *A Private View*, all experience conflicts between their abilities and the views of others about their abilities. Both plays advocate consciousness raising in the able-bodied community. While they are performed by disabled women, they are 'for' the disabled community only in the sense that they represent experiences which may be common in that community. Similarly, Maria Oshodi's new play for Graeae, *Hounds*, examines the issue of power and personal integrity for blind people, and explores the role of charitable organizations which, according to Graeae, 'often project a helpless image in an effort to gain support'.[31]

Plays such as these assume a diverse audience, and have different functions for different spectators. Because both plays focus on 'women's issues' as well, they function at one level as contributions to the developing body of feminist theatre work focusing on difference (in an actual rather than a theoretical sense).

Like Graeae and Neti-Neti, Clean Break Theatre Company has incorporated a policy aim of raising consciousness of discrimination and limitations on women's lives. But Clean Break operates from a different perspective: the membership is able-bodied, but limited by a different kind of access problem. The members are all ex-prisoners. The company was formed in 1979 by two women ex-prisoners. The company's 'mission statement' best summarizes its aims:

> Clean Break Theatre Company aims to develop and expand the employment and personal choices available to women who have been in prison, before the courts or in drug, alcohol and psychiatric units. Clean Break believes that theatre is a vital means by which individuals can develop their personal skills, creativity and self esteem.

Clean Break currently operates as a professional theatre company limited by guarantee, which offers counselling, training and education programmes as well as experience in theatre production. In addition to offering guidance to ex-offenders, Clean Break has assisted other feminist theatre practitioners: for example, the company worked with Timberlake Wertenbaker when she needed to gain insight into prison conditions as part of the research process for her play *Our Country's Good*.[32] The work has tended to focus on issues relevant to women with limited access, but has larger feminist intent as well. In interview, company administrator Alexandra Ford responded to the questions of whether Clean Break is a feminist company, and a political theatre company, in this way:

> Yes, in a general sense, the company is 'feminist'. . . . It is political in a broad sense through the very nature of its work. We aren't, however, a campaigning group and our productions aren't agitprop, but entertaining theatre.[33]

It is interesting that Clean Break, like Graeae and Neti-Neti, does not wish to be viewed as a maker of agitprop theatre. Each of the companies stresses the importance of the form and style of its work, arguing that its concerns are best expressed through 'entertaining theatre' rather than through polemic. Both Graeae and Clean Break have commissioned plays from outside the companies, from playwrights with experience of feminist theatre work: for instance, Graeae commissioned Tash Fairbanks and Maria Oshodi. Clean Break has commissioned several feminist theatre writers, including Bryony Lavery, who wrote *Wicked* for the company in 1989, Sarah Daniels, who wrote *Head-rot Holiday* in 1992, and Paulette Randall, who has also worked with Women's Theatre Group and Theatre of Black Women.

9 Yonic Blackwood as Angela, behind bars in *24%*, by Paulette Randall, for Clean Break Theatre Company, 1991.

Recurrent themes, rules and exceptions

Certain themes and scenarios have emerged repeatedly in the feminist theatres of the past two decades. These include mother–daughter relationships, incest, rape, child abuse, the plight of single mothers and lesbian mothers, eating disorders, lesbian friendships and sexual relationships, the process of 'coming out', and the act of self-representation. This suggests not only that women find these themes interesting (if not necessary) to express, but also that these themes have been part of a developing feminist consciousness in the theatre. The themes, which are based on the experiences of the writers and performers as women, have informed the development of feminist theatres. The theatre has in turn functioned as a public forum for representation of these issues – a framework within which women may 'see themselves' and their own experiences, often by experimenting with the representation of self and gender in a multiplicity of ways. The operative thematic cycle of women's theatre has progressed from topics such as birth control and 'care and control' to some of the most contentious topics of the 1990s: commercialism, political revolutions in Eastern Europe and elsewhere, the spread of AIDS, and the threat of environmental disaster. With such changes in social climates come changes in the images created by theatre makers in different cultures.

Similarly, changes in sources of funding encourage and influence changes in the nature of that which is funded. As Jane Edwardes noted in her report on the cuts which resulted from the abolition of the Greater London Council, 'fewer productions, smaller casts and safer bets are already a fact of life'. WTG and the other companies discussed in chapter 3 have already faced these 'facts' – facts which became harsher when revisions to state benefit schemes meant that actors looking for work could not 'sign on' (i.e., qualify for unemployment benefit), thus initiating a split between the desire for work and the need for a guaranteed income.[34] 'Safer bets' have had to become even safer since 1988. Such a shift in control over the means certainly affects the ends of feminist theatre: groups are formed regularly, but lack of adequate funding often forces them to close and to regroup. Some new companies duplicate work which has already been done, a function of the lack of comprehensive networks between companies, and of the lack of a written feminist theatre history.

Cycles of productivity within feminist theatre can also be traced, from the early work of Mrs Worthington's Daughters and the Women's Street Theatre Group in England, and the San Francisco Women's Street Theatre Group and the Women's Experimental Theatre in the United States, through to the work of Tattycoram, Trouble and Strife, Split Britches and the Omaha Magic Theatre. A few companies – WTG, Monstrous Regiment, Gay Sweatshop, Siren, etc. – have evolved over the years, and still form the backbone of British feminist theatre. Similar studies have been conducted on American feminist theatres as well. The trends suggest the image of the chameleon – of theatre companies changing shape, size and image in order to survive in changing external conditions, while retaining the internal structure and ideologies which define them as 'feminist'. The increasing accessibility of cable television and the feasibility of multimedia productions with wider audience potential have affected women's theatre, and all theatre, in terms of what Patrice Pavis has recently termed (in a different context) the 'mediazation' of the theatre.[35]

What Patrice Pavis has described as 'the mediazation of theatre' can, for instance, be explored in relation to the strategies of feminist theatre makers, and of political campaigners and journalists who use theatrical techniques to convey their messages and to influence public opinion. Here, though, it is important to note that the 'mediazation' of theatre has had real implications for women's theatre work of less directly confrontational kinds. Many women's companies have adapted to the mass-media age by incorporating video and film into theatre productions, in order to enhance the theatre event itself with other media, and in order to make theatre work accessible to larger audiences and to younger audiences.[36] For example, NE1 Theatre (now disbanded) combined with Tynewear TIE in

1985–6 to produce a video for young women, *It's OK to Say No*, about sexual abuse and sexual self-defence. Kay Hepplewrite, spokeswoman for the project, had this to say about the relation of the video project to the larger project of feminist theatre: 'All this work has been approached from a feminist perspective and, as it is performed to young women in non-theatre spaces, is one of the least visible aspects of feminist theatre but is . . . a very valid and important output.'[37]

One example of an individual feminist theatre writer who writes occasionally, and successfully, for television is Gilly Fraser; another is Sarah Daniels, who has written for *Eastenders* and *Grange Hill* in addition to her theatre work. Polly Teale has recently been commissioned by the BBC; and, of course, Caryl Churchill began writing for television and radio.[38] Tash Fairbanks of Siren was commissioned by Channel Four television to write a television drama in 1989. She wrote *Nocturn*, a play about lesbian desire, produced entirely by women, which was the first explicitly lesbian play to be broadcast on 'prime time' television. Donna Franceschild has written television drama, as has Timberlake Wertenbaker. Jackie Kay began work in 1990 on a commission for a television drama about women who kill their children (a topic suggested by Kay). The video age adds a new dimension to the range of possibilities open to writers of plays, in separate or multiple media. Debbie Horsfield has not only moved success-fully from theatre writing to television drama writing, but has also had her series *Making Out* renewed by the BBC for several seasons. Yet the relative success of these women is the exception, rather than the rule.

Similarly, feminist theatre as genre – and not only women's work or 'plays about women' – is beginning to receive some mainstream awards. It is significant that of the feminist playwrights who have been com-missioned to write television drama (noted above), many have also received awards for their theatre work. Public recognition of theatre clearly has some influence on the choice of playwrights commissioned to work in other media. To cite only a few examples, Sarah Daniels was named the 'Most Promising Playwright' in 1983. In 1985, the *Plays and Players* Award for the 'Most Promising Playwright' went to Timberlake Wertenbaker (for *The Grace of Mary Traverse*) with Anne Devlin, Debbie Horsfield and Louise Page all as contenders. That same year, Deborah Warner was given a special *Drama* award for her work with Kick Theatre. In 1987, Churchill's *Serious Money* won the *Plays and Players* Award for 'Best New Play'. In 1988, Timberlake Wertenbaker won several awards for *Our Country's Good*, including the Olivier 'Play of the Year' Award.[39]

These awards are best considered critically. They are exceptions rather than rules. They cannot be assumed to reflect any radical change in the valuing of feminist work. The aims, intents and contents of feminist theatres are not necessarily 'established' over time, but are rather continually rede-fined and often (mis)interpreted from year to year, with changing fashions and shifting definitions of 'feminism', and changing economic and political contexts. Like panty girdles, to borrow Sarah Daniels' metaphor, feminist theatres are subject to the changing needs and values of their respective cultures. The 'new directions' which those theatres take will reflect the (cross-)cultural valuing of feminism and theatre as well as developments in theatre practice.

8

BRITISH FEMINIST THEATRE IN AN INTERNATIONAL CONTEXT

The shifting status of feminism, developments in theatre practice, and academic approaches to (women's) theatre studies all tend to influence the development and reception of feminist theatres. The first part of this chapter examines some of the practical problems which theatres and individuals face, and some of the partial solutions which companies have employed in order to meet changing circumstances. The second part provides a brief summary of key points in previously articulated theories of feminist theatre, and concludes with an outline of an original theory. This developing theory draws upon and extends the work of the book as a whole in arguing for a flexible but critical approach to the study and making of different feminist theatres, by way of placing this study of British feminist theatre into the larger picture of women's theatre and feminist practice in cross-cultural perspective(s).

PRACTICAL PROBLEMS AND PARTIAL SOLUTIONS

Despite the various innovations of feminist theatres in terms of form, style, intent and content, there are still practical problems facing the makers, spectators, and critics of feminist theatres. The first problem in theorizing about feminist theatre(s) is that of defining the term. I have argued that it was most useful for the purposes of this book to adopt a basic definition and to modify it throughout. So, in the introduction and first chapter, I defined feminist theatre as 'political theatre oriented toward change, produced by women with feminist concerns'. As each playwright, director or theatre group was discussed, it became necessary to modify the definition of feminist theatre – to take an individual woman's political perspective into consideration, to think about the effect of having come from a specific class background or culture, from one generation rather than another, etc. In discussing theatre groups, it was necessary to distinguish between groups which considered themselves 'feminist' according to their own definitions of the term, and those which are 'feminist' according to the tentative definition I proposed.

Issues of objectivity, subjectivity and positionality entered in; it became easier to see the significance of distinguishing between women's theatre and feminist theatre, but harder to do so in practice. Then the issue of cultural representation muddied the waters still further: where do theatres such as Talawa and Sistren fit in? Are such theatres 'feminist', and if so, according to whose standards – theirs or someone else's? What about European and Eastern European women's theatres? If it is difficult to compare the theatres of the United States with those of Canada, Britain and Australia, how do we begin to think of comparison in other cultures and languages, where other sets of values have influenced the development of theatres and feminist theories? And we're back to the question of valuing again, and must look not only at the question of 'standards,' but also at who defines them, and to what end(s).

This brings me back to the seriously humorous idea which I quoted in my Introduction: Jane Wagner's comic concern that the concept of 'quality control' may have been designed to mask an underlying suspicion about what might happen if 'control' were not exercised. Would quality 'get out of hand'? Would it still be possible to 'control' cultural standards, and to discuss the reading lists of universities, or the production schedules of major subsidized theatres? Quality control is a fine idea for those 'in control'. But of course, those who act as the guardians of culture or of literary and dramatic standards must have positions (situated perspectives) and agendas of their own. The expression of feminist political ideas, or indeed of the desire to effect social change through the theatre, does not necessarily meet these standards. But does a discussion of 'aesthetics' really solve the problem? I wonder . . .

My writing is informed and inspired by my active exploration of the theatre – in practical terms – as well as by my study of feminist theatres. Thus, the questions which I pose about feminist theatre are not merely rhetorical expressions of academic concern, but are practical questions to which I hope to find some answers. In the attempt to find answers, I begin with one basic idea: making theatre can be an effective means of effecting social change. In this respect, I want to argue that the tension between the 'role' of the academic and that of the practitioner is not always significant in the theatre space, where we meet and deal with each other as individuals. The trouble is that most theorists and academics who also work in the theatre do so in particular theatres and for particular reasons – working out theoretical ideas with students and colleagues in university theatre spaces, for instance, rather than getting involved in community theatres and professional theatres. Partly, this choice of work spaces for academic practitioners is less a choice and more a practical decision based on availability of resources and requirements of practical work with students, etc. But the result, as evidenced by the prevalence of privileged Oxbridge graduates making experimental performance art/theatres in Britain, for instance, is often an effective disjunction between theorists and practitioners, with a handful of women who have studied feminist theory making theatre influenced by it.

Here, I want to return to three of the quotations from playwrights cited in the beginning of Chapter 1, focusing this time on particular ideas expressed in them: Sarah Daniels' idea that 'feminism is now, like panty girdle, a very embarrassing word'; Caryl Churchill's cross-cultural comparison of American and British feminism (her view of British feminism as 'more closely connected with socialism'); and Joan Lipkin's argument that 'you have to take a stand if you make political theatre or feminist theatre' and that such theatre should 'not necessarily offer solutions, but raise provocative questions that help us to think about issues differently'.[1]

These views are illustrative of the complexities and contradictions of working as a feminist in contemporary theatre(s). There are indeed 'values' attached to the word 'feminism': it does seem to be more or less 'in fashion' from one year to the next. Yet, as Daniels points out, there is an intrinsic value to doing feminist work, whatever the 'fashion value' of feminism is at any given point in time. And, as Churchill observed, there are differences in the forms of feminism which emerge in the United States and Britain, yet it is possible to make feminist theatres in many different cultures. Most importantly, Joan Lipkin argues for taking a position. The position which all these women take is feminism. Within that position, there are many sub-positions. These make a definition difficult to agree upon, but need not make the politics of the theatres any less cohesive.

Differences between the perspectives of those involved in academic debates and those involved in theatre work, between those with higher degrees and those with practical experience, are as difficult to manage as are differences based on gender, race and class. But as bell hooks has argued in the context of a 'discussion about race and class', contradiction is not necessarily a bad thing:

> We live in a culture that makes it seem as though having contradictions is bad – most of us try to represent ourselves in ways that suggest we are without contradictions. . . . We have to be willing as women and as feminists and as other groups of people, including as men who enter feminist discussion, to work with those contradictions and almost to celebrate their existence because they mean we are in a process of change and transformation.[2]

The term 'feminist theatre' is still very difficult to define. I hope that it will continue to be so – that the ways in which many different women around the world find of expressing their commitment to feminist ideas – through cultural representations in their theatres – will keep the term flexible, and in need of continual re-vision. I also hope that, rather than reinforcing tired notions of definitive values, I have opened up the issue of defining terminology sufficiently to show that feminist theatres are most usefully viewed as committed active theatres, whichever specific brands of feminism are supported by their members. Yet in arguing that the term 'feminist theatre' is a flexible one, I do not mean to argue that it can include anything.

Here, the thorny issue of 'aesthetic standards' rises like the proverbial phoenix once again. In reference to the development of a 'new poetics' in feminist theatre, Sue-Ellen Case has argued that 'it is useful to locate the project of feminist theory within the realm of political practice', because this will keep women thinking about issues of real concern in the public sphere, rather than in the 'ivory tower'.[3] I could not agree more. Feminist theory which builds upon other theories with no reference to the lives of living women is of little use to most of us in the 'real world'. Moreover, such abstract theorizing runs the risk of alienating women who 'act' or 'perform' or 'demonstrate' their allegiance to feminism in more direct ways – through working in the world, and sometimes through making theatres.

I would qualify Case's idea with a simple addition: it is also useful to locate feminist theory within the realm of theatre practice, to look at the similarities and differences in approach, to think about the role of the practitioners in relation to the theory, to see what each has to offer the other. When this happens, both feminist theory and feminist theatre begin to approach the truly political. The women involved in making theories and making theatres may then meet each other, on the stage or in the audience or on a conference platform, and they may begin to see the similarities as well as the differences between their aims and objectives. The process of translating these connections into a tenable theory – one which will be useful in practice – is complex. The moments of insight gained by individuals, whether from watching particular performances or participating in debates at festivals and conferences, will not necessarily be carried out into the world, or on to the stage of everyday life. But when these insights are applied outside the theatre space or conference hall, then feminist theatre – as an academic subject and as a form of cultural representation – can be infused with the potential to effect social change.

This idea is developed in the work of Patrice Pavis, who has argued that the relationship between theory and practice in contemporary theatres is difficult to determine 'because it is ceaselessly displaced in theatre activity' – because it does not belong exclusively to pre-production work, nor to the production itself, nor to the post-production critical consideration of and response to any given theatre piece.[4] Rather, theory informs the cultures in which theatre productions are conceived, devised, rehearsed, produced, performed and reperformed, received, reviewed, criticized and theorized. Theory is an intrinsic part of the total context of theatre production; it is one aspect of the total process of cultural representation. Theory cannot be separated from theatre practice. Yet the relationship between theory and practice remains ambiguous.

The positioning of feminist theatre *vis-à-vis* the mainstream also remains problematic. Entrance into the mainstream may be desired by some feminist women, but certainly not by all. When some women do find it possible to stage their work in mainstream theatres, the accusation of 'selling out' is often heard. There are, of course, exceptions. Caryl Churchill has established herself and her work in alternative and feminist theatres, mainstream subsidized repertory theatres, and commercial West End theatres (as well as on Broadway, television and radio). She has done so though her work is undeniably and strongly feminist in terms of content and intent, and is also highly progressive and unconventional in terms of form. Yet few other women have been so successful in so wide a range of media.

In Britain, for instance, women such as Genista McIntosh and Janet Suzman have 'become the mainstream', while Jules Wright is continually manipulating the boundary separating the fringe from the mainstream with her work at both the Women's Playhouse Trust and the Royal Court. And now a younger generation of women works primarily in the mainstream, led by Deborah Warner at the National Theatre (previously at the RSC). Yet for most women working in the theatre, and indeed for most audiences, feminist critics and theorists, the relationship which feminist theatre bears to the traditional 'apparatus' is still problematic.

Publication is also a continuing problem for many feminist playwrights (as for many playwrights in general), though, as noted in Chapter 1, the problem has been addressed in the past few years. The continuing problem of publication for feminist theatres is related to the issue of production, or re-production of the plays themselves. As Elizabeth Natalle points out in her account of *Feminist Theatre: A Study in Persuasion* (1985), very few plays by feminist theatre groups are ever performed by other groups or theatres, or adopted into the canon of available works for performance. The reasons for this are many and varied, and are related to the production/publication cycle which generates 'popular success' and which filters down by way of lack of funds, lack of space, lack of accessible outlets for critique of alternative theatre productions (let alone publication of the texts) into 'alternative' theatre spaces.

There are exceptions to this rule. In addition to the recent publication of playscripts by Women's Theatre Group, Monstrous Regiment, Gay Sweatshop and Siren, and by feminist playwrights such as Bryony Lavery, there have been some concerted efforts made by established venues and production companies to publish the plays they produce. The Royal Court Theatre has published the texts of plays performed on its main stage – though not of plays staged in the Theatre Upstairs, where most new plays and plays by women are produced – in the form of paperback playtexts published in conjunction with Methuen, and sold at the theatre box office. The Royal Court's policy has contributed to the immediate availability of such plays as Timberlake Wertenbaker's *Our Country's Good* and Caryl

Churchill's *Ice Cream*, Charlotte Keatley's *My Mother Said I Never Should* and Sarah Daniels' *Beside Herself*, among others. It marks a major development from the days in the 1970s when feminist publishing was beginning to develop, and self-publishing was common for many new writers. Of course, immediate availability of playtexts may pose more problems than it solves; Sarah Daniels, for instance, warned in interview that 'the texts published in those programme/playtexts are based on production scripts; it's important to buy second editions, because that's where I usually put back in everything that was cut for production'.

Plays International publishes one new playtext each month, and has in the past made several plays by women accessible, including Winsome Pinnock's *A Hero's Welcome* and Catherine Johnson's *Boys Mean Business*. In addition, the Women's Playhouse Trust publishes the plays it produces, and has thereby made available plays ranging from Aphra Behn's *The Lucky Chance*, to Ntozake Shange's *Spell No. 7*, to Louise Page's *Beauty and the Beast*, to Sarah Daniels' *Beside Herself*. Yet the recent publication of plays by women has not had time to filter through the system: many playwrights and theatre companies are unaware of the work of earlier writers and companies. Thus, there is still considerable overlap of titles and company names, as well as themes, in feminist theatre work. This 'cycle' seems to be indicative of a continuing problem of accessibility.

What is true in the publishing industry is also true for many other industries, and especially for those involving high levels of training and education, leading to posts of relatively high 'status' or profile, such as those in higher education and the media. The proportions of women teaching at university level is notoriously low (though the number of women teaching drama may be slightly higher than the average for other subjects), as is the number of women in power-holding and policy-making positions at the major television stations, for instance.

Significantly, the Feminist Theatre Survey found the highest level of positive response, among both operative and disbanded companies, was to question five, regarding content and intent of plays produced: 69 of the 98 companies reported having 'feminist intent' and 86 of the 98 reported having 'feminist content,' at least to some extent, or in some of the work produced. In terms of future work, it seems (judging by the comments of practitioners interviewed, as well as from compiled statistics) that the status of women in the theatre, and the number of women entering the mainstream, are slowly continuing to improve; that a trend toward combining theatre with multimedia projects is becoming more common; that women's work in TIE, YPT, community theatre work, performance theatre, and increasingly, in stand-up comedy and cabaret, is also being developed as an 'option' in the face of funding cuts.

Yet the increasing commercialization of the theatre causes particular problems for feminist theatre. Feminist theatre, like most fringe and alternative theatre, is generally excluded – by nature of its non-commercial, non-authoritarian structure – from the lucrative commercial success of West End productions in London, or Broadway productions in New York. There are exceptions. The obvious example of a play by a feminist produced successfully in London's West End is Caryl Churchill's *Serious Money*. But of course this is a play by a feminist writer, and not specifically a 'feminist play'. *Serious Money* is about upwardly mobile young people. Churchill's play, set in the Stock Exchange, includes more male parts than female. The play depicts individual personalities who are lost to the mechanisms of the money-making industry. *Serious Money* is a very powerful play by a British socialist feminist, which is not in itself particularly 'feminist' either in terms of its content or intent. The play is political in the sense that it deals with topical subjects such as capitalism, 'yuppy greed', and the anonymity of people caught up in commercial structures. But the musical format, the verse style, the largess and 'showiness' of the play in performance, all combined to produce a general comment on capitalism rather than the story of particular individuals. It is not immaterial that Churchill herself was a 'proven commodity' when this play was produced, nor that the play was transferred only after it also had 'proved itself' in a trial run at the Royal Court.

Very few West End plays of the past five years have had any kind of feminist content. For a feminist play to succeed in the mainstream in Britain, it is often necessary to underwrite feminist content with 'larger' messages, and to employ a format or style which does not emphasize the connections between the personal and the political. These problems are not limited to feminist theatre work; in fact, they are common to most fringe theatre work and even some mainstream work. As funds diminish or fail to keep up with rising rates of interest and inflation, theatre of all levels of 'acceptability' is affected increasingly. These problems are especially prevalent among non-traditionally structured groups like co-operatives, precisely because the co-operative method stresses process over product, co-operation over competitiveness at the individual level.

While some successful fringe productions do transfer to the West End, and while some writers, directors and performers are comfortable moving between the sectors, this kind of mobility is not common to feminist theatre. The only avowedly feminist theatre company which might have been considered 'mainstream' was the disbanded RSC Women's Project (which was viewed as a finite project, rather than as an on-going company). Playwrights such as Caryl Churchill and Timberlake Wertenbaker may now be considered 'mainstream', in that they have had considerable Royal Court and West End successes, but the RSC – apart from the recent production of Wertenbaker's *The Love of the Nightingale* – and the National Theatre have been slow to recognize them. The Women's Playhouse Trust has begun to bridge the gap by introducing women's work to some of the main stages. For all its successes, however, WPT had no venue of its own until 1991. Of the subsidized Theatres National, the WPT was most frequently housed at the Royal Court (often at the Theatre Upstairs, rather than the main stage).

I do not mean to suggest that the 'potential problems' facing feminist theatres are all financial or practical. Many are more complicated, spanning larger questions of the cultural valuing of women's work and of the theatre itself. Here, Jane Wagner's *The Search for Signs of Intelligent Life in the Universe* (1986) is an important exception to all the general rules. This play opened in a major Broadway venue. It was extremely successful for the length of its run, and was the first playtext since the 1960s to be included on the American 'best seller' list. The play was also adapted for major film release. But what is most significant about the play is the acceptance – in the Broadway context – of a one-woman play which deals in non-linear story-telling and comic narrative, portraying a wide range of characters, including several outspoken feminists. The play depicts feminism in a comic light which does not undercut its serious intent. It portrays likeable characters at odds with a world which does not value their feminist ideas. It also portrays lesbian relationships in a positive way.

Perhaps most significantly, Wagner cast one of the central characters, Trudy, as a wise woman overlooked by a class-conscious capitalist society. Trudy is a 'bag lady', a homeless woman who has the first and last words of the play. She is the chosen woman whom the 'superior' beings from another planet use as their contact with humans, as they search for signs of intelligent life. She is a good choice. She, like Shakespeare's fools, is way ahead of the rest of us. It is she who worries about 'quality control', and who considers the possibility that Andy Warhol might be on to something as she mutters (in what becomes a running gag): 'art, soup, soup, art', as if she is trying to make sense of the distinction. She knows that the 'value' of soup, and of art, depends upon who does the 'valuing' and for what reasons. For Trudy, the homeless woman who knows hunger first-hand, soup fills a need which art does not.

It is Trudy who takes these intergalactic visitors to watch Lily Tomlin perform Jane Wagner's one-woman show on Broadway. But as she reveals in the closing scene, she 'forgot to tell 'em to watch the play: they'd been watching the audience!' In that line, Trudy reveals part of the power of this play. The signs of intelligent life which are 'found' are not those presented on stage, but those of the other people out there in the audience, without whom, as Lily Tomlin says in her greeting at the show's opening, 'there'd be little point in [her] being here'. This is a very humorous play, which makes all the most important points about feminist theatre: it is written by a woman and played by a woman. It portrays a variety of different female characters, and raises issues of importance to women's lives. It urges social reflection and change. It asks questions about the valuing of art, and of theatre. It suggests that the audience plays a crucial role in finding answers, or deciding whether answers must be found.

In her published 'Afterword' to the play, Marilyn French discussed the designation of 'high art' as opposed to popular culture, arguing that such valuing is assigned from a traditional 'masculinist' perspective infused with power and privilege, as well as bias. It is from this perspective, she argues, that feminist art is often criticized for 'belaboring its points', for defending its right to be what it is, rather than using the same energy to create something new. There is some truth to this. Much feminist theatre since 1968 has used polemic, and some has jeopardized its popular success and its claim to 'literary or dramatic integrity' by emphasizing feminist politics at the expense of the theatrical event. But a defensive attitude is not misplaced in feminist politics or theatre. As Mary McCusker has pointed out in regard to her work with Monstrous Regiment, there are always those who ask certain questions about feminist theatre work, and who take their 'answers' and apply them inappropriately, seeming to look at the work from 'totally the wrong angle'. Perhaps, as Joan Lipkin has suggested, the obstruction is caused by 'excess cultural baggage' getting in the way of clear vision. But it is too easy to question the play rather than the apparatus which measures its 'worth'.

In my view, *The Search for Signs of Intelligent Life in the Universe* is an exemplary piece of feminist theatre for all of the reasons listed above and for one other reason, which Marilyn French articulated when she wrote that the play

> simply takes it as a given that a mass audience will accept feminist attitudes, that proceeds on the assumption that these attitudes are shared and that therefore does not lecture, hector or even underline.... Underlying the gentle laughter that is a Tomlin/ Wagner hallmark is the conviction that we have some power to alter the course of our world as well as our own lives. And that message is received by the audience.[5]

In the second part of this chapter, I will list some other plays and performance pieces which I consider to be 'good feminist theatre'. First it is important to clarify a point.

Some of this discussion of the valuing of feminist theatre has assumed that all judgments come from on high – from the apparatus, its architects and designated operators. Not so. Feminist theatre work is judged by its makers, audiences, and by sympathetic feminist critics. All have something at stake, and all want to be sure that quality is controlled to some extent, while providing space for the airing of subversive ideas. For those of us whose job it is to criticize and review theatre, as well as to make it and theorize about it, the issue of sisterly solidarity is a minefield of conflicting values and allegiances.

The same issues of diversity and difference, or 'identity politics', which separated some women from men, and some women from other women in the theatre groups of the early 1970s, can still be seen to be separating women working in feminist theatres, or writing about them, today. And of course, one of the most pressing 'potential problems' of feminist theatres is the relationship between practice and theory – between the values of theatre makers and academic critics. But, as I have argued elsewhere, these are 'potential problems', not inevitable or insurmountable ones. They can be solved partially, or at least mitigated, by the concerted effort of both practitioners and theorists to see (if not see from) the perspective of the other.[6]

The reconciliation of practice and theory is obstructed when issues of multi- or transculturalism are considered. It is hard enough to reconcile the practices and theories of women making and studying feminist theatres in Britain. When the different economic and political patterns of the United States are considered by way of comparison, the differences between practices and theories become more numerous, if not necessarily more complex. When the cultural contexts of Third World nations and First World peoples are also considered, it becomes almost impossible to draw up a list of practices and theories which feminist theatres share. First, it is difficult to define 'feminism' in a way which might possibly be relevant to so many different contexts. But perhaps more importantly, the very idea that all these cultural contexts have the same needs for feminist theatres – or for any forms of theatre – is highly suspect. Different cultures have different ideas about 'culture', and about theatre. Some cultures use ritual drama in religious ceremonies. This is also theatre. Some of the richer world nations have highly class-specific forms of entertainment such as the 'Royal and National' Theatres of England. This is theatre. It is not necessarily transcultural: it will not necessarily appeal to people from non-English cultures.

I have discussed some of the implications of multiculturalism within British and American theatres. Experimental theatres have begun to work with multilingual texts and multicultural casts. Alternative forms of communication – such as Sign Language, body language and mime – have been incorporated into theatre work, in order to extend the reach of theatre languages. What theatre languages are, or can be, or consist of, are huge questions. Whether there may be a 'women's language in the theatre' is one of the many questions related to this larger search for the meaning of theatre as a form of communication and a reflection of social relations. Sue-Ellen Case has analysed the idea of a 'women's morphology', discussing the formal expression of non-linearity in some women's theatre work, as well as issues of 'women's language' *per se*.[7] This area of study deserves much more attention, with regard to a range of issues within and outside feminist theoretical discourses. Case's conception of a 'women's morphology,' for instance, may be extended by other scholars in future, with reference to bilingual and multilingual theatres, and in relation to the 'search for a women's language' in the theatre.

Though linguists and fiction writers have examined the idea of a 'women's language', and though Suzette Haden Elgin has created Láadan (an original language with its own vocabulary, offering new words to express concepts and ideas particular to women's experiences), these kinds of languages have not yet been used in the theatre. It may be the case, in fact, that the creation of a 'women's language' such as Láadan is not compatible with the aims of those feminist theatres which seek to convey political messages and to effect social change. It is difficult enough to do this with a shared language such as English. Yet a 'women's language' might be suited to some women's theatre – might even be created or generated by it. And in this sense, the theatre may be the most constructive forum for the devising of a new 'women's language' which could incorporate body language and gesture, as well as the spoken word.

Yet even the suggestion that such an idea might be explored seems to 'gesture' toward essentialist conceptions of 'the female'. Can it be assumed, for instance, that there is a set of 'women's gestures' or ways of moving and interacting in space? In Native American Indian ritual dramas and in the Kabuki and Nō of Japan, movement is both stylized and gender-specific. The cultural specificity of certain ways of moving, certain gestures, is of course related to social norms of women's representation: costume (in everyday life as well as in the theatre) and women's freedom of expression are to be considered. Yet surely each set of gestures, rituals, costumes and customs is culturally specific, is defined in relation to cultural ideas about 'women's roles' which are not necessarily translatable across cultures. For this reason, it is difficult to make any informed and responsible statements about 'women's gestures' or 'women's ways of moving' *per se*.

Before moving on to discussion of some theoretical perspectives and their possible contributions to feminist theatre practice, I want to examine the basic idea that cultural specificity informs different feminist theatres. Gayatri Chakravorty Spivak and Nadine Gordimer have written, in very different contexts, about the complexities of cultural specificity. In an interview in which she discussed her views on the role(s) of feminist theory, reader reception theory and literary criticism, Spivak was asked whether she thought that 'literary criticism can be a kind of, let's say, feminist literary guerrilla warfare towards the readers'. The strange wording of the question suggests that feminist literary criticism attacks its readers from the margins, and does so in an aggressive and rather underhand way. Spivak replied:

I suppose it can be. But then again, would one have to assume a sort of 'kneecapping' position, as if women are history transcendent? Of course there is a sort of euphoria in that. But, nonetheless, I think as a long-term proposition, it won't last in the wash. Guerrilla warfare takes place where guerrilla warfare takes place, and that's not literary criticism.[8]

In other words, Spivak accepts the idea that some feminist literary criticism may operate like 'guerrilla warfare', as a kind of attack from the margins on mainstream literary critical ideas, but she questions the notion that this is a general characteristic of feminist literary criticism. Most importantly, she questions this idea because of its implicit assumption that women might be 'history transcendent' – that women as a group can be identified with each other and assigned to the margins, or that they can transcend the history of marginalization through writing feminist literary criticism, or (her words suggest) through any other activity.

In an essay on 'The essential gesture', which explores the relationship of 'the writer's freedom' to social and political contexts in European, Third World and South African literatures, Nadine Gordimer has written:

It remains difficult to dissect the tissue between those for whom writing is a revolutionary activity no different from and to be prac- tised concurrently with running a political trade union or making a false passport for someone on the run, and those who interpret their society's demand to be 'more than a writer' as something that may yet be fulfilled through the nature of their writing itself.[9]

Like Spivak, Gordimer sees writing as a political activity or tool, but also distinguishes between those who set out to use writing in this way, and those for whom writing is an end, or art, in itself. There is a compelling similarity between Gordimer's conception of writing as a revolutionary activity, and Spivak's acceptance of the idea that writing feminist literary criticism may, for some, be a form of 'guerrilla warfare'. Neither critic presents the political aims of writing as a negative characteristic. Neither suggests that there would be anything wrong with using writing – whether of literary criticism or other forms of literature – as political weapons or tools. It is therefore interesting to go back to the statement made in interview by playwright Pam Gems, quoted in chapter 1. Gems said: 'I think the phrase "feminist playwright" is absolutely meaningless because it implies polemic, and polemic is about changing things in a direct political way. Drama is subversive.'[10]

These words echo those of Spivak and Gordimer in interesting ways. What Gems perceives is the nature of the theatre – distinguishing it from literature or literary criticism – as a live art form in which political change can be effected directly, as in guerrilla warfare. And of course, many of the earliest feminist theatre groups in Britain and America developed out of 'Guerrilla Street Theatres' – political companies delivering direct polemical statements through their theatres. In the context of contemporary feminist theatres, then, Gems' perspective is important. What might be read as a denial of the feminist theatre label can be re-read as an informed statement about the imprecision of that label, about the need for accuracy in terminology, especially when theatre (or writing) is to be used in direct political ways.

The exigencies of defining the terms and specifying the aims of feminist theatres here emerge, once again, as potentially problematic. But rather than interpreting these 'potential problems' in negative ways, it may be best to see them as enabling problems – ones which call for further examination and consideration, and which thereby keep the theory of feminist theatre alive by questioning it, and pushing its boundaries further toward practice.

In conclusion, perhaps it is most important to emphasize that despite all the 'potential problems' facing feminist theatres, the work of WTG, Monstrous Regiment, Gay Sweatshop and some 243 other feminist and pro-feminist theatre groups continues, with or without adequate funding or public recognition and awards. New groups are continually formed, while others disband and regroup. Thus, all manner of surveys, questionnaires, interviews and empirical studies are helpful in the project of studying feminist theatre in relation to the 'standards' of British theatre. Yet a new theory of feminist theatre is needed – one which would incorporate the views of practitioners and of audiences. Such a theory, in my view, should not be focused exclusively on certain varieties of feminist thought, but rather should accommodate differences of perspective. It should also be flexible enough to change with the times. In this kind of approach, theory might instructively and constructively meet practice.

BRINGING PRACTICE TOGETHER WITH THEORY

Feminist approaches to the theory of performance

In 1984, Susan Bassnett published a key paper entitled 'Towards a theory of women's theatre'.[11] Bassnett cited developments in the theatres and cultures of Western Europe and the United States as well as of Britain. She concluded that the subject of women's theatre would benefit from extended debate, and would necessarily involve consideration of 'women's experience', and also of audience involvement in the development of new theatrical forms. Bassnett's work, and that of others since, has contributed substantially to a growing body of scholarship on the subject of 'women's theatre' in an international context. Some of this work has dealt with 'feminist theatre', variously defined, but little has had any particular resonance for the study of cross-cultural theatres.

In defining feminist theatre as distinct from women's theatre, and in surveying practical developments in the field, this book has begun to articulate some of the elements to be incorporated into a new theory of feminist theatre. Theoretical ideas articulated by women such as Susan Bassnett and Jill Dolan have contributed substantially to this project. In addition, in recent years various feminist film, literary, and social theorists have been engaged in the process of developing a theory, or set of theories, to help analyse and criticize the images of women which are encoded in the cultural representations of contemporary societies. These have been incorporated in the body of the book, where they have informed the study of different kinds of feminist theatre, and of different plays.

Before outlining my own contribution 'toward a theory of feminist theatre', I will consider briefly some of the most relevant contributions made by others. All of these, significantly, involve consideration of the role of the audience. Indeed, most contemporary performance theory (feminist or not) has included discussion of the audience.

Gillian Elinor's essay on 'Performance as an audience activity', though little known, is worthy of attention as it offers an account of the subversive potential of feminist theatre. Elinor has argued that feminist theatre in performance subverts the expectations of the men and non-feminist women in its audiences, in ways which they may find pleasing despite themselves.[12] This argument is significant for two reasons: first, because it assumes an audience of critical spectators, and second, because it conceives of a potential for change in relation to the perspectives of a wide range of people. Rather than argue that the feminist theatre audience is important because it is feminist (i.e., because it is composed of feminist women), Elinor argues that the audience is important because of the diversity of perspectives of its members, and because of the theatre's potential to 'convert' some spectators to a feminist way of seeing. In this view, feminist theatre does more than 'preach to the converted': it affects a range of spectators in different ways.

In *The Feminist Spectator as Critic*, Jill Dolan argued that the feminist audience of the late 1980s was significantly different from that of the 1970s or early 1980s – that audiences had grown increasingly cynical and critical.[13] In arguing that the feminist performer, critic and spectator all engage in the process of redirecting the gaze, Dolan introduced the idea of the 'spectator as critic' into the theoretical vocabulary. In some of her later work, she reformulated this idea with reference to gender, arguing that one of the most significant aspects of feminist theatre is the shift in the gendered perspective of its audience – that the traditional dramatic canon has assumed a male or male-biased spectatorship which called itself 'universal', whereas feminist performance offers the possibility of a female spectatorship which does not call itself universal, does not subsume the male spectator, but rather allows for differences of perspective.

Dolan's work has clearly influenced academics such as Loren Kruger, whose conception of the 'spectacle' of feminist performance is quoted in the keynote. In another discipline, social theorists such as Erving Goffman have discussed the implications of 'performing self' in society.[14] It is this complicated idea which is at the root of developing theories of self in performance such as those which inform Lesley Ferris' work on the subject of 'acting women'. The basic idea is that women represent self in acting, both on stage and in life. But the idea is not as simple as it sounds. The dynamic of the theatre – as opposed to the performances of everyday life – is unique in terms of the presence of an immediate and critical body of spectators. The theatre space encourages immediate reactions from the audience, and permits a level of criticism which is not deemed appropriate in most forms of social interaction. Therefore, developing theories of self in performance must consider the unique qualities of the live theatre performance.

But consideration of academic views alone is not sufficient. Practitioners have also expressed views about the role of the audience. For instance, Deborah Levy has acknowledged her interest in and dependence upon the audiences of her plays, an interrelation which she describes as 'structuring the audience's attention'. Levy contends that:

> Ideology is buried implicitly in the structures of our creative work: in our writing for the theatre, we place the audience by picturing it, and place our words on the page by visualizing their presence in the mouths of performers, in the playing space, the space of address, where we assemble our attentions, direct them and let them be perceived by others.[15]

Here, Levy implicitly connects performance practice to the theory of the audience, by emphasizing the effects of space, language, ideology, theory and criticism, on the writer and on her intended audience.

The live audience and its physical proximity to the performance space is the factor which distinguishes theatre from film and television, lending an immediacy to spectatorship in and of the theatre, which electronically mediated forms do not share (for even in 'live' television, the performers cannot see the spectators, and the interaction is therefore not as reflexive or as complete). In the absence of audience involvement, the capacity for redirecting the gendered gaze is greatly reduced. In film, the camera (or director) refocuses the gaze for the spectator. In the theatre, however, the audience must redirect its own gaze, with 'directions' or cues provided by the director, but cues which originate from a shared sense of the performance's overall dynamic. In the theatre, the spectator is not only the critic, but also an actor – a person who actively engages in the dynamic of performance by directing her or his own gaze, and interpreting accordingly. In criticizing by participating, and finally, by giving the immediate 'reward' of applause, the live theatre audience provides both the stimulus and response which allow the performance – as on-going project, staged night after night – to continue.

The role of the audience in any performance, whether it be a theatre production, a political demonstration or an academic lecture, is inevitably influenced by gender. Gender is a particularly important consideration in terms of theatre audiences, due to the female majority of theatre-goers (shown in chapter 2 to hold fairly steadily across all sections of the theatre community). Yet the gender of the audience in feminist theatres is most significant, for in feminist theatre, it is not only the number of women which influences the stage–audience dynamic, but also the level of identification between performers and spectators, or what can be called the extra-scenic gendered gaze.

The concept of the 'gendered gaze' has informed discussion throughout the book. The theory of the gaze is useful in that it provides a framework for analysis of values associated with seeing and interpreting images. In locating the dynamics of gender and power associated with the gaze, some theorists have become caught up in analysis of visual images and points of view. This kind of approach emphasizes the spectator's role in the performance, and usefully so. But an increasing emphasis on the spectator, as Jill Dolan has argued, may not only extend the idea of 'the death of the author', but may also – in the extreme instance – begin to conflate the specific roles of writers, directors and performers. That is, the importance of the spectator's active engagement within the performance may begin to displace more practical concerns: the intentions of practitioners are not best served by ignoring their 'roles' altogether. Rather, a balanced and interactive exchange between stage and audience is the most effective dynamic. The audience is important, but so is the performance. The active engagement of the audience and the active roles of practitioners are both necessary to the process of change which is the aim of feminist theatre.

In terms of cultural value, feminist theatre functions as a form of self-representation by women. The idea that women's performance is a form of public spectacle can be examined in the light of a number of different theoretical perspectives. The perspective which has most relevance to performance, however, is not theoretical but practical. Making theatre involves entering the public domain, becoming part of the spectacle of women's changing roles in society. The study of 'women's roles' in the theatre, in society, and in popular culture is related to and complicated by theoretical notions of agency, positionality, subjectivity and difference. Thus, I argue for a theory influenced by practice. With this kind of theory, it might be possible to reconsider Loren Kruger's concept of the ambiguous identity of feminist theatre in a way which contributes to a new theory of feminist theatre. Women have long been thought to 'make spectacles of themselves', but have only recently been recognized as the creators or makers of legitimate spectacles worthy of public attention and critical consideration. In the theatre – and particularly in feminist theatre, which self-consciously represents the concerns, and often the bodies, of women – the making of theatrical spectacle not only 'usurps' the power of creation, but also assumes the right to re-view the criteria according to which creative work is valued.

And here again, the issue of 'standards' rears its ugly head. Feminist criticism of feminist theatre is not easy to write, or to read. We all have so much at stake, and there are so many land mines buried beneath the surface, including the honest expression of differences within feminisms and the personal preference for certain kinds of theatre, but also the danger of being accused of 'cat-fighting' or of being unsisterly when we offer constructive criticism. How to take others seriously enough to criticize them, without running the risk that our criticism will encourage others to take them less seriously, or to ignore them altogether? These are real issues. In a British context, where so few women have made so much feminist theatre, and where so few women have positions as critics with notable presses, it is unlikely that the woman or company whose work you write about will not know you, will not take your criticism at a personal (rather than professional) level. But the answer cannot be 'sisterly' approval and praise for everything.

Both feminist critics and feminist theatre practitioners are aware of the problems involved in writing critically about feminist work. Perhaps, in thinking critically about the function of theatrical and academic feminist work, it may be possible to find a way to inform feminist criticism with a sense of its larger political importance. But of course, this is easier said than done. Joan Lipkin has responded to this point in interview. She said:

> It's very difficult not to take criticism personally. But it was crucial for me to learn to do so, or at least to try. And you know, that's where feminism comes in.
>
> . . . Feminism saved my life. It helped me to realize that I wasn't personally responsible for everything – that some of the limitations I seemed to butt up against as a woman had to do with my role, my social construction in society, and the economic and political and social forces that were at work. Now, having recognized those forces, I have to ask myself: what are my strategies for intervening and taking responsibility for myself and my choices in society? . . . From that position of recognition, it's possible to feel encouraged and empowered, and you can develop creative strategies for what you're going to do next. That's very important.[16]

The issue of personal responsibility which Lipkin identifies relates to critics and academics as well as to theatre makers. Feminists in many different contexts have had to come to terms with the issue of 'blaming the victim',

and it is time that the survivors of this process came together in a constructive way.

Exemplary plays and performance pieces

In the effort to instigate further debate on the matter of 'what makes good
feminist theatre', I offer a selection of what I consider to be exemplary
British feminist plays and performance pieces.

1. Gay Sweatshop's *Care and Control*: because it took the social issue
   of child custody out of the courts and onto the stage, relying on
   real-life stories and effecting social change through the depiction
   of those stories in the public sphere; because it offered positive
   representations of lesbian women and heterosexual women united
   in the attempt to address a common problem; and because the
   play was inspired by the demands of an audience who wanted to
   see more 'women's issues' addressed in the work of Gay Sweatshop
   (this creation of a play in response to an identifiable feminist
   audience is very important).

2. Caryl Churchill's *Top Girls*: because it is experimental in form,
   using overlapping dialogue and skewed time frames; because it
   'reclaims' women from history and gives them voices; because it
   brings together many different people in its audiences, encouraging
   contemporary women and men to look at the situation of the
   working mother and career woman, without suggesting that there
   are easy answers or that everyone should try to be a 'superwoman';
   and because it reached massive audiences and focused public
   attention on the real conflicts which many women face in juggling
   work and family responsibilities, in the context of societies which
   do not yet provide adequate resources for working women.

3. Sarah Daniels' *Masterpieces*: because it takes one of the most controversial issues in the study of cultural representation and gender
   (pornography) and puts it on the stage in a direct political way.
   While the play can be criticized for its prioritizing of feminist
   politics above 'literary value', this is hollow criticism which misses
   its mark. The play is undoubtedly and unashamedly feminist. It
   urges social thought and action, while providing a riveting theatre
   experience.

4. Bryony Lavery's *Her Aching Heart*: because it represents lesbian
   experience in a serious and a comic way; because it is so well
   written, so clever, so moving and so entertaining; because the
   quality of the writing and the use of language is extraordinarily
   refined; because it subverted audience expectation and theatrical
   'traditions' with and through the medium of comedy.

5. Black Mime Theatre Women's Troop's *Mothers*: because it communicates through gesture, mime, spoken language and body language (thereby making itself accessible to a very wide audience); because it depicts the situations of black women in realistic ways, and does so with the help of humour and song; because it does not suggest that 'black women's experiences' are completely different from those of other women, but rather shows the effects of poverty and class/race-based prejudices on the lives of a few black British women.

6. Women's Theatre Group's *Lear's Daughters*: because of its potential to infuse young audiences with a budding feminist consciousness, as it takes a standard text often studied in schools and reframes it, creating women characters and putting them centre-stage.

7. Monstrous Regiment's *Medea*: because it is clearly informed by feminist thought on the subject of giving voice to women who have been silenced in the past; because it re-presents a mythic character in a way which makes it possible to understand her, but does not imply that the audience should necessarily like or admire her; because it raises issues of linearity and formal structures influenced by gender, but does so indirectly and does not 'preach' at the audience; because it dares to show the dilemma of a woman torn between her own values and the value of loyalty to another woman; and most of all, because it dares to pose questions and not to offer easy answers.

8. Victoria Worsley and Caroline Ward's *Make Me A Statue*: because it offers visual, physical, engaging viewing while it inspires thought about the treatment of women artists; because it is so clearly informed by feminist theory, and by a continental training in movement and physical theatre; because it challenges the traditional boundaries between dance and theatre and performance art, and does so implicitly, in the context of the moving story of one woman, portrayed by one (moving) woman who makes statues.

Another performance piece which can be viewed either as 'British' or as 'international' is the Magdalena Project's *Midnight Level Six*, a large-scale performance piece which puts twelve women on stage (a rare thing in itself) and which provides the opportunity for those women to tell their stories, while also giving space to larger themes of social relevance to women and men, and while offering a (sometimes harrowing and sometimes frustrating, but always engaging) 'good night out'. An American play and a South African play deserve mention as well: Jane Wagner's *The Search for Signs of Intelligent Life in the Universe* is closely observed, sardonic, hilariously funny at points; and it represents women's everyday

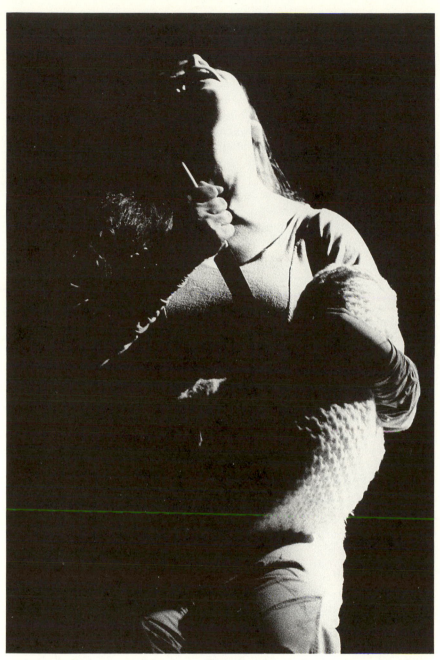

10 Susan Vidler in the Magdalena Project's *Midnight Level 6*, directed by Jill Greenhalgh, 1991.

life experiences in an amusing and thought-provoking way, while challenging assumptions about the forms and themes which are appropriate for main-stage (Broadway) audiences. Gcina Mhlophe's *Have You Seen Zandile?* uses the oral story-telling tradition (a form which is accessible to women around the world, despite class and race oppression and access to education) and offers the experiences of a South African black woman in a way which is engaging, entertaining, moving and humorous, as well as effective in raising consciousness of racial prejudice and cultural politics. These two plays are completely different in style, form, content and intent. They are both feminist in some sense, depending upon who is defining the term, and to what purpose.

My list is eclectic. I might write a different one tomorrow, or if the purpose were different (if, for instance, I were trying to defend feminist theatre in a mainstream context, rather than inviting thoughtful response from a self-selecting audience of readers and critics). The list includes a few plays which might be considered to have 'literary worth', yet it is primarily composed of plays and performance pieces which are chosen for their feminist content and intent, or for their form. Most are available in print, though *Make Me A Statue* and *Medea* have not been published. Several of these plays involved male as well as female performers. All were written and most were directed by women.

A few of these plays and performance pieces incorporate elements of visual theatre, physical theatre and mime, while others are more traditionally text-based. Some are devised and some are 'authored'. Some are plays and some are performance pieces and some fall outside the scope of such distinctions. Thus, the list does not reflect one set of standards, but rather offers a series of possible guidelines for measuring the 'value' of feminist theatre work. Yet this list may offer a starting place for dialogue about the nature of feminist theatre work, and the ambiguous identity of a 'feminist aesthetic' in British and international theatres.

The reasons for 'valuing' each of the plays and performances are all quite different. Yet each has to do with a social significance to the work, which may or may not be combined with literary or dramatic integrity. Of course, each piece 'works' in some way, or it would not be worth watching. Some work through comedy, some through political consciousness-raising, and others through that amorphous thing generally called 'entertainment' (while some combine two or more of these measures of 'value').

I expect that many, perhaps most, readers of this book – all of whom read and write from different perspectives and for different reasons – will disagree with my choices. So it should be. But here, my key phrase 'to each her own' will not work. Of course each critic and reader and practitioner will have slightly different sets of criteria for measuring 'standards', and will be influenced by personal preferences and political bias, sexual orientation, generation, culture, class and race, as well as gender. Yet if we each stubbornly defend our own ideas of 'what makes good (feminist) theatre', no dialogue will develop. Opening up the dialogue, across cultures and between feminisms, might lead to social change of a very important kind – to communication among those interested and active in the making and reviewing of feminist theatres.

I'd like to add two other performances to the list. Neither has been published or is available in printed form. Neither is a 'play' as such. The first is Reno's *Reno Once Removed*, a one-woman piece conceived, written and performed by Reno, one of New York's most outrageous feminist comic performers.[17] The performance is very engaging and extremely funny – filled with contemporary political satire and observational humour. But more important than the text is its performance context. The show was included in the New York Shakespeare Festival's 1991 Season at the Public Theatre. The performance has absolutely nothing to do with Shakespeare (several of the shows in that season did not), and some audience members clearly had not known what to expect. The staging of *Reno Once Removed* – whether accidentally or intentionally – had the effect of a hit and run on some conservative members of the audience. It was definitely not 'preaching to the converted', but it did, it seemed, raise a few consciousnesses as well as eyebrows.

The other non-scripted feminist performance which deserves attention on very different grounds is Mara de Wit's 'academic paper' for the 'Creation, Process, Output' conference on 'Twentieth-Century Perspectives on Women and Theatre', held at Warwick University in 1990.[18] Mara de Wit trained as a performer, choreographer and theatre director and has worked extensively in Holland, India, Nepal, the United States, England and Wales. In 1983, she founded the Research and Navigation Dance/ Theatre Company, based in mid-west Wales. She currently works primarily in London, as an actress and Lecturer in Performing Arts (she did an M.A. in 'gender, self, and performance'). At the Warwick conference, de Wit offered an academic lecture, or what was billed as such in the day's schedule. When her time to talk came around, however, she entered the auditorium from the back of the room, in frilly costume and exotic (wild, long blond) wig, singing. She made her way to the podium and began to perform her solo/lecture. She read some words, but upstaged herself as she spoke by removing the wig and undressing herself. The audience members – including myself – were torn between trying to pay attention to her words and watching her actions, asking ourselves just what she was up to and wanting to laugh or applaud, but not sure whether we should. This performance, which de Wit calls *Self as Source*, was the most powerful demonstration of the 'coming together of practice and theory' which I have ever witnessed.

Reno's mainstreamed feminist comedy is difficult to compare with Mara de Wit's academic performance. These 'shows' were performed in different countries, in different types of venue and to different audiences. Yet both shows worked with similar means, combining the expected with the unexpected, using feminist ideas and personal experiences to make larger points, while being quite careful to entertain their audiences in the process. These two shows are not what most people think of when they hear the term 'feminist theatre'. That is, in part, why I have taken the space to include them here.

These, like the thirteen plays listed above, are all forms of feminist theatre. They are controversial choices for a list of exemplary productions. The guardians of 'quality control' would argue, no doubt, that a more rigid set of 'standards' is needed for the judging of exemplary feminist theatre work. But I have chosen this eclectic set of performances for this very reason – in order to illustrate that, whatever set of criteria is assigned for 'controlling' or measuring the quality of feminist theatre, some excellent work will fall through the cracks, into the interstices of definitions and standards.

But this is not to say that there should be no set values. Certainly, not everything made by feminists is 'good feminist theatre'. Any critical apparatus must be critical, must offer both a framework for discussion and a set of criteria which can be used to measure relative values. The problem is finding a set of criteria which is flexible enough to take into account very different forms of 'quality'. It is for this reason that most of those who write on the subject skirt the question of aesthetic values. While no single set of criteria will 'suit' every kind of feminist theatre, it is nevertheless important to outline a broad and flexible set of considerations which might usefully be applied to the study of feminist theatre. In developing my set of criteria, theory has followed practice. That is, the criteria which follow have been drawn from a close study of British feminist theatre work, with more limited access to theatres of the United States, Canada, Mexico, Italy, Bulgaria, Jamaica and South Africa. The 'values' which evolve from the following attempts to build up a 'new theory' of feminist theatre are based upon the (stated and perceived) needs of practitioners and academics in those cultures.

Toward 'a new theory' of feminist theatre(s)

How to arrive at one theory for the many and varied forms of feminist theatres? And what would make such a theory, if one could be agreed upon, 'new' if it develops from previous ideas and developments in theatre practice? The attempt to articulate one such theory is overly ambitious even within the British context, and ludicrous in a larger international framework. Yet it's worth a try. Rather than propose an ambitious and all-encompassing theory, this section outlines some of the criteria which would best be included in the development of a new theory of feminist theatres. It draws upon and extends the findings of the book as a whole, focusing on the ideas which have emerged as appropriate to the critical study of feminist theatre. In summarizing the findings of the book, however, a 'new theory' does begin to emerge. 'Aesthetic' considerations have a place in this theory, as do the requirements of performance.

Five major ideas have emerged from the argument of this book:

1. The importance of the role of the audience.
2. The importance of taking account of working practices and the views of practitioners in any developing theory (influenced by the discovery that a great deal of feminist theatre has been created by a very small group of women).
3. A recognition of a diversity of feminist approaches and ideas.
4. The need to develop ways of assessing and evaluating feminist theatre which do not simply borrow from established traditions of literary criticism.
5. The importance of recognizing the shifting nature of both feminist ideas and theatrical forms and structures.

These five ideas can contribute to the development of a new theory of feminist theatre.

The role of the audience is significant for two reasons: because it informs the making of feminist theatre, and because the making of the theatre is informed by it. The process is reciprocal. The making of feminist theatre is informed by the role of the audience in so far as practitioners have conceptualized a new audience for their theatre (in the significant shift in gender, or assumed gender, of the spectator). This conceptualization of audience has influenced the choice of themes and the forms of representation chosen by practitioners. Yet feminist theatre is not only received and interpreted, but also influenced by its audience. It does not merely 'preach to the converted', but challenges traditional images and ideas, and may thereby 'convert' some members of its audience by redirecting their views on (or ways of viewing) representations of women in culture. In return, the responses of audiences – in the form of applause, reviews and funding, for instance – influence the theatre itself. When feminist theatres survey their own audiences, the reciprocity of the stage–world dynamic is extended.

The reciprocal relationship between the stage and the audience, the makers and spectators of feminist theatre, is related to the second idea which has emerged from the book: the importance of taking account of working practices and the views of practitioners in any developing theory. A theory based on ideas of interpretation and reception without reference to working practices would fall short of the needs of the theatre itself, while a discussion of theatre practice alone would have only a limited value in on-going theoretical debates.

This book has considered theory in relation to practice, in order to build the foundations for future study. The Feminist Theatre Survey, and studies of audiences and particular theatre companies and working practices, have been intended to ground the theoretical material, not only for this book but also for future work. The discovery of a few key women whose contributions account for a great deal of post-1968 British feminist theatre is important for this same reason. Interviewing these women and recording their views (while they are still alive and making theatre) has added a certain degree of long-term value to the study. The book has built up a base of published and recorded information which may be of use to future practitioners and critics, in that it helps to fill the gap in existing scholarship, and to form an archive of accessible material on cross-cultural feminist theatres.

The third idea which has emerged from the book is a recognition of a diversity of feminist approaches and ideas. Feminist theatres encourage a gender-aware gaze, but do not restrict the range of possible gazes within any play or performance dynamic. They are created largely by women informed by the post-1968 women's movements, though the concerns of the seven demands articulated by that movement (in Britain and the United States) have gradually spread to include more generalized feminist concerns. The marginalization of many black women and women of colour, working-class women and lesbians within feminism has also begun to be recognized. Feminist theatre is informed by a very wide range of different perspectives, and by the views of both practitioners and theorists who are engaged in the creative processes of making and evaluating the same work. The reciprocal dynamic of feminist theatre is not limited to the relationship between the performance and the audience, but also informs and enriches the relationship between practitioners and critics of different generations and with different 'situated perspectives'.

The fourth idea emerging from this book, and the one which has framed the book in a sense, is the need to develop ways of assessing and evaluating feminist theatre which do not simply borrow from established traditions of literary criticism. These traditions are relevant to some extent, and the discussion of particular plays (primarily in the second part of the book) has shown that some measures of literary criticism can be applied to feminist theatre. This discussion, however, has been equally informed by reference to other disciplines: cultural studies, film studies and feminist theory. My approach does not exclude literary or 'aesthetic' arguments; nor does it privilege them. My concern has been to focus on the working practices of feminist theatre in the belief that a proper appraisal of that theatre should be based on a careful consideration of its existing forms and styles, with regard to production and performance contexts.

As Brecht's reference to the position of his own work in relation to the dominant critical 'apparatus' points out, measures of value are informed by many different factors, and may be constructed in different ways, for different purposes. Canonical values are based in part on certain 'aesthetic criteria', but have also been influenced by the structures of the academy. By contrast, commercial values are influenced by market forces. The same play might 'suit' one set of criteria, but not the other. One play might 'suit' both, or neither. Feminist theatres, like other forms of cultural representations, can be evaluated in accordance with different measures of value, depending upon the perspectives of different spectators and critics.

Feminist theatre has had a particularly problematic relationship, not only with measures of literary criticism, but also more immediately with the form of criticism found in mass-market newspaper reviews. A few reviews of feminist plays have been referred to, mainly in the context of illustrating the ways in which plays are received from the situated perspectives of (mostly male) reviewers. There is more to be said, however, about the operative dynamic of gender and power in theatre reviewing, not only in relation to reviews by men, but also in relation to (positive and negative) reviews by women, and to the larger problem of perspective associated with any writing for the popular press. There is space here only to outline the problem: theatre critics work for newspapers which have audiences of their own, in the form of readerships who buy certain papers for particular reasons. That is, reviews are encoded with certain sets of values. The readership of the newspaper, along with the power of the critic to influence the public reception of any play, are complicated by the situated perspectives of individual readers. And of course, in reviewing feminist theatre, the male majority of mainstream reviewers has a significant influence as well.

Future studies might focus on the relationship between theatre reviewing in the press and critical writing about the theatre in academia. Future work on the subject of feminist theatres might also develop the arguments outlined regarding the many different sets of criteria for measuring the 'value' of a form such as feminist theatre. Finally and most importantly, future studies might build upon the basic idea that feminist criticism can be constructively critical of feminist work.

Feminist theatre work is not placed above criticism by its feminist politics. Rather, it may invite negative criticism when politics are seen to take precedence over form or style. But the role of feminist reviewers must itself be considered in a critical light. The hesitation of many feminist critics to criticize feminist theatre is not based on an uncritical celebration of all feminist plays, nor is it solely motivated by a sense of loyalty or sisterhood among feminists. Rather, the hesitation of many critics, self included, to criticize feminist theatre work is based in large part on the difficulty of arriving at any fair set of measures for the valuing of feminist work, and on the basis of an awareness that there are more than enough unsympathetic reviewers (female as well as male) out there already.

Jill Dolan has observed that the male dominance of theatre reviewers is not the only problem. Female reviewers may also be unjust to feminist theatre, though for 'all the right reasons'. In Dolan's words:

> The feminist press has been slow to develop a feminist critique of performance. When they do cover theatre by women, feminist reviewers seem caught between applauding the woman's efforts and critiquing the work against a standard that is yet to be defined in the balance between ideology and art.[19]

Feminist theatres do tend to be defined and criticized in an (as yet unspecified) gap between 'ideology and art'. And as the opening reference to Brecht's conception of a dominant critical 'apparatus' points out, most sets of values are influenced by the vested interests of a dominant culture.

Because feminist theatre was formed and has developed in opposition to the hierarchical structures of patriarchal (dominant) culture, it seems particularly unjust to apply the standards of that culture to the valuing of feminist theatre. But without some set of measures or values for discussion of feminist theatre, the work may be in danger of being undervalued. In the current economic climate, the silence of reviewers may have devastating effects on theatre companies. Receiving negative reviews is at times (commercially) preferable to being ignored. The best means of silencing the voices of feminist (theatre) workers is to ignore them, or to 'damn with faint praise', thereby undermining the social significance of the work. Reviewers are powerful, and so are theorists and academics. Yet until very recently, feminist theatre has been largely ignored by academic critics.

At one level, this book has taken an academic approach to the subject of feminist theatre. It has explored the relationship between the content and intent of feminist theatre work. Yet there is a great deal still to be gained from further academic study of feminist theatre. An adequate 'standard' for measuring the relative value of feminist plays has not yet been defined. Perhaps this is because, as I have argued, no single set of measures is appropriate to all the different kinds of feminist theatre. Yet there are some basic and generally agreed criteria for evaluating the 'well-made play'. The most important and most relevant of these is the idea that form should match or 'suit' content. This idea need not limit the scope of possible forms of feminist theatre; it can be applied equally well to a study of a social realist play or an experimental performance theatre piece.

For instance, a performance piece such as *Make Me a Statue* might be considered in terms of the close correlation between its theme and its style. A deliberate and effective contrast between form and style might also be considered, as in Caryl Churchill's *Lives of the Great Poisoners*, wherein the multiple story-lines and fractured characters are paralleled by formal shifts from operatic song to overlapping conversation. Churchill's best work has been highly experimental in terms of language patterns and levels of interaction between characters, yet has been balanced by her talent for using language in eloquent as well as structurally effective ways. A play such as *Care and Control* is harder to define as aesthetically pleasing, yet it can be evaluated in different terms – as an effective social realist work which affected its audiences in positive ways. Comparing Wandor's work with Churchill's is not comparing like with like. Agitprop and social realism are not easily comparable with performance theatre, or with a story-telling narrative-based theatre such as Gcina Mhlophe's or Djanet Sears'. While formal considerations are relevant to the literary critical project of evaluating particular plays, other considerations may be more relevant to the project of evaluating feminist theatre as a form of cultural representation. A new theory of feminist theatre would allow for literary and formal criticism of individual plays, but would also distinguish between the 'valuing' of particular plays and of the larger genre of feminist theatre.

Lastly, a new theory of feminist theatre should recognize and accommodate the shifting nature of both feminist ideas and theatrical possibilities. In this, the phrase 'bringing theory together with practice' would become more than a phrase. While it is true that 'the forms of representation are determined by the dominant philosophical systems in culture at large', it is also true that these systems touch the lives of individuals, some of whom are the makers of theatre, and many of whom can understand theoretical jargon if they must, but prefer to communicate by other means.[20] Theory is important, and indeed necessary. But it must include some link not only to theatre practice, but also to an accessible language and set of ideas interesting to non-specialists.

In addition to the 'new poetics' which Case defines as informed by semiotic theory and French feminist theory, I want to argue for something much more practical: for a renewed interest in the 'performance' side of 'performance studies'. This would not cut short the work of theorists, but would rather begin to make their work more accessible to others – to students and theatre-goers, as well as theatre-makers. The relationship between the means and the ends of all theatre production is continually shifting. A theory of feminist theatre, therefore, must be a flexible one designed to take into account the contingencies of shifts in cultural climates and developments in feminist thought and activism.

A new theory of feminist theatre would most usefully encompass all 'brands' and subfactions within feminism, and various working methods and forms of theatrical representation as well. But as feminist theatre becomes more 'established', it runs the risk of becoming associated with the establishment. Such an association risks a further fracturing of feminist theatre. This fracturing may be re-viewed as a positive process – a breaking-off, regrouping and refocusing of the feminist theatre project.

With a flexible definition like that proposed in this book, which allows for differences between feminists, takes the needs and interests of practitioners into account and accommodates the politics of production, it may be possible to construct a broad and workable theory of 'feminist theatre'. Or rather, it may be possible to construct a theory of feminist theatre which informs, and is informed by, practice. Such a theory might usefully prioritize the role of the audience – in emphasizing the action involved in watching and interpreting the feminist performance, and in recognizing the political element of any such active spectatorship, the theory of feminist theatre could take a considerable step forward.

In any union of theory and practice, however, one must not be 'valued' above the other. Women's roles in life and in the theatre are always informed by each other. To some extent, they tend – like much of Caryl Churchill's dramatic dialogue – to overlap. Each individual chooses her own position in relation to those roles, and comes to her own conclusions about relative 'values' in making and evaluating cultural representations of different kinds.

Any useful critical apparatus must be flexible enough to 'suit' feminist theatre over time, as both feminism and the theatre continue to change. That is why it is crucial to emphasize, and re-emphasize, the basic tenet of this book: feminist theatre is a form of cultural representation affecting and affected by many and various disciplines. It is shaped and influenced by cultural as well as literary and dramatic factors. Thus, the term 'feminist theatre' can replace the terms 'art' and 'literature' in the following quotation:

> Art is first of all a social practice rather than an object to be academically dissected. We may see literature as a *text*, but may also see it as a social activity, a form of social and economic production which exists alongside, and interrelates with, other such forms.[21]

It may seem strange for an author born and raised in the United States – in a period when socialism was not widely taught in the New York public school system, and particularly now that the 'new world order' is questioning Marxist values on life and art – to align a basic Marxist definition of the value of art to her study of feminist theatres. Or is it strange? It is crucial to the feminist project of striving toward social change that all political perspectives and ways of seeing be examined and considered for their possible contributions 'toward a new theory of feminist theatre'.

I would state the basic tenets of such a tentative 'theory of feminist theatre' in this way: feminist theatres are those theatres created (primarily) by women with political concerns influenced by the development of the post-1968 women's movement(s), and/or by issues of real importance to the daily lives of women, both in terms of the concerns of local communities and of women around the world. These theatres may have many different functions. They may serve to entertain or to enlighten, to raise consciousness or to argue political points, or to represent women's life experiences in ways which make them 'real' subjects in public representation. The specification of 'what makes feminist theatre feminist' will vary from culture to culture, with the influence of social need and availability of resources to women and to theatre.

More importantly, the answer to the question 'what makes feminist theatre good theatre?' can be answered in terms of a flexible scale of values. If it serves a real purpose, to the bettering of women's lives or public understanding of women's lives, then it is 'good feminist politics' and perhaps also 'good theatre'. If it provides enlightenment or entertainment without dismissing or undermining women in the process, then perhaps it is 'good theatre'. (These same criteria might be applied to any number of plays by men whose work – while it is considered to have 'literary and dramatic value' – might be found to be 'bad theatre' on the grounds that it reinforces negative stereotypes of women.) If feminist theatre happens to have a high degree of 'literary value' or 'dramatic worth' as determined by traditional standards, that does not necessarily render it 'good theatre'.

Aesthetic value may enhance a play or performance as a work of art. Yet a play's aesthetic value will not bring about social change. The best feminist theatre invokes social change, whether on a large or an individual scale. It does so by making people think, by asking questions of itself and its audience – questions such as: What is a text? Is it a script, a performance, a reading, an idea collaboratively devised and never recorded? How do we define the relationship between texts and contexts? Is the performer's body a text of sorts? If so, who is in the best position to 'interpret' it? In an international context, issues raised by translation are duly translated into the playing space by the complex question of intertextuality in three dimensions, performed in the public sphere and interpreted by a critical audience of active spectators, in many different languages, including body language and gesture. Is there a women's voice in theatre? If so, can it be inscribed as a 'text'? Such questions will be differently posed from culture to culture, from generation to generation. Whether there's a woman in the text is one question; whether theatre must involve texts, and what kinds, is another. The answers will surely be sorted out in the playing space.

Of course, some might argue that my approach would allow for the creation and 'valuing' of some very boring theatre. Phrases such as 'preaching to the converted' will undoubtedly arise, as will arguments about the right of the audience to watch theatre which is visually engaging and entertaining. I argue in response to these anticipated objections that the audience does indeed have the right to be stimulated by theatre, to engage with theatre and possibly to be entertained. But this is not the same as saying that theatre must adhere to the 'quality control' guidelines of 'aesthetic worth'. Contemporary theatres abound with highly 'aesthetic', beautifully designed and extremely boring and predictable versions of the classics, from re-production of Greek plays to Ibsen and Shaw. This is fine. These plays are also available, under the heading 'dramatic literature', on the library shelves.

Feminist theatres do not pose a threat to other forms of theatre and drama, but only to those individuals and institutions who wish to elevate certain kinds of dramatic expression above others, under the guise of 'quality control'. Yet the extent to which the subject of feminist theatre – and indeed of Theatre Studies, though not to the same extent – is marginalized within academia seems to be a 'sign' that, as Jane Wagner's character Trudy observed, there are those who are afraid that it may all 'get out of hand'. Perhaps the fear is not wholly unfounded.

Despite the relative marginalization of the subject, and despite continual and continuing funding cuts, feminist theatres – in theory and in practice – continue to develop. Contemporary feminist theatres can be evaluated in relation to many different feminist perspectives and political frameworks, and in relation to both texts and contexts. Feminist theatre is an appropriate subject for academic study, and is also the form of cultural representation chosen by many different feminist women. A new theory of feminist theatre – or several new theories – might do well to balance these points in order to 'suit' the needs of the makers, as well as the spectators and critics, of feminist theatre. I hope that this book may contribute something original to the multiplicity of voices now expressing their views on the subject of feminist theatre. More importantly, however, I hope that the book will be of interest to the women who make feminist theatres, and who make this a subject 'worth' writing about.

CONCLUSION

I have argued that a new theory of feminist theatre would best be informed by the views of practitioners and the interpretations of audiences, as well as the ideas of critics and theorists; that feminist theatre is a form of cultural representation which can be considered in light of the relationship between practice and theory in feminism and cultural studies; and for the recognition of 'difference' not only as a theoretical term, but also as a practical approach to making feminist theatres.

Future work in this area might expand to include truly 'international studies' of feminist theatres, written by (not only about) women of colour and women of many different cultures. Yet there has been space in this book only to focus on Britain, with but a few sideways glances at the theatres and feminisms of other cultures. I have argued that British feminist theatres can be analysed in terms of class distinctions and gender hierarchies within a socialist government structure (albeit one which has been radically reshaped by the influence in recent years of Thatcher's and Major's Conservative policies), whereas in the United States, analysis of feminist theatres must take account of the political concerns of a capitalist economy.

Consideration of class issues is particularly relevant to the study of British feminist theatres, but is also a factor in the theatres and feminisms of other cultures. For instance, many feminist theatre practitioners (like the academics who write about them) are middle-class and reasonably well educated. In England, Caryl Churchill, Michelene Wandor, the members of Trouble and Strife and of Tattycoram all attended Oxbridge, and benefited from the relative wealth of student theatres, before 'going professional'. Similarly, many American feminist playwrights and directors come from reasonably well-off backgrounds and have had access to some higher education: Joan Lipkin could not criticize her critics so accurately if she had not been a critic herself; American performance artists could not construct such effective deconstructions of traditional art forms if they had not been taught about those traditions. In fact, many of the early American 'Guerrilla Theatres' were based at university and college cam-

241

puses, and many of the founders of British feminist theatres were college-educated activists. This is not a negative statement about privilege, but rather an important point to keep in mind in the current debates about academic language and the silencing of practitioners: the divide may not be as wide, nor as treacherous, as it sometimes appears to be. To some extent – and I'd like to believe, to a large extent – the 'gap between theory and practice' is itself an artificial construct.

Perhaps most important is the evidence provided of a generation of women who have created and attended most of the feminist theatres and feminist theatre productions in Britain since 1968. The same generation of women has had a significant influence in American feminist theatres, and – the early findings of a few researchers suggest – also in Australian and Canadian feminist theatres.[1] Many speakers at the 'Breaking the Surface' festival/conference held in Calgary observed that Canadian women's theatre has experienced similar generational trends, though many also argued that some of the work currently being produced in Canada continues to work with agitprop forms and themes, to a greater extent than the theatres of Britain and the United States.

Similarly, international conferences in Italy and Germany have revealed differences in approach to women's work in the theatre.[2] This is hardly surprising: cultural differences in approaches to feminism are bound to affect the development of women's theatres. The influence of conservative universities and funding bodies should not be ignored: at academic conferences and government-sponsored festivals, the politics of the events are most often expressed within the 'dominant ideology' of those power structures, and the women who organize are not always free to say and do as they like (or to invite anyone they please). Yet even in countries where feminism is not so strongly embraced by many of those running the theatres, there are nevertheless conferences and festivals on the subject of women's theatre. There must be some strong and determined feminists making these things happen.

While most feminist theatres of the 1970s were made by a relatively small group of women, the influence of those diverse theatres has been very profound. The audiences have been large and diverse. Their ways and means of questioning (and representing the questioning of) dominant social norms have affected a new generation's feminist work with the result that today it is possible and not unusual to discuss political action in theatrical terms, and theatre in political terms, from a feminist perspective and within any number of larger cultural frameworks.

One exemplary feminist theatre piece discussed in these pages is Mara de Wit's *Self as Source*. There are, of course, many others. From the performance art theatre of de Wit and Tattycoram, to the agitprop and feminist 'issue' plays discussed earlier, women in Britain have found many different ways of 'making spectacles'. Feminist theatre, as art form and as platform, continues to offer a means whereby women can perform personal politics and 'make spectacles' of their own. The differences between these spectacles, like the politics which inspire them and the individuals who create them, are situated in terms of politics, age, race, class, sexual orientation and access to higher education. Thus, contemporary feminist theatres take many forms and use many different working methods. They may embrace text and performance in different measures and for different reasons. Yet nearly all contemporary feminist theatres – and theories of those theatres – focus to some extent on the role of the audience, and on the theme of self-representation or 'self in performance'.

The multiplicity of perspectives represented, both on stage and in the role playing of everyday life, give feminist theatres their uniquely effective 'ambiguous identities'. At times, the ambiguity seems destructive and it is tempting to cry wolf, to argue that we must define or redefine 'feminism' and 'feminist theatre' – to determine a clear set of standards in order to prevent the genre from being dismantled altogether. But of course, the ambiguous identity of feminist theatre(s) is a tremendous strength. As one reviewer wrote, in describing the latest performance piece by the Omaha Magic Theatre: 'There is nothing quite like it in either Omaha or many other places.'³ Perhaps Dorothy was right, and we're not in Kansas any more. Or perhaps we haven't moved at all, but the landscape has changed and we can now see places and ideas worth exploring which have not yet been added to the map. These places are new kinds of feminist theatre, and new ways of approaching feminism(s) and theatre(s). Ambiguity is a very effective safeguard and can be embraced as an expression of positive difference. The more such differences are recognized and respected, the less treacherous the gap between theory and practice – if there is one, or need be one – may become.

On the eve of the new century and 'the new world order', the spaces and resources available to feminisms and theatres are not clearly designated. In Britain, as elsewhere, resources are dwindling even as interest in making, watching, studying and writing about feminist theatres continues to grow. It is my profound wish that some of the feminist theatres discussed will outlast the paper in this book. If not, then perhaps this book – like its precursors and others sure to follow – may help to keep some of these theatres alive, if only in the archives.

NOTES

INTRODUCTION

1 Nicole Ward Jouve, *White Woman Speaks With Forked Tongue: Criticism as Autobiography* (London: Routledge, 1991).

2 Mary McCusker of Monstrous Regiment, in unpublished interview with Clive Barker, 1985.

3 Plays by the four key feminist companies discussed in chapter 3 have all been published or commissioned for publication in the past few years: cf. Gabrielle Griffin and Elaine Aston (eds), *Herstory: Vols. 1 and 2*, plays by Women's Theatre Group (Sheffield: The Academic Press, 1991); Gillian Hanna (ed.), *Monstrous Regiment: A Collective Celebration* (London: Nick Hern Books, 1991); Philip Osment (ed.), *The Gay Sweatshop: Four Plays and a Company* (London: Methuen, 1989); and Griffin and Aston (eds), *Herstory: Vols. 3 and 4*, plays by Siren Theatre (Sheffield: The Academic Press, forthcoming). A second volume of *Lesbian Plays*, edited by Jill Davis, was published by Methuen in 1989, and a collection of three plays by Bryony Lavery, *Her Aching Heart, Two Marias, Wicked* (produced by Women's Theatre Group, Clean Break Theatre and Theatre Centre), was published by Methuen in 1991. See bibliography for full publication details on these and other new anthologies of plays by women.

4 *The Search for Signs of Intelligent Life in the Universe*, a one-woman play by Jane Wagner. Performed as work in progress in San Diego, Los Angeles, Seattle, Portland, Houston, Lexington, Atlanta, Aspen and Boston. Premiered in finished form by Lily Tomlin at the Plymouth Theater in New York on 26 Sept. 1985. Published with an 'Afterword' by Marilyn French (New York: HarperCollins Publishers, 1986).

5 Henry Lesnik (ed.), *Guerilla Street Theatre* (New York: Avon Books, 1973), p. 317.

6 Virginia Woolf, *A Room of One's Own* (London: Harcourt, Brace, Jovanovich, 1929); Peter Brook, *The Empty Space* (New York and London: Penguin, 1988, first published 1968).

7 I have published a series of Feminist Theatre Interviews in order to inform this and future studies by making current material – and the voices of practitioners – accessible in published form. See *New Theatre Quarterly*, vol. 6, nos. 21–3, 1990; vol. 7 nos. 25 and 28, 1991; and vol. 8, no. 32, 1992, and forthcoming issues.

8 Adrienne Rich, 'When we dead awaken: writing as re-vision', in *On Lies, Secrets and Silence: Selected Prose 1966–1978* (New York: W. W. Norton and Co., 1979), p. 35.

9 cf. Janet Brown, *Feminist Drama: Definition and Critical Analysis* (Metuchen,

244

NJ: Scarecrow Press, 1979); Dinah Luise Leavitt, *Feminist Theatre Groups* (Jefferson, NC: MacFarland and Co., 1980); Karen Malpede (ed.), *Women in Theatre: Compassion and Hope* (New York: Limelight Editions, 1985); Helen Krich Chinoy and Linda Walsh Jenkins (eds), *Women in American Theatre* (New York: Crown Publishers, 1981); Elizabeth J. Natalle, *Feminist Theatre: A Study in Persuasion* (Metuchen, NJ: Scarecrow Press, 1985); and Alice M. Robinson, Vera Mowry Roberts and Milly S. Barranger (eds), *Notable Women in American Theatre: A Biographical Dictionary* (Westport, CT: Greenwood Press, 1989).

10 Helene Keyssar, *Feminist Theatre* (New York: Macmillan, 1984); Sue-Ellen Case, *Feminism and Theatre* (London: Methuen, 1988).

11 Loren Kruger, 'The dis-play's the thing: gender and the public sphere in contemporary British theatre', *Theatre Journal*, vol. 42, no. 1, March 1990, p. 27; Kruger cites Keyssar, *Feminist Theatre* (1984), p. xi.

12 Lynda Hart (ed.), *Making a Spectacle: Feminist Essays on Contemporary Women's Theatre* (Ann Arbor: The University of Michigan Press, 1989).

13 Sue-Ellen Case and Janelle Reinelt (eds), *The Performance of Power: Theatrical Discourse and Politics* (Iowa: The University of Iowa Press, 1991).

14 Loren Kruger, 'The dis-play's the thing', *Theatre Journal*, vol. 42, no. 1, March 1990; Barbara Freedman, 'Frame-up: feminism, psychoanalysis, theatre', *Theatre Journal*, vol. 40, no. 3, Oct. 1988: reprinted in Sue-Ellen Case (ed.), *Performing Feminisms: Feminist Critical Theory and Theatre* (Baltimore: Johns Hopkins University Press, 1990). Also see *Women and Performance* and *TDR: The Drama Review*, both of which are connected with New York University's Tisch School of the Arts.

15 cf. Susan Bassnett (Susan E. Bassnett-McGuire), 'Notes on the work of Monstrous Regiment', in *British Drama and Theatre From The Mid Fifties to the Mid Seventies* (Rostock: Wilhelm-Pieck-Universitat, 1979); 'Towards a theory of women's theatre', in *Linguistic and Literary Studies in Eastern Europe*, vol. 10: *The Semiotics of Drama and Theatre*, eds. Herta Schmid and Aloysius Van Kesteren (Amsterdam and Philadelphia: John Benjamins, 1984); *Feminist Experiences: The Women's Movement in Four Cultures* (London: Allen & Unwin, 1986); *Magdalena: International Women's Experimental Theatre* (Oxford: Berg Publishers, 1989); Michelene Wandor, 'The impact of feminism on the theatre', *The Feminist Review*, vol. 18, Winter 1984; 'The Fifth Column: feminism and theatre', *Drama*, no. 152, 1984, pp. 5–9; *Look Back in Gender: Sexuality and the Family in Post-War British Drama* (London: Methuen, 1987); *Carry on Understudies: Theatre and Sexual Politics*, revised edn (New York: Routledge & Kegan Paul, 1986); (ed.), *Strike While the Iron is Hot: Three Plays on Sexual Politics* (London: Journeyman Press, 1980); Catherine Itzin, *Stages in the Revolution: Political Theatre in Britain Since 1968* (London: Methuen, 1980); Jill Davis (ed.), introductions to *Lesbian Plays*, vols. 1 and 2 (London: Methuen, 1987 and 1989); Lesley Ferris, *Acting Women: Images of Women in the Theatre* (Basingstoke: Macmillan, 1990). Also see James Redmond (ed.), *Themes in Drama II: Women in Theatre* (Cambridge: Cambridge University Press: 1989), and the introductions to the Methuen *Plays by Women* series, ed. Wandor (1982–5), Mary Remnant (1986–90) and Annie Castledine (1991).

1 CONTEMPORARY FEMINIST THEATRES

1 Loren Kruger, 'The dis-play's the thing: gender and the public sphere in contemporary British theatre', *Theatre Journal*, vol. 42, no. 1, March 1990, p. 27.

2 Sarah Daniels, introduction to *Plays: One* (London: Methuen, 1991), p. xii; Pam

Gems, interviewed by Ann McFerran in *Time Out*, 21–7 Oct. 1977 and revised slightly in personal correspondence with Lizbeth Goodman, 22 Jan. 1992; Megan Terry, interviewed in *Interviews with Contemporary Women Playwrights*, ed. Kathleen Betsko and Rachel Koenig (New York: Beech Tree Books, 1987), p. 398; Yvonne Brewster, interviewed by Lizbeth Goodman in *New Theatre Quarterly*, vol. 7, no. 28, Nov. 1991, p. 361; Ntozake Shange, interviewed in *Interviews with Contemporary Women Playwrights*, p. 369; Caryl Churchill, interviewed in *Interviews with Contemporary Women Playwrights*, p. 77; Gillian Hanna, interviewed by Lizbeth Goodman in *New Theatre Quarterly*, vol. 6, no. 21, Feb. 1990, p. 47; Joan Lipkin of That Uppity Theatre Company, St Louis, Missouri interviewed by Lizbeth Goodman, 15 Nov. 1991, Calgary (as yet unpublished).

3 Pam Gems, from personal correspondence in reply to an earlier draft of this section: 22 Jan. 1992.

4 Bertolt Brecht, 'The modern theatre is epic theatre', in *Brecht on Theatre: The Development of an Aesthetic*, trans. John Willet (London: Methuen, 1964), p. 34. Janelle Reinelt cites this same passage in her discussion of 'British Feminist Drama: Brecht and Caryl Churchill' in an unpublished conference paper delivered at a conference on 'Brecht: Thirty Years After', Toronto, Autumn 1986. Also see Reinelt's 'Beyond Brecht: Britain's new feminist drama', in *Performing Feminisms: Feminist Critical Theory and Theatre*, ed. Sue-Ellen Case (Baltimore: Johns Hopkins University Press, 1990).

5 Janelle Reinelt, 'Rethinking Brecht: Deconstruction, Feminism and the Politics of Form', unpublished paper, 1990.

6 cf. Linda Alcoff, 'Cultural feminism versus post-structuralism: the identity crisis in feminist theory', *Signs*, vol. 14, no. 3, Spring 1989; Biddie Martin and Chandra Jalpede Mohanty, 'Feminist politics: what's home got to do with it?', in *Feminist Studies/Critical Studies*, ed. Teresa de Lauretis (Bloomington: Indiana University Press, 1986); Sandra Harding, 'The instability of analytical categories of feminist theory', *Signs*, vol. 12, no. 4, Summer 1987.

7 Roland Barthes, 'The death of the author', in *Image-Music-Text*, trans. Stephen Heath (New York: The Noonday Press, 1977); Laura Mulvey, *Visual and Other Pleasures* (London: Macmillan, 1989); Sue-Ellen Case, *Feminism and Theatre* (New York: Methuen, 1988); and Jill Dolan, *The Feminist Spectator as Critic* (Ann Arbor: The University of Michigan Press, 1988).

8 Jill Dolan, 'Materialist feminism, postmodernism, poststructuralism ... and theory', *TDR: The Drama Review*, T123, Autumn 1989, p. 59. Frances Bonner and I have used this same quotation in the introduction to an interdisciplinary study of 'cultural representations and gender': see F. Bonner, L. Goodman, R. Allen, C. King and L. Janes (eds), *Imagining Women: Cultural Representations and Gender* (Cambridge: Polity Press, 1992).

9 Donna Haraway, 'Situated knowledges: the science question in feminism and the privilege of partial perspective', *Feminist Studies*, vol. 14, no. 3, Autumn 1988, pp. 575–99. Frances Bonner and I have developed this idea in another context, in *Imagining Women* (1992).

10 Diana Fuss, 'Lesbian and gay theory: the question of identity politics', in *Essentially Speaking: Feminism, Nature, Difference* (London: Routledge, 1989), p. 97.

11 Francine Wattman Frank and Paula A. Treichler, 'False Universals', in the chapter 'Special concerns in scholarly writing and other professional activities', in *Language, Gender and Professional Writing: Theoretical Approaches and Guidelines for NonSexist Usage*, ed. Francine Wattman Frank and Paula A. Treichler (New York: Modern Language Association, 1989), p. 227.

12 Toril Moi, 'Feminist, female, feminine', in *The Feminist Reader: Essays in Gender*

and the Politics of Literary Criticism, ed. Catherine Belsey and Jane Moore (London: Macmillan, 1989), p. 117.

13 For an analysis of feminist factionalism with reference to generational and racial differences, see Audre Lorde, 'Age, race, class and sex: women redefining difference', in *Sister Outsider: Essays and Speeches* (Trumansberg, NY: The Crossing Press, 1984). For a complementary argument with reference to race in relation to material and class inequalities, see Elizabeth Spelman's introduction to *Inessential Woman: Problems of Exclusion in Feminist Thought* (Boston: Beacon Press and London: The Women's Press, 1990).

14 These have been published in *How the Vote was Won: And Other Suffragette Plays*, ed. Dale Spender and Carole Hayman (London: Methuen, 1985). Linda Fitzsimmons and Viv Gardner have published *New Woman Plays* (London: Methuen, 1991); and Jan MacDonald has published a contextualized study of 'New women in the new drama', *New Theatre Quarterly*, vol. 6, no. 21, Feb. 1990, pp. 31–42.

15 Lisa Tickner, *The Spectacle of Women: The Imagery of the Suffrage Campaign 1907–1914* (London: Chatto & Windus, 1987).

16 Catherine Itzin, *Stages in the Revolution: Political Theatre in Britain Since 1968* (London: Methuen, 1980).

17 cf. Feminist commentary on the Miss World and Miss America pageants: in Michelene Wandor, *Carry on Understudies: Theatre and Sexual Politics* (London: Routledge & Kegan Paul, 1981), pp. 36–7; Helene Keyssar, *Feminist Theatre* (New York: Macmillan, 1984), p. 18; and Susan Bassnett, *Feminist Experiences: The Women's Movement in Four Cultures* (London: Allen & Unwin, 1986), pp. 155–6.

18 Susan Bassnett, *Magdalena: International Women's Experimental Theatre* (Oxford: Berg Publishers, 1989), p. 16.

19 Helene Keyssar, 'Hauntings: gender and drama in contemporary English theatre', *Englisch Amerikanische Studien*, vol. 8, nos. 3–4, 1986, pp. 459–60.

20 Statistics show the majority of government subsidy in the UK going to the Theatres National and to large-scale Arts organizations. For instance, the Arts Council Sixth Annual Report (1951, p. 33) showed that over half of all funding to the arts from the ACGB went to these five recipients only: Covent Garden, Sadler's Wells, The Old Vic, The London Symphony Orchestra and the Edinburgh Festival. Arts Council Annual Reports 1980–90 show some improvement, but still record vast inequalities for funding recipients. See also The London School of Economics Report, 'The Effects of Inflation on the Subsidized Reps', 1975; and Nicholas de Jongh, 'Deficit could force RSC to leave London', *The Guardian*, 29 Oct. 1990, p. 22, in which de Jongh quotes Terry Hands: 'Between 1984 and 1989 the RSC's subsidy slipped to 27 per cent. The three other national companies were receiving substantially more: English National Opera 45 per cent, the National Theatre 42 per cent, and the Royal Opera House 33 per cent.' For statistics reflecting the relative status of women's theatre, see *Drama*, no. 2, 1984.

21 Sarachild is quoted in Elizabeth J. Natalle, *Feminist Theatre: A Study in Persuasion* (Metuchen, NJ: Scarecrow Press, 1985), p. 133.

22 Kate Millett, *Sexual Politics* (New York: Avon Books, 1969). cf. Toril Moi, *Sexual/Textual Politics: Feminist Literary Theory* (London: Methuen, 1985); 'Feminist literary criticism', in *Modern Literary Theory*, ed. Ann Jefferson and David Robey (London: Batsford, 2nd edn, 1987); Andrea Dworkin, *Our Blood: Prophecies and Discourses on Sexual Politics* (London: The Women's Press, 1982),

pp. 109–10; Arlyn Diamond, 'Practising feminist literary criticism', *Women's Studies International Quarterly*, vol. 1, 1978, p. 151.

23 cf. Gisela Breitling, 'Speech, silence, and the discourse of art', in *Feminist Aesthetics*, ed. Gisela Ecker (Boston: Beacon Press, 1986), p. 163; Lucy Lippard, 'Sweeping exchanges: the contribution of feminism to the art of the 1970s', *Art Journal*, Autumn/Winter 1980, p. 364; Mary Kelly, 'On sexual politics in art', in *Framing Feminism: Art and the Women's Movement 1970–1985*, ed. Rozsika Parker and Griselda Pollack (London: Pandora Press, 1987).

24 Michelene Wandor, introduction to *Understudies: Theatre and Sexual Politics* (London: Methuen, 1981), reprinted in *Carry on Understudies: Theatre and Sexual Politics* (London: Routledge & Kegan Paul, 1981), p. xix. She continues this discussion in *Look Back in Gender: Sexuality and the Family in Post-War British Drama* (London: Methuen, 1987).

25 Lizbeth Goodman, 'Subverting images of the female: an interview with Tilda Swinton', *New Theatre Quarterly*, vol. 6, no. 23, August 1990. This interview was compiled from a series of taped and untaped sessions dated June-October 1989.

26 Susan Bassnett, 'Towards a theory of women's theatre', in *Linguistic and Literary Studies in Eastern Europe*, vol. 10: *The Semiotics of Drama and Theatre*, ed. Herta Schmid and Aloysius Van Kesteren (Amsterdam and Philadelphia: John Benjamins, 1984).

27 Rosalind Coward, 'Are women's novels feminist novels?', *The Feminist Review*, no. 5, 1980, p. 63. This article was written in response to Rebecca O'Rourke, 'Summer reading', *The Feminist Review*, no. 2, 1979.

28 Bassnett, 'Towards a theory of women's theatre', p. 447.

29 Coward, 'Are women's novels feminist novels?', p. 63.

30 Much recent feminist criticism has taken as its subject its own relationship with postmodernist theory and poststructuralist practice, and some has specifically addressed the issue of labelling: cf. Susan J. Hekman, *Gender and Knowledge: Elements of a Postmodern Feminism* (Cambridge: Polity Press, 1990), and Chris Weedon, *Feminist Practice and Poststructuralist Theory* (Oxford: Basil Blackwell, 1987).

31 Claire Yandell, 'Beauty and the Beast: an interview with Louise Page', *Women's Review*, no. 3, Jan. 1986, pp. 30–1.

32 Elizabeth MacLennan, *The Moon Belongs to Everyone: Making Theatre With 7:84* (London: Methuen, 1990).

33 'Writers Revealed', an interview with Timberlake Wertenbaker broadcast on Women's Hour Radio, BBC Radio 4, 20 June 1991. This quotation has been transcribed from an audio cassette recording.

34 Patti P. Gillespie, 'Feminist theatre: a rhetorical phenomenon', in *Women in American Theatre*, ed. Helen Krich Chinoy and Linda Walsh Jenkins (New York: Theatre Communications Group, 2nd edn, 1987), p. 279. This essay first appeared in *The Quarterly Journal of Speech*, vol. 64, 1978, pp. 284–94.

35 Lizbeth Goodman, 'Waiting for Spring to come again: feminist theatre 1978 and 1989: an interview with Gillian Hanna', *New Theatre Quarterly*, vol. 6, no. 21, Feb. 1990, p. 53. This interview was compiled from four taped and untaped sessions, recorded in April–August 1989. It functions in part as an update of a previous interview with Peter Hulton which appeared in the Dartington College *Theatre Papers*, 2nd series, no. 8, 1978.

36 Sally Minogue, *Problems for Feminist Criticism* (London: Routledge, 1990), p. 5.

37 See especially Elizabeth Spelman, *Inessential Woman: Problems of Exclusion in Feminist Thought* (Boston: Beacon Press, and London: The Women's Press, 1990).

38 Sarah Daniels, introduction to *Plays: One* (London: Methuen, 1991), pp. ix and xii.
39 Maggie Humm, *The Dictionary of Feminist Theory* (Hemel Hempstead: Harvester Wheatsheaf, 1989), p. 41.
40 Audre Lorde, 'An open letter to Mary Daly', in *Sister Outsider: Essays and Speeches* (Trumansberg, NY: The Crossing Press, 1984).
41 Jill Dolan, 'Cultural feminism and the feminine aesthetic', in *The Feminist Spectator as Critic* (Ann Arbor: The University of Michigan Press, 1988), p. 83.
42 Ibid., p. 83.
43 Dolan extends this argument in 'Feminists, lesbians, and other women in theatre: thoughts on the politics of performance', in *Themes in Drama 11: Women in Theatre*, ed. James Redmond (Cambridge: Cambridge University Press, 1989), p. 204.
44 Linda Alcoff, 'Cultural feminism versus post-structuralism: the identity crisis in feminist theory', *Signs*, vol. 14, no. 3, Spring 1989.

2 FEMINIST THEATRES 1968–90

1 See Henry Lesnik (ed.), *Guerilla Street Theatre* (New York: Avon Books, 1973).
2 See the short report, 'British feminist theatre: a survey and a prospect', *New Theatre Quarterly*, vol. 8, no. 32, November 1992. The full survey listings and results (112 pages) are forthcoming in the University of Manchester's *Feminist Praxis* series, ed. Liz Stanley, 1992.
3 See bibliography (final section) for details of interviews and correspondence.
4 Judith Zivanovic, 'The rhetorical and political foundations of women's collaborative theatre', in *Themes in Drama 11: Women in Theatre*, ed. James Redmond (Cambridge: Cambridge University Press, 1989), p. 218, n. 15.
5 As calculated by Tony Bilton, Kevin Bonnett, Philip Jones, Michelle Stanworth, Ken Sheard and Andrew Webster, 'Patterns of inequality', in *Introductory Sociology* (London: Macmillan, 2nd edn, 1987), p. 68. This study compares men's and women's average earnings in both manual and non-manual jobs. Also see Veronica Beechey and Tessa Perkins, *A Matter of Hours: Women, Part-Time Work and the Labour Market* (Cambridge: Polity Press, 1987), pp. 147–9, 150–2, 175, 194–5.
6 Lizbeth Goodman, 'Waiting for Spring to come again: feminist theatre 1978 and 1989: an interview with Gillian Hanna', *New Theatre Quarterly*, vol. 6, no. 21, Feb. 1990, p. 48.
7 This and the following quotation are from 'Structuring the Audience's Attention', an unpublished discussion paper delivered by Deborah Levy to the Graduate Women and Literature Seminar, St John's College, Cambridge, 7 Feb. 1990.
8 Susan Bennett, *Theatre Audiences: A Theory of Production and Reception* (London: Routledge, 1991).
9 cf. William J. Baumol and William G. Bowen, 'Audiences – some face-sheet data', in *Sociology of Literature and Drama*, ed. Elizabeth and Tom Burns (London: Penguin, 1973). This is a comparative study of American and British audience trends, primarily concerned with questions of audience composition by economic strata (class), age and occupation, which uses only two surveys, both based at the National Theatre, as its entire database on 'British theatre'. Also see 'Barbican Centre: Research into Audience Potential' (London: Industrial Market Research, 7 Nov. 1980), which provides economic breakdowns of potential audiences for the subsidized theatre based at Barbican Centre; and John

Myerscough, *The Economic Importance of the Arts in Britain* (London: Policy Studies Institute, 1988), which provides a regionally representative account of the statistics and economic conditions related to the Arts as 'industry'. The most recently compiled information has been put together by the Arts Council's Research and Statistics Unit: 'Seat Prices in the Subsidized Theatres of Britain 1989/90' and 'Drama Attendances England 1988/89, 1989/90, 1990/91', both compiled by Ferzana Butt, 1991. Neither of these reports is concerned with women in theatre audiences, or with the composition of women's theatre audiences.

10 Caroline Gardiner for the Society of West End Theatres (SWET), 'The City University Audience Survey 1985/86'. The survey is available in two forms: the long version published by SWET, and the more concise version incorporated into Gardiner's unpublished Ph.D. thesis: 'The West End Theatre Audience 1981–1986', Dept of Arts Policy and Management, City University, 1988.

11 Gardiner has compiled statistics on 'Frequency of Theatre-Going by Sex' and on 'Percent Attendance Accounted for by Men and Women by Area of Residence' (in her SWET Survey).

12 All points cited from Caroline Elizabeth Gardiner, 'The West-End Theatre Audience: 1981 to 1986', unpublished Ph.D. dissertation (London: City University, Department of Arts Policy and Management, Jan. 1988), chapter 3 (section 2), pp. 141–6.

13 Caroline Elizabeth Gardiner, 'The City University Audience Survey for SWET: The West End Theatre Audience 1985/6', London: City University and SWET, 1986, summary sections 2.1.5 and 2.1.6.

14 Ibid., summary section 2.1.7.

15 Survey conducted by Black Mime Theatre Women's Troop on tour with their first play, *Mothers*, 1990–1, directed by Denise Wong; administrator in charge of surveys: Mel Jennings.

16 Caroline Gardiner's paper to the 'Theatre Under Threat' conference, St John's College, Cambridge, 20 Oct. 1990.

17 Cheryl McGuire, interview with Jules Wright, 12 Oct. 1989. Unpublished transcript from a taped interview. The *Observer* is a fairly liberal non-partisan 'quality' newspaper published in England.

18 Further information about British theatre funding can be found in *The ABSA Sponsorship Manual 1988/89* (London: The Association for Business Sponsorship of the Arts, 1989), and in the Arts Council's annual reports and publications.

19 The Arts Council, 'The Glory of the Garden: The Development of the Arts in England', 1984. cf. 'The Poverty of the Garden', *The Guardian*, 27 March 1987. Monstrous Regiment also replied to this report in their own eleven-page (untitled, unpublished) document, written by Sandy Bailey (administrator) and the company. Quoted with permission.

20 Catherine Itzin, *Stages in the Revolution: Political Theatre in Britain Since 1968* (London: Methuen, 1980), p. 6.

21 From an unpublished interview with John Hoyland, 1978, quoted in Itzin, *Stages in the Revolution* (1980), p. 39.

22 Ibid., p. 39.

23 Published in *Strike While the Iron Is Hot*, ed. Michelene Wandor (London: Journeyman Press, 1980). First performed 1974.

24 From an unpublished article about Red Ladder by Chris Rawlence and Steve Trafford quoted in Itzin, *Stages in the Revolution* (1980), p. 48.

25 From Broadside's response to reading the manuscript of Itzin's *Stages in the Revolution*: Itzin (1980), p. 48.

26 Chris Rawlence and Steve Trafford quoted in Itzin, *Stages in the Revolution* (1980), p. 50.

27 Kathleen McCreery, from an untitled paper delivered to the Judith E. Wilson Conference on Political Theatre, St John's College, Cambridge, 1978. McCreery's paper relates her work in such socialist groups as the AgitProp Street Players, Red Ladder and Broadside Mobile Worker's theatre to the terms 'realism' and 'popularity'. Extract from p. 30 of the unpublished conference transcript.

28 Judith Zivanovic has studied these interconnections in 'The rhetorical and political foundations of women's collaborative theatre', in *Themes in Drama, vol. 11: Women in Theatre*, ed. James Redmond (Cambridge: Cambridge University Press, 1989). She refers extensively to Kathryn Cos Campbell, 'The rhetoric of women's liberation: an oxymoron', *Quarterly Journal of Speech*, vol. 59, no. 1, 1973.

29 Sue-Ellen Case, *Feminism and Theatre* (New York: Methuen, 1988), p. 98.

30 'New perspectives on theatre today: theatre collectives: alive and kicking', *Platform*, no. 4, 1982. Subsequent references are from this same section of the discussion paper.

31 Ibid., p. 2.

32 *Heresies*, by Deborah Levy. First performed by the Royal Shakespeare Company Women's Group, the Pit, Barbican, London, 16 Dec. 1986; directed by Susan Todd, designed by Iona McLeish, original musical score by Ilona Sekacz. cf. reviews, in order of reference, such as Monica Suswin, 'Women's theatre at the stake', *The Independent*, 10 Dec. 1986; Peter Hepple, 'Sludgy concoction that goes to pot', *The Stage*, 24 Dec. 1986; and Milton Shulman, 'Naïve feminist notions', *The Evening Standard*, 17 Dec. 1986. Reviews are collected in full in the RSC archives (copies received from Genista McIntosh: May 1988).

33 *Platform* discussion, p. 2.

34 Recent figures suggest that the situation is growing worse. cf. *The Arts Funding Guide* (London: Directory for Social Change, 1989) and the following Arts Council documents: 'Criteria for Grant-in-Aid' (May 1983); 'The Glory of the Garden: The Development of the Arts in England' (1984); 'Guidelines to Applicants for Drama Project Subsidy' (1 April 1986, 31 March 1987); 'Marketing and Fundraising Guide' (December 1988); 'Arts and Disability Organizations and Projects' (1989); 'Arts Council Scheme for Writers and Theatre Companies 1989/90' (1989); and the Autumn '90 Theatre Campaign Updates (1990–1).

35 Michelene Wandor, *Strike While the Iron is Hot* (London: Journeyman Press, 1980), pp. 7–8.

36 The origins and aims of the Actress' Franchise League have been described by others: cf. Michelene Wandor, *Carry on Understudies: Theatre and Sexual Politics* (New York: Routledge & Kegan Paul, revised edn, 1986), pp. 2–3; Dale Spender and Carole Hayman (eds), *How the Vote was Won: And other Suffragette Plays* (London: Methuen, 1985); and Julie Holledge, *Innocent Flowers: Women in Edwardian Theatre* (London: Virago, 1981), pp. 2–3.

37 Very little has been written about the RSC Women's Group: see Wandor, *Carry on Understudies* (1986), pp. 37–8, and Sue-Ellen Case, *Feminism and Theatre* (1988), p. 66. Further information about the RSC Women's Project was provided in interview by both Deborah Levy and Genista McIntosh (see bibliography for details).

38 Catherine Itzin, *Stages in the Revolution* (1980), pp. 230–1.

39 From an unpublished interview with Anne Engel, 1975, quoted in Itzin, *Stages in the Revolution* (1980), p. 231.
40 The status and memberships of WTG and The Women's Company are accounted for differently by Wandor and Itzin.
41 The only published information on the group appears in Wandor, *Carry on Understudies* (1986), pp. 84–5. A brief history of the company also appears in a programme for a show entitled *Alison's House*, by Susan Glaspell: original copy of the programme provided by Maggie Wilkinson, 9 Feb. 1990. The company archives are dispersed among the personal files of ex-company members.
42 Personal correspondence: letter from Julie Holledge, 17 April 1990.
43 Telephone interview with Anne Engel, 22 Jan. 1990; telephone interview with Maggie Wilkinson, 3 Feb. 1990.
44 Telephone interview with Engel, 22 Jan. 1990. Engel explained that all but the man, Stephen Ley, had trouble finding jobs in the theatre after the disbanding of Mrs Worthington's Daughters. Holledge moved to Australia, where she is now a university lecturer. Charlesworth and Wilkinson did eventually continue their careers in performance. Engel left the theatre altogether when the company disbanded.
45 Catherine Itzin, *Stages in the Revolution* (1980), p. 230.
46 Chris Rawlence, introduction to *A Woman's Work is Never Done, or Strike While the Iron is Hot* in *Strike While the Iron is Hot*, ed. Michelene Wandor (London: Journeyman Press, 1980), p. 19.

3 FOUR COMPANIES

1 For example, Catherine Itzin, *Stages in the Revolution: Political Theatre in Britain Since 1968* (London: Methuen, 1980); Sue-Ellen Case, *Feminism and Theatre* (New York: Methuen, 1988); Helene Keyssar, *Feminist Theatre* (New York: Macmillan, 1984): Michelene Wandor, 'The impact of feminism on the theatre', *The Feminist Review*, vol. 18, winter 1984, pp. 76–91; *Carry on Understudies: Theatre and Sexual Politics* (New York: Routledge & Kegan Paul, revised edn, 1986); *Look Back in Gender: Sexuality and the Family in Post-War British Drama* (London: Methuen, 1987).
2 Women's Theatre Group: company brochure, 1985.
3 Some of the plays have recently been published. See *Herstory: Vols. 1 and 2*, ed. Gabrielle Griffin and Elaine Aston (Sheffield: The Academic Press, 1991), including six of WTG's playscripts: *Lear's Daughters, Pinchdice and Co., Witchcraze, Anywhere to Anywhere, Love and Dissent* and *Dear Girl*.
4 Review of *Double Vision* quoted in the WTG company brochure, 1985.
5 Local Governments Act 1988 (London: HMSO, 1988), Chapter 9, Section 28. The section includes a 'prohibition on promoting homosexuality by teaching or publishing material'.
6 WTG company brochure, 1985.
7 *Mortal*, by Maro Green (Penny Casdagli) and Caroline Griffin. Directed by Claire Grove, designed by Karen Hood, with Sandra James-Young, Elizabeth Kelly, Alison MacKinnon and Kay Purcell. First performed at the Young Vic, London, 12 Feb. 1990 (followed by national tour).
8 Company brochure, 1985.
9 Ibid.
10 Itzin describes this play and its critical reception, both during the run and four years later, when a controversy arose regarding its suitability as educational material for distribution in schools, in *Stages in the Revolution* (1980), pp. 228–30.

11 Telephone interview with WTG administrator Jenny Clarke, 24 July 1990.

12 WTG policy statement, from the company files.

13 Ibid.

14 Telephone interview with Jenny Clarke, 24 July 1990. All the following information on present policy and future plans is taken from this and a follow-up telephone interview.

15 Correspondence: letter from Jonquil Panting, marketing officer, 20 March 1991.

16 From the brochure distributed to all mailing list members in Jan. 1992.

17 From the Monstrous Regiment company brochure, 1985. The first Monstrous Regiment book – *Monstrous Regiment: A Collective Celebration* (London: Nick Hern Books, 1991) – includes four plays (*Scum, Island Life, Love Story of the Century* and *My Sister in This House*) along with background material about the company, by Gillian Hanna with input from the management collective.

18 A complete list of contributors to and participants in Monstrous Regiment productions (up to 1989) is included in the company brochure, 1985.

19 The list of Hanna's work has been extracted from Lizbeth Goodman, 'Waiting for the Spring to come again: feminist theatre 1978 and 1989: an interview with Gillian Hanna', *New Theatre Quarterly*, vol. 6, no. 21, Feb. 1990, p. 43.

20 See the photograph of Gillian Hanna as Shakespeare's Sister, reading Virginia Woolf's *A Room of One's Own* (Fig. 1).

21 Lizbeth Goodman, 'Waiting for the Spring to come again', 1990, p. 44.

22 This quotation is from the unedited transcript of my published interview with Gillian Hanna (1990). The transcript was compiled from taped and untaped interviews held 18 April, 11 May and 20 June 1989. This particular quote was cut from the published version.

23 Unpublished response to the Arts Council, 'The Glory of the Garden' (London: ACGB, 1984) by Sandy Bailey on behalf of Monstrous Regiment Ltd, 1984, p. 1. Held in the Regiment archives.

24 Unedited version of my interview with Gillian Hanna (1990).

25 For example, a multimedia project (based on the life of the Italian painter Artemesia Gentileschi) mentioned in the 1984 report and still awaiting funding in 1992.

26 Quoted from the advertisements for workshops in the New Playwrights' Trust Newsletters nos. 46 (March 1990) and 49 (July 1990). Information regarding Fairbank's residency was obtained from a telephone interview with Mary McCusker, 24 July 1990.

27 Unpublished report by Sandy Bailey (1984), p. 10. The creation of this post was made possible by newly acquired funds – specifically designated for a writer – from the Arts Council and Greater London Arts.

28 Monstrous Regiment in an unpublished interview with Clive Barker, 1985.

29 Unedited version of my interview with Gillian Hanna (1990).

30 The Monstrous Regiment archives contain extensive files of reviews and articles about the company from 1976 to the present. See especially the extended debate in response to Polly Toynbee's dismissive article on women's theatre companies in The *Guardian*, 16 July 1979; and responses by Eileen Pollack, Eve Bland and Noreen Kershaw in The *Guardian*, 19 July 1979; by Susan Glanville, Susan Todd, Eileen Pollack, Anne Engel and Anita Mascara for Beryl and the Perils, Bloomers, Monstrous Regiment and Mrs Worthington's Daughters, and by Caryl Churchill in The *Guardian*, 26 July 1979; and a letter from Chris Bowler, Josephine Cupido, Gus Garside, Gillian Hanna and Veronica Wood on behalf of Monstrous Regiment in The *Guardian*, 20 July 1990.

31 Nancy Diuguid and Kate Crutchley, 'Women's work', *Time Out*, 25 Nov. to 1 Dec. 1977, p. 14.
32 From an undated and unsigned one-page answer to this hypothetical question put by a previous researcher or interviewer, in Nancy Diuguid's personal files.
33 Wandor, *Carry on Understudies* (1986), p. 56.
34 Letter to me from Suad El-Amin, 27 July 1990, providing additional information, in response to an earlier draft of this chapter which was distributed to the three key companies for comment and approval.
35 Telephone interview with Suad El-Amin, 24 July 1990.
36 Telephone interviews with Jackie Kay, June 1991.
37 A complete history of Gay Sweatshop is included in Philip Osment (ed.), *The Gay Sweatshop: Four Plays and a Company* (London: Methuen, 1989).
38 Telephone interview with Suad El-Amin, 24 July 1990. The next two quotations are also taken from this interview.
39 Company publicity material reprinted in the Calendar of Events for the Junction Arts Centre, Cambridge (Nov./Dec. 1990).
40 Autumn '90 Theatre Campaign Factsheet Update, May 1991.
41 Sources for Siren include: responses to the Feminist Theatre Survey; the company brochure; a letter from Tash Fairbanks (6 June 1989); written information appended to a set of postal interview questions which were returned with a letter from Tash Fairbanks and Jane Boston, 12 Aug. 1990; and an interview with Tash Fairbanks, London, 21 Feb. 1991.
42 Siren history, from the company brochure.
43 Ibid.
44 Personal correspondence: letter from Tash Fairbanks, 6 June 1989.
45 Siren company brochure.
46 The *Guardian*, theatre listings, 10 July 1990, p. 36. A telephone interview with the company confirmed that this listing refers to a different company altogether. The new black women's company's change of name is recorded in a review by Betty Caplan in The *Guardian*, 20 Feb. 1991, p. 36. See the Conclusion in this volume for a brief reference to Cynthia Grant and Toronto's Company of Sirens.
47 From an interview with Tash Fairbanks, London, 21 Feb. 1991.
48 Written information appended to a set of postal interview questions which was submitted to the company with an earlier draft of this chapter. Received with a letter from Tash Fairbanks and Jane Boston, 12 Aug. 1990.
49 Monstrous Regiment in an unpublished interview with Clive Barker, 1985.

4 COMMON WORKING METHODS OF FEMINIST THEATRES

1 These factors have been analysed in 'The Women's Employment Working Party Interim Report', The Director's Guild of Great Britain with the Association of Directors and Producers, second draft, Dec. 1984 (unpublished); and The Conference of Women Theatre Directors and Administrators, 'Collected Papers', 1979–81, and 'The Status of Women in British Theatre', 1982–3 (collected and unpublished conference papers). Also see Jenny Armitage, 'The privatization of women', *Theatre Writers' Union Journal*, Winter 1983.
2 Note that many groups use several different methods.
3 See Jane Edwardes, 'Closing stages', *Time Out*, 23–30 March 1988, p. 41. The article begins: 'The final curtain is coming down all over the London theatre scene as government cuts take their effect'. Among the groups most affected were Women's Theatre Group, The Black Women's Theatre Cooperative, Clean

Break, The Women's Playhouse Trust, The King's Head (base for The Cave of Harmony Women-Only Cabaret), etc.

4 See Lizbeth Goodman, 'Art form or platform? On women and playwriting: an interview with Charlotte Keatley', *New Theatre Quarterly*, vol. 6, no. 22, May 1990, p. 128.

5 Olwen Wymark, from a discussion paper delivered to the 'Theatre Under Threat' Conference, St John's College, Cambridge, 20–1 Oct. 1990.

6 Caryl Churchill on the process of writing *Vinegar Tom*, in her introduction to the play in *Plays: One* (London: Methuen, 1985), p. 129.

7 Geraldine Cousin, *Churchill: The Playwright* (London: Methuen, 1989), p. 15.

8 Colin Chambers and Mike Prior, *Playwright's Progress: Patterns in Postwar British Drama* (Oxford: Amber Lane Press, 1987), p. 190. For a more political analysis of Churchill's work, see Linda Fitzsimmons, ' "I won't turn back for you or anyone": Caryl Churchill's socialist-feminist theatre', in *Essays in Theatre*, vol. 16, no. 1, Nov. 1987.

9 Interview with Mel Gussow, 'Caryl Churchill: genteel playwright with an angry voice', *The New York Times*, 22 Nov. 1987, p. 26.

10 Chambers and Prior, *Playwright's Progress* (1987); see also the interview with Gussow and the entry on Churchill in Stanley Weintraub (ed.), *The Dictionary of Literary Biography*, vol. 13: British Dramatists Since World War Two (Detroit: Book Tower, 1982).

11 Churchill, *Plays: One* (1985), p. xi.

12 Elizabeth Taylor, 'An Investigation into the Role of the Interaction between Actor and Writer in the Creating of a Script for Performance, Illustrated by Four Plays by Caryl Churchill', unpublished MA thesis (including notes from Churchill's personal files), Royal Holloway and Bedford New College, University of London, May 1986. It was necessary to paraphrase this reference in the past tense, because Joint Stock has disbanded since Taylor's dissertation was written.

13 Caryl Churchill, *Plays: One* (1985), p. 129.

14 Chambers and Prior use the phrase 'belief in the possibility' in a more critical context in *Playwright's Progress* (1987), p. 193. For sociological studies of language patterns and notation which add to a reading of either *Top Girls* or *Serious Money*, see Jim Schenkein (ed.), *Studies in the Organization of Conversational Interaction* (New York: Academic Press, 1978), especially Schenkein, 'Sketch of an analytic mentality for the study of conversational interaction' and Harvey Sacks, Emanuel Schlegoff and Gail Jefferson, 'A simplest systematics for the organization of turn taking for conversation', with notations developed by Jefferson.

15 Interview with Caryl Churchill following a playwriting workshop at the Women's Playhouse Trust Workshop Series, the Lyric Theatre Hammersmith, London, 14 July 1988.

16 *Mad Forest*, premiered at the Central School of Speech and Drama, Chalk Farm, London, July 1990; toured before transferring to the Royal Court Theatre (main stage) in Oct. 1990.

17 The first version of the script was devised by the company with Priscilla Allen. The company at the time included Kate Crutchley, Nancy Diuguid, Kate Phelps, Michael Kellan, Helen Barnaby and Tash Fairbanks. The first production was designed by Mary Moore, with music by Terri Quaye.

18 Interviews with Nancy Diuguid and personal correspondence with Tash Fairbanks (see Bibliography for details).

19 From an unpublished interview with Nancy Diuguid: transcript compiled from taped and untaped sessions dated June 1988 to Feb. 1990.

20 Personal correspondence from Michelene Wandor, in response to an earlier draft of this section: letter received 1 Feb. 1992.

21 From a letter accompanying the survey response for Siren Theatre Company from Tash Fairbanks (and Jane Boston), 12 Aug. 1990. The first Fairbanks knew of the discrepancy was receipt of a draft chapter of this book.

22 Natasha Morgan, *By George!*, unpublished. First performed on tour with That's Not It Theatre Company in 1982. The programme notes read: 'written by Natasha Morgan, devised by the company'. The company at that time included Morgan, Nancy Diuguid and Noel Greig, among others. Programme and reviews provided by Diuguid in interview, 4 Aug. 1988.

23 Representative reviews for this play were cited in chapter 2 (p. 00 and n. 32).

24 Elaine Feinstein and Women's Theatre Group, *Lear's Daughters*. Published in *Herstory, Volume One*, ed. Gabrielle Griffin and Elaine Aston (Sheffield: The Academic Press, 1991). First performed 12 Sept. 1987 and then on tour, second tour ('by popular demand') in 1988.

25 Notes taken by Peter Holland on the devising and writing of *Lear's Daughters*, from a group discussion following the performance in The School of Pythagoras, St John's College, Cambridge, 5 Nov. 1987; supplemented by notes from interviews with the company (see bibliography for details).

26 *The London Theatre Record*, no. 24, 1987, p. 1256; programme, handbill and performance notes from the 1987 tour.

27 *The London Theatre Record*, no. 18, 1988, p. 1178. Jane Edwardes: '. . . based on the original idea by Elaine Feinstein (whose name seems mysteriously to have been dropped from the programme)'.

28 Personal correspondence (letter dated 19 Aug. 1988) from Kathleen Hamilton, administrator for Women's Theatre Group.

29 Sonja Lyndon and Trouble and Strife, *Now and In The Hour of Our Death*, unpublished. First performed at the Corner Theatre, London, 26 Jan. to 14 Feb. 1988; tour; Young Vic Studio 5–23 July 1988; tour; Dublin Theatre Festival 26 Sept. to 8 Oct. 1988; final tour.

30 Interview with Sonja Lyndon, 18 March 1989, and follow-up conversations after Lyndon sent a copy of her original manuscript *Poetry in Motion* as a reference source.

31 Interview with Abigail Morris, director of Trouble and Strife, 13 Nov. 1990. Morris responded directly to an earlier draft of this chapter section.

32 Ibid.

33 This and the next two quotations are taken from personal correspondence: letter from Finola Geraghty for Trouble and Strife (dated 22 Jan. 1989); cf. supporting documents and promotional materials sent by Judith Dimant, administrator, 26 Jan. 1989. Interviews and feature articles on the show are printed in *What's On* (Jan. 1988), *Vogue* (July 1988), *Cosmopolitan* (July 1988), The *Guardian* (July 1988), and *Elle* (Jan. 1989).

34 Interview with Bryony Lavery, 20 July 1988; cf. reviews from the Monstrous Regiment archives.

35 Gillian Hanna, interviewed by Peter Hulton, *Dartington College Theatre Papers*, second series, no. 8, 1978; cf. recent personal correspondence (see bibliography for details).

36 In Stephen Lowe (ed.), *Peace Plays* (London: Methuen, 1985).

37 Telephone interview with Tanya Myers, in response to a previous draft of this chapter: 5 March 1992.

38 Performed at Chapter Arts Centre, Cardiff (in association with the Magdalena Project), 29 Oct. 1990.

39 cf. wife–husband teams Franca Rame and Dario Fo (political comedy) in Italy, and Margaretta D'Arcy and John Arden (political drama) in Ireland. Churchill/ Lan's *A Mouthful of Birds* has recently been the subject of extended feminist critical debate, including Sue Smith's reading of the play as paradigm for 'The Other Bisexuality', an unpublished paper delivered at the Warwick University Conference, 'Twentieth Century Perspectives on Women and Theatre: Creation, Process, Output', 19 May 1990.

40 *About Face*, first performed as a one-woman show at the Edinburgh Festival, 1985: performed by Cordelia Ditton, directed by Maggie Ford; then on tour with ReSisters Theatre Company until Nov. 1985. Published in Mary Remnant (ed.), *Plays by Women*, vol. 6 (London: Methuen, 1987). All quotations are from a 'conversation' between Ditton and Ford, published with the playtext.

41 For detailed discussion of the work of these and other comediennes, see my chapter on 'Gender and humour' in *Imagining Women: Cultural Representations and Gender*, ed. F. Bonner, L. Goodman, R. Allen, C. King and L. Janes (Cambridge: Polity Press, 1992).

42 *More*: first performed as a reading in the Women's Writing Workshop at the Arts Theatre, London, 19 Oct. 1984 (funded by an Arts Council Bursary); given a second reading as part of Gay Sweatshop's x10 Festival at the Drill Hall, London, 1 Nov. 1985. First staged by Gay Sweatshop on 28 March 1986 at the Drill Hall, London. The show toured in England, Canada, America and Hong Kong (funded by GLA). Published in Mary Remnant (ed.), *Plays by Women*, vol. 6 (London: Methuen, 1987).

43 Published in Caroline Griffin, *Passion is Everywhere Appropriate* (London: Only-Women Press, 1989).

44 Written notes from Caroline Griffin, attached to the revised transcript of an earlier draft of this section. The following quotations are also taken from the revised transcript.

45 From an interview with Penny Casdagli, 4 April 1991, which was revised and extended with written notes from Caroline Griffin.

46 Ibid.

47 Ibid. (and following quotation).

5 LESBIAN THEATRES AND THEORETICAL PERSPECTIVES

1 Elizabeth Wilson, 'Borderlines', *The New Statesman and Society*, vol. 3, no. 125, Nov. 1990, p. 31.

2 Sue-Ellen Case lists several American lesbian feminist theatre groups: see *Feminism and Theatre* (New York: Methuen, 1988), pp. 76–81.

3 Jill Davis (ed.), *Lesbian Plays* (London: Methuen, 1987), and *Lesbian Plays: Two* (London: Methuen, 1989). Siren's plays are forthcoming from the Sheffield Academic Press (1992). A few plays by lesbian authors are also included in the *Plays by Women* series, vols. 1–4 ed. Michelene Wandor, vols. 5–6 ed. Mary Remnant (London: Methuen, 1982–7). In America, lesbian plays are compiled in Kate McDermott (ed.), *Places Please! The First Anthology of Lesbian Plays* (Santa Cruz, CA: Aunt Lute Book Co., 1985) and are included in volumes such as Myrna Lamb's *The Mod Donna and Scyklon Z: Plays of Women's Liberation* (New York: Merit Books, 1971). In contrast to their two volumes of lesbian plays, Methuen has published four volumes of *Gay Plays*, ed. Michael Wilcox (London: Methuen, 1986, 1987, 1989, 1990). Lesbian and gay plays are pub-

lished in Philip Osment (ed.), *The Gay Sweatshop: Four Plays and a Company* (London: Methuen, 1989). In America, gay plays are collected in William Hoffman (ed.), *Gay Plays: The First Collection* (New York: Avon Books, 1979).

4 Jill Davis (ed.), *Lesbian Plays* (1987), p. 9.

5 Judith Butler, 'Performative acts and gender constitution: an essay in phenomenology and feminist theory', *Theatre Journal*, vol. 40, no. 4, Dec. 1988, p. 527.

6 Teresa de Lauretis, 'Sexual indifference and lesbian representation', *Theatre Journal*, vol. 40, no. 2, May 1988, p. 172. De Lauretis refers to Marilyn Frye, 'To be and be seen', in *The Politics of Reality* (Trumansberg, NY: The Crossing Press, 1983), pp. 167–9.

7 De Lauretis, *Theatre Journal*, 1988, pp. 172–3.

8 Michel Foucault, *The History of Sexuality. Volume One: An Introduction* (New York: Vintage Books, 1980), p. 101. See Mandy Merck, 'Lianna and the lesbians of art cinema', in *Films for Women*, ed. Charlotte Brunsden (London: BFI, 1986) for critical exegesis of lesbian film as a genre distinct from 'high art', culture, society and their respective (Foucaultian) discourses.

9 Katie Mack, 'Romantic Outsiders: A Study of Lesbian Romantic Fiction from the 1950s to the 1970s', unpublished BA thesis, 1988.

10 Ibid. In this section of her argument Mack cites: Frank Mort, 'Sexuality: regulation and contestation', in *Homosexuality: Power and Politics*, ed. The Gay Collective (London: Alison and Busby, 1980); Jeffrey Weeks, *Sexuality, Politics, and Society* (New York: Longmans, 1981) and *Coming Out: Homosexual Politics in Britain, from the Nineteenth Century to the Present* (London: Quartet, 1977); Lillian Faderman, *Surpassing the Love of Men* (London: The Women's Press, 1981).

11 Gayle Rubin, 'Thinking sex: notes for a radical theory of the politics of sexuality', in *Pleasure and Danger: Exploring Female Sexuality*, ed. Carole S. Vance (London: Routledge & Kegan Paul, 1984).

12 Celia Kitzinger, *The Social Construction of Lesbianism* (London: Sage, 1990).

13 Interviews with Nancy Diuguid: Aug. 1988 to Feb. 1989 (see bibliography for details).

14 Kate McDermott, *Places Please! The First Anthology of Lesbian Plays* (1985).

15 Tucker Pamella Farley, 'Lesbianism and the social function of taboo', in *The Future of Difference*, ed. Hester Eisenstein and Alice Jardine (New Brunswick, NJ: Rutgers University Press, 1987), p. 267.

16 Jeffrey Weeks, *Coming Out* (1977), pp. 65–6.

17 Published in Bryony Lavery, *Her Aching Heart, Two Marias, Wicked* (London: Methuen, 1991).

18 cf. Kate Davy, 'Constructing the spectator: reception, context, and address in lesbian performance', *Performing Arts Journal*, 29, vol. 10, no. 2, 1986, p. 45. The construction of desire in the 'lesbian gaze' is also discussed in E. Ann Kaplan, 'Is the gaze male?', in *Women and Film: Both Sides of the Camera* (London: Methuen, 1983), and in *Powers of Desire: The Politics of Sexuality*, ed. Ann Snitow, Christine Stansell and Sharon Thompson (New York: New Feminist Library/ Monthly Review Press, 1983).

19 See Lorraine Gamman and Margaret Marshment (eds.), *The Female Gaze: Women as Viewers of Popular Culture* (London: The Women's Press, 1988); Jackie Stacey's essay 'Desperately seeking difference' focuses on the gendered gaze in narrative and popular cinema: pp. 112–29.

20 Laura Mulvey, 'Visual pleasure and narrative cinema', *Screen*, vol. 16, no. 3, Autumn 1985, pp. 6–18.

21 See the photograph from Siren Theatre Company's production of *Pulp* (Fig. 3). Also see the production photograph from Bryony Lavery's *Her Aching Heart*

(Fig. 4) depicting two courtly lovers engaged in a battle of wits in which looking and speaking are weapons related to class difference as well as to gender and sexual politics.

22 Judith Barry and Sandy Flitterman, 'Textual strategies: the politics of art-making', *Screen*, vol. 21, no. 2, 1980, p. 37.

23 E. Ann Kaplan, 'Is the gaze male?', in *Women and Film* (1983), p. 29. cf. Mary Ann Doane, 'The Woman's Film: Possession and Address', a paper delivered at the Conference on Cinema History, Asilomar, Monterey, May 1981; quoted in Kaplan, *Women and Film*, p. 28.

24 Farley, 'Lesbianism and the social function of taboo', 1987, p. 269.

25 *Care and Control*, scripted by Michelene Wandor from material devised by the company for Gay Sweatshop in 1977. Directed by Kate Crutchley, designed by Mary Moore, music by Terri Quaye. Published in Wandor (ed.), *Strike While the Iron is Hot* (London: Journeyman Press, 1980); textual quotations are from this published version of the play.

26 Interviews with Sarah Daniels (all unpublished): London, 11 July 1988; London, 20 Aug. 1988; and Cambridge, 8 March 1989. Daniels also provided written notes on a previous draft of this section, which have been taken into account in revision (Winter 1990/1).

27 Sarah Daniels, *Neaptide* (London: Methuen, 1986). First performed at the Cottesloe, National Theatre, London, 26 June 1986. Directed by John Burgess, designed by Alison Chitty.

28 In her unpublished BA thesis (1988), Katie Mack notes that a parallel argument can be directed at literary criticism itself, at the tendency in some well-known liberal (mostly American) feminist criticism to present only 'narrow and homo-geneous literary production, chiefly that of white middle-class heterosexual women'. Mack (p. 14) lists these texts as her examples: Mary Ellmann, *Thinking About Women* (New York: Harcourt, 1968), Patricia Myer Spacks, *The Female Imagination: A Literary and Psychological Investigation of Women's Writing* (New York: Knopf, 1975), Ellen Moers, *Literary Women: The Great Writers* (Oxford: Oxford University Press, 1976), and Elaine Showalter, *A Literature of Their Own: British Women Novelists from Brontë to Lessing* (Princeton, NJ: Princeton University Press, 1977).

29 Interview with Sarah Daniels: London, 11 July 1988.

30 Ibid.

31 Programme printed and distributed for the National Theatre, available from the National Theatre Book Shop (stock).

32 Alison Lyssa, *Pinball*. First produced at the Nimrod Theatre Downstairs, Sydney, Australia, 9 Sept. 1981. Directed by Chris Johnson, designed by Kate JasonSmith. Published in Michelene Wandor (ed.), *Plays by Women*, vol. 4 (London: Methuen, 1985).

33 For actual custody cases and statistics on the number of custody cases awarded to heterosexual mothers (almost all) versus those awarded to lesbian mothers in the court systems of England and Wales, see Gillian E. Hanscombe and Jackie Forster, *Rocking the Cradle: Lesbian Mothers: A Challenge to Family Living* (London: Peter Owen, 1981).

34 See Lizbeth Goodman, 'Art form or platform? on women and playwriting: an interview with Charlotte Keatley', *New Theatre Quarterly*, vol. 6, no. 22, May 1990. Compiled from taped and untaped sessions dated April–Sept. 1989. In the long, unedited version of this interview, Keatley described the devices with which she would build up audience expectation of male characters present just off-stage, always about to enter but never actually appearing.

35 Mel Gussow, 'Women playwrights: new voices in the theatre', *New York Times Magazine*, 1 May 1983.
36 Alison Lyssa, 'Feminist theatre: a monologue to start discussion', *Australasian Drama Studies*, vol. 2, April 1984, pp. 37–8.
37 Brian Hoad, review in *The Bulletin*, 29 Sept. 1981, p. 85, quoted by Lyssa in her postscript to *Pinball*, in Michelene Wandor (ed.), *Plays by Women*, vol. 4, p. 157.
38 Jackie Kay, *Twice Over*. Commissioned by Theatre Centre. First performed as a rehearsed reading in Gay Sweatshop's x10 Festival, at the Oval House, March 1987. Performed at the Drill Hall 27 Sept. to 15 Oct. 1988, directed by Nona Shepphard, designed by Kate Owen. Published in Philip Osment (ed.), *The Gay Sweatshop: Four Plays and a Company* (1989).
39 The same criticism might be made of Jackie Kay's first play, *Chiaroscuro*, written for Theatre of Black Women and given a reading at Gay Sweatshop's x10 Festival (Spring 1985). First produced at the Soho Poly, 19 March 1986; toured the Drill Hall, the Oval House, the Cockpit Theatre and various community arts centres in London. Directed by Joan Ann Maynard, designed by Helena Roden. Published in Jill Davis (ed.), *Lesbian Plays* (1987).
40 Jill W. Fleming, *The Rug of Identity*. First performed at the Oval House, London, by Hard Corps on 5 Feb. 1986. Directed by Jude Alderson, designed by Amanda Wilson. Published in Jill Davis (ed.), *Lesbian Plays* (1987). All textual quotations are from this published version of the play.
41 Liz Lochhead – one of the most radical Scottish feminist playwrights and poets of the 1980s and 1990s – has written an ironic poem with the title 'Everybody's Mother', published in Rosemary Palmeira (ed.), *In The Gold of the Flesh* (London: The Women's Press, 1990), pp. 146–8. American columnist Erma Bombeck has defined and described 'everybody else's mother' as 'a person used frequently in children's arguments, she is a woman who likes live-in snakes, ice cream before dinner and unmade beds. . . . She is a myth, that's who she is.' Erma Bombeck, 'Bombeck on Bombeck', *Family Circle*, 3, 14, 21 Jan. 1984. Cited in *A Feminist Dictionary*, ed. Cheris Kramarae and Paula A. Treichler (London: Pandora Press, 1985), p. 145.
42 Caryl Churchill, *Cloud Nine*, in *Plays: One* (London: Methuen, 1985), pp. 307 and 309.
43 Jill Davis' list was compiled for use in an unpublished paper, 'Theatre and the lesbian community', delivered to the 'Gender, Text, Image: Women in Theatre' Conference at Nene College, Northampton, 19 Nov. 1988. The list and thematic breakdown were provided by Davis in personal correspondence, 5 Dec. 1988.
44 Kate Davy, 'Reading past the heterosexual imperative', *TDR: The Drama Review*, vol. 33, Spring 1989.
45 See Sande Zeig, 'The actor as activator: deconstructing gender through gesture,' *Woman and Performance*, vol. 2.2, 1985, p. 14.
46 *Donna Giovanni* by Companias Divas of Mexico, directed by Alicia Urretta and Alberto Cruzprieto. US tour, performance at Purchase, NY, Summerfest 1987 (festival director, Peter Sellars).
47 *Dress Suits to Hire* by Holly Hughes, in collaboration with Peggy Shaw and Lois Weaver for New York's Split Britches. Designed by Joni Wong, performed by Peggy Shaw and Lois Weaver. First English performance at the Drill Hall, Sept. 1988. Reviewed in *The London Theatre Record*, 1988, 26 Aug. to 8 Sept., pp. 1185–6.
48 Split Britches and Bloolips in *Belle Reprieve*, devised and performed by Lois Weaver with Peggy Shaw, Bette Bourn and Precious Pearl. Music by Laka

Daisical and Phil Booth; set design by Nancy Bardawil and Mathew Owens; costumes by Susan Young; light design by Lizz Poulter. A co-production of the Drill Hall, London and La Mama ETC, New York. Performed at the Junction Arts Centre, Cambridge on 11–12 Feb. 1992 as part of a second British tour.

49 Sue-Ellen Case, *Feminism and Theatre* (1988), p. 80.

50 See Jill Dolan, 'Women's theatre program ATA: creating a feminist forum', *Woman and Performance*, vol. 1.2, 1984; and the major discussion of her theories in 'Toward a Critical Methodology of Lesbian Feminist Theatre', unpublished MA thesis, New York University, 1983.

51 Zeig and Wittig, discussed in Sue-Ellen Case, *Feminism and Theatre* (1988), pp. 79–81.

52 Jill Davis (ed.), *Lesbian Plays* (1987), p. 11.

53 See my article 'Comic subversions in feminist theatre', in *Imagining Women: Cultural Representations and Gender*, ed. F. Bonner, L. Goodman, R. Allen, L. Janes and C. King (Cambridge: Polity Press, 1992).

54 From an interview with Joan Lipkin, 15 Nov. 1991, the revised version of which is scheduled for publication in *New Theatre Quarterly*, vol. 9, no. 34, May 1993. Further quotations are also taken from the transcript of this taped interview (approved by Lipkin).

55 From the unpublished (1989) script provided by Lipkin.

56 Interview with Joan Lipkin, 15 Nov. 1991.

57 Ibid.

58 Jill Davis, 'Archetypes and Stereodykes', an unpublished paper delivered at the 'Archetype, Stereotype, Prototype' Conference at the University of Warwick, 16 May 1992.

6 BLACK FEMINIST THEATRES IN CULTURAL CONTEXT

1 Sandra J. Richards, 'Women, Theatre and Social Action', unpublished paper delivered at the international conference/festival held at the University of Calgary, 13–17 Nov. 1991.

2 Kathy A. Perkins (ed.), *Black Female Playwrights: An Anthology of Plays Before 1950* (Bloomington and Indianapolis: Indiana University Press, 1990); and Ann Allen Shockley (ed.), *Afro-American Women Writers 1746–1933: An Anthology and Critical Guide* (New York: Meridian Books, 1988).

3 See Helen Krich Chinoy and Linda Walsh Jenkins (eds), *Women in American Theatre* (New York: Theatre Communications Group, 2nd edn, 1987) and some of the interviews in Kathleen Betsko and Rachel Koenig (eds), *Interviews with Contemporary Women Playwrights* (New York: Beech Tree Books, 1987). In addition, Ruby Cohn discusses the work of Alice Childress and Adrienne Kennedy in a chapter titled 'Black on black', in *New American Dramatists 1960–1990* (Basingstoke: Macmillan, 1991; first published 1982).

4 See especially Nesha Z. Haniff, *Blaze a Fire: Significant Contributions of Caribbean Women* (Ontario: Sister Vision Press, 1988), which chronicles the work of women involved in various aspects of the Arts, from education to the development of different languages, to dance and the theatre.

5 Michelene Wandor, *Carry on Understudies: Theatre and Sexual Politics* (London: Routledge & Kegan Paul, 1981), p. 183.

6 Catherine Itzin, *Stages in the Revolution: Political Theatre in Britain Since 1968* (London: Methuen, 1980), pp. 53–4.

7 Cecilia Green argues this case in 'Towards a "weapon of theory" for black

and working class women's liberation', a review of Angela Davis' *Women, Race and Class* (New York: Random House, 1981). Green's provocative essay appears in *The Issue is 'Ism: Women of Colour Speak Out* (Ontario: Sister Vision Press, 1989), *Fireweed* issue no. 16.

8 Helene Keyssar (1984) has discussed these four women. Other black women playwrights, Chicana women playwrights and Native American coalition theatre workers are discussed in Sue-Ellen Case, *Feminism and Theatre* (New York: Methuen, 1988), pp. 100–11. Lynda Hart's anthology *Making a Spectacle* (Ann Arbor: The University of Michigan Press, 1989) includes several articles on black women's theatre (focused primarily on playwrights and their plays), and on Japanese American and Chicana women's work in the theatre. Karen Malpede's anthology *Women in Theatre* (New York: Limelight Editions, 1985) includes a section on Lorraine Hansberry (pp. 163–76). Methuen's two volumes of *Black Plays*, ed. Yvonne Brewster (1987 and 1989), include plays by women and brief introductions to them. In Ann Considine and Robyn Slovo's anthology of new plays by young women, *Dead Proud* (London: The Women's Press, 1987), the work of a few young black women is published and discussed in connection with the community importance of the Second Wave Project's work at the Albany Empire Theatre in East London.

9 Sue-Ellen Case, *Feminism and Theatre* (1988), p. 104.

10 *Chiaroscuro* is published in Jill Davis (ed.), *Lesbian Plays* (London: Methuen, 1987).

11 See *Money to Live* in *Plays by Women*, ed. Michelene Wandor, vol. 5 (London: Methuen, 1986) and *Basin* in *Black Plays*, ed. Yvonne Brewster (London: Methuen, 1987).

12 Feminist Theatre Survey response, received in 1988.

13 Listings and resources for black theatres are included in two new Arts Council documents: Susan Okoken's 'An Introductory Guide to Travel Opportunities for Black Arts Practitioners', ACGB, August 1991; and 'Women in Arts: Networking Internationally', the Arts Council in collaboration with the Women Artists' Slide Library, 1991.

14 Jatinder Verma, 'Marginalized like me', *Artrage*, Winter 1988, p. 5.

15 *Blackwright*: A report for the Advisory Panel of the New Playwrights Trust, Towards the Production of the New Playwrights Trust and Black Audio Film Collectives' Black Playwrights Directory and Black and Third World Screen Writers Directory. Researched and compiled by Julie Reid, August 1991. Copies available upon request from the New Playwrights Trust, London.

16 Taslima Hossain Rana, 'The Contingencies Affecting the Participation of Bengali Sylheti Speaking Women of All Ages in the Devising Process and Performance of a Bilingual Play: A Guide to the Writer', April 1991. Copies available upon request from the New Playwrights Trust, London.

17 Bernardine Evaristo's paper on 'Theatre of Black Women: an odyssey through the 80s' is forthcoming in *Sphinx Arts Journal*.

18 Interview with Bernadine Evaristo, 28 March 1991, London. The following quotations are all taken from this interview.

19 Ibid. The transcript from that interview was checked and approved by Evaristo.

20 The information on Talawa in this section is taken from my published interview with Yvonne Brewster: 'Drawing the black and white line/Defining black women's theatre', *New Theatre Quarterly*, vol. 7, no. 28, Nov. 1991 – an edited version of the transcript of a taped interview, conducted at the (former) Talawa Theatre Offices, Africa Centre, Covent Garden, London on 27 Feb. 1991. Brewster is the editor of Methuen's two volumes of *Black Plays* (1987 and 1989)

and is currently editing a third volume for the series (expected date of publication: late 1992).

21 Lizbeth Goodman, 'Drawing the black and white line . . . an interview with Yvonne Brewster', 1991, p. 361.

22 Personal correspondence: Brewster to Goodman, 6 Feb. 1991.

23 My interview with Yvonne Brewster (1991).

24 This information is extracted from Talawa's 1990 response to my 'Feminist Theatre Survey'.

25 Work produced includes 1985/6: *The Black Jacobins* by C. L. R. James; 1986/7: *An Echo in the Bone* by Dennis Scott; 1987/8: *O Babylon!* by Derek Walcott; 1988/9: Wilde's *The Importance of Being Earnest*, 1989/90: *The Gods Are Not to Blame* by Ola Rotimi; 1990/1: *The Dragon Can't Dance* by Earl Lovelace; 1991/2: Shakespeare's *Antony and Cleopatra*; Ntozake Shange's *The Love Space Demands*.

26 Lizbeth Goodman, 'Drawing the black and white line . . . an interview with Yvonne Brewster', 1991. The following quotations are from the same interview.

27 Sue-Ellen Case, *Feminism and Theatre* (1988), p. 102.

28 Elean Thomas, 'Lionhearted women: Sistren Women's Theatre Collective', *Spare Rib*, no. 172, Nov. 1986, p. 15.

29 Ibid., pp. 15–16.

30 Didi Elliott in interview with Elean Thomas, in Thomas, 1986, p. 16.

31 Interview remarks quoted in Thomas, 1986, p. 18.

32 Sistren Theatre Collective with Honor Ford Smith, *Lionheart Gal* (London: The Women's Press, 1990). Elean Thomas lists a few other publications which have been inspired by or written about Sistren. See Thomas, 1986, p. 19.

33 Sistren videos and magazines are available by post from the Sistren Theatre Collective, 20 Kensington Crescent, Kingston 5, Jamaica.

34 The 'Breaking the Surface' Festival/Conference was held at the University of Calgary, 13–17 Nov. 1991. This event is discussed in more detail in the conclusion to this book.

35 Annie May Blake, quoted in Sistren Theatre, 'Sistren profile', *Sistren*, vol. 13, no. 1, July 1991, p. 3

36 From an unpublished transcript of an interview with Denise Wong, director of the Black Mime Theatre Women's Troop, 4 April 1991, London. All further quotations are taken from this interview, the transcript of which was read and approved by Denise Wong and Mel Jennings (company administrator).

37 *Mothers* was devised by the Black Mime Theatre Women's Troop, directed by Denise Wong. It was first performed on national tour in Nov. 1990; it played in London at the International Mime Festival in Jan. 1991.

38 Unpublished interview with Denise Wong, April 1991.

39 *Have You Seen Zandile?*: a play originated by Gcina Mhlophe, with Maralin Vanrenen and Thembi Mtshali (Johannesburg: Skotaville Publishers, 1988). First produced at the Market Theatre, Johannesburg, 6 Feb. to 8 March 1986; performed in England as part of the London International Festival of Theatre (LIFT), 1991.

40 The play has received academic attention in England: Dennis Walder has written about the play and introduced an audio cassette containing extracts from Gcina Mhlophe's performance. This work is part of a new fourth-level Open University Course, 'Post-Colonial Literatures in English' (forthcoming 1993: available only to Open University students and staff, due to restrictions on copyright).

41 Djanet Sears, *Afrika Solo* (Ontario: Sister Vision Black Women and Women of Colour Press, 1990).
42 From the 'Afterword' to *Afrika Solo*, p. 95.
43 Published by Sister Vision Press, Ontario, Canada.
44 Nigel Hunt, 'Fringe of Toronto', *Theatrum*, Sept./Oct. 1991, p. 32.
45 Cecilia Green, 'Towards a "weapon of theory" for black and working class women's liberation', 1989.
46 Valerie Smith, 'Black feminist theory and the representation of the "other"', in *Changing Our Words: Essays on Criticism, Theory, and Writing by Black Women*, ed. Cheryl A Wall (London: Routledge, 1989), p. 47.

7 NEW DIRECTIONS IN FEMINIST THEATRE(S)

1 cf. Sue-Ellen Case, *Feminism and Theatre* (New York: Methuen, 1988), pp. 56–61; Jeanie Forte, 'Female body as text in women's performance art', in *Women in American Theatre*, ed. Helen Krich Chinoy and Linda Walsh Jenkins (New York: Theatre Communications Group, 2nd edn, 1987), p. 378.
2 This has been argued by Moira Roth (ed.), *The Amazing Decade: Women and Performance Art 1970–1980* (Los Angeles: Astro Artz, 1982), by RoseLee Goldberg, *Performance Art: From Futurism to the Present* (London: Thames & Hudson, revised edn, 1988); and by several newspaper journalists in recent months. See, for instance, Naseem Khan, 'Mime time for the Euro art form', *The Guardian Guide*, 4–5 Jan. 1991, p. vii; and Deborah Orr, 'Unmasking the world of dreams', The *Guardian*, 11 Jan. 1991, p. 34.
3 Texts by some of the American performance artists mentioned in this section have been published in Lenora Champagne (ed.), *Out From Under: Texts by Women Performance Artists* (London: Nick Hern Books, 1990).
4 Interview with the company following a performance of *Three Sisters in I Want to Go to Moscow*, at the Traverse Theatre, Edinburgh, 30 Aug. 1988 (the Edinburgh Festival). The following quotations, unless otherwise noted, are from this and subsequent interviews with company members (see final section of Bibliography for details).
5 Quoted from the letter which served as the follow-up to a series of conversations (with Susannah Rickards and Victoria Worsley), Dec. 1988 to Feb. 1989.
6 Telephone conversation with Caroline Ward re critical reactions to *Make Me a Statue* after the London run at the ICA, 3 April 1990. See the production photograph of Worsley as Camille Claudel, holding the weight of the paternalistic legacy of Rodin's art on her shoulders (p. 187 above).
7 Peter Holland, 'Reading to the Company', a paper delivered to the Graduate Drama Seminar, Selwyn College, Cambridge, 24 Oct. 1989; published in Hanna Scolnicov and Peter Holland (eds), *Reading Plays: Interpretation and Reception* (Cambridge: Cambridge University Press, 1991).
8 Terry Eagleton, 'The author as producer', in *Marxism and Literary Criticism* (London: Methuen, 1976), p. 59.
9 Jill Dolan, 'Materialist feminism, postmodernism, poststructuralism . . . and theory', *TDR: The Drama Review*, T123, Fall 1989, p. 59.
10 Interview with Sheila Yeger, 24 June 1988.
11 Terry Browne, *Playwrights' Theatre: The English Stage Company at the Royal Court* (London: Pitman, 1975), p. 37. This text includes a chronology of all the plays produced at the Royal Court, highlighting the 'Sunday Night productions without decor' (seventy in all).
12 Ann Jellicoe quoted in Richard Findlater, *At the Royal Court* (Ambergate:

Amberlane Press, 1981), p. 56. cf. George Devine, 'The right to fail', *The Twentieth Century*, vol. 169, Jan. 1961.

13 For further information about the work of Jane Howell and Pam Brighton at the Court, see Philip Roberts, *The Royal Court Theatre 1965–72* (London and New York: Routledge & Kegan Paul, 1986).

14 Small-scale groups such as Player-Playwrights and the Playwrights' Cooperative (London), and larger networks such as the Pub Theatre Network, CWTDA (the Standing Conference of Women Theatre Directors and Administrators), the New Playwrights' Trust, ITC (the Independent Theatres Council), and TWU (the Theatre Writers' Union) are just a few of these organizations. SCYPT (the Standing Conference of Young People's Theatre) was set up in 1975 to cover TIE and YPT schemes; SESAME and SHAPE (national) and AIM (Arts Integration Merseyside) are just a few of the many organizations making theatre by and for disabled and disadvantaged people. Further details and addresses in *The British Alternative Theatre Directory* (London: Conway and McGillivray, 1988 and annually).

15 Sarah Daniels, *Beside Herself* (originally titled *The Power and the Story*). Funding for this rehearsed reading was provided in part by GLA and the London Borough Grants Scheme (grant for WPT for 1988–9) and from private 'angels' and local sponsors of the Women's Playhouse Trust.

16 After sitting in on rehearsals, I discussed and corresponded with Daniels about the process. Rehearsals for the rehearsed reading of *Beside Herself* took place from Tuesday 16 to Saturday 20 Aug. 1988; the rehearsed reading was 'performed' on the evening of 20 Aug. 1988. All these stages in the process took place in the Theatre Upstairs, the Royal Court Theatre. Quotations and observations, unless otherwise cited, are from notes taken at rehearsal breaks (no notes could be taken during rehearsals).

17 Daniels has explained that the first draft which was presented to the director was revised before it was shared with the performers in rehearsal. Daniels made further revisions to the text during the rehearsal process.

18 Notes from rehearsal of *Beside Herself*, 20 Aug. 1988.

19 See the production photograph from the staged production (not from the reading) of the characters Evelyn and Eve (Fig. 8). The characters embody divided aspects of the same person. Their separation is represented as divided spatially by a domestic appliance (the refrigerator) and emotionally by antagonistic denial of each other (suggested in their facial expressions).

20 In Daniels' words: 'These were the only revisions made in the rehearsal process, and they were not included in the final staged and published version'. Personal correspondence quoted with permission, Feb. 1991.

21 Notes from rehearsal of *Beside Herself*, 20 Aug. 1988.

22 Michael Billington, 'Wounded child, haunted woman', The *Guardian*, 6 April 1990, p. 37.

23 Julie Wilkinson, report to the Theatre Writers Union, Winter 1988. cf. Richard Pinner, 'Contract in Writing: A Report About Writing in and for TIE and Community Theatre today' (London: TWU, 1984).

24 TWU newsletter, Feb. 1989, p. 5. Also see my short report on a group discussion/workshop on the subject of TIE (participants included Julie Wilkinson and Kathleen McCreery), 'Devising as writing', *TDR: The Drama Review*, T126, Summer 1990. The long transcript, 'The (woman) writer and TIE', is published in two parts in *MTD: Journal of the Performance Arts*, Part 1 in no. 3 (Winter 1990) and Part 2 in no. 4 (Summer 1991).

25 See Ann Jellicoe, *Community Plays: How to Put Them On* (London: Methuen, 1987).

26 While there are as yet no 'academic' sources on this subject, some of this work has been written about in newspaper articles: cf. 'A Graeae area of the Arts', *GLA Quarterly*, no. 11, 1987–8; reviews on a double-bill of bilingual women's plays by The Asian Theatre Cooperative, *The London Theatre Record*, no. 24, 1988; Common Stock's recent work on a common theatre for the deaf and the hearing.

27 Berta Freistadt, *The Celebration of Kokura*. First performed by Freistadt's pupils at the Deanery High School for Girls, East London, 1970; published in Stephen Lowe (ed.), *Peace Plays* (London: Methuen, 1985), authors' notes pp. 45–6. Women's Theatre Group, *My Mother Says I Never Should*. First performed at the Oval House Theatre, 1975, then on tour; published in Michelene Wandor (ed.), *Strike While the Iron is Hot* (London: Journeyman Press, 1980). Charlotte Keatley, *My Mother Said I Never Should*. First performed at the Contact Theatre, Manchester, 25 Feb. 1987, directed by Brigid Larmour, opened at the Royal Court 28 Feb. 1989; published by Methuen, 1988. Lou Wakefield and WTG, *Time Pieces*. First performed at the Oval House Theatre, Jan. 1982; published in Michelene Wandor (ed.), *Plays by Women*, vol. 3 (London: Methuen, 1984).

28 Interview with Penny Casdagli (aka Maro Green), revised with notes from Casdagli and Caroline Griffin (1991).

29 Ibid., supplemented with information from promotional materials and reviews of the plays.

30 Interview with Steve Mannix, Graeae administrator, 28 March 1991, London.

31 From the publicity blurb released in Jan. 1992. The play had not yet been produced when this book went to press, but the press release has billed it as 'the first ever professional play to be performed by blind people and written by a writer who is herself blind; . . . an account of the experiences and struggles encountered by disabled people'.

32 Timberlake Wertenbaker in interview, 'Writers Revealed', on *Woman's Hour* BBC Radio 4, 20 June 1991.

33 Postal interview following telephone conversations with Alexandra Ford, 1991: see final section of bibliography for details.

34 Jane Edwardes, 'Closing stages', *Time Out*, 23–30 March 1988, p. 41.

35 Patrice Pavis, *Theatre at the Crossroads of Culture*, trans. Loren Kruger (London: Routledge, 1992), p. 99.

36 For example, the 'Women Live' annual festivals, Operation Pearl, the Manchester Women and Theatre Group TIE, NE1 Theatre Co., Tynewear TIE and the Girls' Video Project, etc. Details on these projects provided in part by Janet Mantle (on behalf of herself and Sue Ashby, for the Manchester Women and Theatre Group): personal correspondence, 31 May 1988.

37 Kay Hepplewrite for NE1 and the Girls' Video Project, personal correspondence: letter and promotional materials, 2 June 1988.

38 Gilly Fraser, *A Bit of Rough*. Unpublished script (dated Oct. 1987) available through Judy Daish Associates, London.

39 Yearly listings of theatre awards in *The London Theatre Record*, year-end reports, 1983–7. Newspapers commonly list Olivier award winners: see, for example, The *Observer*, The *Guardian* (for 1988–90 listings).

8 BRITISH FEMINIST THEATRE IN AN INTERNATIONAL CONTEXT

1 Sarah Daniels, introduction to *Plays: One* (London: Methuen, 1991), p. xii; Caryl Churchill, interviewed in Kathleen Betsko and Rachel Koenig (eds), *Interviews with Contemporary Women Playwrights* (New York: Beech Tree Books, 1987), p. 77; Joan Lipkin of That Uppity Theatre Company, St Louis, Missouri, interviewed by Lizbeth Goodman, 15 Nov. 1991.
2 From Mary Childers and bell hooks, 'A conversation about race and class', in *Conflicts in Feminism*, ed. Marianne Hirsch and Evelyn Fox Keller (London: Routledge, 1990), p. 70.
3 Sue-Ellen Case, *Feminism and Theatre* (New York: Methuen, 1988), p. 112.
4 Patrice Pavis, 'Theory as one of the Fine Arts', in *Theatre at the Crossroads of Culture*, trans. Loren Kruger (London: Routledge, 1992), p. 89.
5 Marilyn French, 'Afterword' to Jane Wagner, *The Search for Signs of Intelligent Life in the Universe* (New York: HarperCollins Publishers, 1986), p. 222.
6 This is the basic tenet of the keynote paper which I wrote and delivered (with video illustrations provided by Jill Greenhalgh and Janise Browning-Levesque) at the 'Breaking the Surface' Conference/Festival, held at the University of Calgary, 13–17 Nov. 1991.
7 See Sue-Ellen Case, *Feminism and Theatre* (1988), pp. 127–32.
8 Gayatri Chakravorty Spivak, interviewed by Walter Adamson in 1986: 'The problem of cultural self-representation' in Spivak, *The Post-Colonial Critic*, ed. Sarah Harasym (London: Routledge, 1990), p. 52. This interview was first published in *Thesis Eleven*, no. 15, 1986.
9 Nadine Gordimer, 'The essential gesture', in *The Essential Gesture: Writing, Politics and Places*, ed. Stephen Clingman (New York: Alfred A. Knopf, 1988), p. 291.
10 Ann McFerran, 'An interview with Pam Gems', *Time Out*, Oct. 1977, pp. 21–7.
11 Susan Bassnett (Susan E. Bassnett-McGuire), 'Towards a theory of women's theatre', in *Linguistic and Literary Studies in Eastern Europe*, vol. 10: *The Semiotics of Drama and Theatre*, ed. Herta Schmid and Aloysius Van Kesteren (Amsterdam and Philadelphia: John Benjamins, 1984), p. 445.
12 Gillian Elinor, 'Performance as an audience activity', *Feminist Art News*, Summer 1980.
13 Jill Dolan, *The Feminist Spectator as Critic* (Ann Arbor: The University of Michigan Press, 1988), pp. 99 and 101.
14 Erving Goffman, *The Presentation of Self in Everyday Life* (New York: Penguin Books, 1959). cf. studies of the role of the audience in ritual drama: Mary Jo Deegan, *American Ritual Dramas: Social Rules and Cultural Meanings* (Westport, CT: Greenwood Press, 1989); and in dance: Judith Lynne Hanna, *The Performer –Audience Connection: Emotion and Metaphor in Dance and Society* (Austin: The University of Texas Press, 1983).
15 Deborah Levy, 'Structuring the Audience's Attention', unpublished discussion paper delivered at a Graduate Women and Literature Seminar, St John's College, Cambridge, 1989.
16 From the transcript of a taped interview with Joan Lipkin of That Uppity Theatre Company, St Louis, Missouri; interviewed in Calgary, 15 Nov. 1991. The revised version of this interview is scheduled for publication in *New Theatre Quarterly*, vol. 9, 1993.
17 *Reno Once Removed*, developed and directed by Eyan Yionoulis, with original music by Mike Yionoulis, staged at the Public Theatre, New York, Dec. 1991. First staged as part of the Serious Fun! Festival at Lincoln Center, New York, on 24 July 1991.

18 The conference was held at the University of Warwick on 19 May 1990. 'Self as source', in *Women and Theatre Occasional Papers 1*, ed. Maggie Gale and Susan Bassnett, 1992.

19 Jill Dolan, 'Bending gender to fit the canon: the politics of production', in *Making a Spectacle: Feminist Essays on Contemporary Women's Theatre* (Ann Arbor: The University of Michigan Press, 1989), p. 336.

20 Sue-Ellen Case, *Feminism and Theatre* (1988) p. 114.

21 Terry Eagleton, 'The author as producer', in *Marxism and Literary Criticism* (London: Methuen, 1976), p. 60.

CONCLUSION

1 Charlotte Canning, 'Performing Community: Feminist Theatre of the Early Second Wave in the United States', and Peta Tait, 'Gender Roles Offstage', unpublished papers delivered at the 'Breaking the Surface' Conference/Festival, The University of Calgary, 13–17 Nov. 1991.

2 See the following reports on international women's theatre conferences and festivals: my short report on the 'Women and Theatre International' initiative, with a draft of the 'Call to Action' is published in *Women and Theatre Occasional Papers 1*, ed. Maggie Gale and Susan Bassnett, 1992. See the report by the 'Breaking the Surface' conference organizers – Susan Bennett, Tracy Davis and Kathleen Foreman – in *New Theatre Quarterly* vol. 8, no. 30, May 1992, pp. 187–93. For details or a copy of the International Working Party membership list and drafts of the Canadian, British and Australian versions of the 'Call to Action', please write to The Organizers, 'Breaking the Surface', c/o Dept of Drama, University of Calgary, 2500 University Drive, NW, Calgary, Alberta, Canada TN2 1N4. Joan Lipkin has published her report on 'Breaking the Surface' in *Callboard*, a monthly magazine published by Theatre Bay Area, San Francisco, CA, Feb. 1992. Peta Tait has published her report in the Australian *Women and Theatre Newsletter*.

A brief account of the first Divina conference held in Turin is published in *New Theatre Quarterly*, vol. 7, no. 25, pp. 97–9; and a report on the second Divina conference is published in *New Theatre Quarterly*, vol. 8, no. 30, May 1992. Some of the contributions to the first Divina Conference have been collected for publication in Antonia Spaliviero (ed.), *Divina: Stories of Life and Theatre* (Turin: Tirrenia Stampatori, 1992).

Also see Rita Much's report 'Voices of authority: a report from Toronto', *New Theatre Quarterly*, vol. 7, no. 28, Nov. 1991, pp. 390–1; and Lisa Ann Johnson's report, 'Grieving my ghetto', *Theatrum* (Canada), no. 25, Sept./Oct. 1991, pp. 4–5.

3 Jim Delmont, 'Play blends words, images', *The Omaha World-Herald*, 11 Jan. 1992, p. 25c.

BIBLIOGRAPHY

Plays and performance pieces discussed in the text which are not available in any printed form are cited in the notes only. Printed sources are separated into three categories: playtexts and anthologies; published reference sources; and unpublished reference sources. A separate section at the end of the bibliography lists details of primary sources such as interviews and correspondence.

PLAYTEXTS AND ANTHOLOGIES

Arden, Jane, *Vagina Rex and the Gas Oven*, London: Calder and Boyers, 1981.

Barlow, Judith E. (ed.), *Plays by American Women: The Early Years*, New York: Avon Books, 1981. Including: Anna Cora Mowatt, *Fashion*; Rachel Crothers, *A Man's World*; Susan Glaspell, *Trifles*; Zona Gale, *Miss Lulu Bett*; Sophie Treadwell, *Machinal*.

—— (ed.), *Applause: Plays By American Women, 1900–1930*, New York: Theatre Book Publishers, 1985. Including: Rachel Crothers, *A Man's World*; Susan Glaspell, *Trifles*; Zona Gale, *Miss Lulu Bett*; Georgia Douglas Brown, *Plumes*; Sophie Treadwell, *Machinal*.

Beckett, Samuel, *Waiting for Godot*, London: Faber and Faber, 1986.

Behn, Aphra, *Five Plays*, introduced by Maureen Duffy, London: Methuen, 1990.

Brewster, Yvonne (ed.), *Black Plays*, London: Methuen, 1987. Including: Jacqueline Rudet, *Basin*.

—— (ed.), *Black Plays: Two*, London: Methuen, 1989. Including: Winsome Pinnock, *A Rock in Water*; Maria Oshodi, *Blood Sweat and Fears*.

Busch, Charles, *Vampire Lesbians of Sodom* and *Sleeping Beauty, or Coma*, New York: Samuel French, 1985.

Casdagli, Penny, *Only Playing, Miss!*, London: Neti-Neti Theatre Company, 1989.

Castledine, Annie (ed.), *Plays by Women Nine*, London: Methuen, 1991. Including: Marieluise Fleisser, *Purgatory in Ingolstadt, Pioneers in Ingolstadt, Avant-garde, Early Encounter*, and *I Wasn't Aware of the Explosive*; Maureen Lawrence, *Tokens of Affection*; Sheila Yeger, *Variations*.

Champagne, Lenora (ed.), *Out From Under: Texts by Women Performance Artists*, London: Nick Hern Books, 1990. Including: Holly Hughes, *World Without End*; Beatrice Roth, *The Father*; Laurie Anderson, from *United States*; Karen Finley, *The Constant State of Desire*; Rachel Rosenthal, *My Brazil*; Laurie Carlos, Jessica Hagedorn and Robbie McCauley, *Teeny Town*; Leeny Sack, *The Survivor and the Translator*; Lenora Champagne, *Getting Over Tom*; Fiona Templeton, *Strange to Relate*.

Churchill, Caryl, *Softcops and Fen*, London: Methuen, 1983.

—— *Plays: One*, London: Methuen, 1985.

—— *Serious Money*, London: Methuen, 1987.

—— *Three More Sleepless Nights*, first published in *British Women Writers*, ed. Dale Spender and Janet Todd, New York: Peter Bedrick Books, 1989.

—— *Ice Cream*, Royal Court Programme/Text, London: Nick Hern, 1989.

—— *Plays: Two*, London: Methuen, 1990.

—— *Mad Forest*, London: Nick Hern Books, 1990.

—— *Lives of the Great Poisoners*, unpublished author's copy of the text/libretto, 1991.

—— *Shorts*, London: Nick Hern Books, 1991. Including: *Three More Sleepless Nights, Lovesick, The After-Dinner Joke, Abortive, Schreber's Nervous Illness, The Judge's Wife, The Hospital at the Time of the Revolution, Hot Fudge, Not not not not not Enough Oxygen* and *Seagulls*.

Churchill, Caryl and Lan, David (for the Joint Stock Theatre Company), *A Mouthful of Birds*, London: Methuen, 1986.

Circle of the Witch Feminist Theatre Collective, *Sexpot Follies*, 'A satire on sexism from our own lives and experiences', unpublished.

Considine, Ann and Slovo, Robyn (eds), *Dead Proud, for Second Wave Young Women Playwrights*, Livewire Series, London: The Women's Press, 1987. Including: Marie Wilson, *Shopping Spree*; Briony Binnie, *Forshore*; Roselia John Baptiste, *Back Street Mammy*; Angie Milan, *Dead Proud*; Nandita Ghose, *Ishtar Descends*; Lisselle Layla, *When Did I See You Last*; Pauline Jacobs and The Bemarro Theatre Group, *A Slice of Life*; Cathy Kilcoyne and Robyn Slovo, *A Netful of Holes*; Roselia John Baptiste, *No Place Like Home*; Polly Teale (developed with Carol Pluckrose), *Fallen*.

Curino, Laura, *Passione*, unpublished (a brief summary of the play's action and references in English, by the author, is available from Teatro Settimo, Turin), 1991.

Curino, Laura and Settimo Teatro, *Stabat Mater*, unpublished, 1990.

Daniels, Sarah, *Masterpieces*, London: Methuen, 1984.

—— *Neaptide*, London: Methuen, 1986.

—— *Ripen our Darkness and The Devil's Gateway*, London: Methuen, 1986.

—— *Birthrite*, London: Methuen, 1987.

—— *Beside Herself*, London: Methuen, 1990 (text revised 1991).

—— *Plays: One*, London: Methuen, 1991.

Davies, Andrew, *Prin*, in *Plays International*, vol. 5, no. 3, Oct. 1989, pp. 38–49.

Davis, Jill (ed.), *Lesbian Plays*, London: Methuen, 1987. Including: Jill Posener, *Any Woman Can*, 1975; Libby Mason for WTG, *Double Vision*, 1982; Jackie Kay, *Chiaroscuro* (1986); Jill W. Fleming, *The Rug of Identity*, 1986.

—— (ed.), *Lesbian Plays: Two*, London: Methuen, 1989. Including: Debby Klein, *Coming Soon*; Catherine Kilcoyne, *Julie*; Sandra Freeman, *Supporting Roles*; Sue Frumin, *The Housetrample*; Cheryl Moch, *Cinderella, the Real True Story*.

Delaney, Shelagh, *A Taste of Honey*, London: Methuen, 1989 (first published 1959).

Devlin, Anne, *Ourselves Alone* (with *The Long March* and *A Woman Calling*), London and Boston: Faber and Faber, 1986.

Dunbar, Andrea, *Three Stage Plays: Rita, Sue and Bob Too, The Arbor, Shirley*, London: Methuen, 1988.

Fairbanks, Tash, *Curfew*, 1982, *From the Divine*, 1983; *Pulp*, 1985/6; *Hotel Destiny*, 1988, all unpublished scripts.

Ferris, Lesley, *The Subjugation of the Dragon*, unpublished author's copy, 1981.

Finley, Karen, *The Constant State of Desire*, *TDR: The Drama Review*, T117, Spring 1988.

Fitzsimmons, Linda and Gardner, Viv (eds), *New Woman Plays*, London: Methuen, 1991. Including: Elizabeth Robins, *Alan's Wife*; Cicey Hamilton, *Diana of Dobson's*; Elizabeth Baker, *Chains*; Githa Sowerby, *Rutherford and Son*.

Fo, Dario and Rame, Franca, *Female Parts: One Woman Plays*, London: Pluto Plays, 1981.

Fornes, Maria Irene, *Plays*, New York: PAJ Publications, 1986.

—— *Promenade and Other Plays*, New York: PAJ Publications, 1987.

France, Rachel (ed.), *A Century of Plays by American Women*, New York: Richards Rosen Press, 1979. Including: Megan Terry, *Ex-Miss Copper Queen on a Set of Pills*; Rosalyn Drexler, *Skywriting*; Maria Irene Fornes, *Dr Kheal*; Clare Boothe Luce, *Slam the Door Softly*; Joan Holden, *The Independent Female*; Karen Malpede, *Lament of Three Women*; Martha Boesing, *Pimp*.

Fraser, Gilly, *A Bit of Rough*, London: Judy Daisch Associates, Oct. 1987.

Furnival, Christine, *The Petition*, 1970, rewritten 1982; *The Starving of Sarah*, 1980; *The Jewel of the Just*, 1984; *The White Headscarves*, 1986; *The Flame You Gave Me*, 1971, unpublished scripts.

Gee, Shirley, *Warrior*, playtext published in *Plays International*, vol. 5, no. 2, Sept. 1989, pp. 36–50.

Gems, Pam, *Three Plays*, New York: Penguin Books, 1985.

Goorney, Howard and MacColl, Ewan (eds), *Agit-prop to Theatre Workshop: Political Playscripts 1930–50*, Manchester: Manchester University Press, 1986.

Green, Maro (aka Penny Casdagli) and Griffin, Caroline, *The Memorial Gardens*, unpublished authors' copy, 1988.

Griffin, Gabrielle and Aston, Elaine (eds), *Herstory: Volume One*, Sheffield: The Academic Press, 1991. Including: Women's Theatre Group and Elaine Feinstein, *Lear's Daughters*; Julie Wilkinson, *Pinchdice and Co*; Bryony Lavery, *Witchcraze*.

—— (eds), *Herstory: Volume Two*, Sheffield: The Academic Press, 1991. Including: Elisabeth Bond, *Love and Dissent*; Tierl Thompson and Libby Mason, *Dear Girl*; Joyce Holliday, *Anywhere to Anywhere*.

Hanna, Gillian (ed.), *Monstrous Regiment: A Collective Celebration*, London: Nick Hern Books, 1991. Including: Claire Luckham and C. G. Bond, *Scum*; Wendy Kesselman, *My Sister in this House*; Jenny McLeod, *Island Life*; Marta Tikkanen, *Love Story of the Century*.

Hardie, Victoria, *Sleeping Nightie*, in *First Run Two*, ed. Kate Harwood, London: Nick Hern Books, 1990.

Harwood, Kate (ed.), *First Run: New Plays by New Writers*, London: Nick Hern Books, 1989. Including: Clare McIntyre, *Low Level Panic*; Winsome Pinnock, *Leave Taking*.

—— (ed.), *First Run Two*, London: Nick Hern Books, 1990. Including: Victoria Hardie, *Sleeping Nightie*; Trish Cook, *Back Street Mammy*.

Hoffman, William M. (ed.), *Gay Plays: The First Collection*, New York: Avon Books, 1979. Including: Susan Miller, *Confessions of a Female Disorder*; Jane Chambers, *A Late Snow*; William M. Hoffman and Anthony Holland, *Cornbury*.

Honey, Joan, *The Play-Reading*, London: English Theatre Guild, 1971.

Horsfield, Debbie, *The Red Devils Trilogy*, London: Methuen, 1986.

Jellicoe, Ann, *The Knack, a Comedy*, London: Faber & Faber, 1962.

—— *Shelley, or The Idealist*, London: Faber & Faber, 1966.

—— *The Rising Generation*, London: Hutchinson Playbooks, no. 2, 1969.

—— *The Giveaway*, London: Faber & Faber, 1970.

—— *The Sport of My Mad Mother*, London: Faber & Faber, 1985 (first published 1958).

Johnson, Catherine, *Boys Mean Business*, published playtext in *Plays International*, Nov. 1989.

Johnson, Terry, *Unsuitable for Adults*, London: Faber and Faber, 1985.

Karge, Manfred, *Man to Man* in *Plays International*, 1987.

Keatley, Charlotte, *My Mother Said I Never Should*, London: Methuen, 1988.

Kendall (ed.), *Love and Thunder: Plays by Women in the Age of Queen Anne*, London: Methuen, 1988. Including: Susanna Centlivre, *The Adventures of Venice*, 1700; Mary Pix, *The Spanish Wives*, 1696; Catherine Trotter, *Love At A Loss, or Most Votes Carry It*, 1700; Jane Wiseman, *Antiochus the Great, or The Fatal Relapse*, 1701–2.

Kilgore, Emile S. (ed.), *Landmarks of Contemporary Women's Drama*, London: Methuen, 1992. Including: Marsha Norman, *Getting Out*; Wendy Kesselman, *My Sister in This House*; Lynn Siefert, *Coyote Ugly*; Tina Howe, *Painting Churches*; Anne Devlin, *Ourselves Alone*; Caryl Churchill, *Serious Money*; Lucy Gannon, *Keeping Tom Nice*.

Kroetz, Franz Xaver, *Request Programme*, unpublished script adapted by Nancy Diuguid (director), trans. Judy Waldman. Written 1971; performed in English adaptation 1987. Director's annotated copy.

Lamb, Myrna, *The Mod Donna and Scyklon Z: Plays of Women's Liberation*, New York: Merit Books, 1971. Including: *The Mod Donna and Scyklon Z; But What Have You Done for Me lately?; Monologia; Pas de Deux; The Butcher Shop; The Serving Girl and the Lady; In the Shadow of the Crematorium*.

LaTempa, Susan (ed.), *New Plays by Women*, Berkeley, CA: Shameless Hussy Press, 1979. Including: Toni Press, *Mash Note to an Old Codger*; L. M. Sullivan, *Baron's Night, or Catch as Catch Can*; Susan LaTempa, *The Life of the Party*; Helen Ratcliffe, *The Railroad Women*; Madeline Puccione, *Laundromat*; Betsy Julia Robinson, *The Shanglers*; Susan Boyd, *St Mael and the Maldukian Penguins*.

Lavery, Bryony, *Time Gentlemen Please*, unpublished script available from the Monstrous Regiment archives, 1978.

—— *Witchcraze*, unpublished author's copy, 1985.

—— *Kitchen Matters*, unpublished script available from the Gay Sweatshop archives, 1990.

—— *Her Aching Heart, Two Marias, Wicked*, London: Methuen, 1991.

Lessing, Doris, *Play With a Tiger*, New York: John Cushman Associates, 1962.

Levy, Deborah, *Heresies and Eva and Moses*, London: Methuen, 1987.

Lipkin, Joan, *Sketch for the ATHE Paper*, to accompany discussion of the play *He's Having Her Baby*, unpublished, 1990.

Lipkin, Joan and Clear, Tom, *Some of My Best Friends Are: A Gay and Lesbian Revue for People of all Preferences*, unpublished author's copy, 1989.

—— *He's Having Her Baby: A Pro-Choice Musical Comedy*, unpublished author's copy, 1990.

Lowe, Stephen (ed.), *Peace Plays*, London: Methuen, 1985. Including: Adrian Mitchell, *The Tragedy of King Real*, 1983; Berta Freistadt, *The Celebration of Kokura*, 1970; Deborah Levy, *CLAM*, 1985; Stephen Lowe, *Keeping Body and Soul Together*, 1984; Tanya Myers for Common Ground, *The Fence*, 1984.

Luckham, Claire, with Bond, C. G. and the Co., *SCUM*, unpublished script filed in the Monstrous Regiment archives, 1976.

MacDonald, Sharman, *When I Was a Girl I Used to Scream and Shout, When We Were Women, The Brave*, London: Faber and Faber, 1990.

Malpede, Karen, *A Monster Has Stolen the Sun and Other Plays*, Marlboro, VT: The Marlboro Press, 1987. Including: *The End of War* and *Sappho and Aphrodite*.

McDermott, Kate (ed.), *Places Please! The First Anthology of Lesbian Plays*, Santa Cruz: Aunt Lute Book Co., 1985. Including: Terry Baum and Carolyn Myers, *Dos Lesbos*; Sarah Dreher, *8 × 10 Glossy*; Julia Willis, *Going Up*; Terry Baum,

Immediate Family; Mariah Burton Nelson, *Out of Bounds*; Sarah Dreher, *Ruby Christmas*; Ellen Gruber Garvey, *Soup*.

McGrath, John, *Watching for Dolphins*, unpublished, 1991.

McIntyre, Clare, *Low Level Panic*, in *First Run: New Plays by New Writers*, ed. Kate Harwood, London: Nick Hern Books, 1989.

—— *My Heart's a Suitcase*, London: Nick Hern Books, 1990.

Mebarek, Gilli, *Treading on My Tale*, unpublished script available from the Clean Break Theatre Company archives, 1986. Broadcast on Channel Four television, March 1989.

Mhlophe, Gcina, with Vanrenen, Maralin and Mtshali, Thembi, *Have You Seen Zandile?*, Johannesburg: Skotaville Publishers, 1988.

Miles, Julia (ed.), *The Women's Project: Seven New Plays by Women*, New York: PAJ Publications 1980. Including: Joyce Aaron and Luna Tarlo, *Acrobatics*; Kathleen Collins, *In the Midnight Hour*; Penelope Gilliat, *Property*; Rose Leiman Goldemberg, *Letters Home*; Lavonne Mueller, *Killings on the Last Line*; Phyllis Purscell, *Separate Ceremonies*; Joan Schenkar, *Signs of Life*.

—— (ed.), *The Women's Project 2: Five New Plays by Women*, New York: PAJ Publications, 1984. Including: Kathleen Collins, *The Brother*; Lavonne Mueller, *Little Victories*; Carol K. Mack, *Territorial Rites*; Terry Galloway, *Heart of a Dog*; Paula Cizmar, *Candy and Shelley go to the Desert*.

—— (ed.), *Women Heroes: Six Short Plays from the Women's Project*, New York: Applause Theatre Book Publishers, 1987. Including: Lavonne Mueller, *Colette in Love*; Gina Wendkos and Ellen Ratner, *Personality*; Jessica Litwak, *Emma Goldman*; Denise Hamilton, *Parallax*; Cynthia Cooper, *How She Played the Game*; Susan Kander, *Milly*.

Mitchell, Ann with Todd, Susan, *Kiss and Kill*, unpublished script filed in the Monstrous Regiment archives, 1977–8.

Morgan, Natasha, *By George!*, 1982, *An Independent Woman*, 1986, unpublished scripts.

Monstrous Regiment (Caryl Churchill, Bryony Lavery, Michelene Wandor and David Bradford), *Floorshow*, unpublished script filed in the Monstrous Regiment archives, 1977–8.

Moore, Honor (ed.), *The New Women's Theatre: Ten Plays by Contemporary American Women*, New York: Vintage Books, 1977. Including: Corinne Jacker, *Bits and Pieces*; Tina Howe, *Birth and After Birth*; Honor Moore, *Mourning Pictures*; Myrna Lamb, *I Lost a Pair of Gloves Yesterday*; Eve Merriam, *Out of Our Father's Houses*; Alice Childress, *Wedding Band*; Joanna Halpert Kraus, *The Ice Wolf*; Joanna Russ, *Window Dressing*; Ursula Molinaro, *Breakfast Past Noon*.

Munro, Rona, *Saturday Night at the Commodore*, in *Scot-Free: New Scottish Plays*, ed. Alasdair Cameron, London: Nick Hern Books, 1990.

Murray, Melissa, *Coming Apart*, in *The Verity Bargate Awards: Short Plays*, London: Methuen, 1984.

Myers, Tanya, *The Fence*, author's annotated copy, 1984. Also published in *Peace Plays*, ed. Stephen Lowe, London: Methuen, 1985.

Norman, Marsha, *Night Mother*, New York: Dramatists Play Service, 1983.

Osborne, John, *Look Back in Anger*, London: Faber and Faber, 1957.

Osment, Philip (ed.), *The Gay Sweatshop: Four Plays and a Company*, London: Methuen, 1989. Including: Noel Greig, *Dear Love of Comrades*; Andy Kirby, *Compromised Immunity*; Philip Osment, *This Island's Mine*; Jackie Kay, *Twice Over*.

Page, Louise, *Salonika and Real Estate*, London: Methuen, 1984.

—— *Golden Girls*, London: Methuen, 1985.

—— *Beauty and the Beast*, London: Methuen, 1986.

—— *Plays: One*, London: Methuen, 1991.

Perkins, Kathy A. (ed.), *Black Female Playwrights: An Anthology of Plays Before 1950*, Bloomington and Indianapolis: Indiana University Press, 1990.
Pinnock, Winsome, *A Hero's Welcome*, in *Plays International*, vol. 4, no. 9, April 1989.
Playwrights Press (ed.), *Female Voices*, London: The Playwrights Press, 1987. Including: Juliet Aykroyd, *The Clean-up*; Anne Caulfield, *The Ungrateful Dead*, Elizabeth Gowans, *Casino*; Claire Schrader, *Corryvreken*; Susan Yankowitz, *Alarms*.
Poland, Albert and Mailman, Bruce (eds), *The Off-Off Broadway Book*, New York: Bobbs-Merrill, 1972. Including: Ruth Krauss, *A Beautiful Day*; Gertrude Stein, *What Happened*; Rosalyn Drexler, *Home Movies*; Tom Eyan, *Why Hanna's Skirt Won't Stay Down*; Rochelle Owens, *Futz*; Megan Terry, *Massachusetts Trust*; Maria Irene Fornes, *Molly's Dream*; Julie Bovasso, *Gloria and Esperanza*; Adrienne Kennedy, *A Rat's Mass*.
Rame, Franca, *The Mother* and *I Don't Move, I Don't Scream, My Voice is Gone*, trans. by La Commune and published in *Red Notes: Fo/Rame Workshops at Riverside Studios*, London: April/May 1983.
Randall, Paulette, *24%*, unpublished script available from the Clean Break Theatre Company archives, 1990.
The Raving Beauties (eds), *No Holds Barred: New Poems by Women*, performed as theatre pieces, London: Women's Press, 1985.
Ray, Brenda, *Pregnant Pauses*, 1981, rewritten for WTG rehearsed reading of 1985; *Dressing Up*, 1983; *Remember*, 1985/6; *Small Print*, 1987, unpublished scripts.
Reid, Christina, *Two Belfast Plays: Joyriders and Tea in a China Cup*, London: Methuen, 1987.
Remnant, Mary (ed.), *Plays by Women*, vol. 5, London: Methuen, 1986. Including: Pam Gems, *Queen Christina*, 1977; Lorraine Hansberry, *A Raisin in the Sun*, 1959; Rona Munro, *Piper's Cave*, 1985; Jacqueline Rudet, *Money to Live*, 1984.
—— (ed.), *Plays by Women*, vol. 6, London: Methuen, 1987. Including: Cordelia Ditton and Maggie Ford, *About Face*, 1985; Maro Green and Caroline Griffin, *More*, 1984; Bryony Lavery, *Origin of the Species*, 1984; Deborah Levy, *Pax*, 1985; Eve Lewis, *Ficky Stingers*, 1986.
—— (ed.), *Plays by Women*, vol. 7, London: Methuen, 1988. Including: Kay Adshead, *Thatcher's Women*, 1987; Claire Dowie, *Adult Child/Dead Child*, 1987; Lisa Evans, *Stamping, Shouting and Singing Home*, 1986; Marie Laberge, *Night (L'Homme Gris)*, 1985; Valerie Windsor, *Effie's Burning*, 1987.
—— (ed.), *Plays by Women*, vol. 8, London: Methuen, 1991. Including: April de Angelis, *Ironmistress*; Mary Cooper, *Heartgame*; Janet Cresswell and Niki Johnson, *The One-Sided Wall*; Ayshe Raif, *Caving In*; Ena Lamont Stewart, *Towards Evening and Walkies Time*; Joan Wolton, *Motherlove*.
Robson, Cheryl (ed.), *Female Voices, Fighting Lives: Seven Plays by Women*, London: Aurora Metro, 1991. Including: Eva Lewin, *Cochon Flambe*; April de Angelis, *Crux*; Jan Ruoppe, *Cut It Out*; Nina Rapi, *Ithaka*; Jean Abbott, *Forced Out*; Ayshe Raif, *Fail/Safe*; Cheryl Robson, *The Taking of Liberty*.
Royal Court Writers Series, *The Mayday Dialogues*, London: Methuen, 1990. Including: Julie Burchill, *How Now Green Cow*; Sue Townsend, *Disneyland it Ain't*; Jeannanne Crowley, *Goodnight Siobhan*.
Sears, Djanet, *Afrika Solo*, Ontario: Sister Vision Black Women and Women of Colour Press, 1990.
Shange, Ntozake, *For Colored Girls who have Considered Suicide when the Rainbow is Enuf*, London: Methuen, 1984.
Shaw, George Bernard, *Plays Unpleasant*, New York: Penguin Books, 1981.
Spender, Dale and Hayman, Carole (eds), *How the Vote Was Won and Other Suffragette Plays*, London: Methuen, 1985.

Stewart, Ena Lamont, *Men Should Weep*, Edinburgh: 7:84 Publications, 1983 (revival).

Sullivan, Victoria and Hatch, James (eds), *Plays by and About Women*, New York: Vintage Books, 1974. Including: Lillian Hellman, *The Children's Hour*; Clare Booth, *The Women*; Megan Terry, *Calm Down Mother*; Maureen Duffy, *Rites*; Alice Childress, *Wine in the Wilderness*.

Temerson, Catherine and Kourilsky, Françoise (eds.), *Plays by Women: An International Anthology*, New York: UBU Repertory Theatre Publishers, 1988. Including: Denise Bonal, *A Picture Perfect Sky*; Michele Fabien, *Jocasta*; Abla Farhoud, *The Girls From the Five and Ten*; Fatima Gallaire-Bourega, *You Have Come Back*; Simone Schwarz-Bart, *Your Handsome Captain*.

Terry, Megan, *Goona, Goona*, New York: Broadway Play Publishing, 1991.

Théâtre de l'Aquarium, *Shakespeare's Sister*, trans. by Monstrous Regiment for their English-language performance, unpublished, 1982.

Thomas, Heidi, *Indigo*, Oxford: Amber Lane Press, 1988.

Tilton, Charles and The Theatre Workshop, *Oh What a Lovely War!*, London: Methuen, 1982. Director, Joan Littlewood.

Townsend, Sue, *Bazaar and Rummage, Groping for Words, Womberang*, London: Methuen, 1984.

Van Twest, Patricia, *The Importance of Being Emulated*, 1981/2; *Scared*, 1982/3; *Odd Man Out*, 1984; *Lego, or Builders of Babylon*, 1987, unpublished scripts.

Vincent, Hannah, *The Burrow*, unpublished author's copy, 1989.

Wagner, Jane, *The Search for Signs of Intelligent Life in the Universe*, New York: Harper-Collins Publishers, 1986.

Wandor, Michelene, *Five Plays*, London: Journey/Playbooks, 1967.

—— (ed.), *Strike While the Iron is Hot*, London: Journeyman Press, 1980. Including: Red Ladder Theatre (Kathleen McCreery and Co.), *Strike While the Iron is Hot*; Gay Sweatshop (Michelene Wandor, scripted), *Care and Control*; Women's Theatre Group, *My Mother Says I Never Should*.

—— *Whores D'Oeuvres*, in *Hecate: A Women's Interdisciplinary Journal*, vol. 6, no. 2, 1980.

—— (ed.), *Plays by Women*, vol. 1, London: Methuen, 1982. Including: Caryl Churchill, *Vinegar Tom*, 1976; Pam Gems, *Dusa, Fish, Stas and Vi*, 1976; Louise Page, *Tissue*, 1978; Michelene Wandor, *Aurora Leigh*, 1979.

—— (ed.), *Plays by Women*, vol. 2, London: Methuen, 1983. Including: Maureen Duffy, *Rites*, 1969; Rose Leiman Goldemberg, *Letters Home*, 1979; Claire Luckham, *Trafford Tanzi*, 1980; Olwen Wymark, *Find Me*, 1977.

—— (ed.), *Plays by Women*, vol. 3, London: Methuen, 1984. Including: Pam Gems, *Aunt Mary*, 1982; Debbie Horsfield, *Red Devils*, 1983; Sharon Pollock, *Blood Relations*, 1980; Lou Wakefield and WTG, *Time Pieces*, 1982.

—— (ed.), *Plays by Women*, vol. 4, London: Methuen, 1985. Including: Caryl Churchill, *Objections to Sex and Violence*, 1975; Grace Dayley, *Rose's Story*, 1984; Liz Lochhead, *Blood and Ice*, 1984; Alison Lyssa, *Pinball*, 1981.

—— *Wanted*, London: Playbooks, 1988.

Wertenbaker, Timberlake, *The Love of the Nightingale and The Grace of Mary Traverse*, London: Faber and Faber, 1989.

—— *Our Country's Good*, London: Methuen in association with the Royal Court Theatre, 1989 (revised); first published 1988.

Wilcox, Michael (ed.), *Gay Plays*, vol. 1, London: Methuen, 1985. Including: Tom McClenaghan, *Submariners*, 1980; Mordaunt Shairp, *The Green Bay Tree*, 1933; Martin Sherman, *Passing By*, 1975; Michael Wilcox, *Accounts*, 1981.

—— (ed.), *Gay Plays*, vol. 2, London: Methuen, 1986. Including: Roger Gellert,

Quaint Honour, 1958; Timothy Mason, *Bearclaw*, 1969; Martin Sherman, *Cracks*, 1984; C. P. Taylor, *Lies About Vietnam*, 1975.

—— (ed.), *Gay Plays*, vol. 3, London: Methuen, 1988. Including: Richard Crowe and Richard Zajdlic, *Cock and Bull Story*, 1987; Paul Selig, *Terminal Bar*, 1985; Timothy Mason, *Levitation*, 1984; J. R. Ackerley, *The Prisoners of War*, 1925.

Wood, Victoria, *Good Fun and Talent*, London: Methuen, 1988.

Worsley, Victoria and Ward, Caroline, *Make Me A Statue*, unpublished author's copy, 1989/90.

Wymark, Olwen, *The Gymnasium and Other Plays*, London: Methuen, 1971.

—— *Lunchtime Concert*, in *Gambit: International Theatre Review*, vol. 10, no. 38, 1981.

Yeger, Sheila, *Endlessly Playing With Possibilities*, 198?; *The Lizzy Papers*, 1987; *Self Portrait; Dancing in the Dark*, 1987/8, unpublished scripts.

—— *Free 'n Lovely*, London: Theatre Venture, 1984.

PUBLISHED REFERENCE SOURCES

Abel, E. and Abel, Emily K. (eds), *The Signs Reader: Women, Gender and Scholarship*, Chicago: The University of Chicago Press, 1983.

Alcoff, Linda, 'Cultural feminism versus post-structuralism: the identity crisis in feminist theory', *Signs: Journal of Women in Culture and Society*, vol. 14, no. 3, Spring 1989.

Ambrose, B. (ed.), *An Actor's Aide Memoire*, from *Fowler's Technical Terms of Rhetoric, Grammar, Logic, Prosody, Diplomacy, Literature, etc.* by permission of Oxford University Press, London: Composium, 1983.

Andrews, Dennis, 'New drama and the Arts Council of Great Britain', *Gambit: International Theatre Review*, vol. 3, no. 10, 1969, pp. 90–2.

Anon., 'Five important playwrights talk about theatre without compromise and sexism', *Mademoiselle*, no. 75, Aug.–Oct., 1972.

Anon., 'Women's work', *Time Out*, 25 Nov.–1 Dec. 1977.

Anon., 'Grant aid and political theatre, 1968–77', *Wedge*, nos. 1 and 2, Summer 1977.

Anon., 'Theatre collectives, alive and kicking: new perspectives on theatre today', *Platform*, no. 4, 1982.

Ansorge, Peter, *Disrupting the Spectacle: Five Years of Experimental and Fringe Theatre in Britain*, London: Pitman Publishing, 1975.

Arden, John and D'Arcy, Margaretta, *Presenting the Pretense: Essays on Theatre and its Public*, London: Eyre Methuen, 1977.

Armitage, Jenny, 'The privatization of women', *Theatre Writers Union Journal*, Winter 1983.

Arthurs, Jane, 'Technology and gender: women and television production', *Screen*, vol. 30, nos. 1 and 2, Winter/Spring 1989, pp. 40–59.

Arts Council, 'Criteria for Grant-in-Aid', London: ACGB, May 1983.

—— 'The Glory of the Garden: The Development of the Arts in England', London: ACGB, 1984.

—— 'Guidelines to Applicants for Drama Project Subsidy', London: ACGB, 1 April 1986, 31 March 1987.

—— 'Marketing and Fundraising Guide', London: ACGB, Dec. 1988.

—— 'Arts and Disability Organizations and Projects', London: ACGB, 1989.

—— 'Arts Council Scheme for Writers and Theatre Companies 1989/90', London: ACGB, 1989.

—— 'Seat Prices in the Subsidized Theatres of Britain 1989/90', compiled by

Ferzana Butt, Research and Statistics Planning Department, London: ACGB, Oct. 1991.

—— 'Playlist England, 1990/1', Research and Statistics Planning Department, London: ACGB, Nov. 1991.

—— 'Drama Attendances England 1988/9, 1989/90, 1990/1', compiled by Ferzana Butt, Research and Statistics Planning Department, London: ACGB, Nov. 1991.

—— 'An Introductory Guide to Travel Opportunities for Black Arts Practitioners', complied by Susan Okoken, London: ACGB, Aug. 1991.

—— 'Women in Arts: Networking Internationally', the Arts Council in collaboration with the Women Artists' Slide Library, 1991.

Asquith, Ros, 'The wild bunch: Women's Theatre Group', a review in *Spare Rib*, no. 89, Dec. 1979, p. 43.

Association for Business Sponsorship of The Arts, *The ABSA Sponsorship Manual 1988/89*, London: ABSA, 1989.

Aston, Elaine, 'Feminism in the French theatre', *New Theatre Quarterly*, vol. 2, no. 7, Aug. 1986, pp. 237–42.

Auslander, Philip, 'Just be yourself: logocentrism and difference in performance theory', *Art and Cinema*, vol. 1, no. 1, Summer 1986.

—— 'Towards a concept of the political in postmodern theatre', *Theatre Journal*, vol. 39, no. 1, March 1987, pp. 20–34.

Axarlis, Nick, 'Arts Council theatre enquiry', *Artrage*, no. 15, 1986, pp. 43–4.

Bailey, Martin and de Bruxelles, Simon, 'Crisis over Arts funds may mean curtains', The *Observer*, 12 Nov. 1989, p. 9.

Banks, Morwenna and Swift, Amanda, *The Joke's On Us: Women in Comedy from Music Hall to the Present*, London: Pandora Press, 1987.

Banks, Olive, *Becoming a Feminist: The Social Origins of 'First Wave' Feminism*, Sussex: Wheatsheaf Books, 1986.

Barba, Eugenio, 'The actor's energy: male/female versus *Animus/Anima*', *New Theatre Quarterly*, vol. 3, no. 11, Aug. 1987, pp. 237–40.

Bardsley, Barney, 'The young blood of theatre: women's theatre groups', *Drama*, no. 152, 1984, pp. 25–9.

Barker, Clive and Trussler, Simon (eds), 'Theatre in Thatcher's Britain: organizing the opposition', *New Theatre Quarterly*, vol. 5, no. 18, May 1989, pp. 113–23.

Barreca, Regina (ed.), *Last Laughs: Perspectives on Women and Comedy*, New York: Gordon and Breach, 1988.

Barrett, Michele, 'The concept of "Difference" ', *The Feminist Review*, no. 26, Summer 1987, pp. 29–41.

Barth, John, *Chimera*, New York: Random House/Fawcett Crest, 1972.

Barthes, Roland, *Image-Music-Text*, trans. Stephen Heath, New York: The Noonday Press, 1977.

Bassnett, Susan (Susan E. Bassnett-McGuire), 'Notes on the work of Monstrous Regiment', in *British Drama and Theatre From The Mid Fifties to the Mid Seventies*, Rostock: Wilhelm-Pieck-Universitat, 1979.

—— 'An introduction to theatre semiotics', *Theatre Quarterly*, vol. 10, no. 38, 1980.

—— 'Towards a theory of women's theatre', in *Linguistic and Literary Studies in Eastern Europe*, vol. 10: *The Semiotics of Drama and Theatre*, ed. Herta Schmid and Aloysius Van Kesteren, Amsterdam and Philadelphia: John Benjamins, 1984.

—— *Feminist Experiences: The Women's Movement in Four Cultures*, London: Allen & Unwin, 1986.

—— 'Women experiment with theatre: Magdalena '86', *New Theatre Quarterly*, vol. 3, no. 1, Aug. 1987, pp. 224–33.

—— 'Perceptions of the female role', *New Theatre Quarterly*, vol. 3, no. 1, Aug. 1987, pp. 234–6.

—— 'Women's theatre in search of a history', *New Theatre Quarterly*, vol. 5, no. 18, May 1989, pp. 107–12.

—— *Magdalena: International Women's Experimental Theatre*, Oxford: Berg Publishers, 1989.

Battersby, Christine, *Gender and Genius*, London: The Women's Press, 1989.

Beauvoir, Simone de, *The Second Sex*, New York: Bantam Books, 1970.

Beauman, Sally, *The Royal Shakespeare Company: A History of Ten Decades*, Oxford: Oxford University Press, 1982.

Beechey, Veronica and Perkins, Tessa, *Women, Part-Time Work and the Labour Market*, Cambridge: Polity Press, 1987.

Belsey, Catherine and Moore, Jane, *The Feminist Reader: Essays in Gender and the Politics of Literary Criticism*, London: Macmillan, 1989.

Bennett, Paula, *My Life a Loaded Gun: Dickinson, Plath, Rich and Female Creativity*, Chicago: The University of Illinois Press, 1990.

Bennett, Susan, *Theatre Audiences: A Theory of Production and Reception*, London: Routledge, 1991.

Benstock, Shari, *The Private Self*, London: Routledge, 1988.

Betsko, Kathleen and Koenig, Rachel, *Interviews with Contemporary Women Playwrights*, New York: Beech Tree Books, 1987.

Bigsby, C. W. E., *Contemporary English Drama*, Stratford-Upon-Avon Studies, no. 19, London: Edward Arnold Publishers, 1981.

Billington, Michael, Review of Sarah Daniels' *Masterpieces*, The *Guardian*, 7 Oct. 1983.

—— 'The play's the thing', The *Guardian*, 12 Sept. 1988, p. 34.

—— 'Wounded child, haunted woman', review of Sarah Daniels' *Beside Herself*, The *Guardian*, 6 April 1990, p. 37.

Bilton, Tony, Bonnett, Kevin, Jones, Philip, Stanworth, Michelle, Sheard, Ken and Webster, Andrew, *Introductory Sociology* (including Michelle Stanworth's 'Gender divisions in society'), London: Macmillan, 2nd edn, 1987.

Binns, Mich, Interview with Victoria Wood, *Gambit: International Theatre Review*, vol. 10, no. 38, 1981, p. 20.

—— Interview with Jude Alderson of the Sadista Sisters, *Gambit: International Theatre Review*, vol. 10, no. 38, 1981, pp. 65–71.

Blau, Herbert, *The Audience*, Baltimore and London: Johns Hopkins University Press, 1990.

Boal, Augusto, *Theatre of the Oppressed*, London: Pluto Press, 1979 (first published as 'Teatro de Oprimido' in 1974).

Bonner, F., Goodman, L., Allen, R., Janes, L. and King, C. (eds), *Imagining Women: Cultural Representations and Gender*, Cambridge: Polity Press, 1992.

Boston, Richard, 'Friendly Persuasion', review of Annie Griffin's *Almost Persuaded*, The *Guardian*, 6 April 1990, p. 37.

Bradby, David, James, Louis and Sharratt, Bernard (eds), *Performance and Politics in Popular Drama*, Cambridge: Cambridge University Press, 1981.

Bradley, Harriet, *Men's Work, Women's Work*, Cambridge: Polity Press, 1989.

Brater, Enoch (ed.), *Feminine Focus: The New Women Playwrights*, New York and Oxford: Oxford University Press, 1989.

Brecht, Bertolt, *Brecht on Theatre: The Development of an Aesthetic*, trans. John Willet, London: Methuen, 1964.

Brehm, Sharon S., *Seeing Female: Social Roles and Personal Lives*, Contributions in Women's Studies no. 88, New York and London: The Greenwood Press, 1988.

Brennan, Teresa (ed.), *Between Feminism and Psychoanalysis*, London: Routledge, 1989.

Brewster, Yvonne, 'Homeless, black, and gifted: what does 1992 hold in store for black theatre', *City Limits*, 19–26 April 1990, pp. 80–1.

Brook, Peter, *The Empty Space*, New York and London: Penguin Books, 1988 (first published 1968).

—— *The Shifting Point*, London: Methuen, 1988.

Brown, Frederick, *Theatre and Revolution*, New York: The Viking Press, 1980.

Brown, Janet, *Feminist Drama: Definition and Critical Analysis*, Metuchen, NJ: Scarecrow Press, 1979.

Brownmiller, Susan, *Femininity*, London: Hamish Hamilton, 1984.

Brunsdon, Charlotte (ed.), *Films for Women*, London: BFI, 1986.

Brustein, Robert, *Critical Moments: Reflections on Theatre and Society 1973–9*, New York: Random House, 1980.

Burns, Elizabeth and Tom (eds), *Sociology of Literature and Drama*, London: Penguin, 1973.

Butcher, Helen, 'Images of Women in the Media', Stencilled Occasional Paper for the Centre for Contemporary Studies, no. 31, Birmingham: The University of Birmingham, Nov. 1974.

Butler, Judith, 'Performative acts and gender constitution: an eassay in phenomenology and feminist theory', *Theatre Journal*, vol. 40, no. 4, Dec. 1988, pp. 519–31.

—— *Gender Trouble: Feminism and the Subversion of Identity*, London: Routledge, 1990.

Cameron, Averil and Kuhrt, Amelie (eds), *Images of Women in Antiquity*, Kent: Croom Helm, 1983.

Campbell, Beatrix, 'A feminist sexual politics', *Feminist Review*, no. 5, 1980.

Cantarella, Eva, *Pandora's Daughters: The Role and Status of Women in Greek and Roman Antiquity*, Baltimore, NJ: Johns Hopkins University Press, 1987.

Capek, Mary Ellen S., *The Women's Thesaurus*, New York: Harper and Row, 1987.

Caplan, Betty, 'Towards another other place', The *Guardian*, 2 Sept. 1989, p. 20.

—— 'Setting a stage for women', The *Guardian*, 13 Jan. 1990.

—— 'Zofia Kalinska and the demonic woman: work in progress', *MTD: Music, Theatre, Dance: A Journal of the Performance Arts*, no. 2, Summer 1990, pp. 49–51. Reprinted in Cheryl Robson (ed.), *Female Voices, Fighting Lives: Seven Plays by Women*, London: Aurora Metro, 1991.

Carlson, Susan, 'Comic collisions: convention, rage and order', *New Theatre Quarterly*, vol. 3, no. 12, Nov. 1987, pp. 303–15.

—— 'Process and product: contemporary British theatre and its communities of women', *Theatre Research International*, vol. 13, no. 3, Autumn 1988, pp. 249–63.

Case, Sue-Ellen, 'Classic drag: the Greek creation of female parts', *Theatre Journal*, Oct. 1985, pp. 317–27.

—— *Feminism and Theatre*, New York: Methuen, 1988.

—— (ed.), *Performing Feminisms: Feminist Critical Theory and Theatre*, Baltimore, NJ: Johns Hopkins University Press, 1990.

—— 'The power of sex: English plays by women, 1958–1988', *New Theatre Quarterly*, vol. 7, no. 27, Aug. 1991, pp. 238–45.

Case, Sue-Ellen and Forte, Jeanie, 'From formalism to feminism', *Theatre*, vol. 16, no. 2, Spring 1985, pp. 62–5.

Case, Sue-Ellen and Reinelt, Janelle (eds), *The Performance of Power: Theatrical Discourse and Politics*, Iowa: The University of Iowa Press, 1991.

Chambers, Colin, *Other Spaces: New Theatre and the RSC*, London: Methuen, 1980.

Chambers, Colin and Prior, Mike, *Playwright's Progress: Patterns of Postwar British Drama*, Oxford: Amber Lane Press, 1987.

Chesler, Phyllis, *Mothers on Trial*, New York: McGraw-Hill, 1986.

Chester, Gail and Neilson, Sigrid (eds), *In Other Words: Writing as a Feminist*, London: Century Hutchinson, 1987.

Chinoy, Helen Krich and Jenkins, Linda Walsh, *Women in American Theatre*, New York: Crown Publishers, 1981; 2nd edn, New York: Theatre Communications Group, 1987.

Cixous, Hélène, 'Aller à la Mer', *Le Monde*, 28 April 1977.

—— *Writing the Feminine*, Nebraska: University of Nebraska Press, 1984.

Cohn, Ruby, *New American Dramatists 1960–1990*, Basingstoke: Macmillan, 1991 (first published 1982).

Collins, Patricia Hill, *Black Feminist Thought*, Boston: Unwin Hyman, 1990.

Conway, Robert and McGillivray, David (eds), *The British Alternative Theatre Directory*, London: Conway McGillivray, 1987.

Cooks, Judith, *Director's Theatre*, London: Hodder & Stoughton, 1989.

Coole, Dinah H., *Women in Political Theory*, Sussex: Wheatsheaf Books, 1988.

Cork, Sir Kenneth (ed.), 'Theatre is for All: Report of the Enquiry into Professional Theatre in England', London: The Arts Council of Great Britain, 1986.

Cott, Nancy F., *The Grounding of Modern Feminism*, New Haven: Yale University Press, 1987.

Cotton, Nancy, *Women Playwrights in England c. 1363–1750*, London: Associated University Presses, 1980.

Coult, Tony, 'Class struggles: an appraisal of theatre in education', *Platform*, no. 1, 1979, p. 18.

Cousin, Geraldine, 'The common imagination and individual voice', *New Theatre Quarterly*, vol. 4, no. 13, Feb. 1988, pp. 3–16.

—— *Churchill: The Playwright*, London: Methuen, 1989.

Coute, David, 'Author's Theatre', in *Collisions: Essays and Reviews*, London: Quartet, 1974.

Coveney, Michael, 'For this relief, no thanks', The *Observer*, 11 Feb. 1990, p. 59.

Coward, Rosalind, 'Are women's novels feminist novels?', *Feminist Review*, no. 5, 1980, pp. 53–64.

—— 'Female desire and sexual identity', in *Women, Feminist Identity and Society in the 1980s*, ed. M. Diaz-Diocaretz and I. M. Zavala, Amsterdam and Philadelphia: John Benjamin, 1985.

—— *Female Desire*, London: Granada, 1988.

Coyle, Jane, 'Charabanc motors on', *Theatre Ireland*, no. 18, April–June 1989, pp. 41–2.

Craig, Sandy (ed.), *Dreams and Deconstructions: Alternative Theatre in Britain*, London: Amber Lane Press, 1979.

—— 'A spanner in the works canteen', *Time Out*, no. 463, 2–8 March 1979, p. 17.

Croyden, Margaret, Interview with Joan Littlewood, *The Transatlantic Review*, 1969.

Curb, Rosemary, 'Re/cognition, re/presentation, re/creation in woman-conscious drama: the seer, the seen, the scene, the obscene', *Theatre Journal*, vol. 37, no. 3, Oct. 1985.

Curb, Rosemary, Mead, Phyllis and Pavitts, Beverly Byers, 'Catalogue of feminist theatre, Parts 1 and 2', *Chrysalis* (Los Angeles, CA), vol. 10, 1979/80.

Currie, Dawn and Kazi, Hamida, 'Academic feminism and the process of de-radicalization', *Feminist Review*, no. 25, Spring 1987.

Dahlerup, Drude (ed.), *The New Women's Movement: Feminism and Political Power in Europe and the USA*, London: Sage Publications, 1986.

Daniels, Sarah, 'There are fifty two percent of us', *Drama*, no. 152, 1984, pp. 23–4.

Davies, Andrew, *Other Theatres*, New York: Macmillan, 1987.

BIBLIOGRAPHY

Davis, Jill, ' "This be different" – The lesbian drama of Mrs Havelock Ellis', *Women: A Cultural Review*, vol. 2, no. 2, 1991, pp. 134–48.

Davis, Tracy C., *Actresses as Working Women: Their Social Identity in Victorian Culture*, London: Routledge, 1991.

Davy, Kate, 'Constructing the spectator: reception, context, and address in lesbian performance', *Performing Arts Journal*, 29, vol. 10, no. 2, 1986.

—— 'Reading past the heterosexual imperative', *TDR: The Drama Review*, vol. 33, Spring 1989.

Deegan, Mary Jo, *American Ritual Dramas: Social Rules and Cultural Meanings*, Contributions in Sociology, no. 76, Westport, CT: Greenwood Press, 1989.

De Jongh, Nicolas, 'Culture shock', The *Guardian*, 24 March 1989, p. 30.

—— 'Uneasy lies the head' (the RSC's search for a new director), The *Guardian*, 9 Nov. 1989, p. 21.

—— 'Arts works amazed by £6 million boost', The *Guardian*, 17 Nov. 1989, p. 7.

—— 'RSC theatres go dark to avert ruin', The *Guardian*, 9 Feb. 1990.

—— 'Deficit could force RSC to leave London', The *Guardian*, 29 Oct. 1990, p. 22.

De Lauretis, Teresa, *Alice Doesn't: Feminism, Semiotics, Cinema*, New York: Macmillan, 1984.

—— (ed.), *Feminist Studies/Critical Studies*, Bloomington: Indiana University Press, 1986.

—— 'Sexual indifference and lesbian representation', *Theatre Journal*, vol. 40, no. 2, May 1988, pp. 155–77.

Delphy, Christine, 'A materialist feminism is possible', trans. Diana Leonard, *Feminist Review*, no. 4, 1980.

Devine, George, 'The right to fail', *The Twentieth Century*, vol. 169, Jan. 1961.

Dex, Shirley, *Women's Occupational Mobility: A Lifetime Perspective*, London: Macmillan, 1987.

Diamond, Arlyn, 'Practising feminist literary criticism', *Women's Studies International Quarterly*, vol. 1, 1978.

Diamond, Elin, 'Refusing the romanticism of identity: narrative interventions in Churchill, Benmussa, Duras', *Theatre Journal*, vol. 38, no. 3, Oct. 1985, pp. 273–86.

—— 'Brechtian theory/feminist theory', *TDR: The Drama Review*, vol. 2, no. 1, Spring 1988.

Dickey, Julienne and the London Campaign for Press and Broadcasting Freedom Women's Group, 'Guidelines for eliminating media sexism', *Women in Focus*, 1985.

Dinnerstein, Dorothy, *The Mermaid and the Minotaur: Sexual Arrangements and Human Malaise*, New York: Harper & Row, 1977.

Director's Guild of Great Britain, with the Association of Directors and Producers, 'Women's Employment Working Party Interim Report', Dec. 1984.

Dolan, Jill, 'Gender impersonation onstage: destroying or maintaining the mirror of gender roles', *Women and Performance: A Journal of Feminist Theory*, vol. 2, no. 2, 1985, pp. 3–11.

—— 'The dynamics of desire: sexuality and gender in pornography and performance', *Theatre Journal*, May 1987.

—— *The Feminist Spectator as Critic*, Theatre and Dramatic Studies no. 52, Ann Arbor: The University of Michigan Press, 1988.

—— 'In defense of the discourse: materialist feminism, postmodernism, poststructuralism . . . and theory', *TDR: The Drama Review*, T123, Autumn 1989, pp. 58–71.

Doulton, Anne-Marie, *The Arts Funding Guide*, London: A Directory for Social Change Publication, 1989.

Dunderdale, Sue, 'The status of women in British theatre and survey', *Drama*, no. 152, 1984, pp. 9–11.

Durham, Carolyn A., 'Medea: hero or heroine?', *Frontiers*, vol. 8, no. 1, 1984, pp. 54–9.

Eagleton, Terry, *Marxism and Literary Criticism*, London: Methuen, 1976.

—— *The Significance of Theory*, Oxford: Basil Blackwell, 1990.

Easthope, Antony, *Literary into Cultural Studies*, London: Routledge, 1991.

Eccles, Christine, 'The unsolicited playscript . . . and its almost inevitable return', *New Theatre Quarterly*, vol. 3, no. 9, Feb. 1987, pp. 24–8.

—— 'On the verge: an interview with Juliet Stevenson, Paola Dionisotti and Anna Furse', *Plays International*, April 1989, pp. 8–9.

Ecker, Gisela (ed.), *Feminist Aesthetics*, Boston: Beacon Press, 1986.

Edgar, David, 'Political theatre: part one', *Socialist Review*, no. 1, April 1978, pp. 16–19.

—— 'Political theatre: part two', *Socialist Review*, no. 2, May 1978, pp. 35–8.

—— 'Ten years of political theatre, 1968–78', *Theatre Quarterly*, vol. 8, no. 32, 1979.

Edwardes, Jane, 'Closing stages', *Time Out*, 23–30 March 1988, p. 41.

—— Review of Clare McIntyre's *My Heart's a Suitcase*, reprinted (from *Time Out*) in *The London Theatre Record*, vol. 10, 1990, p. 213.

Eisenstein, Hester and Jardine, Alice (eds), *The Future of Difference*, New Brunswick, NJ: Rutgers University Press, 1987 (first published 1980).

Elam, Keir, *The Semiotics of Theatre and Drama*, London: Methuen, 1980.

Elinor, Gillian, 'Performance as a subversive activity', *Feminist Arts News*, Summer 1980.

Ellmann, Mary, *Thinking About Women*, New York: Harcourt, 1968.

Elsom, John, *Post-War British Theatre*, London: Routledge & Kegan Paul, 1976.

English Collective of Prostitutes, 'Prostitute Women and Aids: Resisting the Virus of Repression', London: King's Cross Women's Centre, 1988.

Equity/New Playwright's Trust, 'Profit Share Code of Conduct', mimeograph, draft version for discussion and debate, March 1989.

Esslin, Martin, *The Field of Drama*, London: Methuen, 1987.

Etherton, Michael, *Contemporary Irish Dramatists*, London: Macmillan, 1989.

Farrell, Joe, 'The Scottish plays: an interview with Liz Lochhead', *Plays and Players*, Feb. 1990, pp. 21–3.

Faux, Marianne, *Roe v. Wade*, New York: Penguin, 1988.

Ferretti, Fred, 'Women in humour confer: is it a man's world?', *The New York Times*, 1 May 1983, style section.

Ferris, Lesley, *Acting Women: Images of Women in the Theatre*, Basingstoke: Macmillan, 1990.

Figes, Eva, *Patriarchal Attitudes: Women in Society*, London: Faber and Faber, 1970.

Findlater, Richard, *The Player Queens*, London: Harrap, 1931.

Finley, Karen, 'On the constant state of desire', *Performing Arts Journal*, 30, vol. 10, no. 3, pp. 42–6.

Fireweed Collective (ed.), *The Issue is 'Ism: Women of Colour Speak Out*, Fireweed Issue no. 16, Ontario: Sister Vision Press, 1989.

Fitzsimmons, Linda, 'First women's playwright's conference', *New Theatre Quarterly*, vol. 5, no. 18, May 1989, p. 123.

—— *File on Churchill*, London: Methuen, 1989.

Fishburn, Katherine, *Women in Popular Culture: A Reference Guide*, Westport, CT and London: Greenwood Press, 1982.

Foley, Helene P., *Reflections on Women in Antiquity*, New York: Gordon and Breach, 1981.

Forte, Jeanie, 'Women's performance art: feminism and post-modernism', *Theatre Journal*, vol. 40, no. 2, May 1988, pp. 217–35.

—— 'Realism, narrative, and the feminist playwright: a problem of reception', *Modern Drama*, vol. 32, no. 1, March 1989, pp. 115–25.

Foucault, Michel, *The History of Sexuality. Volume One: An Introduction*, New York: Vintage Books, 1980.

Frank, Francine Wattman and Treichler, Paula A. (eds), *Language, Gender and Professional Writing: Theoretical Approaches and Guidelines for Nonsexist Usage*, Commission on the Status of Women in the Profession, New York: Modern Language Association, 1989.

Franklin, Sarah, Lury, Celia and Stacey, Jackie, 'Feminism and cultural studies: pasts, presents, futures', *Media, Culture and Society*, vol. 13, 1991, pp. 171–92.

Franks, Helen, 'Nice girls don't, do they? Interviews with women's theatre companies', *The Sunday Times Magazine*, 27 July 1980, pp. 50–1.

Franks, Helen, Norris, Stephanie and Fairweather, Eileen (eds), 'The Writer is a Woman', London: The Writer's Guild of Great Britain, 1989.

Freedman, Barbara, 'Frame-up: feminism, psychoanalysis, theatre', *Theatre Journal*, vol. 40, no. 3, Oct. 1988, pp. 375–97.

Frye, Marilyn, *The Politics of Reality: Essays in Feminist Theory*, Trumansberg, NY: The Crossing Press, 1983.

Fuss, Diana, *Essentially Speaking: Feminism, Nature, and Difference*, London: Routledge, 1989.

Gallop, Jane, *The Daughter's Seduction*, London: Macmillan, 1982.

Gambit Discussion, 'Subsidy for alternative theatre', *Gambit: International Theatre Review*, vol. 6, no. 24, 1974, pp. 15–19.

Gamman, Lorraine and Marshment, Margaret (eds), *The Female Gaze: Women as Viewers of Popular Culture*, London: The Women's Press, 1988.

Gardiner, Caroline Elizabeth, 'The City University Audience Survey for SWET: The West End Theatre Audience 1985/6', London: City University and SWET, 1986. Long report no longer available except through consultation with permission of the Arts Council.

—— 'What Share of the Cake? The Employment of Women in the English Theatre', London: Women's Playhouse Trust, 1987.

Garnault, Ruth, 'The economic importance of the Arts in Britain', *CUE: Technical Theatre Review*, no. 56, Nov./Dec. 1988, p. 9.

Gems, Pam, 'Imagination and gender', in *On Gender and Writing*, ed. Michelene Wandor, London: Pandora, 1983.

Giannachi, Gabriella, 'Report on women's theatre in Italy: Divina Two', *New Theatre Quarterly*, vol. 8, no. 30, May 1992, pp. 193–4.

Gilder, Rosamond, *Enter the Actress: The First Women in the Theatre*, New York: Theatre Art Books, 1960.

Gillespie, Faith and Lane, Helen R. (trans.), *The Three Marias: New Portuguese Letters*, New York: Paladin, 1975 (first published London: Gollancz, 1975; New York: Doubleday, 1975).

Gillespie, Patti P., 'Feminist theatre: a rhetorical phenomenon', *The Quarterly Journal of Speech*, vol. 64, 1978; reprinted in Chinoy and Jenkins (1987).

Gluck, Victor, 'Major women in theatre review: their progress', *Backstage*, 22 July 1983.

Goffman, Erving, *The Presentation of Self in Everyday Life*, New York: Penguin Books, 1959.

—— *Frame Analysis*, New York: Penguin Books, 1974.

—— *Gender Advertisements*, New York: The Society for the Anthropology of Visual Communication, 1976 and London: Macmillan, 1979.

Goldberg, RoseLee, *Performance Art: From Futurism to the Present*, London: Thames & Hudson, revised edn, 1988.

Gooch, Steve, *All Together Now: An Alternative View of Theatre and the Community*, London: Methuen, 1984.

Goodman, Lizbeth, 'Waiting for Spring to come again: feminist theatre 1978 and 1989: an interview with Gillian Hanna', *New Theatre Quarterly*, vol. 6, no. 21, Feb. 1990, pp. 43–56.

—— 'Art form or platform? On women and playwriting: an interview with Charlotte Keatley', *New Theatre Quarterly*, vol. 6, no. 22, May 1990, pp. 128–40.

—— 'Subverting images of the female: an interview with Tilda Swinton', *New Theatre Quarterly*, vol. 6, no. 23, Aug. 1990, pp. 215–28.

—— 'Devising as writing: British women theatre writers and educators demand contractual status', *TDR: The Drama Review*, T126, Summer 1990, pp. 17–19.

—— 'The (woman) writer and TIE', *MTD: Journal of the Performance Arts*, Part 1, no. 3 (Winter 1990), Part 2, no. 4 (Summer 1991).

—— 'Drawing the black and white line/defining black women's theatre: an interview with Yvonne Brewster', *New Theatre Quarterly*, vol. 7, no. 28, Nov. 1991, pp. 361–8.

—— British feminist theatre: a survey and a prospect', *New Theatre Quarterly*, vol. 8, no. 32, Nov. 1992.

—— *British Feminist Theatre: Survey and Analysis*, Feminist Praxis, The University of Manchester Monograph Series, double issue no. 29–30, 1992.

Goodman, Lizbeth and Giannachi, Gabriella, 'A theatre for urban renewal: an Interview with Teatro Settimo', *New Theatre Quarterly*, vol. 7, no. 25, Feb. 1991.

Goorney, Howard, *The Theatre Workshop Story*, London: Methuen, 1981.

Gordimer, Nadine, 'The essential gesture', in *The Essential Gesture: Writing, Politics and Places*, ed. Stephen Clingman, New York: Alfred A. Knopf, 1988.

Gordon, Linda, 'What's new in women's history?', in *Feminist Studies/Critical Studies*, ed. Teresa de Lauretis, Bloomington: Indiana University Press, 1986.

Gottlieb, Vera, 'Thatcher's theatre: or after Equus', *New Theatre Quarterly*, vol. 4, no. 14, May 1988, pp. 99–104.

—— 'Theatre in crisis', *Modern Drama*, vol. 33, no. 1, March 1990, pp. 57–8.

Greater London Arts, 'Policies, Priorities, and Funding Guidelines for the Performing Arts', 1987/8.

Greater London Enterprise Board, 'Enterprising Women', a pamphlet on job discrimination and alternative careers held by women, London, 1986.

Greene, Gayle and Kahn, Copelia (eds), *Making a Difference: Feminist Literary Criticism*, London: Methuen, 1985.

Greenfield, Myrna, 'Acting pregnant? The split-up of Beryl and the Perils', *Spare Rib*, no. 110, Sep. 1981.

Greenhalgh, Jill, 'Director's discourse', *The Magdalena Grapevine*, no. 6, Dec. 1991, pp. 2–3.

Greer, Germaine, *The Female Eunuch*, London: Granada Publishing, 1981 (first published 1968/9).

Griffiths, Trevor P. and Woodis, Carole (eds), *Theatre Guide*, London: Bloomsbury, 1988.

Griffiths, Viv. *Using Drama to Get at Gender: Studies in Sexual Politics*, Manchester: Department of Sociology Educational Development Handbook no. 9, 1986.

Gussow, Mel, 'Women playwrights: new voices in the theatre,' *New York Times Magazine*, 1 May 1983.

—— 'Caryl Churchill: a genteel playwright with an angry voice', *The New York Times*, 22 Nov. 1987.

Hackney Council/Stop the Clause Campaign, 'Special Report on Clause 28', *Spare Rib*, no. 189, April 1988.

Hamid, Rizu, 'The cripple: theatre of black women', *Spare Rib*, no. 177, April 1987, p. 33.

Hands, Terry, 'Why the RSC must stage new writing', *Plays International*, Sept. 1989, p. 12.

Haniff, Nesha Z., *Blaze a Fire: Significant Contributions of Caribbean Women*, Ontario: Sister Vision Press, 1988.

Hanna, Gillian, 'Feminism and theatre', an interview with Peter Hulton in the *Dartington College Theatre Papers*, 2nd series, no. 8, Devon: Dartington College, 1978.

Hanna, Judith Lynne, *The Performer–Audience Connection*, Austin: The University of Texas Press, 1983.

Harding, Sandra, 'The instability of the analytical categories of feminist theory', *Signs: Journal of Women in Culture and Society*, vol. 12, no. 4, Summer 1987.

Harpe, Wendy, 'Equal opportunities: a question of equity', *Local Arts UK*, no. 8, Oct. 1990, p. 13.

Harris, John S., *Government Patronage to the Arts in Great Britain*, Chicago and London: The University of Chicago Press, 1970.

Hart, Lynda (ed.), *Making a Spectacle: Feminist Essays on Contemporary Women's Theatre*, Ann Arbor: The University of Michigan Press, 1989.

Hayman, Ronald, *British Theatre Since 1955*, Oxford: Oxford University Press, 1979.

Hedges, Elaine and Wendt, Ingrid (eds), *In Her Own Image: Women Working in the Arts*, New York: The Feminist Press, 1980.

Hedley, Philip, 'My battle royal', The *Guardian*, 23 Oct. 1989, p. 36.

Heilbrun, Carolyn G. and Miller, Nancy K. (eds), *The Poetics of Gender*, Columbia: Columbia University Press, 1986.

Hekman, Susan J., *Gender and Knowledge: Elements of a Postmodern Feminism*, Cambridge: Polity Press, 1990.

Helms, Lorraine, 'Playing the women's part: feminist criticism and Shakespearean performance', *Theatre Journal*, vol. 41, no. 2, May 1989, pp. 190–200.

Henriques, Julian, Holloway, Wendy, Urwin, Cathy, Venn, Caize and Walkerdine, Valerie, *Changing the Subject: Psychology, Sexual Regulation and Subjectivity*, London: Methuen, 1984.

Herbert, Ian, 'Prompt corner', *The London Theatre Record*, vol. 10, no. 1, 12–25 Feb. 1990, p. 211.

Hess, Thomas B. and Baker, Elizabeth C. (eds), *Art and Sexual Politics*, London: Collier-Macmillan, 1973.

Hewison, Robert, *Too Much: Art and Society in the Sixties 1960–75*, London: Methuen, 1986.

Hewson, David, 'Arts Council grants: shift of emphasis from London to the regions divides Arts world', *The Times*, 21 March 1984.

Heys, Sandra, *Contemporary Stage Roles For Women: A Descriptive Catalogue*, London and Westport, CT: Greenwood Press, 1985.

Hirsch, Marianne and Keller, Evelyn Fox, *Conflicts in Feminism*, London: Routledge, 1990.

HMSO, The Local Governments Act, Chapter 9, Section 28, London: HMSO, 1988.

Hodgson, Terry (ed.), *The Batsford Dictionary of Drama*, London: Batsford, 1988.

Holland, Peter, 'The director and the playwright: control over the means of production', *New Theatre Quarterly*, vol. 3, no. 11, Aug. 1987.

Holledge, Julie, *Innocent Flowers: Women in Edwardian Theatre*, London: Virago, 1981.

Holloway, Wendy, 'Gender differences and the production of subjectivity', in *Changing the Subject: Psychology, Social Regulation and Subjectivity*, London: Methuen, 1984.

Homden, Carol, 'Right on the borderline', an interview with Trouble and Strife, *Everywoman*, April 1989, p. 14.

Hornbrook, David, 'Background on drama in education', *New Theatre Quarterly*, vol. 1 no. 4, Nov. 1985, and vol. 2, no. 5, Feb. 1986.

Humm, Maggie, *The Dictionary of Feminist Theory*, Hemel Hempstead: Harvester Wheatsheaf, 1989.

Industrial Market Research, 'Barbican Centre: research into audience potential,' London: Industrial Market Research, 7 Nov. 1980.

Ingram, Angela J. C., *In the Posture of a Whore: Changing Attitudes to 'Bad' Women in Elizabethan and Jacobean Drama*, Salzberg Studies in English Literature, vol. 2, no. 93, Salzburg: Institut fur Anglistik und Amerikanistik Universität Salzburg, 1984.

Irigaray, Luce, *This Sex Which Is Not One*, trans. Catherine Porter, Ithaca, NY: Cornell University Press, 1977 (first French edition by Editions de Minuit).

Itzin, Catherine, 'The case for a British Theatre Institute', *Theatre Quarterly*, vol. 1, no. 3, 1971.

—— 'Arts Council eyes still fixed on higher things', *Tribune*, 20 Jan. 1978.

—— 'The Albany rises from the ashes', *Time Out*, 12 Jan. 1979, p. 28.

—— *Stages in the Revolution: Political Theatre in Britain Since 1968*, London: Methuen, 1980.

—— (ed.), *Directory of Playwrights, Directors, Designers*, Sussex: John Offord Publications, 1983.

Jacobus, Mary (ed.), *Reading Woman: Essay in Feminist Criticism*, London: Methuen, 1986.

Jardine, Alice A., *Gynesis: Configurations of Woman and Modernity*, Ithaca and London: Cornell University Press, 1985.

Jardine, Lisa, *Still Harping on Daughters*, NJ: Barnes & Noble, 1983.

Jefferson, Ann and Robey, David (eds), *Modern Literary Theory*, London: Batsford, 2nd edn, 1987.

Jellicoe, Ann, 'Some Unconscious Influences in the Theatre', published version of the Judith E. Wilson Lecture, Cambridge: Cambridge University Press, 1967.

—— *Community Plays: How To Put Them On*, London: Methuen, 1987.

Jenkins, Hugh (Minister for the Arts 1974–6), *The Culture Gap: An Experience of Government and the Arts*, London and Boston: Marion Boyers, 1979.

Johnson, Lisa Ann, 'Grieving my ghetto: a report on the Toronto Women Playwrights' Conference', *Theatrum*, no. 25, Sept./Oct. 1991, pp. 4–5.

Jones, Derek (ed.), *Ordinary People: Why Women Become Feminists*, transcript based on the Channel 4 TV series produced by Christina Burnett and Janine Marmot, London: Channel 4, 1990.

Kaplan, E. Ann, 'The case of the missing mother: maternal issues in Vidor's *Stella Dallas*', *Heresies*, vol. 4, no. 4, issue 16, 1983.

—— *Women and Film: Both Sides of the Camera*, London: Methuen, 1983.

Kay, Jackie, Interview with Caryl Churchill, in *The New Statesman and Society*, April 1989, pp. 41–2.

Kelly-Gadol, Joan, 'The social relation of the sexes: methodological implications of women's history', *Signs, A Journal of Women in Culture and Society*, vol. 1, no. 4, Summer 1976.

Keyssar, Helene, *Feminist Theatre*, New York: Macmillan, 1984.

—— 'Hauntings: gender and drama in contemporary English theatre', *Englisch Amerikanische Studien*, vol. 8, nos. 3–4, 1986.

Khan, Naseem, 'Cowboys and contraception: Pam Gems and the Women's Group at the Roundhouse', *Time Out*, no. 223, 7–13 July 1974.

—— 'Theatre on the rocks', *Time Out*, no. 228, 12–18 July 1974, pp. 12–15.

—— 'Women in the Arts', *The New Statesman*, 30 Oct. 1987.

—— 'Stealing the Show (new ethnic women's theatre project and sponsorship', The *Guardian*, 6 Dec. 1989, p. 19.

—— 'Mime time for the Euro art form', *The Guardian Guide*, 4–5 Jan. 1991, p. vii.

King's Cross Women's Co-operative, 'Out of the Clause, into the Workhouse', *Centrepiece 7*, London: King's Cross Women's Centre, 1988.

Kirk, G. S., *Myth: Its Meaning and Functions in Ancient and Other Cultures*, Berkeley CA: The University of California Press, 1970.

Kishtainy, Khalid, *The Prostitute in Progressive Literature*, London and New York: Alison and Busby, 1982.

Kitzinger, Celia, *The Social Construction of Lesbianism*, London: Sage Publications, 1990.

Klein, Ethel, *Gender Politics: From Consciousness to Mass Politics*, Cambridge, Mass.: Harvard University Press, 1984.

Koedt, Anne, Lavine, Ellen and Rapone, Anita (eds), *Radical Feminism*, New York: Quadrangle Books, 1973.

Kramarae, Cheris and Treichler, Paula A., *A Feminist Dictionary*, London: Pandora Press, 1985.

Kruger, Loren, 'The dis-play's the thing: gender and the public sphere in contemporary British theatre', *Theatre Journal*, vol. 42, no. 1, March 1990, pp. 27–47.

Kuhn, Annette, *The Power of the Image: Essays on Representation and Sexuality*, London and New York: Routledge & Kegan Paul, 1985.

Landreth, Jenny, 'Donna and Kebab: two good Greek girls', *Spare Rib*, no. 189, April 1988, pp. 20–2.

Lamb, Margaret, 'Feminist criticism', *TDR: The Drama Review*, vol. 18, no. 3, 1974.

Lauter, Estella, *Women as Mythmakers: Poetry and Visual Art by Twentieth-Century Women*, Bloomington: Indiana University Press, 1984.

Leavitt, Dinah Luise, *Feminist Theatre Groups*, Jefferson, NC: MacFarland and Co., 1980.

Lenz, Carolyn Ruth Swift, Greene, Gayle and Neely, Carol Thomas (eds), *Feminist Criticism of Shakespeare*, Illinois: The University of Illinois Press, 1980.

Lesnick, Henry (ed.), *Guerilla Street Theatre*, New York: Avon Books, 1973.

Lidington, Tony, 'New terms for old turns: the rise of the alternative cabaret', *New Theatre Quarterly*, vol. 3, no. 10, May 1987, pp. 107–19.

Lipkin, Joan, 'Report on Breaking the Surface', in *Callboard*, San Francisco, CA: Theatre Bay Area Publications, Feb. 1992.

Lipman, Amanda, 'Denise Black and the Kray Sisters', *Spare Rib*, no. 163, Feb. 1986, pp. 25–6.

Lippard, Lucy, 'Sweeping exchanges: the contribution of feminism to the art of the 1970s', *Art Journal*, Autumn/Winter 1980.

Local Arts, UK, 'Not so wild about Wilding: a report on the Wilding Report', *Local Arts, UK*, no. 3, Nov. 1989, pp. 20–1.

Lorde, Audre, 'Age, race, class and sex: women redefining difference', in *Sister Outsider: Essays and Speeches*, Trumansberg, New York: The Crossing Press, 1984.

Luce, Richard, 'Parliamentary Statement on the Wilding Report', 13 March 1990.

Lyssa, Alison, 'Feminist theatre: a monologue to start discussion', *Australasian Drama Studies*, vol. 2, April 1984.

MacArthur, Colin, 'The Arts in society; not leisure escapism but a major means of change and growth', *Tribune*, 23 July 1976.

MacDonald, Jan, 'New women in the new drama', *New Theatre Quarterly*, vol. 6, no. 21, Feb. 1990, pp. 31–42.

Mackinnon, Catherine A., *Feminism Unmodified*, Cambridge, Mass.: Harvard University Press, 1987.

MacLennan, Elizabeth, *The Moon Belongs to Everyone: Making Theatre with 7:84*, London: Methuen, 1990.

Macqueen-Pope, W., *Ladies First: The Story of Woman's Conquest of the English Stage*, London: W.H. Allen, 1952.

Mairowitz, David Zane, 'God and the Devil: the latest work of Caryl Churchill', *Plays and Players*, Feb. 1977, pp. 24–5.

Maitland, Sara, *Vesta Tilley*, London: Virago, 1986.

Malpede, Karen, *Women in Theatre: Compassion and Hope*, New York: Limelight Editions, 1985.

Marcus, Jane, *Art and Anger: Reading Like a Woman*, Ohio: Ohio State University Press, 1988.

Marhol, Joseph, 'De-realized women; performance and identity in *Top Girls*', *Modern Drama*, no. 3, Sept. 1987, pp. 376–88.

Markham, E. A., Interview with Sistren Theatre Collective, *Artrage*, no. 15, 1986, pp. 4–6.

Marks, Elaine and de Coutrivon, Isabelle, *New French Feminisms*, New York: Schocken Books, 1981.

Marks, Laurence, 'A problem for Peter: scandal awaiting the new Arts Council chairman', The *Observer*, 26 March 1989, p. 43.

Marowitz, Charles and Trussler, Simon (eds), *Theatre at Work: Playwrights and Politics in the Modern British Theatre*, London: Methuen, 1967.

Martin, Biddie and Mohanty, Chandra Jalpede, 'Feminist politics: what's home got to do with it?', in *Feminist Studies/Critical Studies*, ed. Teresa de Lauretis, Bloomington: Indiana University Press, 1986.

Martin, John, 'Directing women: a difference of perspective. Interviews with Sheila Hancock and Nancy Meckler', *Drama*, no. 152, 1984, p. 18.

Martin, William, 'Theatre as social education: events leading to a situation from which people find themselves unable to escape', *Theatre Quarterly*, vol. 2:8, Oct.–Dec. 1972.

Mayne, Judith, 'The female audience and the feminist critic', in *Women and Film*, ed. Janet Todd, New York: Holmes and Meier, 1988.

McFerran, Ann, 'Caught napping: ITC campaign to increase Arts Council grants', *Time Out*, no. 468, 6–12 April 1979, p. 13.

McGrath, John, 'The theory and practice of political theatre', *Theatre Quarterly*, vol. 4, no. 35, 1979.

—— *A Good Night Out: Popular Theatre: Audience, Class and Form*, London: Methuen, 1985.

—— *The Bone Won't Break*, London: Methuen, 1990.

McRobbie, Angela, 'The politics of feminist research: between talk, text and action,' *The Feminist Review*, no. 12, 1982.

Merck, Mandy, 'The cause without a rebel: Nighhawks Gay Theatre', *Time Out*, no. 464, 9–15 March 1979, pp. 14–15.

Merrall, Ann (ed.), *Contacts: Stage, Television, Screen and Radio*, London: The Spotlight, 1988–9.

Miller, Casey and Swift, Kate, *The Handbook of Non-Sexist Writing*, London: The Women's Press, revised British edn, 1981.

Miller, Sally M. (ed.), *Flawed Liberation: Socialism and Feminism*, Westport, CT: Greenwood Press, 1981 (originally published as Contributions to Women's Studies no. 19).

Millett, Kate, *Sexual Politics*, New York: Avon Books, 1969.

Minogue, Sally, *Problems for Feminist Criticism*, London: Routledge, 1990.

Mitchell, Juliet, *Women: The Longest Revolution: On Feminism, Literature and Psychoanalysis*, New York: Pantheon Books, 1984.

Moers, Ellen, *Literary Women: The Great Writers*, Oxford: Oxford University Press, 1976.

Moi, Toril, *Sexual/Textual Politics: Feminist Literary Theory*, London: Methuen, 1985.

Monaghan, Patricia, *Women in Myth and Legend*, London: Junction Books, 1981.

Monk, Erika, 'The rites of women', *Performing Arts Journal*, 29, vol. 10, no. 2, 1987.

Moraga, Cherrie and Anzaldúa, Gloria (eds), *This Bridge Called My Back: Writings by Radical Women of Colour*, Watertown, Mass.: Persephone Press, 1981.

Mordin, Lynda, 'Arts and money', *The Sunday Correspondent Guide to the Arts*, Part 1, Jan. 1990 (published in association with the ACGB), pp. 26–7.

Morgan, Fidelis, *The Female Wits: Women Playwrights of the Restoration*, London: Virago, 1981.

Morgan, Robin, 'Lesbianism and feminism: synonyms or contradictions?', Pittsburg, PA: Know., 1973 (reprinted from *Second Wave*, vol. 2, no. 4).

—— *The Demon Lover: On the Sexuality of Terrorism*, London: Methuen, 1989.

Moss, Jane, 'Women's theatre in France', *Signs: A Journal of Women in Culture and Society*, vol. 13, no. 3, Spring 1988.

Much, Rita, 'Voices of authority: a report from Toronto', *New Theatre Quarterly*, vol. 7, no. 28, Nov. 1991, pp. 390–1.

Mulvey, Laura, 'Visual pleasure and narrative cinema', *Screen*, vol. 16, no. 3, Autumn 1985.

—— *Visual and Other Pleasures*, London: Macmillan, 1989.

Myerscough, John, *The Economic Importance of the Arts in Britain*, London: Policy Studies Institute, 1988.

Mylon, Caroline, Review of Sarah Daniels' *The Devil's Gateway*, in *Spare Rib*, no. 136, Nov. 1983, p. 41.

Natalle, Elizabeth J., *Feminist Theatre: A Study in Persuasion*, Metuchen, NJ: Scarecrow Press, 1985.

Nava, Mica, 'Everybody's views were just broadened: a girls project and some responses to lesbianism', *Feminist Review*, no. 10, Spring 1982.

Nead, Lynda, *Myths of Sexuality: Representations of Women in Victorian Britain*, Oxford: Basil Blackwell, 1988.

Newton, Judith Lowder, *Women, Power, and Subversion: Social Strategies in British Fiction*, Georgia: University of Georgia Press, 1981.

Newton, Judith and Rosenfelt, Deborah (eds), *Feminist Criticism and Social Change*, London: Methuen, 1985.

Nisedzwiecki, Patricia, 'About "thespian" characteristics of women's language', *IAW*, European Workshop on Language, Sexism and Education, Europaische Akademie Berlin, 1985.

Norden, Barbara, 'Paying lip service to alternative comedy', *Everywoman*, Feb. 1990, pp. 14–15.

Nye, Andrea, *Feminist Theory and the Philosophies of Man*, London: Routledge, 1990.

Oddey, Alison, 'Devising theatre', *MTD: Music, Theatre, Dance: A Journal of the Performance Arts*, no. 2, Summer 1990, pp. 45–8.

Olauson, Judith, *The American Woman Playwright: A View of Criticism and Characterization*, Troy, New York: The Whitson Publishing Co., 1981.

Orr, Deborah, 'Unmasking the world of dreams', The *Guardian*, 11 Jan. 1991, p. 34.

Page, Louise, 'Emotion is a theatrical weapon: the playwright interviewed by Elizabeth Sakellaridou,' *New Theatre Quarterly*, vol. 6, no. 22, May 1990, pp. 174–82.

Palmeira, Rosemary (ed.), *In the Gold of the Flesh*, London: The Women's Press, 1990.

Pankhurst, E. Sylvia, *The Suffragette Movement*, London: Virago, 1977.

Parker, Rozsika and Pollack, Griselda (eds), *Framing Feminism: Art and the Women's Movement, 1970–1985*, London: Pandora Press, 1987.

Parrish, Sue, 'The Women's Playhouse Trust', *Drama*, no. 152, 1984, p. 13.

Paterman, Carole and Gross, Elizabeth (eds), *Feminist Challenge: Social and Political Theory*, London: Allen and Unwin, 1986.

Pavis, Patrice, *Theatre at the Crossroads of Culture*, trans. Loren Kruger, London: Routledge, 1992.

Petchesky, Rosalind Pollack, 'Antiabortion, antifeminism and the rise of the New Right', *Feminist Studies*, vol. 7, no. 2, Summer 1981, p. 229.

Peters, Adrienne and Weston, Ann, 'Cutting the cake: public ownership vs Free Enterprise', *Spare Rib*, no. 104, March 1981.

Phelan, Peggy, 'Feminist theory, poststructuralism, and performance', *TDR: The Drama Review*, T117, Spring 1988, pp. 107–27.

Philips, Deborah, 'Beyond the fringe', a review of the work of the Millies, Beryl and the Perils, and others, *Women's Review*, no. 12, 12 Oct. 1986, p. 43.

Pick, John, *Managing the Arts? The British Experience*, London: Rhinegold Publishers, 1986.

Pitt, Angela, *Shakespeare's Women*, London: David and Charles, 1981.

Polan, Dana B., *The Political Language of Film and the Avante-Garde*, Studies in Cinema Series, Michigan: University of Michigan Press, 1985.

Pomeroy, Sarah B., *Goddesses, Whores, Wives and Slaves: Women in Classical Antiquity*, New York: Schocken Books, 1975.

Practical Arts, 'Training and Standards Development in the Arts and Entertainment Industry', a summary report of the Practical Arts Research Study commissioned by the Training Agency, London: Practical Arts, Sept. 1989.

Pribram, E. Deirdre (ed.), *Female Spectators: Looking at Film and Television*, London: Verso, 1989.

Rea, Charlotte, 'Women's theatre groups', *TDR: The Drama Review*, vol. 16, no. 2, June 1972.

Redmond, James (ed.), *Themes in Drama 7: Drama, Sex and Politics*, Cambridge: Cambridge University Press, 1985.

—— (ed.), *Themes in Drama 11: Women in Theatre*, Cambridge: Cambridge University Press, 1989.

Reinelt, Janelle, 'Beyond Brecht: Britain's new feminist drama', *Theatre Journal*, May 1986, pp. 154–64.

Rhinegold Publishers (ed.), *The British Performing Arts Yearbook*, London: Rhinegold Publishers, 1988 and annually.

Rich, Adrienne, *Of Woman Born: Motherhood as Experience and Institution*, New York: W. W. Norton, 1976.

—— *On Lies, Secrets and Silence: Selected Prose 1966–1978*, New York: W. W. Norton and Co., 1979.

Rich, B. Ruby, 'In the name of feminist film criticism', *Heresies*, no. 9, 1980, pp. 74–81.

Ritchie, Rob, *The Joint Stock Book: The Making of the Theatre Collective*, London: Methuen, 1987.

Roberts, Helen (ed.), *Doing Feminist Research*, London: Routledge & Kegan Paul, 1981.

Roberts, Philip, *The Royal Court Theatre: 1965–72*, London and New York: Routledge & Kegan Paul, 1986.

Robinson, Alice M., Roberts, Vera Mowry and Barranger, Milly S. (eds), *Notable Women in the American Theatre: A Biographical Dictionary*, Westport, CT: Greenwood Press, 1989.

Robson, Cheryl, Georgeson, Vania, and Beck, Janet (eds), *The Women Writers' Handbook*, London: Aurora Metro, 1990.

Roden, Suzanne, 'Black feminists: organizing on both sides of the Atlantic', *Spare Rib*, no. 171, Oct. 1986, pp. 20–4.

Rose, Helen, 'The crux of the matter: an interview with April de Angelis', *Plays and Players*, April 1990, pp. 18–19.

Rose, Jacqueline, *Sexuality in the Field of Vision*, London: Verso, 1986.

Roth, Martha, 'Notes toward a feminist performance aesthetic', *Women and Performance: A Journal of Feminist Theory*, vol. 1, no. 1, Spring/Summer 1983, pp. 5–14.

Roth, Moira (ed.), *The Amazing Decade: Women and Performance Art 1970–1980*, Los Angeles: Astro Artz, 1982.

Rothenberg, Diane, 'Social art/social action', *TDR:, The Drama Review*, vol. 32, no. 1, Spring 1988, pp. 31–7.

Rothstein, Mervyn, 'Women playwrights: themes and variations', *The New York Times*, Section 2, 7 May 1989, pp. 1, 2 and 42.

Rowbotham, Sheila, Segal, Lynne and Wainwright, Hilary (eds), *Beyond the Fragments: Feminism and the Making of Socialism*, London: Merlin Press, 1979 (first published Newcastle Socialist Centre and Islington Community Press, 1979).

Rowell, George and Jackson, Anthony, *The Repertory Movement: A History of Regional Theatre in Britain*, Cambridge: Cambridge University Press, 1984.

Rubens, Robert, Interview with Ann Jellicoe, *The Translantic Review*, 1963.

Rutter, Carol, *Clamorous Voices: Shakespeare's Women Today*, ed. Faith Evans, London: The Women's Press, 1988.

Ryan, Mary P., *Women in Public: Between Banners and Ballots*, Baltimore and London: Johns Hopkins University Press, 1990.

Sakellaridou, Elizabeth, 'NTQ Checklist No. 6: Louise Page', *New Theatre Quarterly*, vol. 6, no. 22, May 1990, pp. 183–7.

Schenkein, Jim (ed.), *Studies in the Organization of Conversational Interaction*, New York: Academic Press, 1978.

Schlueter, June (ed.), *Modern American Drama: The Female Canon*, London and Toronto: Associated University Presses, 1990.

Scolnicov, Hanna and Holland, Peter (eds), *Reading Plays: Interpretation and Reception*, Cambridge: Cambridge University Press, 1991.

Searle, G. R., *Eugenics and Politics in Britain: 1900–1914*, Leyden, The Netherlands: Noordhoff Int. Pb., 1976.

Sedgwick, Elizabeth, *Between Men: English Literature and Male Homosocial Desire*, New York: Columbia University Press, 1985.

Shaw, Phyllida, 'Theatre: danger in the wings', *National Campaign for the Arts Newsletter*, no. 9, Spring 1988.

Shaw, Roy, 'An Open Letter to Peter Palumbo', The *Guardian*, 4 April 1989, p. 38.

Sheehy, Margaret, 'Why aren't there more women directors?', *Drama*, no. 152, 1984, p. 12.

Sherman, Alfred and Ivens, Michael, 'How to Get Money from the GLC and other Left-Wing Authorities', London: The Aims of Industry, Feb. 1984.

Shewell, Debbie, 'Women in entertainment', *Drama*, no. 152, 1984, p. 14.

Shockley, Ann Allen, *Afro-American Women Writers 1746–1933: An Anthology and Critical Guide*, New York: Meridian Books, 1988.

Showalter, Elaine, *A Literature of Their Own: British Women Novelists from Brontë to Lessing*, Princeton, NJ: Princeton University Press, 1977.

Shulman, Milton, Review of Clare McIntyre's *My Heart's a Suitcase*, reprinted (from The *Evening Standard*) in The *London Theatre Record*, vol. 10, 1990, p. 214.

Siltanen, Janet and Stanworth, Michelle, *Women and the Public Sphere: A Critique of Sociology and Politics*, London: Hutchinson and Co., 1984.

Sistren Theatre, 'Sistren profile', *Sistren*, vol. 13, no. 1, July 1991, p. 3.

Smith, Eric (ed.), *A Dictionary of Classical Reference in English Poetry*, Cambridge: D. S. Brewer, 1984.

Smith-Rosenberg, Carroll, 'The new woman and the new history', *Feminist Studies*, vol. 3, nos. 1/2, 25–7 Oct. 1974.

Snell, Mandy, 'The Equal Pay and Sex Discrimination Acts: their impact in the workplace', *Feminist Review*, no. 1, 1979.

Snitow, Ann, Stansell, Christine and Thompson, Sharon (eds), *Powers of Desire: The Politics of Sexuality*, New York: Monthly Review Press/New Feminist Library, 1983.

Spacks, Patricia Myer, *The Female Imagination: A Literary and Psychological Investigation of Women's Writing*, New York: Knopf, 1976.

Spaliviero, Antonia (ed.), *Divina: Stories of Life and Theatre*, Turin: Tirrenia Stampatori, 1992.

Spare Rib Collective, 'Theatre: four women's groups affected by drastic funding cuts', *Spare Rib*, no. 89, Dec. 1979.

Spelman, Elizabeth V., *Inessential Woman: Problems of Exclusion in Feminist Thought*, Boston: Beacon Press and London: The Women's Press, 1990.

Spender, Lynne, *Intruders on the Rights of Men: Women's Unpublished Heritage*, London: Pandora Press, 1983.

Spivak, Gayatri Chakravorty, *The Post-Colonial Critic: Interviews, Strategies, Dialogues*, ed. Sarah Harasym, London: Routledge, 1990.

Sprague, Joey, 'The other side of the banner: toward a feminization of politics', in *Seeing Female: Social Lives and Personal Lives*, ed. Sharon S. Brehm, New York: The Greenwood Press, 1988.

Stafford-Clark, Max, 'Victims of a gale-force farce: the closing of the Theatre Upstairs', The *Guardian*, 25–6 March 1989, p. 19.

—— 'Looking back in anger', The *Guardian*, 28 May 1991, p. 29.

Stallybrass, Peter and White, Allon, *The Politics and Poetics of Transgression*, Ithaca: Cornell University Press, 1986.

Steinem, Gloria, *Outrageous Acts and Everyday Rebellions*, London: Fontana, 1984.

Stourac, Richard and McCreery, Kathleen, *Theatre as a Weapon*, London: Routledge & Kegan Paul, 1986.

Swanson, Michael, 'Mother/daughter relationships in three plays by Caryl Churchill', *Theatre Studies*, nos. 31–2, 1984–6, pp. 49–66.

Swanwick, H. M., *I Have Been Young*, London: Victor Gollancz, 1935.

Szanto, George H., *Theatre and Propaganda*, Austin: University of Texas Press, 1975.

Taylor, Dave, 'Raymond Williams: building a socialist culture: interview', *The Leveller*, no. 24, March 1979, pp. 25–7.

Taylor, John Russell, *The Second Wave: British Drama for the Seventies*, London: Methuen, 1971.

—— *Anger and After: A Guide to the New British Drama*, London: Methuen, 1983.

Taylor, Paul, 'Scrambled egos: review of Sarah Daniels' *Beside Herself*', The *Independent*, 6 April 1990.

Thomas, Elean, 'Lionhearted women: Sistren Women's Theatre Collective', *Spare Rib*, no. 172, Nov. 1986, pp. 14–19.

Thomson, Ann and Wilcox, Helen (eds), *Teaching Women: Feminism and English Studies*, Manchester: Manchester University Press, 1989.

Tickner, Lisa, *The Spectacle of Women: Imagery of the Suffrage Campaign 1907–1914*, London: Chatto & Windus, 1987.

Todd, Susan (ed.), *Women and Theatre: Calling The Shots*, London: Faber & Faber, 1984.

Tolland, V. G. et al., 'Where are the women dramatists?', a letter to *The Stage*, 19 March 1981; followed by numerous responses from Michelene Wandor, Pat Van Twest and others in issues up to 23 April 1981.

Trussler, Simon, 'Political playwrights in Britain', *Theatre Quarterly*, vol. 6:24, Winter 1976.

Tuttle, Lisa, *An Encyclopedia of Feminism*, London: Arrow Books, 1987.

Tweedy, Colin, 'Business in the Arts', *CUE: Technical Theatre Review*, no. 56, Nov./Dec. 1988, pp. 15–16.

Vaughan, Jenny, 'Revolting women', a review of Cunning Stunts' TV show (broadcast 22 Jan. 1981), *Spare Rib*, no. 104, March 1981, pp. 44–5.

—— 'Shakespeare's Sister: Monstrous Regiment/Theatre de l'Aquarium', *Spare Rib*, no. 104, March 1981, pp. 44–5.

Verma, Jatinda, 'Marginalized like me: funding for Tara Arts Group', *Artrage*, Winter 1988, p. 5.

Vernant, Jean-Pierre, *Myth and Society in Ancient Greece*, trans. Janet Lloyd, London: Methuen, 1982.

Walby, Sylvia, *Patriarchy at Work*, Cambridge: Polity Press, 1986.

Walkowitz, Judith R., *Prostitution and Victorian Society: Women, Class, and the State*, Cambridge: Cambridge University Press, 1980.

Wandor, Michelene, 'Women are uncharted territory', an interview with Pam Gems, *Spare Rib*, Sept. 1977.

—— 'Free collective bargaining', *Time Out*, no. 467, 30 March to 5 April 1979, pp. 14–16.

—— *Understudies: Theatre and Sexual Politics*, London: Methuen, 1981.

—— (ed.), *On Gender and Writing*, London: Pandora, 1983.

—— 'The impact of feminism on the theatre', *The Feminist Review*, vol. 18, Winter 1984.

—— 'The Fifth Column: feminism and theatre', *Drama*, no. 152, 1984, pp. 5–9.

—— *Look Back in Gender: Sexuality and the Family in Post-War British Drama*, London: Methuen, 1987.

—— *Carry on Understudies: Theatre and Sexual Politics*, London: Routledge & Kegan Paul, 1981, revised edn, New York: Routledge & Kegan Paul, 1986.

Wardle, Irving, *The Theatres of George Devine*, London: Methuen, 1979.

Warner, Marina, *Alone of All Her Sex: The Myth and Cult of the Virgin Mary*, London: Weidenfeld and Nicolson, 1976.

—— *Monuments and Maidens: The Allegory of the Female Form*, London: Weidenfeld and Nicolson, 1985.

Weedon, Chris, *Feminist Practice and Poststructuralist Theory*, Oxford: Basil Blackwell, 1987.

Weeks, Jeffrey, *Coming Out: Homosexual Politics in Britain, from the Nineteenth Century to the Present*, London: Quartet, 1977.

Weick, Ann, 'Other ways of seeing: the female vision', in *Seeing Female: Social Lives and Personal Lives*, ed. Sharon S. Brehm, New York: The Greenwood Press, 1988.

Weimann, Robert, 'Text, author-function, and appropriation in modern narrative: toward a sociology of representation', *Critical Inquiry*, vol. 14, no. 3, Spring 1988.

Weintraub, Stanley (ed.), *The Dictionary of Literary Biography*, vol. 10: Modern British Dramatists 1900–45, vol. 13: British Dramatists Since World War Two, Detroit: Book Tower, 1982.

Westwood, Chris, 'The woman and theatre project, 1980–1981', *Australasian Drama Studies*, vol. 1, Oct. 1982.

White, Victoria, 'Towards post-feminism? Women in theatre in Ireland', *Theatre Ireland*, vol. 18, April–June 1989, pp. 33–5.

Wilding, Richard, 'Supporting the Arts: the Wilding Report', London: ACGB, 1989.

Williams, Raymond, 'The social history of dramatic forms', in *The Long Revolution*, London: Penguin, 1965 (first published 1961).

—— *Drama in Performance*, London: Penguin, 1972 (first published 1961).

—— *Keywords: A Vocabulary of Culture and Society*, London: Fontana Press, 1976.

—— 'Drama in a dramatized society', in *Writing in Society*, London: Verso, 1983.

Williamson, Judith, *Consuming Passions: The Dynamics of Popular Culture*, London: Marion Boyers, 1986.

Willmott, Nigel, 'The "One of Us" board game: the broadcasting bill and new-look regulatory bodies', The *Guardian*, 15 Jan. 1990, pp. 21 and 23.

Wilson, Elizabeth, 'Borderlines', The *New Statesman and Society*, vol. 3, no. 125, Nov. 1990, p. 31.

Woddis, Carole, 'Support, not competition: interviews with designers Amanda Fiske and Di Seymour', *Drama*, no. 152, 1984, p. 20.

—— 'In her Wright mind: an interview with Jules Wright', *Plays and Players*, April 1990, pp. 14–16.

—— *Sheer Bloody Magic: Conversations with Actresses*, London: Virago, 1991.

Wolf, Matt, 'Staying upstairs: a report on the Theatre Upstairs', *Plays and Players*, Feb. 1990, pp. 24–5.

Wolff, Janet, *The Social Production of Art*, London: Macmillan, 1981.

Woolf, Virginia, *A Room of One's Own*, London: Harcourt, Brace, Jovanovich, 1929.

Wyland, Faith, 'Motherhood, Lesbianism and Child Custody', a working pamphlet for Wages Due Lesbians, London, 1977.

Yandell, Claire, 'Beauty and the Beast: an interview with Louise Page', *Women's Review*, no. 3, Jan. 1986, pp. 30–1.

Young, Alison, *Femininity in Dissent*, London, Routledge, 1990.

Ziff, Trish and Barnett, Jo, 'The dessert, or what's for afters: cunning stunts?', *Spare Rib*, no. 98, Dec. 1979, p. 43.

Zivanovic, Judith, 'The rhetorical and political foundations of women's collaborative theatre', in *Themes in Drama 11: Women in Theatre*, ed. James Redmond, Cambridge: Cambridge University Press, 1989.

UNPUBLISHED REFERENCE SOURCES

Bailey, Sandy (administrator) and Monstrous Regiment, Unpublished reply to the Arts Council's 'The Glory of the Garden' Report, 1984.

Barker, Clive, Unpublished draft of an interview with Monstrous Regiment, 1985.

Butcher, Peggy, Abstract of an unpublished dissertation on 'A Brief History of Feminism and Fringe Theatre in Britain', 1985.

Canning, Charlotte, 'Performing Community: Feminist Theatre of the Early Second

BIBLIOGRAPHY

Wave in the United States', unpublished paper delivered at the 'Breaking the Surface' Conference, The University of Calgary, 13–17 Nov. 1991.

Conference of Women Theatre Directors and Administrators, Collected, unpublished conference papers 1979–81.

—— *The Status of Women in British Theatre*, collected, unpublished 1982–3 conference papers.

Craze, Tony (ed.), Soho Poly Theatre Forum transcript: discussion on 'What Writers Want', Spring 1989.

Croft, Susan, *Bibliography: Plays by Women and Books on Women in Theatre*, unpublished author's copy; copyright Susan Croft, 1986.

Croft, Susan and de Angelis, April, 'An Alphabet of Apocryphae: Collaboration and Explorations in Women's Theatre', unpublished authors' copy; forthcoming in *Women Dramatists Since 1958*, ed. Trevor R. Griffiths and Margaret Llewellyn Jones, Milton Keynes: The Open University Press, 1991.

Davis, Jill, 'Theatre and the Lesbian Community', unpublished paper delivered at the Conference on 'Women and Theatre: Gender, Text, Image', held at Nene College, Northampton, 19 Nov. 1988 (prior to release of her second volume of *Lesbian Plays*). Also taped.

—— A list of lesbian theatres and plays, sent by Davis on 5 Dec. 1988.

Eastern Arts Association, 'Future Structure for Arts Funding', an internal memorandum from Jeremy Newton, director, along with associated factsheets and facsimile of a letter from Richard Luce to Peter Palumbo, distributed to the Council of Members, Eastern Arts, 23 March 1990.

Gardiner, Caroline Elizabeth, 'The West-End Theatre Audience: 1981 to 1986', unpublished Ph.D. dissertation, London: Department of Arts Policy and Management, City University, Jan. 1988.

Harpe, Wendy, 'A Question of Equity: Women in the Arts Research', a report funded by Merseyside Arts, April 1990.

Lipkin, Joan, 'The Male Media Reception of *He's Having Her Baby: a Pro-Choice Musical Comedy*', unpublished paper delivered at the 'Breaking the Surface' Conference, The University of Calgary, 13–17 Nov. 1991.

—— 'A Report from Canada's "Breaking the Surface: An Interactive Festival/Conference of Women, Theatre and Social Action" ', in *The Riverfront Times*, St Louis, Missouri, 1992.

Mack, Katie, 'Romantic Outsiders: A Study of Lesbian Romantic Fiction from the 1950s to the 1970s', unpublished BA thesis, 1988.

McGuire, Cheryl, Interview with Sian Evans, Oct. 1990, London. Transcribed from a taped interview session. Unpublished.

—— Interview with Kate Harwood, 26 Oct. 1989, London. Transcribed from a taped interview session. Unpublished.

—— Interview with Jules Wright, 12 Oct. 1989, London. Transcribed from a taped session. Unpublished.

Miles, Julia, et al. Listings of Productions, Workshop Productions and Rehearsed Readings of the Women's Project at the American Place Theatre. Unpublished papers dated 1978–85.

Morgan, Charles, 'Autumn '90 Theatre Campaign Factsheet', distributed at the 'Theatre Under Threat' Conference, Cambridge, 20–1 Oct. 1990. Updated: May 1991.

New Playwrights Trust, Unpublished pamphlets: 'New Playwrights Trust Development Plan 1988–90', 'New Writing Venues', 'Regional Workshops and Other Contacts', 1989. All available from the Trust.

—— Pamphlet: 'The Contingencies Affecting the Participation of Bengali Sylheti

295

Speaking Women of all Ages in the Devising Process and Performance of a Bilingual Play: A Guideline to the Writer', prepared by Taslima Hossain Rana, April 1991.
—— 'Blackwright: Towards the Production of the New Playwrights Trust and Black Audio Film Collectives' Black Playwrights Directory and Black and Third World Screen Writers Directory', prepared by Julie Reid, Aug. 1991 (revised edition: Sept. 1991).
Rana, Taslima Hossain, See New Playwrights Trust.
Reid, Julie, See entry for New Playwrights Trust.
Reinelt, Janelle, 'British Feminist Drama: Brecht and Caryl Churchill', unpublished paper, 1990.
—— 'Rethinking Brecht: Deconstruction, Feminism and the Politics of Drama', unpublished paper, 1991.
RSC, Company Files: Complete Press/Review Pack on the RSC Women's Project, provided by the company, 2 May 1990. Reviews too numerous to be listed separately.
Tait, Peta, 'Gender Roles Offstage', unpublished paper delivered at the 'Breaking the Surface' Conference, The University of Calgary, 13–17 Nov. 1991.
Taylor, Elizabeth, Notes from research for an MA thesis on 'An Investigation into the Role of the Interaction between Actor and Writer in the Creating of a Script for Performance, Illustrated by Four Plays by Caryl Churchill', London: Royal Holloway and Bedford New College, May 1986.
Theatre Writers Union, Report: 'Playwrights: A Species Still Endangered?', statistics compiled by David Edgar et al., distributed by TWU London, Oct. 1987.
Theatre Writers Union and the Theatres National Committee, 'Writer's Contract' agreement in draft; negotiations were frozen when the draft was released, March 1989.
Thomas, Polly (ed.), Conference minutes for 'Out of the Attic: Women and Theatre', 14 July 1990. Available from the New Playwright's Trust.
Todd, Susan, Unpublished paper delivered to the Judith E. Wilson Conference on Political Theatre, King's College, Cambridge, 1978.
Various authors, Judith E. Wilson Conference on Political Theatre Papers. Unpublished. King's College, Cambridge, 1978 and St John's College, Cambridge, 1982.
Women's Hour Radio, 'Writers Revealed': an interview with Timberlake Wertenbaker. Broadcast 20 June 1991. Notes transcribed from an audio cassette recording.
Writer's Guild of Great Britain, and the Theatre Writers Union, 'Questionnaire Re: Commissioning Policy in UK Theatres', compiled and distributed through TWU, Autumn 1988.

INTERVIEWS AND CORRESPONDENCE

*Indicates papers delivered at the Judith E. Wilson conference on Theatre Under Threat, 20–1 Oct. 1990, St John's College, Cambridge, organized by Lizbeth Goodman and Gabriella Giannachi. A report on the conference was published in *New Theatre Quarterly*, vol. 7, no. 25, Feb. 1991.

Eve Adams (of Donna and Kebab) Interview 10 May 1991.
Morwenna Banks Written correspondence 1988. Telephone conversation 6 Oct. 1989. Workshop and interview 18 Nov. 1990.
Marion Baraitser Interview and workshop 20 June 1989.

BIBLIOGRAPHY

Susan Bassnett Workshop at the Magdalena Conference Dec. 1987. Intermittent written and oral correspondence thereafter.

Jane Boston (of Siren) Written correspondence 1988, 1989 and 12 Aug. 1990.

Jacky Bratton Interview 28 March 1988, London.

Eleanor Bron Written correspondence Aug.–Nov. 1989.

Janet Brown Written correspondence 14 Dec. 1987 and Jan. 1988.

Morna Burdon Written correspondence May 1988. Interview 11 Aug. 1988.

Helen Carr Telephone conversation 3 Feb. 1990.

Tasleen Carstairs Telephone interview 5 April 1990.

Penny Casdagli (aka Maro Green) Interview 4 April 1991. Written and taped correspondence May–June 1991.

Clair Chapman (Spare Tyre) Interview 27 June 1991, London.

Caryl Churchill Playwriting workshop and follow-up interview/discussion 14 July 1988. Telephone conversation and written correspondence April–May 1991.

Jenny Clarke Telephone interviews 24 July and 1 Nov. 1990.

Norma Cohen Interview and workshop 9 Nov. 1989.

Kate Corkery Written correspondence 2 May 1989.

Julie Covington Written correspondence Oct. 1989.

Susan Croft Meetings and correspondence 1987 to Sept. 1990.

Laura Curina (of Teatro Settimo) Meetings and discussions after performances and talks at the Divina Conferences, 1989 and 1991. Taped interview is published in *New Theatre Quarterly*, vol. 7, no. 25, Feb. 1991, pp. 27–34.

Sarah Daniels Playwriting workshop and interviews 11 July 1988, 17–20 Aug. 1988. Letter 19 Feb. 1989. Interview 8 March 1989. Telephone interviews Oct. 1989. Meetings 8 Nov. 1989 and 30 Jan. 1990. Discussion 30 Jan. 1990. Meetings 23 April 1990, 27 Feb. 1991.

Jill Davis Written correspondence 5 Dec. 1988. Telephone conversation Summer 1989. Written correspondence 8 Dec. 1989. Meeting 30 March 1990.

Judith Dimant Written correspondence 26 Jan. 1989.

Nancy Diuguid Interviews 4 Aug. 1988, 18 Aug. 1988, 8 Feb. 1989, 18 April 1989, 20 June 1989, 12 July 1989, 1 Aug. 1989, 29 Aug. 1989. Written correspondence Sept. and Oct. 1989, and 12 Feb. 1990. Previous draft sections of this manuscript were approved by post, 14 Feb. 1992.

Donna and Kebab (Eve Adams and Martha Lewis) Interview 10 May 1991.

Suad El-Amin Telephone interview 4 July 1990.

Anne Engel Telephone interview 22 Jan. 1990.

Etheldreda (Louise Rennison and Jane Bassett) Workshop, followed by written correspondence Dec. 1988 to Feb. 1989. Interview 2–4 Feb. 1989. Written correspondence 2 March 1989.

Bernardine Evaristo Interview regarding her work with Theatre of Black Women 28 March 1991, London.

Tash Fairbanks Written correspondence 6 June 1989 and 12 Aug. 1990. Interview and discussion 21 Feb. 1991, London. Follow-up postal correspondence.

Lesley Ferris Meeting 20 June 1989. Written correspondence 13 July 1989. Meetings 21 Nov. 1989, 23 May 1990 and 30 May 1990.

Alexandra Ford (administrator of Clean Break Theatre Company) Written and telephone correspondence April–June 1991. Completed postal interview received 1 July 1991.

Maggie Fox (of Lip Service) Written correspondence 1988–90. Interview 14 May 1991.

Christine Furnival Written correspondence and telephone interviews Feb.–June 1988.

Caroline Gardiner Written correspondence 1988–90. Telephone interview 20 Aug. 1990. Conference paper delivered 20 Oct. 1990.*

Pam Gems Written correspondence 21 July 1988 and 22 Jan. 1992 (in response to an earlier draft of parts of this book).

Finola Geraghty Written correspondence 22 Jan. 1989.

Faith Gillespie Interviews 18 April 1989 and Aug. 1989.

Lisa Goldman Interview 22 March 1990.

Jill Greenhalgh Meetings at Magdalena Project events 1987–91. Interviews about *Midnight Level Six* after a performance at Phoenix Arts Centre, Leicester, 25 Sept. 1991, and at the 'Breaking the Surface' Conference, The University of Calgary, 13–17 Nov. 1991. Written correspondence in regard to previous drafts of this book, 1991–2.

Germaine Greer Written correspondence Aug.–Nov. 1989. Telephone conversation 7 Jan. 1990. Meetings 10 Jan. 1990 and 25 March 1990.

Caroline Griffin Written correspondence April–June 1991.

Caroline Grimshaw Telephone conversation 3 Feb. 1990.

Kathleen Hamilton Written correspondence 19 and 31 Aug. 1988.

Gillian Hanna Written and oral correspondence 31 Aug. 1988. Interviews 18 April 1989, April–Aug. 1989.

Victoria Hardie Written correspondence 2 Feb. 1990.

Julie Holledge Written correspondence 17 April 1990.

Debbie Horsfield Interviewed on camera for a BBC/Open University programme on women in TV, 'Taking the Credit', part of the Issues in Women's Studies Course (producer: Meg Sheffield; academic: Lizbeth Goodman), 1991.

Pamela Howard Conference paper delivered 20 Oct. 1990.

Sheila Hyde Interview 27 June 1991, London.

Ann Jellicoe Written correspondence and interview 20 July 1988.

Mel Jennings (administrator for Black Mime Theatre Women's Troop) Telephone and postal correspondence Jan.–March 1991. Audience surveys and video received Feb. 1991.

Frances Jessup Meeting 18 March 1989.

Judith Johnson Interview 18 March 1989.

Zofia Kalinska Discussions at the second Divina Conference, The University of Turin, 1–5 Dec. 1991.

Jackie Kay Written correspondence and telephone conversations Feb.–June 1991.

Charlotte Keatley Playwriting workshops and writers group meetings 1988–9. Interviews 12 April, 27 April, 8 May and 17 May 1989.

Naseem Khan Written and oral correspondence July–Oct. 1990. Conference paper delivered 21 Oct. 1990.

Bryony Lavery Written correspondence and interview 20 July 1988. Written correspondence and telephone conversations Dec. 1990 to May 1991.

Helen Lederer Interview 2 May 1991.

Deborah Levy Playwriting workshop and interview 4–6 Dec. 1987. Second workshop and interview 14 July 1988. Occasional meetings and correspondence Oct. 1989 to Nov. 1990. Conference paper delivered 20 Oct. 1990.*

Martha Lewis (of Donna and Kebab) Interview 10 May 1991.

Lip Service (Maggie Fox and Sue Ryding) Written correspondence 1988–90. Interview 14 May 1991.

Joan Lipkin Taped interview 15 Nov. 1991 and discussions at the 'Breaking the Surface' Conference, The University of Calgary, 13–17 Nov. 1991. Follow-up written and telephone correspondence in response to previous drafts of this book Dec. 1991 to March 1992.

BIBLIOGRAPHY

Sonja Lyndon Interview 18 March 1989. Meeting and workshop 20 June 1989. Telephone conversations Oct. 1989 and March 1992.

Kathleen McCreery Interview 18 March 1989. Further correspondence 13 April 1989.

Mary McCusker Telephone interview 24 July 1990.

Claire MacDonald Occasional written and oral correspondence throughout 1989–90. Conference paper delivered 21 Oct. 1990.*

Genista McIntosh Telephone and written correspondence March–May 1990. Interview 2 May 1990.

Steve Mannix (administrator for Graeae Theatre) Interview 28 March 1991, London.

Miriam Margolyes Written correspondence Aug.–Nov. 1989. Telephone and written correspondence re: *Dickens' Women* May–June 1991.

Natasha Morgan Written correspondence May 1988.

Abigail Morris Interview 13 Nov. 1990.

Tanya Myers Written correspondence 24 May and June 1988. Telephone interviews in response to previous drafts of parts of this book 25 Jan. and 5 March 1992.

Mica Nava Written correspondence Aug. 1989.

Penny O'Connor Written correspondence 12 June 1988. Interview 18 March 1989.

Jonquil Panting (marketing officer for Women's Theatre Group) Written correspondence 20 March 1991 regarding the company's change of name.

Kathryn Pogson Meeting 30 Jan. 1990.

Harriet Powell (Spare Tyre) Interview 27 June 1991, London.

The Raving Beauties (Anna Carteret, Fanny Viner, Sue Jones-Davis) Interview 13 Nov. 1987.

Brenda Ray Written correspondence 26 June 1988 to Feb. 1990.

Sue Ryding (of Lip Service) Written correspondence 1988–90. Interview 14 May 1991.

Joanna Scanlan Written correspondence Oct.–Nov. 1989. Workshop and interviews 18 Nov. 1989 and 20 May 1990.

Jo Ann Schmidmann (artistic director of Omaha Magic Theatre) Discussions following the performance of *Body Leaks*, The University of Calgary, 15 Nov. 1991.

Rose Sharpe (Monstrous Regiment administrator) Interview and granted access to archives Summer 1987. Telephone interviews 24 July 1990 and 1 Nov. 1990.

Sistren Discussions after their talks and performances at the 'Breaking the Surface' Conference, The University of Calgary, 13–17 Nov. 1991.

Spare Tyre (Clair Chapman, Harriet Powell, Katina Noble) Workshop 17 July 1989, Cambridge. Interview 27 June 1991, London.

Diane Speakman Interview 30 Nov. 1989.

Tilda Swinton Interviews 8 June, 20 June, 26 June, 3 Aug., 9 Aug., 17 Aug., and 7 Sept. 1989.

Tattycorum Interview 30 Aug. 1988. Follow-up correspondence and telephone conversations with Susannah Rickards and Victoria Worsley Dec. 1988, Jan. and Feb. 1989. Written correspondence 4 Oct. 1989.

Polly Teale Interview 13 April 1988.

Megan Terry (founder and playwright for Omaha Magic Theatre) Discussions following the performance of *Body Leaks*, The University of Calgary, 15 Nov. 1991.

Polly Thomas (New Playwrights Trust) Written and oral correspondence and meetings 1988 to Dec. 1990.

Emma Thompson Written correspondence: Oct.–Nov. 1989, 5 Sept. 1989. Telephone discussion 14 Aug. 1990.

Susan Todd Telephone interview 25 April 1989.

Sandi Toksvig Written correspondence Oct.–Nov. 1989. Letter 18 Sept. 1989.

Trouble and Strife Meeting 3 Nov. 1989.

Patricia Van Twest Correspondence April–June 1988. Interview 24 June 1988.

Clare Venables Conference paper delivered 21 Oct. 1990.*

Richard Vranch (formerly of The Millies) Correspondence, followed by telephone interview 17 Jan. 1990.

Harriet Walter Written correspondence re: the RSC Women's Project 15 Jan. 1990.

Michelene Wandor Written correspondence May 1988. Workshop and interview 20 June 1989. Further correspondence regarding draft sections of this manuscript, approved by post 1 Feb. 1992.

Caroline Ward Telephone interview 3 April 1990. Interviews 26–8 April 1990.

Maggie Wilkinson Telephone interview 3 Feb. 1990. Written correspondence 9 Feb. 1990.

Julie Wilkinson Written and oral correspondence Dec. 1988 to March 1989. Interview and discussion 18 March 1989. Written correspondence 8 May 1989.

Women's Theatre Group Meeting 5 Nov. 1987.

Denise Wong Interview April 1991, London.

Victoria Worsley Written and oral correspondence Nov.–Dec. 1989. Interviews 26–8 April 1990.

Amanda Wray Interview 18 March 1989. Written correspondence 7 May 1989.

Jules Wright Interview 11 July 1988. Interviews/workshops 17–20 Aug. 1988. Discussion 30 Jan. 1990. Conference paper delivered 21 Oct. 1990.

Olwen Wymark Occasional written correspondence 1987–9. Conference paper delivered 20 Oct. 1990.*

Sheila Yeger Correspondence May 1988. Interview 24 June 1988.

INDEX

301